Critical Disability Theory

Law and Society Series
W. Wesley Pue, General Editor

The Law and Society Series explores law as a socially embedded phenomenon. It is premised on the understanding that the conventional division
of law from society creates false dichotomies in thinking, scholarship,
educational practice, and social life. Books in the series treat law and
society as mutually constitutive and seek to bridge scholarship emerging
from interdisciplinary engagement of law with disciplines such as politics,
social theory, history, political economy, and gender studies.

A list of the titles in this series appears at the end of this book.

Edited by Dianne Pothier
and Richard Devlin

Critical Disability Theory: Essays in Philosophy, Politics, Policy, and Law

UBCPress · Vancouver · Toronto

Anyone requiring an electronic version to facilitate conversion to an alternate format should direct enquiries to the volume editors (dianne.pothier@dal.ca or richard.devlin@dal.ca) or the publisher (www.ubcpress.ca).

15 14 13 12 11   5 4 3

Printed in Canada on ancient-forest-free paper (100% post-consumer recycled) that is processed chlorine- and acid-free, with vegetable-based inks.

Library and Archives Canada Cataloguing in Publication

Critical disability theory : essays in philosophy, politics, policy, and law / edited by Dianne Pothier and Richard Devlin.

(Law and society)
Includes bibliographical references and index.
ISBN-13: 978-0-7748-1203-0 (bound); 978-0-7748-1204-7 (pbk.)
ISBN-10: 0-7748-1203-6 (bound); 0-7748-1204-4 (pbk.)

1. People with disabilities – Government policy. 2. People with disabilities – Legal status, laws, etc. 3. Discrimination against people with disabilities. I. Devlin, Richard F. (Richard Francis), 1960- II. Pothier, Dianne III. Series: Law and society series (Vancouver, B.C.)

HV1559.C3C747 2005   362.4   C2005-904165-X

UBC Press gratefully acknowledges the financial support for our publishing program of the Government of Canada through the Book Publishing Industry Development Program (BPIDP), and of the Canada Council for the Arts, and the British Columbia Arts Council.

This book has been published with the help of a grant from the Canadian Federation for the Humanities and Social Sciences, through the Aid to Scholarly Publications Programme, using funds provided by the Social Sciences and Humanities Research Council of Canada.

Printed and bound in Canada by Friesens
Set in Stone by Artegraphica Design Co. Ltd.
Copy editor: Judy Phillips
Proofreader: Dianne Tiefensee
Indexer: Lillian Ashworth

UBC Press
The University of British Columbia
2029 West Mall, Vancouver, BC V6T 1Z2
604-822-5959 / Fax: 604-822-6083
www.ubcpress.ca

Canadä

For our parents:

Ona and Charles
Geraldine and Tom

Contents

Figures and Tables

Preface

This collection brings together twenty-three scholars from a variety of disciplines, scholars who are deeply concerned about conventional understandings of politics targeted at persons with disabilities and legal responses for them. As editors we want to thank the contributors for their willingness to share their ideas and insights in this collaborative enterprise. We also want to express our gratitude to Dalhousie Law School, the Canadian Law and Society Association, and the Canadian Association of Law Teachers for facilitating this project. Wes Pue and Randy Schmidt at UBC Press have offered generous guidance and the Aid to Scholarly Publications Programme has provided a much appreciated publication grant. We especially want to thank Dean Dawn Russell for her institutional support and the McIntosh Fund for its significant financial assistance in bringing this project to fruition. Last but not least, we wish to express our gratitude to David Dzidzornu for his superior editorial assistance and to Molly Ross for her wizardry with computers.

Critical Disability Theory

Introduction: Toward a Critical Theory of Dis-Citizenship

Richard Devlin and Dianne Pothier

North American societies take pride in promoting themselves as bastions of liberty, equality, and inclusion. In Canada, politicians never tire of proclaiming that it is the best country in the world to live in (Chrétien 2003), and judges and lawyers seldom miss the opportunity to celebrate the *Canadian Charter of Rights and Freedoms* and its commitment not only to liberty but also equality (L'Heureux-Dubé 2001). There is little doubt that, relatively speaking, the majority of North Americans do enjoy a high standard of living and that the quality of life, for most, when measured on a worldwide scale, is quite good.

However, not all share equally in the good life, or feel adequately included. Among those who face recurring coercion, marginalization, and social exclusion are persons with disabilities. Depending on how and what one counts, the disabled comprise from 6 percent to 15 percent of the Canadian population. Traditionally, responses to the needs of persons with disabilities have oscillated between charity on the one hand and welfarism on the other. As the following chapters will argue, both responses (despite their probably well-intentioned nature) have failed to adequately respond to the needs of persons with disabilities and, indeed, may have compounded the problems experienced by many of the disabled. The consequence, we suggest, is a system of deep structural economic, social, political, legal, and cultural inequality in which persons with disabilities experience unequal citizenship, a regime of dis-citizenship.

The issue of citizenship has garnered quite significant academic attention in the last decade or so (Hobson and Lister 2002). For some, citizenship has relatively formal significance, for example, the ability to hold a passport and to vote. For others, citizenship is more substantive: it is about the capacity to participate fully in all the institutions of society – not just those that fit the conventional definitions of the political, but also the social and cultural. This latter approach emphasizes that citizenship is not just an issue of individual *status*; it is also a *practice* that locates individuals in the larger community. As such, the substantive approach raises questions of access and participation, exclusion and inclusion, rights and obligations, legitimate governance and democracy, liberty and equality, public and private, marginalization and belonging, social recognition and redistribution of resources, structure and agency, identity and personhood, and self and other (Kabeer 2002). Building on Hammar's (1990) concept of denizens to describe guest workers, who have some social rights but no political rights, in countries such as Germany, we want to suggest that because many persons with disabilities are denied formal and/or substantive citizenship, they are assigned to the status of "dis-citizens," a form of citizenship minus, a disabling citizenship.

In response to this dis-citizenship regime, this book posits that we need new ways to conceptualize the nature of disability, a new understanding of citizenship that encompasses the disabled, new policies to respond to the needs of the disabled, and a new legal vision of the entitlements of the disabled. More precisely, we hope to develop an anti-necessitarian understanding of disability that focuses on genuine inclusiveness, not just abstract rights. Such an agenda we will characterize as critical disability theory.

This introduction is, therefore, an inquiry into the possibilities and parameters of a critical disability theory. Our central arguments are that disability is not fundamentally a question of medicine or health, nor is it just an issue of sensitivity and compassion; rather, it is a question of politics and power(lessness), power over, and power to. While liberalism has been subjected to a number of prescient and persuasive critiques in the last few decades (from feminists, communitarians, critical race theorists, and gay/lesbian/queer theorists, among others) we will suggest that, because of the particular needs of the disabled, critical disability theory gives rise to its own particular set of challenges to the core assumptions of liberalism. Indeed, we think that in some respects critical disability theory poses more fundamental challenges than do other critical theories. Liberalism, as a dominant ideology and principle of social organization, has a particularly hard time dealing with disability. As we will elaborate below, liberalism's approach to disability incorporates embedded assumptions that conceptualize disability as misfortune, and privilege normalcy over the abnormal. The corollaries are presumptions that the structures for societal organization based on able-bodied norms are inevitable, and that productivity is essential to personhood. The goal of critical disability theory is to challenge these assumptions and presumptions so that persons with disabilities can more fully participate in contemporary society.

To frame our overview, we organize our argument around four central themes: (1) language, definitions, and voice; (2) contextual politics and the politics of responsibility and accountability; (3) philosophical challenges; and (4) citizenship/dis-citizenship.

Language, Definitions, and Voice

A primary concern of critical disability theory is an interrogation of the language used in the context of disability. There are several layers.

First, what is the most appropriate descriptor to employ? The reader will have noticed that thus far we have referred to "the disabled" and "persons with disabilities" interchangeably. Contributors to this book invoke a number of other possibilities: "disabled persons," "people with impairments," people who experience "activity limitations," and "people who live with impairments." We believe that the range of descriptors is a reflection of a significant level of discomfort with what the English language seems to be able to offer as the available options.

In early discussions, the terms "handicapped" and "disabled persons" were common, but they generated criticism on the basis that it is inappropriate to convey the idea that the entire person is disabled because of a specific impairment. This led to the adoption by the Canadian federal and provincial governments of an explicit policy to use the term "persons with disabilities" instead, while strongly discouraging the use of "disabled persons" (Titchkosky 2001, 126). Yet, "persons with disabilities" or other "person first" language has its detractors. Without particularly defending the use of the term "disabled persons," Titchkosky offers a sociological critique of person-first language as an apolitical, individualized, and inappropriate means by which to "dismember disability from the self" (129, 134). Titchkosky is not seeking to ban the use of person-first language but, rather, to challenge its ubiquitous status and normalizing potential. While we think Titchkosky's critique, as a sociologist, is an important one, we, as lawyers, think an alternative perspective on the significance of person-first language should also be taken into account.

In legal terms, the concept of personhood is significant to equality rights: for example, in the contexts of race, gender, and sexual orientation. Before the Civil War in the United States, this was starkly illustrated by provisions in the 1787 American Constitution that officially counted enslaved persons as only three-fifths of a free person in determining each state's representation in the House of Representatives (e.g., article I, section 2, cause 3). In Canada, the recognition by the Judicial Committee of the Privy Council of women as legal persons under the *British North America Act* (1867), persons capable of being named as senators, was a crucial landmark on the road to women's equality (*Edwards v. A.G. Canada* 1930). Kathleen Lahey's book, *Are We "Persons" Yet? Law and Sexuality in Canada,* uses full legal personhood as the test of whether gays, lesbians, bisexuals, and the transgendered have obtained full equality (Lahey 1999). Viewed in this historical and legal context, it can be argued that "persons with disabilities" or other person-first language is not so apolitical after all. To be a person is to have the capacity to appear on the political radar screen. Yet, the first-person, or "with," language does still have the potential to disconnect the disability or to make it appear that the disability is of a second order nature; we do not speak of "persons with a gender" or "persons with a race."

Part of the difference in language is that while the words "race" and "gender" do not themselves designate a specific subset of the population (and in that sense they are facially neutral), "disability" does explicitly engage in targeting (and in that sense is ideologically loaded). Moreover, in its origins, the term "disability" is clearly pejorative. The 1989 edition of the *Oxford English Dictionary* defines "disability" as "want of ability ... inability, incapacity, impotence" and "disable" as, among other things, "to pronounce incapable; hence to disparage, depreciate, detract from, belittle." The disability movement has had some success in reclaiming the word "disability" to remove its negative connotations, which may explain in part the re-emergence of the terms "the disabled" and "disabled persons." This is parallel to the transformation of "queer" from a derogatory slang word into a badge of pride for gays, lesbians, and bisexuals. Yet, on the disability front, the transformation has been far from complete. As an example, when someone is on the "disabled list" of a sports team, not only are they ineligible to play the game, they don't even count among the allowable number of players – a rather stark example of exclusion. This book is part of the project of trying to rid the term "disability" of its pejorative and exclusionary origins. For our purposes, we have chosen to use the descriptor "persons with disabilities," as we believe that currently it is the least worst option.[1]

Second, if we are prepared to use the word "disability," what qualifies as a disability? This is crucial because, as Mary Ann McColl, Alison James, William Boyce, and Sam Shortt demonstrate in Chapter 1, depending on how the definition is constructed, it can have a determinative impact on how people identify themselves and on how they are perceived by others. Equally importantly, it has a huge impact on the numbers question. As Dana Lee Baker points out in Chapter 8, in the context of autism, the numbers question can generate huge political and policy shifts. Another aspect of the what-qualifies-as-a-disability issue is equally political: while there is consensus, for example, that being blind or an amputee qualifies as a disability, other conditions are more contentious. What about anorexia, smoking, alcoholism, and gambling? In Chapter 13, Daphne Gilbert and Diana Majury tackle the question of whether infertility is a disability and, in a heterosexual context, whose disability it might be – the man's, the woman's, the couple's? They argue that male infertility cannot be collapsed into a couple's infertility, and also that infertility does not qualify as a disability.

Moreover, even if we could find agreement on what might qualify as a disability, what types of disability exist? A number of authors have suggested different categorizations for various types of disability. Karpin (1999, 284) suggests the triad of psychiatric, physical, and intellectual. Lepofsky (2004) invokes a slightly different triad: physical, sensory, and/or mental disability. McColl and colleagues, on the other hand, suggest in Chapter 1 that it is useful to factor in age, and to distinguish between adult disability and old age disability.

These diverse ways of differentiating among types of disability invoke the challenges of consolidating the subject matter of, as well as the methods and arguments advanced by, critical disability theory. Here we would note the particular challenge of integrating analyses of mental disorder and mental disability as legal and medical categories within the critical disability literature and within the disability rights movement as social phenomena (Herr, Gostin, and Koh, 2003). This literature and social movement have historically been more oriented to challenging dominant conceptions of physical disability than of mental disorder and disability. However, particularly in light of contemporary scientific efforts directed at "unlocking the mysteries of the brain" to produce evidence of biochemical or genetic components of psychiatric disorders (so that they are finally on par with physical disorders) and to identify genetic components of specific forms of mental disability, critical disability theory is increasingly concerned with targeting the problematic assumptions of the biological model in the distinct historical and institutional realms of mental disorder and mental disability. This requires further fundamental challenges to dominant constructions of rationality and reasonableness, of agency and personhood, and of the hierarchical binary of mind and body that critical disability theory has arguably only begun to confront.[2]

The struggle over definitions and categories is important because, historically, we have tended to adopt a binary conception of disability: there are the disabled (them-us) and the able-bodied (us-them). McColl and colleagues (Chapter 1) are skeptical of such a dualistic approach to disability. Carolyn Tyjewski (Chapter 5) is also critical of a binary analysis of disability (as well as of other identity categories), objecting to the failure of American courts to recognize the existence of hybrids. What Tyjewski says about American court decisions is not directly transferable to Canada,[3] but her general point about the fluidity of categories does still resonate.[4] In other words, the binaristic approach to disability engenders a process of "othering" and categorization, when the more nuanced reality is that disability might be better understood as a dynamic and contextualized range. Disability, we argue, has no essential nature. Rather, depending on what is valued (perhaps overvalued) at certain socio-political conjunctures, specific personal characteristics are understood as defects and, as a result, persons are *manufactured* as disabled.

If this is accurate, the vital question is not whether the disability inheres in a particular person, but what is society's response to a particular person's circumstances? This is why we emphasize the importance of context. Whether a person is "disabled" is highly dependent on the social organization of society – not only in the way we construct our buildings and our transport systems, but also in the performance benchmarks we utilize to assess people (see Chapter 4 by Theresa Man Ling Lee and Chapter 9 by Teri Hibbs and Dianne Pothier), and in the ways in which people are expected to engage in the daily activities of work, leisure, and living. As we change our patterns of social organization, so too might we have to change our understanding of what and who qualifies as disabled. Phrased slightly differently, when it comes to disability, there is a duality at play – the particular circumstance of a specific individual, and the larger social context within which that person operates – and the two are mutually constitutive (discussed in Chapter 7 by Kari Krogh and Jon Johnson, and in Chapter 10 by Catherine Frazee, Joan Gilmour, and Roxanne Mykitiuk). A revealing example of this is Darcy MacPherson's anecdote in Chapter 11 of "walking" in his wheelchair into a room full of students. MacPherson's incorporation of wheeling within "walking" can be seen as simply an effort to downplay the difference between moving by legs and moving by wheels. Such use of language, however, could also be a profound political challenge to the privilege society gives to walking in the "normal" way.

MacPherson's anecdote might also lead some readers to believe that the trajectory of the duality is that gradually we are getting better at responding to the needs of persons with disabilities, primarily through accommodation. This we will characterize as the narrative of progress. However, as several of this book's contributors point out, because of changing structural dynamics, things may be getting worse rather than better for some persons with disabilities. Neo-liberal policies of downsizing and retrenchment, for example, have resulted in increased marginalization and impoverishment of many persons with disabilities. Another example is that of computer programs increasingly tied to fancy graphics or to the use of a mouse, creating major barriers for users with visual impairments. The result, by fluke rather than design, is that older computer programs are often more adaptable to the needs of those with visual impairments. Even when new technologies enable the removal of barriers, the actual deployment in practice of such technologies may generate perverse effects. For example, the same technology that now makes it easy to produce large-print versions of a document (enabling a visually impaired person to read otherwise inaccessible text) equally facilitates the production of extremely small-print versions (increasing inaccessibility for the visually impaired).

However, even this contextualist approach to disability may not go far enough. Tremain (2002) suggests an even deeper level of concern. She argues that while the social constructionist understanding of disability is an improvement over traditional essentialist conceptions, it too draws on a problematic dichotomy between impairment, which is understood as a natural defect, and disability, which is understood as society's oppressive characterization of an impairment. Her critique is that "impairment" is itself ideologically loaded, a medicalized discourse that assumes a perfect norm and the impaired (read defective) other. Similarly, in Chapter 10, Frazee, Gilmour, and Mykitiuk examine "impairment as a relational inquiry." In short, there is no apolitical way to think or talk about either impairment or disability, because language itself is an unavoidably political phenomenon. By way of illustration, Bickenbach (1993) has argued that there are at least four distinct ways of thinking about disability – the biological, economic, socio-political, and equality models – and that each approach generates not just different understandings but distinct policy/political responses, ranging from charity, empathy, and pity to surgery, to rights and entitlements. To speak of disability, then, is to already have engaged. As Ravi Malhotra points out in Chapter 3, there is no Rawlsian original position from which to pursue an impartial assessment of the situation of persons with disabilities or the basic institutions of society. One of the reasons we suggest that critical disability theory poses a fundamental problem for liberalism is that most liberal theory assumes that language is a relatively transparent neutral medium through which we communicate. Critical disability theory, however, posits that language itself is deeply partial.

So how do we understand disability? We take our cue from Gilbert and Majury, who suggest in Chapter 13 that stigmatization is pivotal (and on this basis argue that a man's infertility is not a disability). Frazee, Gilmour, and Mykitiuk document in Chapter 10 a particular form of stigmatization in circumstances in which the medical gaze on women with disabilities often transforms patients from human beings into "interesting conditions." While we think the emphasis on stigmatization is important in identifying disability, we want to suggest that the political dimensions of coming to terms with disability are even more entrenched than stigmatization. That is to say, stigmatization is still connected to an intentionalist understanding of disability. A more political/structural analysis would emphasize the existence of exclusionary social practices that are not dependent on intentions. From this perspective, social organization according to able-bodied norms is just taken as natural, normal, inevitable, necessary, even progress. It's just the way things have to be done. The resulting exclusion of those who do not fit able-bodied norms may not be noticeable or even intelligible. For example, most daily practices (e.g., work, leisure, and access to the necessaries of basic survival) are organized on the assumption that people have 20/20 vision, perhaps with the assistance of glasses or contact lenses. If this assumption is inaccurate, persons whose vision does not accord with this measurement run the serious risk of marginalization. Expanding cities are increasingly designed on the basis that people can drive, but if one cannot drive because of his or her eyesight, society is creating barriers for that person to get to work, to buy food, or to play. There may be no stigma involved here, but the consequences are manifestly exclusionary. It is this focus on the combination of assumed inevitability plus social exclusion that leads us to suggest that what is required is an "anti-necessitarian" (Unger 1987) disability theory.

In light of the significance of language and definitions, it is also vital to emphasize the importance of voice. The editors and contributors to this book form a diverse group. Although we all share a commitment to advancing the social status and equality rights of persons with disabilities, there is a range of opinions as to how to accomplish such goals, both theoretically and practically. We also come from a diversity of academic backgrounds: law, politics, disability studies, geography, health policy, public affairs, and cultural studies. Moreover, however one defines the term, we are a mixture of disabled and non-disabled persons. Several of the contributors are persons with disabilities, although most do not self-identify as such in their chapters. However, four of the contributors, Lee (Chapter 4), Tyjewski (Chapter 5), Hibbs (Chapter 9), and MacPherson (Chapter 11), expressly invoke their personal experiences of disability as central features of their analyses. For those who do not do so expressly, we have little doubt that their personal experiences of disability inform their arguments and perspectives.

As editors, the two of us have developed an interest in critical disability theory by different routes. Devlin comes to this through an academic interest in critical theory and a political commitment to radical participatory democracy. Pothier comes to this through an academic interest in constitutional and public law, but with a more personal stake. Pothier's understanding of equality and human rights law has developed alongside her conceptualization of her own disability – visual impairment (on the borderline of legal blindness) since birth, because of albinism. The personal and academic experiences intertwine in challenging ways. Pothier engages in an ongoing process of using theory and legal analysis to reassess her own experiences of how she is treated as someone with a disability, and of using her experiences of how she is treated as someone with a disability to question the adequacy of theory and legal analysis.

Contextual Politics and the Politics of Responsibility and Accountability

The foregoing discussions of language, definitions, experiences of disability, and voice lead directly to a second general theme of critical disability theory: that it is a self-consciously politicized theory. Its goal is not theory for the joy of theorization, or even improved understanding and explanation; it is theorization in the pursuit of empowerment and substantive, not just formal, equality.

The origins of critical disability theory can be traced to a larger movement in politics and law that has become disenchanted with the promises of liberalism (Minda 1995). Liberalism, in its most positive manifestations, was able to promote a welfare state, that is, a web of social and economic relations that went beyond formal equality to facilitate equal opportunity for some. However, liberalism has been unwilling and unable to pursue substantive equality. In response, a number of post-liberal voices – including critical theory, some forms of feminism, queer theory, critical race theory, and critical disability theory – have emerged, identifying both the weaknesses of liberalism and the requirements of a more inclusive democracy (Devlin 2001). This new critical realism, as it might be called, has taken on an increased urgency in the light of both neo-liberalism and globalization, the joint effect of which has been to further marginalize the historically excluded, including persons with disabilities.

Two key political insights undergird critical disability theory: power(lessness) and context. As suggested previously, issues of disability are not just questions of impairment, functional limitations, or enfeeblement; they are issues of social values, institutional priorities, and political will. They are questions of power: of who and what gets valued, and who and what gets marginalized. Critical disability theory interrogates a system of justice that is based on a politics of "just us." This is why context is so important to critical disability theory, because it is theory that emerges from the bottom up, from the lived experiences of persons with disabilities, rather than from the top down, from the disembodying ivory tower. As such, it is a form of embodied theory. But this does not mean critical disability theory does not engage with some of the big questions of philosophy and political theory; it simply means that it comes at them with a sharp awareness of the contexts of inequality based on disability. So, for example, critical disability theory is skeptical of liberalism, not just because it has potential ontological weaknesses (for example, its insufficiently relational understanding of a self) but because of its deep structural assumptions such as its narrative of progress, which many persons with disabilities find hard to imagine given the current context of state downsizing, budget cutting, and retrenchment.

The emphasis on power and context also provides a clue to the philosophical origins of critical disability theory. While some authors, for example Malhotra in Chapter 3, argue that liberalism can be given a radical turn, many critical disability theorists build on the insights of critical theory and feminism. Lee argues in Chapter 4 that even Will Kymlicka's egalitarian liberalism is inadequate to the task.

Liberalism's approach to disability is constrained by limiting normative assumptions. The starting point for liberalism is that disability is about misfortune or bad luck. As MacPherson describes in Chapter 11, tort law conceives of a pre-existing condition of disability as a subtraction from the norm. Conceptualizing disability as a misfortune has very specific implications, and forms the basis of the approaches referred to earlier, ranging from charity to welfarism. If the starting point is misfortune, the first level of engagement must be prevention. As Tremain (2006) points out, the notion of prevention is taken so far as to normalize the selective abortion of impaired foetuses. We, as a society, develop and utilize prenatal testing techniques because we have determined that certain kinds of lives are not worth living. Such an appreciation of disability sends a very powerful message to persons with disabilities who are already born. Second, if disability cannot be prevented, the next level of engagement is treatment and cure. This is where the biomedical model of disability is paramount. The disability is located in the individual, and efforts, often extraordinary efforts, are pursued to eliminate the defect and get rid of the disability. Third, if neither prevention nor cure is possible, the last resort is rehabilitation, where assistive devices, prosthetics, medication and/or training the body to function in non-standard ways are used as means of coping with the disability. In this framework, disability is at best tolerated.

We do not mean to suggest that prevention, cure, or rehabilitation are, in themselves, bad things. But they are not the full picture. To start from the perspective that disability is misfortune is to buy into a framework of charity and pity rather than equality and inclusion. To contextualize and conceptualize disability as misfortune is to create a hierarchy of difference – fortune must be better than misfortune. Although liberalism is perhaps naive and simplistic in terms of what is necessary to achieve equality, in other contexts liberalism can, at a fundamental level, readily reject a hierarchy of difference. Relatively early in its development, liberalism was able to reject as both irrational and wrong the notion of privileging one race over another; in liberal thought, racial origins are obviously irrelevant to the entitlement to equality. Gender equality has been more of a challenge to liberalism, because of biological differences between men and women. While liberalism is still struggling to come to terms with gender difference, and while liberalism is still fixed on the binary conception of gender (Tyjewski, in Chapter 5, discusses the exclusion of intersexuals), the basic premise of gender equality is well established in liberalism. Unpacking and dismantling the social construction of gender is still a challenge, but, at the level of theoretical premise, liberalism can now easily accept that gender is irrelevant to the entitlement to equality. As regards sexual orientation, liberalism is still struggling with whether there is a hierarchy of difference. The current controversy over same-sex marriage is really a debate on whether non-heterosexuals are worthy of the institution of marriage. Opponents of same-sex marriage who claim to be pro-marriage but not anti-gay are preaching tolerance of homosexuals but not full equality; they are invoking a hierarchy of difference. The Supreme Court of Canada, in *Reference Re Same-Sex Marriage* (2004, 46), in ruling that the proposed federal statute to extend the right to civil marriage to same-sex couples is consistent with the *Canadian Charter of Rights and Freedoms,* accepted that the federal initiative represented a furtherance of rights: "The mere recognition of the equality rights of one group cannot, in itself, constitute a violation of the rights of another. The promotion of *Charter* rights and values enriches our society as a whole and the furtherance of those rights cannot undermine the very principles the Charter was meant to foster." In other words, the Charter is meant to foster the elimination of hierarchies of rights and hierarchies of difference.

It is our contention that it is in the context of disability that liberalism has the greatest difficulty in rejecting a hierarchy of difference. In a utopian society, liberalism would not seek to abolish race or gender or sexual orientation. But it would seek to abolish disability, on the basis that human beings are not meant to "suffer" disability. In the practical life of our non-utopian society, not only is the abortion of impaired foetuses routine (Tremain 2006), but the murder of a child with a disability, Tracy Latimer, generates a great deal of public sympathy for the father who killed her. Ridding society of disability, that is, ridding society of the defective and inferior other, is widely seen as understandable and perhaps socially acceptable behaviour. On the theoretical plane, Malhotra's analysis in Chapter 3 points out that Rawls is quite blatant in expressly excluding the disabled from his social contract model, on the premise that their "fate arouses pity and anxiety" (Rawls 1999, 83-84). Similarly, Sampson, in Chapter 12, identifies pity as the core of the Supreme Court of Canada's approach to gender disability in *R. v. Parrott* (2001).

Equality is not about evoking pity or charity. As Krogh and Johnson highlight in Chapter 7, a charitable approach tends to focus on bare survival rather than on genuine participation in society, and is highly susceptible to claims of budgetary restraint. Rioux and Valentine discuss in detail in Chapter 2 the theoretical significance of moving from a charity-based approach to a human rights-based approach. To genuinely adopt a human rights approach means rejecting a hierarchy of disability difference, rejecting a privileging of the "normal" over the "abnormal," to use Frazee, Gilmour, and Mykitiuk's terminology. But it also entails an engagement with what Martha Minow (1990) has described as the "dilemma of difference," that is, when to factor in difference and when to ignore it. Given the diverse nature of different disabilities and the particular impacts a disability may have on different people, as well as the different spheres of life within which a person may operate in any one day, a disability may not have any essential significance. Its significance is contingent on the context. In some situations it will be necessary for both the person with the disability and the larger society to specifically factor in the disability; in other situations, the disability may be safely ignored.

Yet, as a general proposition, disability demands a coming to terms with difference. Critical theory generally challenges the assumption that difference can be ignored. Critical race theorists, for example, challenge the notion (originally in Justice Harlan's dissent in *Plessy v. Ferguson*) that the American constitution should be colour-blind. They argue that to ignore race is to perpetuate racism. Similarly, radical feminists understand that ignoring gender perpetuates patriarchy (MacKinnon 1989). Substantive equality necessitates taking difference into account in order to both identify the systemic nature of inequality and pursue solutions tailored to the goals of full inclusion and participation. This is even more crucial in the context of disability than elsewhere because to ignore the difference of disability is to engender exclusion. If the sign says that all are welcome, then gender or race is not an absolute barrier to getting in the door, but a set of stairs is an absolute barrier for a wheelchair user. Getting in the door may be a long way from full equality, but it is the necessary first step. Formal equality is inadequate for all equality seekers, but it is most inadequate for persons with disabilities where ableist norms that ignore difference, as well as rigid norms of rationality or reasonableness, can make participation simply impossible. Whereas liberalism says that difference should be ignored, critical theory demands that difference be confronted. The challenge is to pay attention to difference without creating a hierarchy of difference – either between disability and non-disability or within disability.

Finally, critical disability theory goes beyond political analysis to pursue a politics of transformation. In this regard it asks not only the traditional question of what is to be done, but also, who is to do it?

Critical disability theory argues that if we adopt an individualist and essentializing conception of disability, the primary responsibility lies with(in) the person with the disability. Hence, the emphases on prevention, cure, and rehabilitation that we identified earlier. If, however, we understand disability as a socially created barrier, then, as Rioux and Valentine (Chapter 2) and Baker (Chapter 8) note, responsibility and accountability shifts to the larger community. As one commentator has noted, "a person is a person through other persons" (Shutte in Kabeer 2002, 37). But this shift in the location of responsibility is only a first step. As we have already emphasized in this Introduction, a variety of options might be available to the larger community, including pity, charity, surgical intervention, accommodation, and transformation. Furthermore, even if the latter two approaches were to be adopted, that would only be the beginning of policy considerations. As Malhotra points out in Chapter 3, a number of possibilities present themselves: "tax subsidies for individual employees to pay for accommodations, greater flexibility in workplace rules mandated through state regulation, tax credits, or possibly even quotas for workers with disabilities." Moreover, the critical analysis continues, the problem is not just the disadvantaging of persons with disabilities but the privileging of those who are perceived to be non-disabled. Again, our previous discussions of computer technology may be illustrative of this concern, as may be the conventional merit-based performance criteria, for example in the university context (discussed by Lee in Chapter 4, and Hibbs and Pothier in Chapter 9).

At the same time, however, critical disability theory does not want to portray persons with disabilities as passive victims. While there are undoubtedly pervasive structures of inequality, as Krogh and Johnson emphasize in Chapter 7, there are also many and diverse agentic practices developed by the disabled to resist the exclusion and oppression (Lepofsky 2004). For every moment and instance of "power over," there are moments and instances of "power to." As the various contributors have demonstrated, at every level, persons with disabilities have engaged with empowering strategies – at the level of the self; in the family; at school; at work; in local, national, and international politics; in the social realm; and in the cultural realm. Even in law. Viewed in this light, questions of responsibility and accountability can be resolved only through the joint efforts of both those who are disabled and those who are non-disabled.

Philosophical Challenges

As we have noted, perhaps the most important critical claim with regard to disability is that it is a social construct. Persons with disabilities may experience functional limitations (*Granovsky* 2000, 703, 721) that non-disabled persons do not experience, but the biggest challenge comes from mainstream society's unwillingness to adapt, transform, and even abandon its "normal" way of doing things. As the Supreme Court of Canada has acknowledged in *Granovsky v. Canada (Attorney General)*, we live "in a world relentlessly oriented to the able-bodied" (*Granovsky* 2000, 703, 723).[5]

Whether the social construct incorporates just disability or disability and impairment, the point is that the problem is not the person with the disability. Rather, it is the pervasive impact of ableist assumptions, institutions, and structures that disadvantage persons with disabilities. As Justice Gérald La Forest has pointed out, "This historical disadvantage has to a great extent been shaped and perpetuated by the notion that disability is an abnormality or flaw. As a result, disabled persons have not generally been afforded the 'equal concern, respect and consideration' that s. 15(1) of the *Charter* demands. Instead, they have been subjected to paternalistic attitudes of pity and charity, and their entrance into the social mainstream has been conditional upon their emulation of able-bodied norms" (*Eldridge* 1997, 668). These comments were made in the context of a claim for state funding of sign language interpretation for deaf patients being treated by doctors or at hospitals, ultimately a fairly modest challenge to the mainstream way of functioning. Where the claim was a more fundamental challenge, a claim on behalf of a child with profound disabilities, a child very different from student peers, the court rejected a presumption of integration of students with disabilities in *Eaton v. Brant County Board of Education* (1997). Similarly, in *Auton v. British Columbia* (2004), arguments that fundamentally challenged the orientation of the health-care system were roundly dismissed.[6] A primary goal of critical disability theory is to force dominant society to break out of the "psychic prison" (McKenna 1997, 160) of ableism and move toward a barrier-free society (*Eldridge* 1997, 689) in which persons with disabilities (both the easy cases and the hard cases) genuinely belong (Michalko 2002). We will have more to say on this below.

The claim that disability is not just an individual impairment but a systematically enforced pattern of exclusion moves the analysis forward in important ways. However, it also raises a number of other questions. For example, as Malhotra points out in Chapter 3, there may be significant differences between a social model, a social constructionist model, and an oppressed minority model, each of which might characterize the problem, and potential solutions, differently.

Even more importantly, there is the question of whether the language of social construction is successful in its attempt to escape the dangers of essentialism. This, in part, is a consequence of a point we referred to previously: the complexity and diversity of disabilities. The range of potential disabilities is enormous, so how does one begin to talk about a group characteristic such as disability without slipping into commonalistic claims that reproduce categories of inclusion and exclusion? A number of authors in this book have struggled with this problem, aware that emphasis on particularism threatens to return us to a medicalized characterization of the circumstances of persons with disabilities.

This is compounded by the issue of intersectionality. As a number of authors argue, disability may run the danger of being too generic because it does not give significant emphasis to other aspects of disabled persons' identities, for example, their ethnicity (Lee, Chapter 4), gender (Sampson, Chapter 12), sexual orientation (Tyjewski, Chapter 5) or class (Hibbs and Pothier, Chapter 9; Frazee, Gilmour, and Mykitiuk, Chapter 10). Most authors agree that it is not helpful to adopt an additive conception in these situations, that is, race + disability + gender = discrimination (to the third degree). Rather, there is the sense of a concatenated experience that is more than the sum of its parts. Sampson, for example, in Chapter 12 offers a critique of the Supreme Court's decision in *Parrott,* claiming that, despite their differences, all the judges completely miss the gendered disability nature of the crime, that is, that an exclusive focus on disability is an inadequate analysis of a crime against a woman with a mental disability. Lee highlights in Chapter 4 the complexity of trying to disentangle interlocking patterns of discrimination based on race and disability. Similarly, Frazee, Gilmour, and Mykitiuk in Chapter 10 question the possible significance of the differences in the composition of the focus groups participating in their study. Wilton in Chapter 6 underscores the significance of factors beyond disability that contribute to the reality of precarious work, providing a sharp insight into the specifics of exclusion depending on one's gender, age, or ethnic background.

On the one hand, these analyses appear to be promising because they help us break the stranglehold of essentialism. However, on the other hand, they may resurrect the fear that without some element of commonality, we cannot analyze the patterns of systemic exclusion, never mind mobilize to ensure greater inclusion and participation. These challenges are intensified by Tyjewski's invocation in Chapter 5 of the descriptor "hybrids" for those who do not fit nicely into preconceived conventional identity categories.

It is important to remember that disabilities range from the highly visible to the highly invisible. Moreover, whether the disability is visible may depend on the context. For example, although a wheelchair is generally a very visible sign of disability, if someone using a wheelchair is seated at a table with others who did not bring their own chairs, the disability may not be obvious to the casual observer (or to someone who cannot see the wheelchair because they cannot see at all). Many disabilities are not apparent unless specific activities impacted by the disability are being engaged in. For example, in a situation where no one is speaking, muteness or deafness may not be discernible. There are also many hidden disabilities that are not obvious unless the person chooses to disclose, or is required to disclose to qualify for benefits or accommodation, as discussed by Frazee, Gilmour, and Mykitiuk in Chapter 10 and Hibbs and Pothier in Chapter 9, respectively.

The reality of hidden disabilities leads to the possibility (and politics) of passing. If marginalization or discriminatory consequences are associated with being categorized as disabled, there may be an incentive to act as though one is not disabled, that is, to try to elude the social construction of disability. Given the negative connotation attributed to disability, the able-bodied majority generates an expectation that persons with disabilities should try to pass (Titchkosky 2003, 66-71). In its purest form, passing is a very deliberate attempt to pretend you are something you are not. People may put a great deal of effort into passing. Rod Michalko, who was diagnosed as legally blind (10 percent vision) at age eleven, describes how he went to great lengths to pass as fully sighted in his high school years. He preferred to attribute his inability to drive to a fictitious, impaired driving licence suspension than to admit he could not see well enough to drive (Michalko 2002, 74).

Even where someone is making no attempt to pass, that person may get caught up in a presumption of normalcy, especially if he or she is not visibly disabled. Most of the time, people are expected to act in an able-bodied way unless there is very specific notice to the contrary. This can have important marginalizing or exclusionary effects. This goes well beyond the issue of intent or denial of access. Pothier witnessed an example of the exclusionary effects of the presumption of normalcy during her appearance at a court hearing with several other lawyers, one of whom was in a wheelchair. The chief justice was noticeably upset by the breach of protocol when this particular lawyer did not, like the other lawyers, stand up at the start of the hearing when her name was called. After a whispered comment from the judge sitting next to him, the chief justice seemed to understand why she had not stood up, but he gave no acknowledgment of his inappropriate reliance on a presumption of normalcy.

Even where the visibility or knowledge of a disability precludes passing in its pure sense, there can be another form of passing. A person with a disability may try to blend in as much as possible, trying to downplay the significance of the disability. This is a process of accommodating oneself to one's environment, while asking and expecting little or no effort of the environment to accommodate the disability. This is a form of passing that Pothier now recognizes as a practice of her younger self. The conceptual shift that Pothier has made in the last fifteen years is to not be satisfied with accommodating herself to her physical and human environment. Rather, she expects the physical and human environment to be welcoming to the presence of disability – hers and that of others.

The foregoing discussions indicate that critical disability theory is not just about the failure of liberalism as a political response to needs of persons with disabilities but also a philosophical challenge to conventional liberal assumptions. Liberalism tends to put great emphasis on the individual, assuming that the self is both sovereign and a foundational unit for analysis. However, critical disability theory forces us to reflect on a number of profound ontological questions. Who is a self? Is there such a thing as an authentic self? What is the significance of disability to the conception of self? Are the answers fundamentally different for those born with a disability than they are for those who acquire a disability after having a previous conception of self? How does the self relate to others? Lee in Chapter 4 considers, but ultimately rejects, the notion of the disabled as members of a cultural group. Krogh and Johnson in Chapter 7 and Frazee, Gilmour, and Mykitiuk in Chapter 10 interrogate how people reconstruct themselves and their sense of self to respond to the dominant norms and expectations of them. As the previous discussion of passing suggests, given the coercive demands of normalcy, are there not enormous barriers to being certain of whom a disabled person might be?

Liberalism also has put great store in the principles of liberty, autonomy, and choice. But once again, critical disability theory invites us to revisit the analytical and strategic utility of such discursive artifacts. Given the reality that some persons with disabilities will necessarily be in situations of intense dependency and reliance, can liberty and autonomy – with their emphasis on freedom from – really be the lodestars liberalism has assumed? Despite liberalism's assumption that dependency is the opposite of autonomy, disability may force a reconciliation between autonomy and dependence. In other contexts, if a person with disabilities (for example, an autistic child, as Baker discusses in Chapter 8) has difficulty, even great difficulty, communicating her or his wishes to others, what work can liberty and autonomy really do? Is "choice" a useful, or realistic, way to discuss some issues of disability? Would a focus on sometimes mutually reinforcing, sometimes competing, coercions provide more insightful analyses and reflections? If it is true, as several authors have suggested, that the language of disability is always and already an exercise in categorization, regulation, and discipline, does this mean that the options are not between liberty and constraint, but between different forms of constraint? Could we not provide more grounded analyses by identifying the competing acts of violence that saturate the lives of persons with disabilities? However, we are also concerned that such a shift in focus and analysis might raise the spectre of paternalism and infantilization. Our goal in making such suggestions is not so much to abandon the discourses of autonomy, liberty, and choice as to decentre them to create space for more context-specific interrogations and analyses.

Citizenship/Dis-Citizenship

At the outset of this introduction, we introduced the concept of dis-citizenship, the idea that persons with disabilities are disabled citizens on both the formal and substantive levels. In immigration law, for example, disability is, under some conditions, explicitly considered a legitimate reason for denying an applicant admission to Canada (Voyvodic 2001). Krogh and Johnson point out in Chapter 7 that if some disabled people are unable to receive home care, they are disempowered from participating in the larger polis; they are privatized and closeted away. In the context of genetic testing, we are witnessing the denial of life, perhaps the most basic citizenship right.

While we obviously believe that the substantivist approach to citizenship is superior to the formalist analysis, we detect even in this literature a tendency to assume that genuine citizenship entails a capacity for productivity, and that if one cannot be productive, one is not worthy of full citizenship. Most of the literature on citizenship has focused on gender, sexual orientation, or race, to argue that the contributions (actual or potential) of women or minorities to the larger polis are being overlooked or undervalued (Kabeer 2002; Hobson and Lister 2002). This, however, raises a number of questions: is the lack of productivity the "fault" of the person with disabilities, or are the social barriers that make productivity impossible on his or her part to blame? What is meant by productivity? What are the criteria? Who gets to make the assessment? And, most importantly, why should productivity (regardless of how we define it) be a legitimate criterion? Embedded in the discourse of productivity is an unavoidable cost-benefit analysis. In our opinion, no matter how well we move toward a barrier-free society, no matter how ameliorative medical interventions become, if one thinks in cost-benefit terms, there is always likely to be a significant segment of our community whose costs can be argued to outweigh the benefits they produce. But is this an appropriate way for us to value each other? Efficiency and productivity are irretrievably ableist discourses that can only condemn (some) persons with disabilities to a presumptive inferior status. An enabling citizenship needs to be unshackled from the ideology of productivity and efficiency.

Thus, we want to suggest that the landscape of citizenship discourse needs to be expanded to respond to the particular experiential circumstances of persons with disabilities. Our hopes in naming the hitherto unnamed are threefold: first, to highlight the unequal status to which persons with disabilities are confined; second, to destabilize necessitarian assumptions that reinforce the marginalization of persons with disabilities; and third, to help generate the individual and collective practical agency of persons with disabilities in the struggles for recognition and redistribution (Fraser 1989).

Structure of the Book

The book is organized into four sections and an Appendix. In Part 1: Setting the Context, McColl and colleagues identify the substantive and methodological significance of the numbers question and illustrate this significance by referring to three distinct policy initiatives: access to health services, income replacement, and human rights. Part 2: Conceptual Frameworks is designed to outline the various theoretical approaches that might underlie a critical disability theory. Rioux and Valentine argue that the reason we have confused and contradicting policy initiatives in Canada is that we have been unclear as to the most appropriate theoretical framework within which to understand disability. Malhotra suggests a solution to this dilemma by subjecting Rawls' theory of justice to a radical reconstruction based on the insights of critical theory. Lee, however, is more cautious and, through a critique of Kymlicka, raises concerns about whether treating persons with disabilities as a cultural group is sufficiently empowering for full citizenship. Tyjewski, through the introduction of the concept of hybrids, goes one step farther by problematizing the legal system's ability to deal with categories.

Part 3: Policy Analyses builds on the theoretical insights of the previous section through several case studies. Wilton analyzes the phenomenon of precarious work, considering how the economic policies of neo-liberalism have had an impact on the employment situation of persons with disabilities. Krogh and Johnson discuss how cutbacks to home care programs can have negative impacts that go beyond the loss of physical support to include reconfigurations of disabled persons' sense of self and their capacities for civic participation. Both studies are careful, however, not to construct persons with disabilities as mere passive victims of the structural forces of globalization and neo-liberalism. Wilton discusses how different individuals find different strategies to respond to their circumstances, while Krogh and Johnson highlight the mobilization efforts of disability rights activist groups. Baker picks up on these insights to provide a comparative study of the impact of autism on public policy in both Canada and the United States to suggest that, given the right configuration of circumstances, there may be opportunities to move issues of disability onto the public policy agenda. Hibbs and Pothier conclude the section by demonstrating how reactive, as opposed to proactive, accommodation policies in the university reinscribe rather than challenge patterns of ableism and exclusion because they remain dependent on an individualizing, biomedical understanding of disability.

Part 4: Legal Interrogations provides four case studies of how the legal system has responded to disability. Frazee, Gilmour, and Mykitiuk analyze how medical and legal paradigms and discourses intersect to oppress and discipline women with disabilities in spite of privacy rights to which they are formally entitled. MacPherson discusses how the tort system's calculation of damages systemically devalues the lives of persons with disabilities. Sampson analyzes how the Supreme Court of Canada has a particularly difficult time in dealing with the equality aspects of gendered disability because it remains ensnared in an ideology of pity. Gilbert and Majury, rounding out the discussion, also pick up on the issue of the relationship between gender and disability to argue that it is a mistake to conceptualize infertility as a disability.

Finally, the Appendix, by Pothier, provides a brief but comprehensive overview of Supreme Court decisions on issues of disability from 1985 to 2004.

Conclusion
We began this introduction by suggesting that critical disability theory is part of a larger movement, the new critical realism, that challenges the promises and potential of liberalism. However, as the Introduction progresses, we suggest that in some respects the challenges posed by critical disability theory are greater than those of other critical realisms, such as feminism, critical race theory, or queer theory. We suggest that, despite

their constitutive identities, women, persons of colour, and gays, lesbians, and transsexuals pose a less radical challenge to the material, if not necessarily the normative, conditions of contemporary North American society. This is not true of many – but not all – persons with disabilities. In part, this is because critical disability theory emphasizes the inevitability of difference, it demands the material reorganization of our basic social institutions, and it challenges the assumptions of sameness and assimilation in a profound way. Furthermore, critical disability theory interrogates not only conceptions of productivity and efficiency – a strategy destabilizing enough on its own – but also taken-for-granted assumptions of adequacy and competency. In short, this collection argues that critical disability theory demands a reconceptualization of the nature of, and the lived relationships among, the citizen, the self, and the community, a reconceptualization that transforms the basic assumptions of contemporary philosophy, politics, policy, and law.

Acknowledgments
Special thanks to Alexandra Dobrowolsky for her theoretical promptings and to Sheila Wildeman for her constructive criticisms, insightful comments, and self-described nitpicky nature.

Notes
1 In an earlier draft of this introduction we experimented with the idea of "PERSONS with disABILITIES" (capitalizing the elements "PERSONS" and "ABILITIES" but leaving lowercase "with" and "dis"). Our aim was to avoid the twin dangers of, on the one hand, overdetermining and essentializing the "dis" aspects of a person's identity and, on the other, underestimating how both the individual person and the larger society respond to disability. After further consideration we decided that, although this was potentially helpful, such a representation would not be easily translatable into the spoken word or alternative formats. Anyone using Braille or voice synthesis would need to be using very particularized settings to appreciate this format. We will, however, return to the identified twin dangers later in this introduction.
2 We would like to thank Sheila Wildeman for the insights articulated in this paragraph. More generally, we note that, with the exception of Sampson (Chapter 12), most of the contributions to this book tend to focus on physical rather than mental disability, a pattern that is common in much disability scholarship. In our forthcoming paper "Discitizenship," to be published by the Law Commission of Canada in 2006, we attempt to partially remedy this problem. For a recent collection specifically focusing on mental disability see Herr, Gostin, and Koh 2003.
3 The majority decision of the Supreme Court of the United States in *Sutton et al. v. United Air Lines, Inc.* (1999), a primary focus of Tyjewski's discussion, is antithetical to the unanimous decision of the Supreme Court of Canada in *Mercier* 2000. See further discussion in the Appendix.
4 In *Granovsky* 2000, the implications of binary thinking in the Supreme Court of Canada are stark for the plaintiff, who is ultimately not disabled enough to succeed in his claim.
5 In drawing this conclusion, the court assumed that impairment is not socially constructed.
6 See the Appendix for further discussion of these issues.

References
Auton v. British Columbia (Attorney General), [2004] 3 S.C.R. 657.
Bickenbach, J. 1993. *Physical disability and social policy*. Toronto: University of Toronto Press.
British North America Act, (1867), 30-31 Vict. c. 3 (U.K.).

Canadian Charter of Rights and Freedoms, Part I of the *Constitution Act, 1982,* being Schedule B to the *Canada Act 1982* (U.K.), 1982, c. 11 [Charter].

Chrétien, J. 2003. Retirement speech. 13 November. Toronto.

Devlin, R. 2001. Jurisprudence for judges: Why legal theory matters for social context education. *Queen's Law Journal* 27: 161-205.

Eaton v. Brandt County Board of Education, [1997] 1 S.C.R. 241.

Edwards v. A.G. Canada, [1930] A.C. 124 (P.C.).

Eldridge v. British Columbia (A.G.), [1997] 3 S.C.R. 624 *[Eldridge]*.

Fraser, N. 1989. *Unruly practices, power discourse and gender in contemporary social theory.* Minneapolis: University of Minnesota Press.

Granovsky v. Canada (Minister of Employment and Immigration), [2000] 1 S.C.R. 703 *[Granovsky]*.

Hammar, T. 1990. *Democracy and the nation state: Aliens, denizens and citizens in the world of international migration.* Aldershot: Avebury.

Herr, S., L.O. Gostin, and H.H. Koh. 2003. *The human rights of persons with intellectual disabilities: Different but equal.* Toronto: Oxford University Press.

Hobson, B., and R. Lister. 2002. Citizenship. In *Contested concepts in gendered social politics,* ed. Barbara Hobson and Ruth Lister, 23-54. Cheltenham: Edward Elgar.

Kabeer, N. 2002. Citizenship and the boundaries of the acknowledged community: Identity, affiliation and exclusion. Working Paper 171, Institute of Development Studies, Brighton.

Karpin, I. 1999. Peeking through the eyes of the body: Regulating the bodies of women with disabilities. In *Disability, divers-ability and legal change,* ed. M. Jones and L. Basser Marks, 283-300. Boston: Martinus Nijhoff.

Lahey, Kathleen. 1999. *Are we "persons" yet? Law and sexuality in Canada.* Toronto: University of Toronto Press.

Lepofsky, D. 2004. The long arduous road to a barrier-free Ontario for people with disabilities: The history of the Ontarians with Disabilities Act – The first chapter. *National Journal of Constitutional Law* 15: 125-333.

L'Heureux-Dubé, C. 2001. Beyond the myths: Equality, impartiality and justice. *Journal of Social Distress and Homelessness* 10, 1: 87-104.

McKenna, I. 1997. Legal rights for persons with disabilities in Canada: Can the impasse be resolved? *Ottawa Law Review* 29: 153-224.

MacKinnon, C. 1989. *Toward a feminist theory of the state.* Cambridge, MA: Harvard University Press.

[Mercier]. *Quebec (Commission des droits de la personne et des droits de la jeunesse) v. Montréal (City) (Re Mercier),* [2000] 1 S.C.R. 665 *[Mercier]*.

Michalko, Rod. 2002. *The difference that disability makes.* Philadelphia: Temple University Press.

Minda, G. 1995. *Postmodern legal movements: Law and jurisprudence at century's end.* New York: New York University Press.

Minow, M. 1990. *Making all the difference: Inclusion and exclusion in American law.* Ithaca, NY: Cornell University Press.

Plessy v. Ferguson, 163 U.S. 537 (U.S.S.C., 1896).

Pothier, D., and R. Devlin. 2006. Dis-citizenship. Ottawa: Law Commission of Canada.

R. v. Parrott, [2001] 1 S.C.R. 178.

Rawls, J. 1999. *A theory of justice.* Rev. ed. Cambridge, MA: Belknap Press of Harvard University Press.

Reference re Same-Sex Marriage, [2004] 3 S.C.R. 698.

Shutte, A. 1993. *Philosophy for Africa.* Randesboch, South Africa: UCT Press.

Sutton et al. v. United Air Lines, Inc., 527 U.S. 471 (6th Cir. 1999).

Titchkosky, T. 2001. Disability: A rose by any other name? "People first" language in Canadian society. *Canadian Review of Sociology and Anthropology* 38, 2: 125-40.

–. 2003. *Disability, self, and society.* Toronto: University of Toronto Press.

Tremain, S. 2002. On the subject of impairment. In *Disability/postmodernity: Embodying disability theory,* ed. Mairian Corker and Tom Shakespeare, 32-47. New York: Continuum Press.

–. 2006 (forthcoming). Anti-realism, bio-politics and the government of impairment in pregnancy. *Hypatia.*

Unger, R.M. 1987. *Politics: A work in constructive social theory.* Cambridge: Cambridge University Press.

Voyvodic, R. 2001. Into the wasteland: Applying equality principles to medical inadmissibility in Canadian immigration law. *Journal of Law and Social Policy* 16: 115-43.

Part 1
Setting the Context

1

Disability Policy Making: Evaluating the Evidence Base

Mary Ann McColl, Alison James, William Boyce, and Sam Shortt

We are fortunate in Canada to have a wealth of population-based information about people with disabilities available for use by researchers and advocates. There is a remarkable storehouse of national, provincial, and regional level data available to Canadian researchers who wish to study a variety of issues and conditions associated with disability. These data are available in public access files and can be readily obtained at no cost. Not least among these are Statistics Canada's 1991 Health and Activity Limitation Survey (HALS) and its successor, the 2001 Participation and Activity Limitation Survey (PALS), which are arguably the international gold standard for disability data. At the time that HALS was conceived and initially administered, no other country in the world was attempting population-based data collection on disability while conforming to the World Health Organization definition of disability.

To successfully influence policy to respond to the issues of people with disabilities, it is essential to be able to make evidence-based arguments based on population information. Population-level evidence for policy arguments has a number of advantages. It is broadly representative of the population as a whole. It provides national coverage, while still allowing for regional comparisons. Population-based surveys are often repeated periodically, making comparisons across time possible. Finally, they include large numbers of participants, making complex multivariate analyses possible, and offering some assurances of methodological rigour and consistency.

Advantages like these attract the attention of politicians, provide planning information for policy makers, and furnish statistics for advocacy groups. For example, using the 1997 Canadian Election Survey, we can identify voting patterns among people with disabilities and explore how they differ from those of the general population. In this way, we can identify the issues that mobilize disabled people to vote in certain ways, and we can assess their political power on the basis of the attention given to these issues. As another example, using the General Social Survey, we can identify socio-economic indicators such as work, education, and income among people with disabilities, to assess the presence or absence of systematic biases in productivity and distribution of wealth in the Canadian population.

Analysis of the disability policy-making process in Canada suggests that research data is one of a number of sources of evidence used by the policy community (Boyce et al. 2001). However, to use the available data to the best advantage, we need to understand the caveats of the database approach, the limitations of the data source, and the generalizability of the findings.

In this chapter, we address three objectives:

1 to identify and describe a sample of people with disabilities in national, population-level survey data
2 to compare the characteristics of disabled people with the general population, and to examine the portrait of disability according to each survey
3 to discuss policy and service implications of subscription to different definitions of disability.

To fulfill these objectives, we have undertaken a comparative study of five population-based national surveys, spanning the decade from 1991 to 2001:

• Health and Activity Limitation Survey, 1991
• General Social Survey, 1994
• Canadian Election Survey, 1997
• National Population Health Survey, 1998-99
• Participation and Activity Limitation Survey, 2001.

Issues in Assembling the Evidence

The first issue in evaluationg population-level databases for their ability to support data-based arguments is the need to be clear about who the data are referring to (Tepper et al. 1997). In other words, when the data refer to people with disabilities, whom do they include? Before attempting any methodological discussion of how disabled people were sampled or how accessible the data-gathering approach was, we must be clear about what we mean by disability. When we make a statement based on the data about what disabled people do or don't do, what their preferences are, or what conditions characterize them, we must be clear about who we are talking about (Kriegsman and Deeg 1999).

The definition of disability has undergone a fascinating and contentious period of development over the past forty years (Pfeiffer 1999). Numerous authors have discussed different definitions of disability, and argued for the benefits of one over another (McColl and Bickenbach 1998; Michaelakis 2003; Donoghue 2003; Roulstone 2003). However, all agree that the bio-medical definition that held sway before the 1970s is inadequate at best, and inappropriate at worst. More modern definitions of disability have lo-cated the origin of disability partially or wholly outside the individual, that is, in the environment, in a society built to serve the average or majority mode of moving, thinking, understanding, sensing, and reacting. This defi-nition is typically associated with the social model of disability. However, the social model has recently also been criticized. Dewsbury and colleagues (2004) claim that the social model merely replaces the biomedical discourse with a sociological discourse and still fails to deal with the real issues facing people with disabilities, such as housing, employment, and human rights.

The current gold standard for defining disability, according to several commentators, is the World Health Organization's 2001 definition (Mehlmann and Neuhauser 1999; Chatterji, Ustun, and Bickenbach 1999). The International Classification of Functioning, Disability and Health (ICF) defines disability as a component of health, rather than a consequence of disease, a determinant of health, or a risk factor. It is "an umbrella term for impairments, activity limitations or participation restrictions" (World Health Organization 2001, 3). This definition incorporates two ideas: that disabil-ity is associated with health, and that it is manifest as activity limitations and participation restrictions. It also includes a number of other ideas that are beginning to permeate the consciousness of health professionals, re-searchers, policy makers, and, perhaps more slowly, the public. For example, the WHO definition incorporates some aspects of what has come to be called the social construction of disability – in other words, the idea that disability is not an objective biomedical reality but, rather, a product of our culture and social institutions. On the other hand, the WHO definition, because of its reliance on the presence of a diagnosable health condition, has been accused of unrelenting positivism and naive realism (Roulstone 2003; Michaelakis 2003). Some authors believe that placing the definition of dis-ability in the realm of health unnecessarily limits the scope of disability and perpetuates the biomedical culture that has historically applied the "sick role" to people with disabilities and treated them as a segregated minority group.

This debate has important implications for measurement and data collec-tion on disability (Rioux et al. 2002). For example, is it appropriate in sur-vey data to ask people with disabilities about specific health conditions, and to make assumptions about the relationship of those conditions to dis-ability? Even more fundamental, is information about health conditions and activity limitations a suitable indicator of population levels of disabil-ity? Should we depend on individuals as the source of information about disability, or should data about disability focus on the structures and institutions that socially construct our potentially disabling society? Should disability information be collected at a higher level of analysis, such as the community, the health region, or the legislative jurisdiction?

Another feature of the WHO definition is its resistance to the notion that disability is a minority concern. Instead, it casts disability as a universal concern of varying degrees (Chatterji, Ustun, and Bickenbach 1999). This idea also has important implications for data collection about disability. Historically, disability has been treated dichotomously – as an on-off switch – by survey methodologists. On the basis of a screening question (or series of questions), individuals are classified as either having a disability or not having one (Cwikel 1999; Mehlmann and Neuhauser 1999; Joslyn 1999). As mentioned above, many Canadian national surveys contain a data field that acts as a screen or flag for disability. However, this approach has been criticized for inaccuracy and misrepresentation of disability. The Canadian Council on Social Development (2001) contends that this threshold approach grossly underestimates the presence of disability, while Cwikel (1999) and Chatterji and colleagues (1999) argue the opposite. Mehlmann and Neuhauser (1999) advocate instead for an ordinal approach to measurement, that is, one that recognizes that there are varying degrees of disability, not simply its presence or absence.

While it is almost impossible to marshal a credible argument against the ordinal approach, the reality faced by people with disabilities in interacting with social institutions is the dichotomous approach. The dichotomous approach responds not to the heterogeneity of disability, but to the dichotomy of the policy response – for example, pension or no pension. People with disabilities are repeatedly required to fulfill eligibility requirements, to seek the label of disability, in order to qualify for benefits and services. Thus, the dichotomous approach pervades the reality of Canadian social and political institutions, and therefore must be dealt with and understood if it is to be administered fairly and equitably, and if it is, ultimately, to be changed.

In this research, we have sought to do just that – to understand what existing data tell us about living in Canadian society with a disability, and how those data and their interpretations vary, depending on how the questions are asked.

Methods

Design
Public access data files were obtained from Statistics Canada through the Social Science Data Centre at Queen's University in Kingston, Ontario, on four national surveys:

- Health and Activity Limitation Survey (HALS), 1991
- General Social Survey (GSS), 1994
- Canadian Election Survey (CES), 1997
- National Population Health Survey (NPHS), 1998-99.

At the time of analysis, only tabular data were available for the 2001 Participation and Activity Limitation Survey, and where possible, these data are furnished as well.

Where comparisons are made with the general Canadian population, these data were taken from the National Population Health Survey. The NPHS was chosen for population comparisons since it is the most recent of the four surveys considered. Figure 1.1 gives more information about the specific objectives of each of the five surveys.

Sample

The sample consisted of all respondents in each of the surveys between twenty and sixty-four years of age. This age range was chosen to capture adult disability and to avoid mixing those with lifelong conditions with those whose disabilities were acquired in old age. Table 1.1 shows the number and sampling proportion of each survey. Information on PALS was incomplete at the time of publication. It can be readily seen from the table that sample sizes varied dramatically across surveys, from 207 for CES to more than 18,000 for HALS. In all instances, sampling weights were applied to correct for sampling proportions, as recommended in the survey documentation. Sampling weights are intended to increase the generalizability of findings to the Canadian population and are used in all subsequent analyses.

Sampling strategies differed by survey, as shown in Figure 1.2. There are a number of factors to note when assessing sampling strategy. First, it is important to note whether the sampling strategy targets the entire population (e.g., census) or particular geographic clusters. Second, it is important to note how respondents were sampled – as individuals or households? Finally, it should be noted if there were particular exclusions in a sampling frame. For example, the NPHS excluded Aboriginal reserves, armed forces, remote areas, and the three northern territories. The CES included Canadian citizens over the age of eighteen only. Most notably, HALS and PALS were population-based surveys, since they accompanied the census. All the others used a cluster sampling technique.

Measurement

The primary variable of interest is the classification of disability, with the underlying definition or construction of disability that is implied by the

Figure 1.1

Purpose of the five surveys

HALS (1991)
To collect data for a national database on disability. HALS collects data on:
- the nature and severity of disabilities;
- the barriers that persons with disabilities face in household tasks, employment, education, accommodation, transportation, finances, and recreation and lifestyles;
- the use of and need for assistive devices;
- the out-of-pocket expenses related to disability.

GSS (1994)
To gather data on social trends in order to monitor temporal changes in the living conditions and well-being of Canadians; and to provide immediate information on specific social policy issues of current or emerging interest. The 1994 survey focused on education, work, and retirement.

CES (1997)
To collect information on vote intention and party identification, interest in election, personal finances ... and national economic conditions, knowledge and rating of parties and leaders, personal position, and socio-demographic background.

NPHS (1998-99)
To collect information related to the health of the Canadian population. The board objectives are:
- to measure the health status of the population and its relationship to the use of health care services and determinants of health;
- to collect data on the economic, social, demographic, occupational, and environmental correlates of health;
- to provide information on a panel of individuals who will be followed over time to reflect the dynamic process of health and illness;
- to allow the possibility of linking survey data to routinely collected administrative data. (Tambay and Catlin, 1995)

PALS (2001)
To collect information on adults and children who have a disability, problem, ... PALS provides essential information on the prevalence of various disabilities, the supports for persons with disabilities, their employment profile, their income and their participation in society. This information will be used by all levels of government, associations, researchers and non-government organizations to support the planning of services needed by persons with activity limitations in order for them to participate fully in society.

operational definition used in the survey. Figure 1.3 details the screening questions used in each of the surveys to classify individuals as disabled or not. All very similar, the questions contain some combination of four elements:

- presence of a long-term disability or handicap
- limitation in kind or amount of activity
- presence of a physical condition, mental condition, or health condition
- location of limitation at home, school, work, or other (e.g., transportation).

Table 1.1

Proportion of sample classified as disabled

Total sample (Ages 20-64)	NPHS (1998-99)	GSS (1994)	HALS (1991)	PALS (2001)	CES (1997)
Disabled-unweighted	15.6%	16.2%	31.4%	*	6.9%
(n)[a]	(1,703)	(7,156)	(18,384)		(207)
Disabled-weighted	14.5%	14.5%	14.1%	10.6%	6.3%
Non-disabled-weighted	85.5%	85.5%	85.9%	–	93.7%

* Unweighted estimates for PALS were not available.
a The symbol (n) refers to the total number of disabled survey respondents.

Figure 1.2

Sampling frame and target population

HALS (1991)
Census-based, individually mailed, subsequent telephone survey

GSS (1994)
Household telephone survey, random digit dialling (RDD), all persons over 15 years of age

CES (1997)
Household, telephone, RDD, Canadian citizens over 18 years of age, probability sampling within household

NPHS (1998-99)
Labour force sampling frame, household, telephone, cluster sample

PALS (2001)
Same as HALS – see screening question in Figure 1.3

Figure 1.3

Screening questions – self-identification as disabled

HALS (1991)
"Are you limited in the kind or amount of activity you can do because of
a long-term physical condition, mental condition, or mental problem – at
home, at school, at work, or at other activities?"
"Do you have a long-term disability or handicap?"

GSS (1994)
"Are you limited in the amount of activity done at home?"

CES (1997)
"Do you have any long-term disability or handicap?"

NPHS (1998-99)
"Are you limited in the kind or amount of activity you can do because of
a long-term physical condition, mental condition, or mental problem – at
home, at school, at work, or at other activities?"
"Do you have a long-term disability or handicap?"

PALS (2001)
"Does a physical condition or mental condition or health problem reduce the
amount or the kind of activity you can do at home? At school or work? In
other activities (transportation or leisure)?"

Results

Prevalence of Disability
The most basic implication of the definition of disability used in population survey research is the proportion classified as disabled based on that
definition. Table 1.1 shows that the prevalence of disability varied significantly between the five surveys, with CES having the smallest proportion of
disabled individuals (6.3 percent), PALS showing just over 10 percent, and
GSS, HALS, and NPHS all at approximately 14 percent. The table is organized by increasing prevalence from left to right. It does not appear that a
temporal trend exists to explain these differences. The very low prevalence
in the CES is surprising, given that the sampling frame and questions were
similar to those of the other surveys. It may be that the method of probability sampling within households somehow systematically decreased the likelihood of participation for disabled household members.

Another interesting reference point is the reported prevalence of disability in other countries. Canadian rates were consistent with rates for other
developed countries, particularly Australia, the United States, and in Europe (Brown 1998). Canadian rates differed significantly from the very low

rates seen in the developing world. For example, rates less than 1 percent were found in Qatar, Bangladesh, and Thailand (Durkin 1996 in Brown 1998). Of course, there are artifactual (i.e., data collection issues) as well as substantive explanations for these differences.

Disability and Health

The remainder of the analyses presented focus on the group labelled as disabled in each of the four surveys of interest. Information on the total Canadian population (taken from the NPHS) is provided as a reference point for comparison and, where available, the most recent information from PALS is also provided.

Table 1.2 compares the information provided on the four surveys of interest about the types of impairments and activity limitations experienced by respondents who self-identified as having a disability. The most notable observation about the data is that dramatic differences occur from survey to survey. Whereas more than half the disabled respondents in both HALS and PALS reported mobility impairments, less than 10 percent of respondents in NPHS reported these types of problems. Pain was reported by over half the respondents in the two instances where it was directly addressed

Table 1.2

Comparison of impairments and activity restrictions (%)

	HALS (1991)	CES (1997)	NPHS (1998-99)	PALS (2001)	Canadian population (1998-99)
Impairments					
Cognitive/Learning	31.5		36.6	35.3	18.9
Emotional	26.1		8.5		2.9
Hearing	25.8	4.8	5.3	24.3	2.3
Mobility	55.1	43.6	9.9	69.1	1.9
Seeing	9.6	10.1	3.9	15.2	1.5
Agility/Dexterity	52.8	13.6	3.5	64.8	0.7
Speaking	6.7		2.0	11.4	0.4
Pain			50.9	77.7	
Other		27.7			13.1
Activity restrictions					
Heavy housework	65.2		44.7		7.5
Meal preparation	49.6		9.4		1.6
Housework	28.1		19.3		3.1
Shopping for necessities	24.2		15.4		2.6
Personal care	4.9		4.5		0.9
Moving about indoors	2.2		5.3		0.9

(PALS and NPHS). Cognitive and learning disabilities were consistently reported by about 35 percent of the disabled participants (except in CES, where this impairment was not addressed).

The same six questions about activity limitations were asked on both NPHS and HALS. Positive responses were higher for HALS, but respondents in both surveys agreed that the most troublesome activities were instrumental activities of daily living, especially heavy chores such as yard work, home maintenance, and snow shovelling. Personal care and mobility difficulties affected less than 5 percent of those who included themselves among the disabled population. In the case of both impairments and activity restrictions, the difference between disabled and non-disabled Canadians is significant and obvious.

Two of the surveys – NPHS and GSS – asked about self-assessed health. Figure 1.4 compares the results of these two surveys, including the general Canadian population rates derived from NPHS. The general population, represented by the dark bars, has a curve that is highly skewed to the right, with over 90 percent of respondents rating their health between good and excellent. The disabled populations in both surveys were more inclined to rate their health poorly. On the NPHS, 70 percent of disabled people reported their health as good to excellent, while 30 percent classified their

Figure 1.4

Proportion of sample in various states of self-reported health

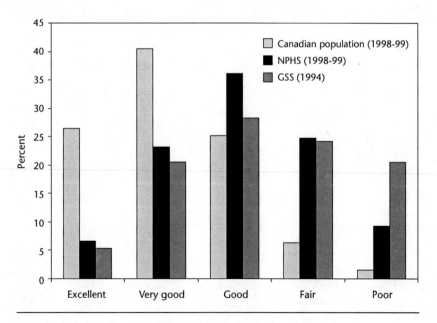

Table 1.3

Comparison of gender (%)

	HALS (1991)	PALS (2001)	NPHS (1998-99)	GSS (1994)	Canadian population (1998-99)	CES (1997)
Males	43.1	44.6	46.1	47.3	49.9	54.9
Females	56.9	55.4	53.9	52.7	50.1	45.1

health as fair or poor. Similarly, on the GSS, only 55 percent reported good to excellent health, while 45 percent reported fair to poor.

Demographic Characteristics
Table 1.3 compares the gender distribution of disabled samples on all five surveys. HALS and CES show the most extreme and, interestingly, opposite distributions of males and females. Whereas the Canadian population of adults between twenty and sixty-four years of age is almost equally divided between men and women, most of the surveys show the disabled population as dominated by women, with the exception of CES, which shows a preponderance of males.

Figures 1.5 and 1.6 offer two ways of looking at the age distributions of the disabled samples on the four surveys. Figure 1.5 shows the prevalence of disability in each of four ten-year age groups; that is, it shows the percentage of the total population in each age group that is classified as disabled. Across all four surveys the prevalence of disability increases with age. Figure 1.6 shows the proportion in each age group within the disabled population alone. Most notable in this figure are the two distinct shapes of the age distribution curve – diagonal to the right with the mode in the highest age group, and curved with the mode in the middle-age groups. This latter curve, evident in NPHS, CES, and the general population, suggests that there is a dropping off of disability after about fifty years of age. This finding warrants further exploration, as the diagonal curve is considerably more intuitive and readily explainable.

Socio-Economic Characteristics
Table 1.4 provides information about education, employment and income for people with disabilities in the four surveys. Between 25 and 45 percent of respondents report not having completed high school, and only between 40 and 50 percent attained any post-secondary education, compared with about 70 percent in the general Canadian population. Again, the explanation of a temporal trend cannot be invoked to explain these findings. Much as we might have hoped that access to higher education had improved for

Figure 1.5

Prevalence of disability in each age group

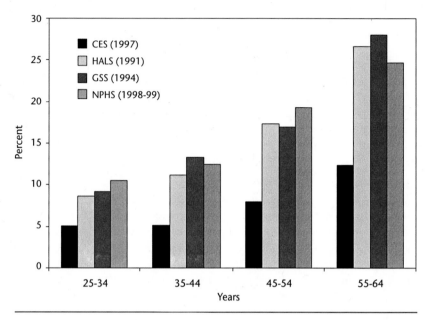

Figure 1.6

Proportion of population in each age group

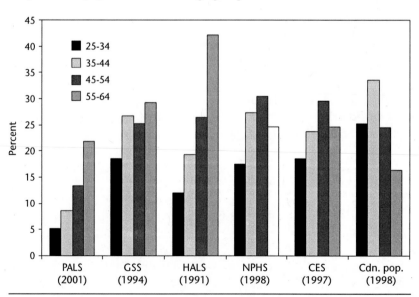

people with disabilities in recent decades, these results do not show a steady increase in either secondary or post-secondary educational attainment. They do, however, show a steady decrease in the proportion that does not complete high school.

The surveys are fairly consistent regarding employment: it hovered somewhere around the 50 percent mark for people with disabilities in Canada in the 1990s. Unemployment varies between 5 percent (close to the population norm) and 15 percent over the four surveys, while the number reported as not being in the labour market declined from 1991 to 1999. With regard to income, the surveys agree that people with disabilities are over-represented at the low end of the scale and under-represented at the high end.

Table 1.4

Comparison of educational attainment, employment, and household income (%)

	HALS (1991)	GSS (1994)	CES[a] (1997)	NPHS (1998-99)	Canadian population (1998-99)
Educational attainment					
Less than secondary	45.7	35.5	33.6	23.9	17.2
Graduated secondary	13.0	15.9	23.3	14.9	15.7
Some post-secondary	34.9	12.2	28.6	29.4	28.5
University/college degree	6.5	36.3	14.6	31.8	38.5
Employment					
Employed	47.9	49.5	41.9	55.1	69.1[b]
Unemployed	7.5	5.4	15.6	7.8	5.0
Not in labour force	44.6	44.8	42.4	37.1	25.9
school		4.5	3.4		6.9
housekeeping		18.8	7.8		13.3
retired		7.3	14.1		3.5
disabled		14.2	17.1		2.2
Income					
<$10,000	38.3	10.5		6.8	4.1
$10-$19,000	21.3	13.4	36.8[c]	14.3	9.0
$20-$29,000	15.6	16.3	15.8	12.7	10.6
$30-$39,000	24.8	15.1	5.3	13.9	13.8
$40-$49,000		15.2	23.7	12.0	13.2
$50-$59,000		10.4	7.9	8.9	11.6
>$59,000		19.0	10.5	31.4	37.7

a CES has small cell sizes; estimates may be unstable.
b Employment characteristics for Canadian population are based on 1994 data.
c This figure represents the $0-$19,000 range.

Summary
When we compare the descriptive information about the disabled population in Canada afforded by the four surveys, several similarities emerge:

- The prevalence of disability increased with age, relative to the general
population.
- People with disabilities were less likely to have post-secondary education
and more likely to lack a completed high school education.
- There was a lower percentage of people with than without disabilities in
the labour force.
- People with disabilities were overrepresented in the low-income categories.
- Women were more likely than men to report disability (except for in the
CES).

However, the surveys were dissimilar in a number of respects, such as the
prevalence of disability (6 percent to 15 percent), the prevalence of particular impairments in the disabled population, the importance of activity restrictions, and the extent of socio-economic disadvantage among people
with disabilities.

Discussion

The Portrait of Disability According to Each of the Four Surveys
In this chapter, we have set out to describe the disabled population in Canada,
using information from four national surveys spanning approximately a
decade. What emerges are four very different portraits of disabled people in
Canada. According to HALS (1991), 14.1 percent of the Canadian population are disabled. Compared with the other surveys, there were high estimates of mobility and agility problems, and instrumental activities of daily
living limitations affected about half the disabled population. Furthermore,
there were more females than males in the disabled population (56.9 percent), and disabled people had the poorest educational attainment and lowest
incomes of the four groups surveyed.

The General Social Survey conducted in 1994 also found that 14.1 percent of the Canadian population was disabled. There was no information
on the nature of disability or impairment, but the disabled population had
high estimates of poor health. Detailed information of socio-economic indicators found disabled people at significant disadvantage compared with
the Canadian population in general.

The lowest prevalence of disability among the four surveys was found in
the 1997 Canadian Election Survey, with a rate of 6.3 percent. The disabled
sample described in the CES was the most incongruent with the samples of
other surveys. For example, the disabled population in the CES had the

lowest percentage of females (45.1 percent), had the poorest record of employment (42 percent), and had the highest percentage of retired people (14.1 percent).

The disability prevalence rate for the NPHS was 14.5 percent, which was the same as for the GSS and HALS. Cognitive and pain problems were dominant in the disabled sample. Activity restrictions were noted, and chronic conditions were reported in detail. However socio-economic indicators were reported most favourably, that is, closest to those of the Canadian population as a whole.

Underlying Constructions of Disability
The purpose of this empirical exploration of disability in Canada is to expose the differences in the way disability is portrayed, depending on how it is defined. As we have shown above, different portraits of disability emerge, depending on the conditions under which data is collected. Admittedly, some of those differences are real. They could be a function of real changes over the decade covered (1991-2001). Perhaps the 1990s saw real improvements in accessibility of the environment, attitudes of society, and policy and service incentives and disincentives. If that were the case, those improvements would be reflected in the way people reported the presence or absence, and the extent, of a disability. However, we cannot dismiss the possibility that to some extent the differences between surveys are artifactual – a by-product of the way data were collected. The differences could be due to the sampling method, the questions asked, or the definition of disability applied. We are most interested in the latter possibility.

We discussed earlier the many definitions of disability that have emerged over time. Figure 1.7 outlines five such definitions. Of these, we are primarily interested in two: the biomedical and the economic. We suggest that the biomedical definition underlies the portrayal of disability in two of the surveys reviewed: NPHS and HALS. Both show a higher prevalence

Figure 1.7

Definitions of disability

Biomedical: the result of underlying illness or impairment
Philanthropic: a human tragedy, a source of sympathy, an object of charity
Sociological: a deviation from societal norms for activity performance
Economic: a social cost resulting from limited productivity and excess service costs
Socio-political: the interface between a person with a health condition and a society designed for non-disabled people

Source: McColl and Bickenbach 1998.

of disability, accompanied by reports of poorer health than that of the general population. They show a disability population with more pain, cognitive and emotional problems, significant activity restrictions, at an older age, with more females.

On the other hand, the other two surveys (GSS and CES) appear to subscribe to the economic definition of disability. They provide little information on health, illness, or impairment, and emphasize the physical limitations associated with disability. They focus on socio-economic indicators and, particularly in the case of CES, they offer a sample with a more substantial proportion of males.

Implications of Definition for Service and Policy

While the differences in these two portraits are important conceptually, they become crucial when we realize that decisions about service and policy may be based on these numbers and the impressions and assumptions that accompany them. In the final section of this chapter, we offer several examples of the ways that the data associated with these two definitions of disability might affect policy and the delivery of goods and services to people with disabilities in Canada. We offer both positive and negative implications of each definition for three types of policy issues: access to health services, income replacement, and human rights. These three policy areas were chosen for their relevance to people with disabilities.

Access to Health Services

The biomedical definition, with its focus on impairment and illness, when applied to health service and policy has the advantage of promoting a high degree of attention and specificity to health issues for people with disabilities. Data derived from HALS and NPHS offer detailed information to health planners for the development and evaluation of health services that meet specific needs of disabled Canadians. However, on the negative side, this same emphasis on underlying health conditions is the very feature for which the biomedical definition has been roundly criticized in recent years. The medicalization of disability has served to distance professionals from people with disabilities, focus on limitations rather than potentialities, and undermine the political power of people with disabilities. By reducing every concern to one of medical diagnosis and treatment, the opportunities for full participation of people with disabilities in Canadian society are limited to their participation in the health-care system.

The economic definition, on the other hand, views access to health services as an issue of service costs, economic incentives, and return to productivity. One advantage of this definition of disability for access to health services may be that it promotes more expedient and timely access, with the expectation of productive occupation and economic independence. On the negative side, the lower prevalence rates that characterize the application of the economic definition probably underestimate the need for service, particularly among members of the disabled community who participate in remunerative employment.

Income Replacement

A broad range of services and policies exist at both the federal and provincial levels, as well as in the public and private sectors, to provide economic benefits to people with disabilities and to ensure equity in the workplace. For most of these programs and benefits, a crucial issue is the establishment of eligibility. Dependence on information from the biomedical tradition in developing and implementing eligibility criteria may have the advantage, as shown in the data provided earlier, of shining some light on problems of an emotional or cognitive nature. Instead of focusing exclusively on physically observable and diagnosable conditions, the biomedical approach to disability appears to take greater consideration of important issues such as pain. The biomedical definition, however, is associated with considerably higher prevalence not only of disability in general but also of particular conditions. Numbers like these make the prospect of income replacement appear very costly indeed, and may decrease both political and public support for these programs.

Application of the economic definition of disability in the area of income replacement has the advantage of focusing attention where it belongs. The economic definition of disability argues that there are systematic inequities in Canadian society that specifically disadvantage people with disabilities. Income replacement programs are one of a variety of strategies designed to redress these inequities. On the negative side, however, the economic approach is sometimes seen as portraying competitive employment as the only legitimate productive goal, to which all should strive. To those for whom competitive employment is not a realistic outcome, this approach may be experienced as promoting two classes of citizens.

Human Rights

The application of the biomedical definition of disability to human rights issues has the advantage of legitimizing claims for consideration by lending to them the authority conferred by medical validation. In our society, medical testimonials and expert opinions are almost incontrovertible sources of evidence of the need for consideration. However, the price of this support is the necessity of adopting the sick role and becoming a patient again, rather than a citizen with full rights and participation.

The advantage of the economic definition for human rights is that it focuses attention on economic inequities rather than on personal characteristics as the basis for consideration. It assumes a structural level of analysis of social inequities, rather than a personal level. On the negative side, it provides little guidance in terms of the types of accommodations needed or the particular problems faced by people with disabilities.

Summary and Conclusions
This chapter has used data from four national surveys to describe and compare portrayals of the disabled community in Canada. We have noted that each of the four surveys provides a slightly different picture of disabled people in Canada, and further, we have suggested that these portrayals are consistent with two traditional definitions of disability:

- the biomedical definition, which portrays disability as existing exclusively within the individual, and resulting directly from medically diagnosable conditions
- the economic definition, which portrays disability as a social condition; more specifically, as a function of the ability of individuals to be economically independent and productive.

We have discussed the positive and negative aspects of each of these definitions for three areas of policy and service that are of particular concern to people with disabilities: access to health services, income replacement, and human rights.

These analyses show the power of data to create a portrait, and the importance of that portrait for subsequent decisions about access to goods and services. They emphasize the need to understand the underlying assumptions on which data are collected and the methodological decisions that flow from those assumptions. While evidence-based positions are arguably the strongest form of advocacy, it is essential to understand the sources and conditions under which data were collected in order to most effectively marshal a case or present an argument. It is our hope that these analyses have shown that different cases can be made on a variety of issues, all on the basis of high-quality, national population-based data. We have been successful in this chapter if we have raised the awareness of the reader to both the benefits and the caveats of evidence-based advocacy.

What then do we recommend to those wishing to make the situation of disabled Canadians more advantageous and equitable? First and foremost, we recommend using the abundant, high-quality data that exist. Second, we recommend using these data with knowledge and sophistication, with an awareness of their inherent strengths and limitations. Third, we recommend a healthy level of skepticism when examining numbers meant to characterize the situation of people with disabilities. We have shown how variable these numbers can be and the necessity of understanding them relative to conditions of sampling, definition, and question construction regarding disability. Finally, we recommend using multiple sources of data for the fullest possible picture of the conditions of life for people with disabilities in Canadian society.

References

Boyce, W., M.A. McColl, M. Tremblay, J. Bickenbach, A. Crichton, S. Andrews, S. Gerein, and A. D'Aubin. 2001. *A seat at the table: Persons with disabilities and policy making.* Montreal: McGill-Queen's University Press.

Brown, S.C. 1998. Demographics of disability. In *Introduction to disability,* ed. M.A. McColl and J. Bickenbach, 29-42. London: W.B. Saunders.

Canada. Statistics Canada. 1991. *Health and activity limitation survey – 1991: User's guide.* Ottawa: Statistics Canada.

–. 1995. *General social survey: Cycle 9, education, work and retirement (1994) – Public use microdata file.* Ottawa: Housing, Family and Social Statistics Division.

–. Health Statistics Division. 2000. *National population health survey* (NPHS) *1998-1999 (Cycle 3): Public use microdata files.* Ottawa: Minister of Industry.

–. Housing, Family and Social Statistics Division. 2002. *A profile of disability in Canada, 2001.* Ottawa: Statistics Canada.

Canadian Council on Social Development. 2001. *Disability information sheet #2.* Ottawa: CCSD.

Canadian Election Survey. 1997. Institute for Social Research, York University, Toronto.

Chatterji, S., B. Ustun, and J. Bickenbach. 1999. What is disability after all? *Disability and Rehabilitation* 21: 396-98.

Cwikel, J. 1999. Different strokes for different folks: Is one standard of disability possible? *Disability and Rehabilitation* 21: 379-81.

Dewsbury, G., K. Clarke, D. Randall, M. Rouncefield, and I. Sommerville. 2004. The anti-social model of disability. *Disability and Society* 19: 145-58.

Donoghue, C. 2003. Challenging the authority of the medical definition of disability: An analysis of the resistance to the social construction paradigm. *Disability and Society* 18: 199-208.

Joslyn, E. 1999. Disability and health care expenditure data: A wide range of user experience is more important than standard definitions of disability. *Disability and Rehabilitation* 21: 382-84.

Kriegsman, D.M.W., and D.J.H. Deeg. 1999. Implications of alternative definitions of disability beyond health care expenditures. *Disability and Rehabilitation* 21: 388-91.

McColl, M.A., and J. Bickenbach, eds. 1998. *Introduction to disability.* London: W.B. Saunders.

Mehlmann, M.J., and D. Neuhauser. 1999. Alternative definitions of disability: Changes in a dichotomous v continuous system. *Disability and Rehabilitation* 21: 385-87.

Michaelakis, D. 2003. The systems theory concept of disability: One is not born a disabled person, one is observed to be one. *Disability and Society* 18: 209-29.

Pfeiffer, D. 1999. The problem of disability definition: Again. *Disability and Rehabilitation* 21: 392-95.

Rioux, M., E. Zubrow, A. Furrie, W. Miller, and R. Bunch. 2002. Barriers and accommodations: Applying the human rights model of disability to HALS. *Abilities* nos. 56-57.

Roulstone, A. 2003. The legal road to rights? Disability premises, *obiter dicta,* and the Disability Discrimination Act, 1995. *Disability and Society* 18: 117-31.

Statistics Canada. 2003. *Participation and activity limitation survey: Disability supports in Canada, 2001.* Ottawa: Housing, Family and Social Statistics Division.

Tambay, J.L., and G. Catlin. 1995. Sample design of the National Population Health Survey. *Health Reports* 7, 1: 29-38.

Tepper, S., J. Sutton, P. Beatty, and G. DeJong. 1997. Alternate definitions of disability: Relationship to health care expenditures. *Disability and Rehabilitation* 19: 556-58.

World Health Organization. 2001. *International classification of functioning, disability and health.* Geneva: WHO.

Part 2
Conceptual Frameworks

2

Does Theory Matter? Exploring the Nexus between Disability, Human Rights, and Public Policy

Marcia H. Rioux and Fraser Valentine

Legal cases, social policies, and programs point to a divergence in the way the legal and social parameters of human rights and equality for people with disabilities are framed. While the concept of human rights is widely accepted as an organizing principle for law, policy, and advocacy, its meaning in practice is widely divergent and actively debated, resulting in a lack of conceptual clarity. This lack of consensus is evident beyond the judicial branch, extending to legislative and administrative developments and to the disability movement. The goal of this chapter is to illustrate theoretical frameworks found in current practice. In particular, we are interested in exploring the tension between promoting rights and enabling citizenship on the one hand, and paternalistic protection, which underlies legal cases, policies, and practices, on the other hand.

The chapter concludes that theory *does* matter because the development of theory associated with disablement and equality has an impact on, first, an understanding of the meaning of disablement and, second, the development of consistent laws, policies, and practices. The shift in meaning of disablement, grounded in current constitutional protection of disability equality rights and in government policy statements, is uneven. The result is a lack of consensus across the various arenas of policy making concerning the relationship between disability and equality.

This debate is complicated because it requires that we unravel the confusion about the meaning of disablement itself, about which there is no general social or legal consensus. This uncertainty about the meaning of disablement both causes and contributes to the ongoing conflict around policies, programs, laws, and advocacy that are purported to be based on equality and human rights.

A critical disability theory approach offers an important lens in unravelling the inherent complexities associated with disablement and equality. It begins with the assumption that theories of human rights and equality provide the necessary foundation for understanding the linkages between the existing legal, economic, political, and social rationales for the full inclusion of people with disabilities, and the systemic barriers and oppression that continue to construct people with disabilities as inherently unequal and disentitled to citizenship rights. Critical disability theory offers a politicized view of the meaning and experience of disablement in contemporary Canadian society.

Theoretical Overview

Since the late 1970s, there has been a consistent trend in both international and domestic developments linking disability and human rights. Indeed, throughout the 1980s and early 1990s, a series of federal initiatives were pursued to advance the political, civil, and social rights of Canadians with disabilities. As part of the constitution, the passage of the *Canadian Charter of Rights and Freedoms* (1982) is perhaps the most significant domestic development affecting Canadians with disabilities. There is, however, an important and noteworthy paradox.

While governments have enshrined formal equality rights in the Charter and in other human rights codes, substantive citizenship rights – especially at the provincial and municipal level – have not been attained in programs and services. Therefore, most people with disabilities continue to be inhibited from achieving full citizenship. Examining policy frameworks in place at the provincial level reveals a profound contradiction in disability politics. Indeed, the fundamental – but unstated – divergence between governments and the disability community resides in two unreconciled views of the meaning of "inclusion" and "citizenship." Since the passage of the Charter, there has been broad agreement on guaranteeing equality of Canadians with disabilities. Federal and provincial human rights legislation extends anti-discrimination measures to the private and public spheres. People with disabilities have taken this to mean that they should have certain entitlements in all government programs. Governments, on the other hand, see equality as limited by their need to contain spending, and so tend not to talk about entitlements but, rather, "discretionary benefits."[1] Because both governments and the community use the terms "citizenship" and "inclusion" but interpret the meanings differently, the language around disability itself creates a circle of tension and confusion.

The pattern of discrimination and inequality remains entrenched even when individuals and the advocacy community have adopted a rights-based approach and have gone to court to confirm their rights and consequent entitlements to certain services. Arguments grounded in economic rationalism or in biomedical views of disablement have led governments to justify their discretion over policy and spending at the expense of the exercise of rights for people with disabilities. This has occurred even in the face of

Figure 2.1

The social and scientific formulations of disability

INDIVIDUAL PATHOLOGY	
Biomedical approach (consequence of biological characteristics)	**Functional approach** (consequence of functional abilities and capacities)
• **Treatment:** through medicine and biotechnology • **Prevention:** through biological or genetic intervention or screening • **Social responsibility:** to eliminate or cure	• **Treatment:** through rehabilitation services • **Prevention:** through early diagnosis and treatment • **Social responsibility:** to ameliorate and provide comfort
SOCIAL PATHOLOGY	
Environmental approach (consequence of environmental factors and service arrangements)	**Human rights approach** (consequence of social organization and relationship of individual to society)
• **Treatment:** through increased individual control of services and supports • **Prevention:** through elimination of social, economic, and physical barriers • **Social responsibility:** to eliminate systemic barriers	• **Treatment:** through reformulation of economic, social, and political policy • **Prevention:** through recognition of conditions of disability as inherent in society • **Social responsibility:** to provide political and social entitlements

the courts, including the Supreme Court of Canada, having confirmed those rights in cases based on the *Canadian Charter of Rights and Freedoms,* human rights legislation, or other statute law. The inherent tension in contemporary debates about disability in Parliament, in the courts, and among disability activists is grounded in the theories that underlie the collective understanding of disablement. The leading formulations of disablement – the social scientific view of disability, which includes the biomedical and functional approaches, and the social pathology view of disability, which includes the environmental and human rights approaches – shed light on why there is such a discrepancy in implementation of rights and equality in the area of disability. Figure 2.1 summarizes these competing views of disability and disablement and the social responsibilities that attach to each formulation (Rioux and Zubrow 2001).

Social and Scientific Views of Disability

How disability is perceived, diagnosed, and treated, scientifically and socially, is reflected in assumptions about the social responsibility toward people with disabilities as a group.[2] The assumptions or postulates about disability are neither mutually exclusive nor temporally chronological. Some disciplines have characterized disability as solely a biomedical condition, a genetic condition, a disease category, or a personal deficit, while others have adopted the framework of disability as a consequence of social, environmental, and political conditions. There are also hybrids of these two major schools of thought. Consequently, there are tensions in the areas of policy and programming, within both the professional sphere and government, that reflect attempts to accommodate these diverse understandings of disability as a status and of how it should be addressed.

There are four identifiable social and scientific formulations of disability reflected in the treatment of people with disabilities in law, policy, programs, and rights instruments. They can be traced to the concept of disability as a consequence of an individual pathology and the concept of disability as a consequence of a social pathology.

Formulations of Disability Based on Individual Pathology

Of the two identifiable formulations of disability that arise from the assumption that disability is an individual pathology, one is grounded in a biomedical approach and the other is grounded in a functional approach, that is, that disability is a consequence of individual functional abilities and capabilities.[3] The two have a number of common characteristics, including:

- approaching disability as a field of professional expertise
- primarily using a positivist paradigm[4]
- emphasizing primary prevention, including manipulation of biological and environmental conditions
- characterizing disability as incapacity in relation to non-disabled persons (a comparative incapacity)
- distinguishing disability and its attached costs as an anomaly and social burden
- portraying the inclusion of people with disabilities as a private responsibility
- using the individual as the unit of analysis for research and policy purposes
- depicting the individual condition as the primary point of intervention.

Generally, the social responsibility, both professional and political, that has attached and continues to attach to this perspective on disablement is directed to the elimination and cure of disability, and where that is not possible, to ameliorate the condition and provide comfort to the individual, identifying as inevitable the disadvantage suffered by the individual. While the role of the state in regulating and correcting disadvantage and inequality may be either expansive or restrictive, in this case, the privatization of the disadvantage justifies and perhaps even mandates a restrictive or passive engagement in its resolution (Rioux and Zubrow 2001; Mishra 2002). From this perspective the disadvantage is privatized, in the sense that it is presented as an individual condition, and thus the scientific rationalism that underlies this characterization of disability justifies the limitation of state intervention to prevention and comfort. A distinction is then made between what falls within the public domain and what falls within the private domain. Limiting economic expenditure to ensuring the relief of private disadvantage is then arguably reasonable. In this way, a cost-benefit analysis is factored into how far one has to go to ensure the rights and citizenship of people with disabilities.

The rise of neo-liberal ideas has led to an increase in policies and programs that view disablement as primarily an individual pathology. In Ontario, for instance, after years of moving policies and programs away from medically oriented, disease-related criteria, in 1995, the provincial government began reintroducing program eligibility criteria primarily based on formulations that characterize disability as a condition of individual pathology. These changes affected almost every area of public life, including social assistance, transportation, housing, health care, and education.

Formulations Grounded in Social Pathology
In contrast to the two approaches to disability based on individual pathology, two identifiable approaches recognize disability as a consequence of social pathology. They both start from a perspective that assumes that disability is not inherent to the individual. Rather, they assume that the disability is a consequence of the social structure and that the social determinants of disability can be identified and addressed. The pathology is that there is something wrong with the society that needs to be fixed, rather than that there is something wrong with the individual that needs fixing (World Health Organization 1980).

These two approaches have a number of shared identifiable characteristics, including:

- assuming that disability is not inherent to the individual, independent of the social structure
- giving priority to political, social, and built environment
- emphasizing secondary prevention rather than primary treatment
- recognizing disability as difference rather than as an anomaly
- portraying the inclusion of people with disabilities as a public responsibility

- using the social structure as the unit of analysis for research and policy purposes
- depicting the social, environmental, and economic structures as the primary points of intervention.

According to the environmental approach, advances in knowledge based on an understanding of disability as a social pathology demonstrate that personal abilities and limitations are the result, not only of factors residing in the individual but also of the interaction between individuals and their environments. Increasingly, researchers find that the impact of disability is compounded by the failure of ordinary environments to accommodate people's differences. Increasingly, there is evidence in policy research showing that the impact of disability can be lessened as environments are adapted to enable participation.[5]

From this perspective, disability is identified as a consequence of the barriers in society that restrict the participation of people with impairments or disabilities in economic and social life. This includes criteria or program parameters that restrict individual determination of needs and individual control of services and supports. Structural barriers to independent living or community living become the site of "therapy" or modification.[6] Prevention, then, is through the elimination of social, economic, and political barriers. Elimination of physical barriers – for example, by building ramps or adopting employment equity or affirmative action policies – is a method of prevention from the perspective of this approach to disability.

The human rights approach to disability is that disability is a consequence of how society is organized and the relationship of the individual to society at large.[7] Research, policy, and law from a human rights approach looks beyond particular environments to focus on broad systemic factors that keep some groups of people from participating as equals in society. The emphasis is on the social determinants of disability. This approach identifies wide variations in cognitive, sensory, and motor ability as inherent to the human condition and, consequently, recognizes the variations as expected events and not as rationales for limiting the potential of persons with disabilities to contribute to society.

Policy from this perspective constructs an analysis of how society marginalizes people and how society can be adjusted to respond more effectively to the presence and needs of those who have been systemically marginalized. Treating the disadvantage is postulated as being the reformulation of social and political policy. Prevention is effected through recognizing the condition of disability as inherent to society. It is presumed that people with disabilities are an inherent part of society, not some kind of anomaly to normalcy.

From this perspective, the measure of whether rights are being advanced is the degree to which civic inequalities have been reduced. In other words, the fewer the social and economic disadvantages, the greater the likelihood that discrimination against people with disabilities will not be experienced. This approach to rights makes clear that the disadvantage that attaches to disablement falls within the public domain. As a consequence, therefore, society is obliged to provide supports and aids and devices enabling social and economic integration, self-determination, and legal and social rights for the disabled. The focus is on the disabling aspects of society and on supporting human diversity and on empowering disadvantaged individuals.

The Ontario Direct Funding Program (ODFP), a relatively recent Ontario policy and program development advocated by the disability rights movement, illustrates a policy framework based on notions of social pathology. The ODFP provides funding for six hundred adults with physical disabilities who can direct their own personal support services (i.e., hire, fire, or manage attendant workers), enabling the individual to become an employer of his or her own attendants. Attendants assist persons with physical disabilities with routine activities of living, such as dressing, grooming, and bathing. The program respects the independence of persons with disabilities, recognizing that they have the skills and knowledge to control the resources affecting their daily lives.

In sum, the complexity found in these various formulations of disability, and the social responsibility inherent in them, have meaning and find expression in law, policy, administrative arrangements, and even in the advocacy demands of the disability movement itself. The lack of consensus in framing the legal and social parameters of what human rights and equality mean for people with disabilities demonstrates that elements found in each of these conceptualizations of disablement exist in tension among governments and the disability movement.

Views of Equality
As a theoretical construct, equality, like disablement, is subject to interpretation.[8] Equal treatment, equality of opportunity, and equal well-being make different claims for the meaning of equality and suggest different burdens of responsibility for governments in regard to equality generally, and arguably even more so in the area of disability. Assumptions about the meaning of equality can be found in the way in which distributive justice is applied to disablement.

If equality depends on sameness (the equal treatment model) and being *similarly situate* (in the same circumstances), the concept of equality requires that "likes" be treated alike and presumes the impartial enforcement of legal and social rights. This standard of equality can be fairly easily met. If, for example, disability is characterized as an individual pathology, the equal treatment standard can be met even in the face of significantly different social and economic entitlements and outcomes, because the difference between a person with and a person without a disability can be demonstrated. This standard of equality justifies many existing policies and services that disadvantage people with disabilities because the policies and services are not designed to recognize their being accessed by a diverse population. Obvious examples are the public education system, which may exclude children with intellectual or learning difficulties; forced therapeutic treatment of people with psychiatric disabilities; and the institutionalization of people with disabilities.

Using an equality of opportunity model for ensuring equality for people with disabilities creates a dilemma in that the model presumes that the natural characteristics of people with disabilities can somehow be overcome, when in fact this is neither possible in an objective sense nor in many cases desirable from a personal perspective.[9] The concept of substantive equality is often based on an assumption that the objective is to provide access to the competitive, individualist market, not to such non-comparable goods as minimal nutrition and medical support. The basis for a claim to equality has to provide the potential for it to be based on citizenship, humanness, or a general egalitarian value assumption so that the claim to resources enables participation, even though in some cases individuals are not likely to be competitive – within the existing social and economic climate – without some sort of ongoing support. The claim is not for support to redress past discrimination or to overcome particular barriers to participation (equality of opportunity). Instead, the claim of people with disabilities is for redistribution of state resources and ongoing systemic support to enable them to exercise the same rights as do all other people.

A model of equality based on well-being as an outcome incorporates the premise that all humans – in spite of their differences – are entitled to consideration and respect as equals, and have the right to participate in the social and economic life of society. It takes into account the conditions and means of participation that may vary for each individual, entailing particular accommodation to enable that participation. Equality, characterized as inclusion and participation, shifts the basis for distributive justice away from economic contribution as the primary factor of entitlement to other forms of participation (Young 1990). The rationale for social institutions, law, and policy is, within this context, to support the outcome of equality of well-being for all citizens.

Views of Citizenship
Citizenship is a strategically important and contentious idea that is central to an understanding of disablement. At the same time, citizenship is a messy

concept, and therefore its boundaries are often contested. It constructs a system of inclusion and exclusion, defining boundaries between who belongs and who does not, who enjoys the privileges (and duties) associated with membership and who is denied such privileges. Kymlicka and Norman (1995, 283) observe in their survey of contemporary literature on the subject that the concept of citizenship evokes an understanding of individual entitlement, as well as attachment to a particular community. Across modern liberal democracies, it brings into focus normative and empirical debates on justice, fairness, rights, identity, and equality. These debates are especially central to the lives of persons with disabilities (among other marginalized groups) who, throughout the twentieth century, have been effectively denied legal and substantive citizenship rights.[10] In Canada, for instance, people with psychiatric disabilities did not get the political right to the federal vote until 1991. Much of the literature on citizenship, however, does not examine how and why people with disabilities are constructed as non-citizens, and are thereby denied their presence as political actors.

Understanding citizenship is important for our purposes because it defines a set of principles for the relationship between individuals and the state, as well as for relationships among individuals; in this respect, it is "the concrete expression of the fundamental principle of equality among members of the political community" (Jenson and Papillon 2000, 5). This conception allows for an assessment of who belongs to and who is excluded from the community, and under what conditions. Citizenship is a dynamic relationship among three complementary dimensions: rights and responsibilities, access, and belonging. Citizenship grants rights and demands the exercise of responsibilities. But citizenship also provides access to public goods and services – to work, to education, to technology, and to social protection. These are the elements, therefore, that take citizenship beyond a passport to a sense of belonging in a community, in a country (Maxwell 2001).

For people with disabilities, citizenship requires the creation of an inclusive generic base of supports, such as child care, education, recreational programs, and accessible architectural environments for *all* citizens – not only those with disabilities. It also requires that portable and flexible supports targeting the particular needs of individuals with disabilities are in place. These include in/out home supports, respite care, education supports, and assistive devices. Citizenship principles allow us to follow the ways that patterns of access are being altered under the pressure of new economic and social realities and public choices (Valentine 2001).

Developments in international and domestic law and policy are indicative of the importance that is being placed on equality and citizenship rights as organizing principles for disability rights. These recent developments have put pressure on governments to clarify the theoretical constructs of disablement and the theoretical constructs of equality, as well as their interaction.

For people with disabilities, however, there is a substantial (and widening) gap between the rhetoric of equality found in both international and domestic policy instruments and the actual policies and programs put in place to enable people to live, work, and play in our communities.

A Need for Consensus: The Intersection of Approaches to Disability, Equality, and Citizenship

The concepts of disability, equality, and citizenship are central to advancing disability rights because the norms, standards, values, and biases on which these theoretical concepts are built lead to particular standards and constructs of policy, programs, and legal status. These in turn have an effect on whether the human rights of people with disabilities are respected or abridged.

For example, if there is a general acceptance that disability is an individual pathology, it is likely that the courts and governments will presume a model of equality that makes equal treatment of people the standard. They will argue that a person's inability to meet the standards or norms that are set for participating in society (in schools, in the workplace, in the recreational arena), justifies policies of exclusion based on individual pathology, that is, on the biological condition or functional anomaly. Consequently, despite equality advancements, a person with a disability is likely to be differentiated on the basis of his or her objective deviation from the presumed norm. This in turn leads to dissimilar social responsibility, legal treatment, and ethical standards. Not being able to participate in the same manner as others is central to the determination of how much equality, equity, and justice is determined to be the responsibility of the state.

Figure 2.2 provides a way to characterize policies, programs, and laws in relation to the underlying premises of the concepts of disability and to various constructs of equality. The intersection of these two important trends shows the types of law and policy that evolve from the ways in which the constructs intersect. Using this framework, it is possible to show the significant tension underlying current policy and law. It illustrates the need for consensus in framing the legal and social parameters of what disability, equality, and citizenship mean for people with disabilities. This lack of consensus on how to address disability has led to confusion about the meaning of equality for people with disabilities and, subsequently, about how to correct inequities in social entitlement and well-being.[11] Figure 2.2 shows three constructs resulting from the intersection of the formulations of disability and equality, and the types of legislation, jurisprudence, political and administrative developments, and policy that result.

Theories of equality are also based on some shared premises and can be loosely classified according to three general ideas.[12] Civil disability, charitable privilege, and citizenship status are theoretical constructs premised

Figure 2.2

Theoretical constructs of entitlement arising from the intersection
of disability and equality

Concepts of equality	Formulation of concept of disability			
	Individual pathology		Social pathology	
	Biomedical approach	Functional approach	Environmental approach	Rights outcome approach
Equal treatment	Civil disability			
Equal opportunity		Charitable privilege		
Equal outcome			Citizenship status	

on the ways in which the norms and standards of equality and disability are
constructed in policy instruments, as well as in the manner in which a
government chooses to meet its commitments to the agreed upon equality
standards.

Civil disability is a theoretical construct of entitlement in which a social
responsibility to protect individuals with disabilities, both legally and socially,
flows from the presumption that disablement is the consequence of an
individual's largely unchanging pathology, coupled with an understanding
of equality premised only on equal treatment. People with disabilities are
given a status that entitles them to protection by the state (both positive and
negative measures) to which others, who do not hold that status, are not
entitled. The state, therefore, assumes responsibility to protect such individuals from the ill effects and limitations of disability and to provide them with
minimal assistance. In practice, this translates into paternalistic decision
making, politics, programs, and services, including, for instance, institutional
living, segregated education, and sheltered workshops.

Charitable privilege has a long and continuing history in the provision of
care and treatment to people with disabilities. It is based on benevolence
and compassion and on forms of paternalism. The social responsibility arises
from the acknowledgment that while there is a functional incapacity inherent to the individual, the physical and social environment may exacerbate
it. If people with disabilities are seen as biomedically and functionally incapable of participating in the social life of their communities, the obligation
of the state is likely to be circumscribed and limited only to humanitarian
relief. Discrimination is rationalized as being good for an individual in these

circumstances – as a mechanism to protect the individual from harm to self and to others. Goods and services, such as medical care, housing, welfare, and therapeutic services, are provided to the individual not as a matter of right but as a matter of charity and compassion. Whether an individual has rights is premised on the ability of service providers to distinguish difference, which is characterized as incapacity. Without clear guidelines to evaluate the individual's capacity to function in a less hostile and restrictive environment, that is, in an adapted environment, the individual will predictably be viewed as different and unequal. Hence, equality of opportunity should be provided to the extent that the disability is a consequence of external factors. When this standard is used, people with disabilities trade rights for charity.

Finally, citizenship status is an emerging standard in which treatment, care, and allocation of resources are based on citizenship rights and equal outcome for people with disabilities. Society's responsibility is to provide for the disabled political and social entitlements that are equal in outcome to those of other citizens. It is built on the acknowledgment that disability is a consequence of social, economic, and political factors, not simply of individual pathology or incapacity. Further, it acknowledges both the historical disadvantages that people with disabilities have faced as well as the role and function of the current structure of society in contributing to their ongoing marginalization.

The legal and social policy consequences of these theoretical constructs show why theory matters. Indeed, there is significant tension and confusion among these three theoretical positions. This is evident in both judicial developments and political and administrative developments affecting disability in Canada. Moreover, the intersection of these constructs – civil disability, charitable privilege, and citizenship status – also provides a means for explaining the incongruous decisions in case law and political and administrative developments involving disability, as well as the discrepancies in international instruments affecting the rights of persons with disabilities.

The Recognition of Disability Rights in International Agreements

International developments have played a key role in advancing the recognition of disability as a human rights issue. A number of events in the past thirty years have led to this recognition (see Figure 2.3). The instruments arising from these developments could put social and economic rights on a par with the earlier entrenched civil and political liberties and rights, and could set a normative standard requiring that nations honour their commitments to these substantive rights without distinction based on category, including disability.[13] These international norms and standards, which are not restricted by the economic and biomedical considerations that often drive policy and programs in nation-states, have both enabled and encouraged a broader perspective of disability rights. Through these norms and standards it has been possible to draw attention to disability within the broader context of human rights. The release of intellectual and practical imagination that has been generated by this international attention to disability rights has spurred domestic developments. Further, they subject the social policy of nation-states, at least nominally, to international norms and monitoring. In the case of disability, this has particular consequence, because the conventional assumptions about disability as a restrictive condition attributable singularly to the inherent biological or medical condition of the person individualize the discrimination. Thus, the restrictions on rights and citizenship are characterized as a cross-national phenomenon.

This internationalization of disability rights has been important in moving toward a greater theoretical and conceptual clarity of the understanding of disability as an issue of rights as distinguished from charity, medicine, or rehabilitation. The *UN Standard Rules on the Equalization of Opportunities*

Figure 2.3

Initiatives undertaken by the United Nations and human rights agencies concerning persons with disabilities

Date	Initiative
1948	Universal Declaration of Human Rights
1971	UN Declaration of the Rights of Mentally Retarded Persons[a]
1975	UN Declaration on the Rights of Disabled Persons
1981	UN International Year of Disabled Persons
1982	Adoption of the World Program of Action on disabled persons
1983-92	UN Declaration of the Decade of Disabled Persons
1984	Appointment of the first UN Special Rapporteur on Disability
1993	Sub-Commission on Prevention of Discrimination and Protection of Minorities releases special report, *Human Rights and Disabled Persons*
1994	Committee on Economic, Social and Cultural Rights issues General Comment No. 5, in which disability is treated as a human rights issue
1998	UN Commission on Human Rights passes a series of resolutions linking human rights and disability (citizenship status)
2002	First meeting of the UN Ad Hoc Committee to discuss a UN convention on the rights and dignity of people with disabilities
2003	Second meeting of the UN Ad Hoc Committee and the establishment of a Working Group to consider the content of a UN convention on the rights and dignity of people with disabilities

---

a Both this and the 1948 declaration fall within the rubric of charitable privilege because they explicitly limit the rights advanced, to the extent that an individual can exercise them and as far as the state can accommodate them. Thus, they are rights circumscribed by disability. They do not make any claim on the state to facilitate the exercise of the rights by distinguishing people with disabilities as regards the way in which the state protects their rights.

for People with Disabilities is important in bridging the domains of rights and service delivery (United Nations 1993). The Rules provide a roadmap for ensuring the development and implementation of services and social development policies and programs that support and contribute to advancing the rights of people with disabilities – not simply providing them with charity and protection. The United Nations, in a series of resolutions in the last half of the 1990s, made clear that rehabilitation, equalization of opportunities, and service delivery related to disability had to have as their end goal the full exercise of human rights by people with disabilities. The resolutions formalized the need for equality provisions to ensure disability rights. In other words, the resolutions recognize that service provision, rehabilitation, and remedial barrier removal would not necessarily be adequate to ensure the enjoyment of rights by disabled people. This is an important underpinning in the context of the current commitment to the development of a UN convention on the rights and dignity of people with disabilities.

There are, however, limitations to the internationalization of disability rights. Perhaps most important to note is that it does not make factual equality the measure of legal and political action in enhancing rights for people with disabilities. In many countries, the way in which inequality for people with disabilities is addressed is through a series of measures contained in a program of action with an attached timetable for the removal of architectural barriers, return-to-work obstacles, and discriminatory practices. While important, this approach does not begin to address issues related to the restructuring of the imbalance found between persons with, and those without, disabilities among the social, political, and economic realms of life.

These international developments have also affected domestic developments in Canada. It has been argued that the pronouncements, declarations, and conventions of the UN's expanded notions of individual and collective citizens' rights have been influential in the pace of development and direction of domestic public policy (Quinn and Degener 2002).

The Recognition of Disability Rights in Canada
The pressure mounted from the disability rights movement and other rights movements, coupled with international developments, succeeded in getting the Government of Canada to embrace the equality rights of Canadians with disabilities (Rioux and Prince 2002). In the 1980s, the most important legislative advances at the national level included the passage of the *Canadian Charter of Rights and Freedoms* (1982), which extended protection against discrimination because of physical and mental disability; the passage of the *Canadian Human Rights Act* (1977), which prohibits employers and service providers from discriminating on the basis of a number of personal characteristics, including physical or mental disability; and the Canadian *Employment Equity Act* (1986) (repealed and replaced 1996), which

requires that all federally regulated employers, Crown corporations, and grant recipients move toward a representative workforce by removing employment barriers faced by four designated groups, including people with disabilities.

The extension of anti-discrimination protections for people with disabilities in each of these legislative frameworks represented a significant advance on the road to full equality. This momentum, however, has not been sustained. After the 1990s, there have only been sporadic advances for disability rights, and most of these were increasingly overshadowed by losses associated with the ascendancy of neo-liberal ideas and policies, which led to correspondingly reconstituted notions of disability, equality, and citizenship. Evidence of shifts away from full citizenship status toward notions of charitable privilege and civil disability status are evident in judicial, political, and administrative developments affecting disability in Canada.

Judicial Developments Affecting Disability in Canada

While the executive and legislative branches of government are central, the passage of the Charter has meant that the judicial branch now plays an important role in building a picture of what human rights and equality mean in practice, and in determining how pervasively the notion of charity and disentitlement continue to attach to disability. A number of recent Supreme Court of Canada cases illuminate the inherent and ongoing tension between various views of disability and conceptions of equality in Canadian society. These decisions draw a line in the sand as to where rights can be exercised by people with disabilities, and where the usual rules, norms, standards, and customs do not require that people with disabilities be treated to equality of citizenship.

In 1986, the Supreme Court in *E. (Mrs.) v. Eve* ruled that no individual could be lawfully sterilized without personally consenting, unless it is a matter of medical necessity. This case represented a significant breakthrough for disability politics and the rights of people with disability in Canada. The court reasoned that the right to procreate or the privilege to give birth is fundamental, and circumscribes the power of the state to restrict fundamental rights based on disability or on the duty of the state to protect vulnerable people. Although framed as a legal issue, in a number of countries, decisions about sterilization have become a forum for debating the status of people with disabilities generally and, in particular, for debating their claim to citizenship and equality.[14] In a similar case in England, the court ruled in *Re B (a minor)* 1987 that it was in the best interests, and clearly within the jurisdiction of the *parens patriae* power of the state, to sterilize a young woman. In other words, the Canadian court used a citizenship status model of law to decide the case, while the English court used a charitable privilege model, basing its decision on the welfare principle.

Ten years later, however, the Supreme Court of Canada decided *Eaton v. Brant County Board of Education,* which contributed to pushing the equality of people with disabilities back toward the margins of mainstream society.[15] This case involved the educational placement of Emily Eaton, a twelve year old with multiple disabilities, in a regular classroom setting with her non-disabled counterparts. Overturning the Ontario Court of Appeal's decision, the Supreme Court of Canada ruled that Emily's interests were best served in a segregated school setting, excluding her from her non-disabled peers. The case is an example of the tension between conceptions of equality and disablement in a model of law based on civil disability and the conceptions of equality and disablement in a model of law based on citizenship. On one hand, the court found that unlike other types of differences (e.g., race and gender), disability involves individual variations and, therefore, may require variable degrees of inclusion and exclusion. The court based its decision on the individual functional characteristics of the child and drew a distinction of those characteristics based on disability and difference (Frazee 2003). At the same time, the court did say clearly that integrated education is preferable for students with disabilities because of the benefits it provides. Thus, while the court made a particular decision in Emily's case, it ruled that wherever possible, regular schools should accommodate students with different learning needs because of section 15 of the Charter. In other words, the court recognized that inclusive education is an important ingredient in citizenship status, based on a social pathology model of disability and an equal outcome approach to equality. Yet, in this case, the court placed more weight on Emily Eaton's functional limitations and her capacity to learn within the conventional non-inclusive pedagogical environment than on the societal benefits to her inclusion based on notions of equality and rights.

In another case in which three people who were deaf were not provided with an interpreter for health-care services in British Columbia, there was another shift in the court's presumption.[16] The decision in *Eldridge v. British Columbia (Attorney General)* reflects a much clearer shift from a charitable privilege model of law and policy to a model of law reflecting citizenship status based on human rights for Canadians with disabilities. It prompts a paradigmatic shift away from both the view that disability is a condition that requires a cure and the consequent policies of exclusion and institutionalization that follow from that view. Indeed, there is both symbolic significance and practical importance to this strengthening by the Supreme Court of Canada of the contention that disability is a human rights issue and an issue of equality in an expansive sense. At a number of particular points, the court made determinations that support a human rights perspective, and that suggest a wider application of the findings of the case. The court's holding that "once the state does provide a benefit, it is obliged to do so in an non-discriminatory manner" (*Eldridge* 1997, para. 73) is important because it gives recognition to the entitlement of people with disabilities to government benefits, an entitlement that is not discretionary or charitable. It recognizes the right of people with disabilities to receive what others receive, as a legitimate claim and not as government largesse. They are not in the role of supplicants, nor are the benefits they receive entitlements based on charitable privilege.

The court also made clear the interpretation of equality that the Charter protects. The denial of equality in *Eldridge* arose from the failure of the government to take action (rather than the imposition of a burden). The discrimination arose from the adverse effects of a public benefit scheme that failed to provide the same level of service to the disabled as to other citizens. In Justice La Forest's opinion, to argue that "governments should be entitled to provide benefits to the general population without ensuring that disadvantaged members of society have the resources to take full advantage of those benefits ... bespeaks a thin and impoverished vision of s. 15(1)" (*Eldridge* 1997, paras. 72-73). The important principle here is that there is a positive obligation on the government to remedy inequality notwithstanding that the benefit scheme appeared neutral and the remedy meant that the government had to spend money. And in this case, the positive obligation deemed communication to be fundamental to the service (medical treatment) that was to be provided. In other words, equal treatment and equality of opportunity would not have met the standards of equality the court was trying to set in this instance.

These cases make clear the divergence in opinions that arise in framing the legal and social parameters of what human rights and equality mean for people with disabilities. While the *Eve* and *Eldridge* cases brought us closer to the goal of full inclusion for people with disabilities in Canada in the context of a citizenship status, the *Eaton* decision moved us back toward a charitable privilege model of law and policy. For our purposes, these cases do not concern the substantive issues of sterilization, education, and health services; rather, they are case studies of the interplay between law, social theory, and disability. They illuminate the tension between promoting equality rights and enabling citizenship, and paternalistic protection, a tension that pervades legal cases and other policy developments (Rioux 1990). More recent Supreme Court cases, as discussed by Pothier in the Appendix, follow from these precedents.

Political and Administrative Developments Affecting Disability in Canada

Throughout the 1990s, the advances in linking disability, equality, and citizenship were largely undercut by the forces of neo-liberalism and instrumentalism, as well as jurisdictional complexities that dominated the disability policy sphere. For instance, the three areas identified for advancement by federal, provincial, and territorial governments in the *In Unison: A Canadian Approach to Disability Issues* (Canada 1998) agreement – namely, disability-related supports, income, and employment programs – have been, at best, limited.[17] In addition, because of the arbitrary nature of the agreement on the three areas, important disability issues have been largely overlooked because they do not fit neatly into those three policy areas. The voices of those in the disability movement who advocated for other areas of importance were not heard. Examples of areas in which there was a good deal of lobbying but little success because of the neo-liberal hegemony of the government's platform are issues related to children with disabilities within the family setting and First Nations people with disabilities. Compounding the continued exclusion of these societal groups is the fact that there has been no major restructuring of the system to remove existing policy and program barriers and to put in place those elements that would enable participation. The result has been that, despite agreement on a policy framework for disability, each level of government has policies and programs in each of those three areas but without any coherent, authoritative clarification of the concept of disability or an understanding of the impact of the overlap and competitive nature of the programs put in place.

This situation is a result of the tension among the three theoretical constructs of entitlement associated with the norms and standards of equality and disability. Some examples illustrate this tension. First, the disability community frames the issues of disablement by equating inclusion with equality, and full citizenship status with the underlying (and largely unstated) assumption that citizenship is essentially based on human rights (i.e., section 15 of the *Canadian Charter of Rights and Freedoms*). Neo-liberal ideas have ushered in a new wave of policies in which the criteria for government disability entitlements still applies some version of the civil disability model of entitlement, that is, a biomedical formulation of disability that does not incorporate the notion that it is the social and legal construction of disability that leads to the individual disadvantage. In practice, this translates into paternalistic decision making policies, programs, and services, including, for instance, institutional living for children and adults with disabilities (especially developmental disabilities), sheltered workshops, services based on professional classification schemes, and rehabilitation protocols, as well as precarious forms of employment such as part-time work and short-term contracts (see Wilton, Chapter 6).

Second, as neo-liberal ideas permeated most aspects of policy making in Canada, driven primarily by the goals of fiscal restraint, deficit reduction, and smaller government, the relationship between the Canadian welfare state and citizens began to shift (Rice and Prince 2000). These shifts led to an increased role for voluntary and charitable organizations in providing to

Canadians, including Canadians with disabilities, supports and services that the state had no interest in offering or capacity to provide to its citizenry. Tension among the three theoretical constructs of entitlement is exhibited in part because the voluntary sector has no clear model for understanding disability, and in part because some people still hang on to the vestiges of charitable privilege of entitlement – a view of people with disabilities as the deserving poor requiring social protection. This falls far short of full citizenship status for persons with disabilities and represents a step backwards. In practical terms, the neo-liberal period has meant that rights and benefits providing income supports and employment for people with disabilities are largely determined according to individual potential for self-reliance.[18] A marked preference and concern for those seen to have the greatest potential for independent functioning is inherent to the goals of prevention and amelioration. However, for the residue – the "deserving poor" – who need some form of long-term care and financial support, benefits are provided as a humanitarian and charitable gesture, rather than as an entitlement based on equality and citizenship.

Third, while using language based on equality, the neo-liberal period has resulted in federal and provincial governments' assuming that achieving inclusion is determined largely by financial capacity; thus, they try to hang on to discretion over spending on disability programs, which has created an uneven mix of policies based on both civil disability and charitable privilege. In short, most policies and programs aimed at promoting the full citizenship status of people with disabilities are underfunded. Perhaps the best example is found in our public schools. Despite the fact that at the international level, Canada – along with the United States – has been a leader in advancing the notion of inclusive education, recent studies on special education indicate that special education policy, practice, and funding are inconsistent across the country. This creates a situation that imposes significant hardships on many Canadian children and their families. A recent study of the well-being of children and youth concluded that "families with children with disabilities are facing cutbacks in teaching assistant and teacher-training for inclusion – and shorter school days for children with disabilities." Moreover, "cutbacks in related services funded under Health and Social Services have further reduced access to education for children with disabilities" (Canadian Institute of Child Health 2000, 248). Children may, in fact, be included in regular classroom settings, but often they are not provided with the supports and services that are responsive to the students' individual needs. That is, the child has no individual supports, nor is there any support for the systemic change that would be needed to enable the child to function without individual support. In other words, a child with low vision may be in a regular classroom but not have adequate access to Braille instruction because of a shortage of funding for itinerant teachers of Braille, and because non-specialist teachers are not required to have the capacity to provide Braille instruction.

For Canadians with disabilities, the tension among these three theoretical constructs of entitlement is more than an academic curiosity. It represents a very real barrier to their full participation in mainstream Canadian society, and goes some distance in explaining the underlying reasons for the ongoing patterns of exclusion and oppression among people with disabilities (including children and their families) from our communities, workplaces, and schools (Valentine 2001).

Conclusion: The Still Unfinished Project of Disability, Human Rights, and Public Policy

In this chapter we sought to illustrate why theory does in fact matter in advancing the rights of Canadians with disabilities. Using an approach to critical disability theory that offers a politicized view of the meaning and experience of disablement, this chapter began by considering the assumptions or postulates about disability evident in the most salient theoretical social and scientific views of disability, and by considering the theoretical constructs of equality and citizenship in contemporary Canadian society. Using a review of the most significant initiatives (at the international and domestic levels) affecting persons with disabilities, we conclude that a lack of consensus exists at the intersection of approaches to disability, equality, and citizenship with respect to persons with disabilities. Despite significant advances in political, administrative, and judicial documents in recognizing disability as a matter of human rights, there continues to be significant tension among three competing theoretical constructs of entitlement – civil disability, charitable privilege, and citizenship status. A review of key developments in the contemporary period reveals a divergence of opinions in regard to advancing the equality right of Canadians with disabilities, and the onset of neo-liberalism has led to increased confusion and tension in framing the legal and social parameters of what human rights and equality mean for people with disabilities. In short, we have confused law and confused policy concerning the meaning of disablement and its intersection with equality.

This confusion is perhaps to be expected in an area of equality rights as complicated as disability. Achieving equality for persons with disabilities, however, requires that all political, administrative, and judicial actors understand the meaning and experience of disablement as nothing short of full citizenship status. Getting to this point, however, will require significant and ongoing debate in our legislatures, in our courtrooms, and in civil society.

Acknowledgments
We would like to thank the participants in the Critical Disability Theory: Legal and Policy Issues conference, which was held as part of the annual meetings of the Canadian Association of Law Teachers and the Canadian Law and Society Association at the Dalhousie Law School, Halifax, 31 May-4 June 2003, for their thoughtful and insightful comments on an earlier draft of this chapter. As well, our thanks to the editors of this collection, Richard Devlin and Dianne Pothier, for their commitment to expanding our knowledge base on critical disability theory.

Notes
1 A recent example would be reforms to the Canada Pension Plan that changed the eligibility criteria for people with disabilities.
2 This section has been adapted from an earlier published article. See Marcia H. Rioux, "Disability: The Place of Judgement in a World of Fact," *Journal of Intellectual Disability Research* 41, 2 (April 1997): 102-11.
3 This distinction was originally developed from an empirical analysis of the ideas, concepts, and programs related to disability. See Rioux 2003; Rioux and Zubrow 2001.
4 In general, the positivist paradigm emphasizes the supremacy of human reason, arguing also that there is a single objective truth that can be discovered through scientific techniques. This paradigm regards the world as a rational and ordered place, with a clearly defined past, present, and future. The positivist paradigm encompasses a variety of perspectives, including the economic, behavioural, cognitive, motivational/trait/attitudinal, and situational.
5 See, for instance, Peggy Hutchinson, Peter Dunn, John Lord, and Andrea Pedlar, *The Impact of Independent Living Resource Centres in Canada* (St. Catharines, ON: Brock University, 1996); Roeher Institute, *Final Evaluation Report on the Direct Funding Initiative* (North York, ON: Roeher Institute, 1997). Finally, on the relationship between disablement and the workplace environment, see National Institute of Disability Management and Research, *Strategies for Success: Disability Management in the Workplace* (Vancouver: NIDMR, 1997).
6 For examples of this approach, see, for instance, the Canadian Association of Independent Living Centres, *A Time for Change/The Time for Choices: A Proposal for Improving Social Security Arrangements for Canadians with Disabilities* (Ottawa: Canadian Association of Independent Living Centres, 1994); Sherri Torjman, *Income Insecurity: The Disability Income System in Canada* (Downsview, ON: Roeher Institute, 1988).
7 A significant body of research is available on this approach. See, for instance, W. Roth, "Disability as a Social Construct," *Society* 20 (1983): 56-61; P. Beresford and J. Campbell, "Disabled People, Service Users, User Involvement and Representation," *Disability and Society* 9 (1994): 315-25; M.H. Rioux and M. Bach, eds., *Disability Is Not Measles: New Research Paradigms in Disability* (North York, ON: Roeher Institute, 1994); Roeher Institute, *Social Well-Being: A Paradigm for Reform* (North York, ON: Roeher Institute, 1993); Canadian Society for ICIDH, "The Handicap Creation Process," *ICIDH International Network* 4 (1991); M. Oliver, *The Politics of Disablement: A Sociological Approach* (London: Macmillan, 1990).
8 This section is taken substantially from M.H. Rioux, "On Second Thought: *Knowledge, Law, Disability and Inequality*," in *The Human Rights of Persons with Intellectual Disabilities*, ed. S. Herr, L.O. Gostin, and H.H. Koh, 287-317 (Oxford: Oxford University Press, 2003).
9 For a critique of the social model from a post-materialist/post-structuralist perspective, see M. Corker and T. Shakespeare, *Disability/Postmodernity: Embodying Disability Theory* (London: Continuum, 2002).
10 These debates also apply to other oppressed and marginalized citizens, including women, gays and lesbians, and First Nations peoples.
11 As Frazee, Gilmour, and Mykitiuk in Chapter 10 of this book, as well as Sampson in Chapter 12, explore in their discussions on the gendered body, the construction of disability for women is an important example of regulation by systems of law and policy.
12 We are not here trying to cover the entire expanse of equality theory, something which is beyond the parameters of this chapter. Rather, we are looking at the general trends of

equality theory as a way to understand that some formulations of disability, in conjunction with particular constructs of equality, will lead to very distinct legal, policy, and program directions and justifications of actions, even when they result in disadvantage. For an analysis of equality, see Malhotra's discussion in Chapter 3.

13 For an extensive review of international human rights instruments in the context of disability, see Quinn and Degener 2002.

14 See further, Marcia H. Rioux, "Sterilization and Mental Handicap," *Leisurability* 17, 3 (1990): 3-11.

15 For three years, Emily Eaton regularly attended elementary school in Brant County, Ontario, with a full-time educational assistant – until an Identification, Placement and Review Committee found that her needs were not being met in the regular classroom. Accordingly, a special educational tribunal decided that Emily should be placed in a special class for students with disabilities. The tribunal reasoned that because of her intellectual and physical disabilities, Emily would not learn in a regular classroom. Wanting her to stay in her neighbourhood school, Emily's parents argued that Emily had the right to inclusive education under section 15 of the *Canadian Charter of Rights and Freedoms.*

16 On 9 October 1997, in a unanimous decision, the Supreme Court of Canada ordered the Government of British Columbia to pay for sign language interpreters when deaf people access health-care services. The failure to provide sign language interpretation, where it is needed for effective communication in the delivery of health-care services, violates the rights of deaf people.

17 The *In Unison* agreement was reached by the federal, provincial, and territorial governments. In it, the governments adopted a common pan-Canadian vision and long-term policy direction in the area of disability. It is a vision based on the values of equality, inclusion, and independence, and which seeks to translate the vision of full citizenship into objectives and policy directions in three interrelated building areas: disability-related supports, employment, and income. This is a commitment the Government of Canada, and some provincial governments, continue to reaffirm in broad-based policy frameworks on disability. See, for instance, Canada, *Advancing the Inclusion of Persons with Disabilities: A Government of Canada Report, December 2002* (Hull: Human Resources Development Canada, 2002); Manitoba, *Full Citizenship: A Manitoba Strategy on Disability* (Winnipeg: Ministry of Family Services and Housing, 2001).

18 An interesting example of post-secondary education and students with disabilities is explored by Hibbs and Pothier in Chapter 9.

References

Canada. Federal, Provincial, and Territorial Ministers Responsible for Social Services. 1998. *In unison: A Canadian approach to disability issues – A vision paper.* Hull: Human Resources Development Canada.

Canadian Charter of Rights and Freedoms, Part I of the *Constitution Act, 1982,* being Schedule B to the *Canada Act 1982* (U.K.) 1982, c. 11 [Charter].

Canadian Human Rights Act, 1977, S.C. 1976-77, vol. 2, 25-26 Eliz. II, c. 33.

Canadian Institute of Child Health. 2000. *The health of Canada's children: A CICH profile.* 3rd ed. Researched and prepared by Karen Kidder, Jonathan Stein, and Jeannine Fraser. Special contributions by Graham Chance. Ottawa: Canadian Institute of Child Health.

E. (Mrs.) v. Eve, [1986] 2 S.C.R. 388.

Eaton v. Brant County Board of Education, [1997] 1 S.C.R. 241.

Eldridge v. British Columbia (A.G.), [1997] 3 S.C.R. 624 [*Eldridge*].

Employment Equity Act, 1986, S.C. 1986, vol. 1, 34-35 Eliz. II, c. 31. Repealed by the *Employment Equity Act,* 1995, S.C. 1995, vol. II, 43-44 Eliz. II, c. 44, in force 24 October 1996.

Frazee, Catherine. 2003. *Thumbs up! Inclusion, rights and equality as experienced by youth with disabilities.* Working Paper Series, Perspectives on Social Inclusion, Laidlaw Foundation, Toronto.

Jenson, Jane, and Martin Papillon. 2000. *The changing boundaries of citizenship: A review and a research agenda.* Ottawa: Canadian Centre for Management Development. http://www.cprn.org.

Kymlicka, Will, and Wayne Norman. 1995. Return of the citizen: A survey of recent work on citizenship theory. In *Theorizing citizenship*, ed. Ronald Beiner, 283-322. Albany: State University of New York Press.

Maxwell, Judith. 2001. *Toward a common citizenship: Canada's social and economic choices.* Ottawa: Canadian Policy Research Networks.

Mishra, Ramesk. 2002. Globalizing social rights. *Man and Development* 24, 4 (December): 155-78.

Quinn, Gerard, and Theresia Degener. 2002. *Human rights and disability: The current use and future potential of United Nations human rights instruments in the context of disability.* UN Doc. HR/PUB/02/1. New York and Geneva: United Nations. http://www.unhchr.ch/html/menu2/hrdisability.htm.

Re B (a minor) (wardship: sterilization), [1987] 2 All E.R. 206 (H.L.).

Rice, James J., and Michael J. Prince. 2000. *Changing politics of Canadian social policy.* Toronto: University of Toronto Press.

Rioux, Marcia H. 1990. Sterilization and mental handicap: A rights issue. *Leisurability* 17, 3: 3-11.

–. 2003. On second thought: Knowledge, law, disability and inequality. In *The human rights of persons with intellectual disabilities,* ed. S.S. Herr, L.O. Gostin, and H.H. Koh, 287-317. Oxford: Oxford University Press.

Rioux, Marcia H., and Michael J. Prince. 2002. The Canadian political landscape of disability: Policy perspectives, social status, interest groups and the rights movement. In *Federalism, democracy and disability policy in Canada,* ed. Alan Putee, 11-29. Kingston: McGill-Queen's University Press.

Rioux, Marcia, and Ezra Zubrow. 2001. Social disability and the public good. In *The market or the public domain: Global governance and the asymmetry of power,* ed. Daniel Drache, 148-71. New York: Routledge.

United Nations. 1993. Standard Rules on the Equalization of Opportunities for People with Disabilities. UN GA Res. 48/96, Annex (48th Session, December 1993).

Valentine, Fraser. 2001. *Enabling citizenship: Full inclusion of children with disabilities and their parents.* Ottawa: Canadian Policy Research Networks.

World Health Organization. 1980. *International classification of impairments, disabilities and handicaps: A manual of classification relating to the consequences of disease.* Geneva: World Health Organization.

Young, Iris Marion. 1990. *Justice and the politics of difference.* Princeton, NJ: Princeton University Press.

3
Justice as Fairness in Accommodating Workers with Disabilities and Critical Theory: The Limitations of a Rawlsian Framework for Empowering People with Disabilities in Canada
Ravi A. Malhotra

John Rawls' classic work, *A Theory of Justice,* originally published in 1971, captured the imagination of a generation of philosophers, policy makers, and advocates of social justice. In articulating a framework for constructing a more just society, Rawls' hotly debated proposals have served as an indispensable starting point for theorists of equality. It is no overstatement to say that the Rawlsian legacy is one of the most significant contributions to contemporary theories of equality. As even libertarian philosopher Robert Nozick remarked, "political philosophers now must either work with Rawls' theory or explain why not" (Nozick 1974, 183). But can a Rawlsian theory of distributive justice adequately provide a model for understanding the marginality faced by workers with disabilities in the labour market?

I begin this chapter with a brief examination of the profound barriers faced by workers with disabilities in Canada as well as an account of the legislative framework and jurisprudence relating to disability discrimination in employment. I then provide a brief overview of the Rawlsian theory of justice as fairness, and I suggest that although Rawls' Difference Principle importantly addresses the question of redistribution to the less advantaged members of society as a legitimate tool of social policy, Rawls' framework is deeply flawed in its capacity to address the myriad issues faced by workers with disabilities because it fails to appreciate how structural barriers handicap people with disabilities. I therefore argue that a commitment to the social model of disablement (Bickenbach 1993, 135-81), focused on addressing the structural barriers in society, is a necessary prerequisite for formulating sound disablement policy to ameliorate the economic marginalization of workers with disabilities in Canada. I further propose four modifications that would thoroughly transform and reconstruct Rawls' model to better respond to the issues faced by workers with disabilities.

These modifications would stipulate that barriers in the structural environment, be they physical or attitudinal, would be eliminated up to the point of undue hardship. Second, the Rawlsian distinction between social and natural goods is collapsed, so that the social basis of all goods is recognized. Third, contracting parties to Rawls' theory of justice in what Rawls calls the original position would have awareness of characteristics such as race, class, gender, and disability that are constitutive of people's essential identities. Critical theory, such as the analysis articulated by Seyla Benhabib, helps to understand the importance of this proposal. Finally, I suggest that an engagement with critical theory, specifically insights from Benhabib's scholarship on models of discourse and public space, radically transforms Rawls' theory of public reason in a way that enables it to more effectively address the marginalization and discrimination faced by people with disabilities. In the final section of this chapter, I evaluate the Canadian approach to disability policy in employment in light of this transformed Rawlsian theory of distributive justice.

Disability Discrimination and Workers with Disabilities in Canada

The Economic Status of People with Disabilities

Labour market status remains a fundamental defining characteristic for most individuals. At a time of significant cutbacks to social programs in many sectors, including health, welfare, and education, the surest path to social inclusion and economic security is obtaining and maintaining a full-time job. In Canada, however, people with disabilities remain largely outside the labour market. Given the widespread barriers to employment, from inflexible work schedules to workplaces inaccessible to wheelchair users to widely held attitudes that have historically regarded people with disabilities as inferior and dependent (Oliver 1990, 90-92; Wilton, Chapter 6, this volume), this is hardly surprising.

According to 1996 Canadian census data, people with disabilities were only half as likely as people without disabilities to be employed and find it particularly difficult to maintain full-time employment throughout the year. Moreover, the labour market participation rate has actually worsened since 1991 for both men and women with disabilities, and is dramatically lower for Aboriginals with disabilities (Canada 2002, 35-38). Indeed, there is some evidence to suggest that Canada's performance on employment for workers with disabilities trails that of other leading advanced industrialized countries. Canadians with disabilities are clearly more likely than are other Canadians to live in poverty. Approximately one in four people with disabilities lives in low-income households, a rate twice that of people without disabilities (Canada 2002, 36, 47).

Marginalization in the labour market surely reflects the contributing impact of discrimination and barriers in other spheres of social life, and the evidence confirms this. Canadian census data from 1996 indicate people without disabilities are more than twice as likely as people with disabilities to have a university degree (Canada 2002, 33). The low levels of education for people with disabilities undoubtedly reflects the financial and physical barriers to obtaining a university education at a time of sharply rising tuition, as well as the fact that children with physical disabilities, regardless of intellectual ability, were largely educated in third-rate segregated schools in Canada until the 1980s (*Adler v. Ontario* 1994, 48-50). In response to such widespread social exclusion and the physical and attitudinal barriers that impede the lives of people with disabilities, Canadian disability rights activists have campaigned vigorously for legislation that prohibits discrimination on the basis of disability in all spheres of social life. This points to a growing acceptance of the social model of disablement, which posits that people with disabilities are primarily oppressed by the structural barriers in society that handicap them. The social model contrasts sharply with the medical model, which regards curing or at least limiting the physiological impairments of the disabled person's body as the quintessentially appropriate policy intervention (Bickenbach 1993, 61-92; Barnes, Mercer, and Shakespeare 1999, 76).

Disability Discrimination Law in Employment in Canada
In 1982, the adoption of the *Canadian Charter of Rights and Freedoms* as one component of the process of repatriating the Canadian constitution was a pivotal moment in Canadian political history. The equality rights provision of the Charter includes a prohibition on discrimination on the basis of mental or physical disability, making Canada one of the first countries in the world to establish equality rights for people with disabilities in its constitution. The political awareness generated by the United Nations Declaration of 1981 as the International Year of Disabled Persons clearly had an impact for Canadian policy makers at a fortuitous time. Disability discrimination has been prohibited under the human rights codes of the various provinces as well as in the federal sphere and, in fact, allegations of disability discrimination in recent years have constituted the most common ground of complaint before both the Ontario and Canadian Human Rights Commissions (Lynk 2002, 52-56; Torjman 2001, 155). In the employment area, the duty to accommodate workers with disabilities up to the point of undue hardship has thus become a central feature of the law as a result of both the relevant statutes and the evolution of jurisprudence, as seen through recent rulings of the Supreme Court (Lynk 2002, 59). At the federal level, employment equity for people with disabilities and other equity-seeking groups has been enacted (Torjman 2001, 156).

A strength of Canadian jurisprudence is the broad definition given to disability for the purposes of accommodation, including mental health disabilities, chronic pain conditions, and alcoholism (Lynk 2002, 61-64). The key principles of anti-discrimination law may be briefly said to consist of the following ideas. Human rights legislation, including the duty to accommodate, has a quasi-constitutional status in Canadian law and therefore must be given significant weight when evaluating the merits of other laws and policies that may conflict with human rights. Furthermore, the fact that a discriminatory policy was not intended to discriminate is irrelevant in evaluating whether it breaches human rights legislation. While employers need not accommodate an employee if it would create an undue hardship, disability accommodation in the workplace is regarded as a significant, not a trivial, obligation and may be considered by labour arbitrators as well as human rights adjudicators (*Renaud* 1992; *BCGSEU* 1999). Although all parties in a unionized workplace must cooperate in avoiding discrimination and accommodating a disabled employee, the employer is primarily accountable for implementing the accommodation since it has control over the workplace. Similarly, even though terms of the collective agreement must be interpreted in light of human rights legislation and may have to be modified to comply with human rights legislation and to facilitate the accommodation, it is the employer who is primarily accountable for the accommodation (Lynk 2002, 59).

Recent Supreme Court of Canada decisions such as the *Meiorin* case (*BCGSEU* 1999) have constrained an employer's ability to claim that an accommodation that alters a work standard or practice constitutes undue hardship. In *Meiorin*, the court held that an aerobic standard for firefighters discriminated against female firefighters who, unlike their male colleagues, generally were unable to comply with the standard. Furthermore, an employer must demonstrate that the standard meets a three-part test: (1) it was adopted for a purpose rationally connected to job performance, (2) it was adopted in good faith and honest belief that it was necessary to fulfill a legitimate work-related purpose, and (3) it is reasonably necessary to accomplish a legitimate work-related purpose. The third part of the test includes a requirement to show that accommodating individual employees is impossible without imposing undue hardship on the employer (Sheppard 2001, 540-41). Therefore, an employer must meet a very high standard, identifying how practices in the workplace may impinge on people with disabilities and how such effects may be redressed, before it will be permitted to claim an undue hardship. Indeed, the new approach outlined is presented at times in the ruling as requiring dramatic change to empower minorities such as people with disabilities (Sheppard 2001, 550).

Nevertheless, other commentators have stressed the ambiguity of the Supreme Court's decision and the uncertainty as to its long-term implications for disability rights law. Pothier (1999, 27-28) argues that the final branch of the test focuses excessively on addressing individual accommodation rather than the systemic barriers frequently faced by workers with disabilities. In reality, the practical results are more muted than they might initially appear because they largely affect the minority of people with disabilities – those who are already in the workforce – while barriers in transportation and education impede the progress of the majority of persons with disabilities.

A broader approach to disability is needed to fully confront the barriers faced. Below, I briefly outline Rawls' theory of justice as fairness before turning to an analysis of its limitations and my proposal to transform it, followed by a brief application of my theory to Canadian employment law.

Rawls' Theory of Justice as Fairness

Influenced by Kantian theory (Rawls 1999, 221-22; Fisk 1975, 56), Rawls' theory of justice as fairness is premised on the idea of formulating the ideal rules that autonomous individuals would select to govern the basic structure of society. As numerous tomes are devoted to the extensive debates on the meaning and consequences of Rawls' theory of justice as fairness, I inevitably can sketch only the highlights here.

Rawls' theory of distributive justice sets out to create a society in which a high degree of equality is one of the key founding principles. The parties would come to decide on these principles, which constitute the core of Rawls' theory of justice as fairness, through a form of social contract. These principles would be reached in what Rawls describes as the original position. In the original position, the mutually disinterested contracting parties make their decisions out of enlightened self-interest as approximate equals behind a veil of ignorance about their own actual socio-economic characteristics. They are also unaware of their own race, gender, and disability status. Furthermore, they would not be aware of any particular individualized conception of the good, the details of a specific life plan, or even the political circumstances and level of economic development of the society in which they live. However, they would have an understanding of the principles of economic theory and the laws of human psychology. Rawls also assumes a relatively high degree of rationality for the parties. While they attempt to maximize their own distributive share of goods, they are not envious nor vain, and do not attempt to deliberately reduce other people's share of goods (Rawls 1999, 118-25; Nagel 1975, 7-8; Wolff 1977, 28; Schwartz 1997, 134-35).

Through a process of reflective equilibrium, where one weighs the merits of alternative conceptions of justice by balancing general insights about moral intuition with contingent facts about specific human institutions, one reaches the two basic principles on which a just society would be founded (Rawls 1999, 42-46; Nagel 1975, 2). However, the basic foundational principles would not regulate every aspect of a highly complex industrialized society. As Pogge (1989, 26) observes, "Rawls focuses on the fundamental 'rules of the game' and not on what moves players are morally free or constrained to make within a particular game in progress."

The two basic principles deal, respectively, with an individual's right to enjoy liberty in a free society and the redistribution of wealth to ensure the maximum possible equality consistent with a society based on liberty. The first principle states that "each person is to have an equal right to the most extensive total system of equal basic liberties compatible with a similar system of liberty for all" (Rawls 1999, 266). The second principle asserts that "social and economic inequalities are to be arranged so that they are both: (a) to the greatest benefit of the least advantaged, consistent with the just savings principle, and (b) attached to offices and positions open to all under conditions of fair equality and opportunity" (Rawls 1999, 266). The first clause of the second principle has famously become known as the Difference Principle.

Rawls has also crafted two priority rules that outline how to interpret the two basic principles. The first priority rule is the Priority of Liberty. It states that

> The principles of justice are to be ranked in lexical order and therefore the basic liberties can be restricted only for the sake of liberty. There are two cases:
> (a) a less extensive liberty must strengthen the total system of liberties shared by all;
> (b) a less than equal liberty must be acceptable to those with the lesser liberty. (Rawls 1999, 266)

The second priority rule is the Priority of Justice over Efficiency and Welfare. It states that

> The second principle of justice is lexically prior to the principle of efficiency and to that of maximizing the sum of advantages; and fair opportunity is prior to the difference principle. There are two cases:
> (a) an inequality of opportunity must enhance the opportunities of those with the lesser opportunity;
> (b) an excessive rate of saving must on balance mitigate the burden of those bearing this hardship. (Rawls 1999, 266-67)

The effect of the first interpretive priority rule is that liberties, such as a right to a fair trial and freedom of the press, are accorded greater weight and priority than the redistribution of wealth in the Rawlsian framework. The second priority rule stipulates that considerations of efficiency must be subordinated to promoting economic justice for the most disadvantaged (Rawls 1999, 266-67). The mechanism that Rawls develops to actualize his vision of redistribution is the maximin rule. This rule states that when faced with alternative choices, one selects the choice that generates the outcome with the least negative outcome for the worst off. In other words, one makes policy choices that maximize the shares of the least advantaged members of society. Given the strict conditions of the original position, the contracting parties would have no basis upon which to make probabilistic calculations because they would simply have no knowledge of their position in society (Rawls 1999, 132-34).

In interpreting these rules, it is crucial to appreciate the distinction between social primary goods and natural primary goods. Liberties, opportunities, the social bases of self-respect, and income are important examples of social primary goods that may be distributed by what Rawls terms the basic structure of society. Rawls places particular emphasis on self-respect, because he cogently argues that in order for the collective redistributionist aspects of his theory to work, members of society need to have high self-respect as a basis for respect for others (Rawls 1999, 155-56). Although Rawls sometimes includes rights as social primary goods, it has been convincingly shown that Rawls' casual inclusion of rights ought to be disregarded. Rights must both be theoretically grounded in the theory of justice that is formulated only later, and flow from the specific social institutions that are created by the type of society in question (Martin 1985, 23). Natural primary goods, on the other hand, include characteristics such as physical health, intelligence, and imagination. While Rawls concedes that the possession of natural goods may be influenced by the basic structure of society, he largely sees their distribution as occurring prior to the impact of society (Rawls 1999, 54). Therefore, the Rawlsian agenda is to focus on the redistribution of social primary goods to the members of the least advantaged class so that they can fulfill their life plans and achieve their goals.

The identification of the least advantaged group in society is a relatively complicated problem in Rawlsian theory. Rawls (1999, 83) argues that there are three main contingencies that may lead individuals to be in the least advantaged group: having a family and class background that is more disadvantaged than are others', having natural endowments that do not allow one to prosper as well as others, and having misfortune and bad luck over the course of their lives leading to relative failure. Remarkably, Rawls argues that all persons in his model have "physical needs and psychological capacities within the normal range" and that examining marginal cases such as people with significant physical or mental disabilities may distract our ability to make accurate moral judgments by "leading us to think of persons distant from us whose fate arouses pity and anxiety" (83-84). I return to this point below.

At the same time, Rawls also states that moral persons in his framework are owed justice. A moral person is defined as anyone who is capable of having a conception of his or her good, as expressed by a rational plan of life, and is capable of having a sense of justice to, at least, a minimal degree

(Rawls 1999, 442; Barry 1989, 211-12). Consequently, Rawls equivocates. He argues that the identification of the least advantaged group has an arbitrary dimension that cannot be precisely resolved and muses that one might select a particular social position, such as unskilled workers, and then identify the least advantaged group as all those with roughly the same or less income and wealth of individuals in this position (Rawls 1999, 84). By using unskilled workers as a proxy group for the least advantaged, Rawls' solution has the effect of ignoring the specific barriers faced by people with disabilities.

Rawls' theory of public reason and the associated notion of deliberative democracy also merit examination. Rawls envisages public reason as applying to government officials and candidates for public office with regard to fundamental political questions. The substantive content of public reason would be provided by a "family of reasonable political conceptions of justice" (Rawls 1997, 767) that includes, but is not limited to, Rawls' theory of justice as fairness. Public reason would therefore apply to debate on the enactment of coercive legislation which citizens would verify to ensure that the principles derived comply with a sense of reciprocity. This refers to the idea that the reasons provided by citizens for legislative changes are sincerely thought to be adequate and that other reasonable citizens would find those reasons to be legitimate as well (770-71). Deliberative democracy includes the idea of public reason, constitutional democratic institutions where public reason may be exercised, and knowledge and desire of citizens to apply public reason in their political conduct (772). Whether Rawls' theory of public reason is a convincing framework for addressing disability discrimination in employment is an issue to which I turn in the next section, where I examine the deficiencies of Rawlsian theory from the perspective of disability studies scholars and through an engagement with critical theory.

The Rawlsian Theory of Distributive Justice and Critical Theory

Transforming the Rawlsian Theory of Justice
As I noted above, the social model of disablement stands for the proposition that it is primarily the structural barriers in society – from staircases in ancient buildings that house educational institutions, to a lack of materials in alternative formats, to the profound attitudinal barriers faced by people with disabilities – that are responsible for the economic marginalization experienced by people with disabilities. Unlike the medical model, which focuses on ameliorating the physiological impairment of a disabled person, the social model or rights-outcome approach (see Rioux and Valentine, Chapter 2), which seeks to transform society, is now the hegemonic approach among disability rights activists and has become increasingly influential in society in the last thirty years. However, it should be emphasized

that there is certainly no single authoritative social model of disablement. Pfeiffer et al. (2003, 141), for example, distinguish between a social model, a social constructionist model, and an oppressed minority model. British versions of the model tend to place greater emphasis on class politics and the bureaucratic tyranny of the welfare state, while American versions are largely influenced by a civil rights paradigm derived from the experiences of the feminist and African-American movements of the 1960s (Barnes, Mercer, and Shakespeare 1999, 76).

If the social model is difficult to grasp in the abstract, a fictional illustration might facilitate comprehension. Consider the situation of a quadriplegic lawyer, Joanna. She works for the provincial government in a challenging position, having graduated from one of the few Canadian law schools with superb wheelchair access. She uses door-to-door public transportation designed for people with disabilities. She must book any non-routine rides twenty-four hours in advance but often cannot get a reservation at the time she requests; yet she has no other option, as the bus and subway systems are still not wheelchair accessible. Even though she is a highly skilled lawyer, she requires assistance with photocopying from support staff, who must balance these accommodation duties with their routine day-to-day tasks since there is no budget for hiring a full-time assistant for Joanna. At home, Joanna requires twenty-four hour attendant care services to assist her with activities of daily living such as cooking, cleaning, and laundry, as well as personal care such as dressing, bathing, and toileting. She therefore must live in an apartment where government-funded attendant care is provided. Hers is located far from her workplace, compounding her already frustrating transportation issues. The wait for a specialized unit closer to her workplace is up to several years. When her wheelchair periodically breaks down, she faces the prospect of both expensive repairs and having to miss work entirely, because there are relatively few wheelchair repair shops and they are largely accustomed to clients willing to wait, since most of them are not in the labour market. In short, Joanna faces systemic and interlocking barriers in all areas of her life, despite enormous efforts on her part to acquire a high level of education.

What might a critic epistemologically committed to the social model of disablement to improve the lives of people in Joanna's situation say about Rawls' theory of distributive justice? Some commentators have noticed how Rawls' framework essentially fails to grapple with the issues faced by people with disabilities (Brighouse 2001, 538; Martin 1985, 186). Martin (1985, 186) argues that people with physical and intellectual disabilities present peculiarly difficult problems for Rawls' theory of justice because of their imputed inability to work. Having noted that neither a policy of full employment nor a social insurance scheme, which is predicated on past labour market participation, is an adequate solution for addressing the employment problems of disabled people, Martin examines the feasibility of two Rawlsian mechanisms: the natural duty of mutual aid and paternalism. Martin argues that mutual aid may require reciprocation, which he feels people with disabilities generally cannot meet, and depends on individual relationships rather than an institutional solution for society as a whole. While advocates of the social model likely would dispute Martin's analysis of mutual aid as ignoring how all individuals are interdependent, including people with disabilities (Drake 1999, 131), I would argue that he correctly dismisses paternalism as inappropriate for adults who are able to reason and otherwise make a contribution to society (Martin 1985, 186-87). Therefore, he cogently argues that this is an appropriate situation in which to apply Rawls' method of reflective equilibrium to take into account new circumstances that had not been previously analyzed. Martin concludes that the apposite solution is to treat unemployed people with disabilities as the least advantaged class and apply the Difference Principle to supplement the income of people with disabilities who cannot work (188-89).

I suggest that applying a social model of disablement to Rawls' theoretical framework calls into question the merits of the distinction between social primary goods and natural primary goods. As I noted, Rawls distinguishes between social primary goods that are to be redistributed pursuant to the Difference Principle and natural primary goods. The former include the liberties, opportunities, income, and social bases of self-respect that all individuals desire, while the latter consist of physical health or lack thereof, intelligence, and imagination (Rawls 1999, 54). For advocates of a social model of disablement, the notion of disability as an inherent and natural characteristic that is simply beyond any critical analysis is completely unacceptable. In fact, advocates of the social model distinguish sharply between physiological impairments and handicaps that are largely the product of the structural environment (Bickenbach 1993). Therefore, health status, intelligence, and imagination need to be regarded as, in part, a socially constructed product of the structural environment, and one needs to be cognizant of how deficits in the provision of primary goods, as demonstrated by the very high rate of disablement among Aboriginal peoples in Canada, can contribute to the creation of physical or mental impairments. As the illustration of the barriers faced by Joanna vividly indicates, no sharp distinction between natural and social goods can be coherently defended because natural primary goods are inextricably rooted in their social environment.

A second issue is recognizing the capacity for people with disabilities to fully participate in the original position as equal contracting parties, a capacity that can exist only if there is an explicit commitment to eradicating both structural barriers that handicap people with disabilities and ableist attitudes that contribute to disability oppression. While some have argued that people with disabilities ought to be regarded as the least advantaged group within Rawls' paradigm (Stein 1998, 1000; Pendo 2003, 248-53), I think that it is more fruitful to address disability oppression by clearly identifying it as a characteristic, like race and gender, which Rawls (1999, 84-85) clearly states ought not to be the basis for discrimination, even if the accommodation requirements of a fluid category such as disability vary dramatically in different contexts. Equating people with disabilities as inevitably the least advantaged class has the effect of ignoring the impact of structural barriers in largely shaping the poor employment outcomes for most people with disabilities and stigmatizing them as inherently marginal figures in public discourse. Just as feminist scholars have correctly noted how structural barriers historically banished women to the bottom of a hierarchical workplace pyramid (Fudge 2002, 87), critical disability theorists need to make the same argument in the context of disability.

This philosophical position would in no way mean that redistribution to people with disabilities who are in fact impoverished would be precluded. It simply rejects the assumption, implicit in Rawls' theory of justice, that people with disabilities will inevitably become destitute and lie outside the theory of justice. As I noted, Rawls has discussed people with disabilities as objects of pity that distract from the ability to make moral judgments. One must instead ensure that a robust theory of equality for people with disabilities is a foundational concept in a transformed Rawlsian theory of justice, and that the theory includes a substantive duty to accommodate disabilities, recognizing that the Rawlsian notion of a rigid line between social primary goods and natural primary goods is blurry and unsustainable, as I suggested above. A rejection of the distinction between social primary and natural primary goods leads directly to a substantive duty to accommodate in order to overcome the effects of arbitrary barriers created by social institutions. This would encompass a wide range of feasible accommodations, from the altering of work schedules to the provision of assistive devices to the modification of work duties. I suggest that it would be entirely in keeping with the rule of Priority of Justice over Efficiency and Welfare to also ensure that any notion of undue hardship is permitted only after very significant efforts have been made to accommodate people with disabilities.

As a contribution to refining a general theory of justice for the basic structure of society, a principle promoting access and accommodation for people with disabilities would leave open for debate, among citizens in a particular polity, how to address the implementation of such a policy, be it through tax subsidies for individual employers to pay for accommodations, greater flexibility in workplace rules mandated through state regulation, tax credits, or possibly even quotas for workers with disabilities, as has been the practice in Germany, France, and Japan (Weber 2000, 892). It would also explicitly recognize that there will always be some people with disabilities who may make a tangible contribution to society, but are, for diverse reasons, unable to work full-time, or in some cases, at all. Such people would be entitled to the full redistributive remedies of the Difference Principle but without the stigma currently imposed on welfare recipients in Canada. Therefore, Martin's endorsement of the Difference Principle as applied to people with disabilities is accepted with the above qualifications.

This also raises a deeper philosophical question, namely, whether the Rawlsian approach is fundamentally flawed because the original position on which the social contract is based excludes far too many characteristics of the contracting parties through the veil of ignorance. Nagel (1975, 7-10) convincingly argues that while it might be entirely appropriate to deny contracting parties any information about their own and other's race, sex, class background, or what he labels natural endowments but which would clearly include physical disabilities, the parties should at least be aware of their own and each party's conception of the good. He maintains that suppressing knowledge of one's conception of the good is unfair and biased because all primary goods are not equally valuable in achieving all conceptions of the good.

However, if one accepts that having a disability has an enormous impact on a person's outlook on life, then one may also argue, going one step beyond Nagel, that having a disability will significantly affect one's conception of the good. As Tremain (1996, 352) has argued, epistemological claims are contextual, value laden, and perspectival. For instance, it is undoubtedly the case that being born with a mobility impairment sometimes leads an individual to decide to embark on a career devoted to disability rights, or to become an occupational therapist providing services directly to people with disabilities, or even to become a professional athlete in wheelchair sports. Just as importantly, it also leads to a conscious awareness of systemic ableism that ranges from rude stares on the street to the lived experience of institutional barriers in all areas of social life. This suggests that knowledge of the contracting parties' identities, whether it is their race, gender, sexual orientation, or disability, ought to pierce the veil of ignorance because such knowledge is a legitimate factor in shaping their conception of the good. A disabled person may feel that a relatively low-paying career as a social worker engaged in advocacy for disabled clients is more rewarding than a comparatively wealthy career as a corporate lawyer, precisely because her or his conception of the good has been fundamentally shaped by the life experience of having a disability. Therefore, disability status is a factor that the contracting parties should be able to take into account in developing principles for a just society.

Moreover, critical theorists such as Seyla Benhabib and others (Jhappan 2002, 227) have made devastating critiques of the Rawlsian framework of the original position that are highly relevant to advocates of disability rights. In critiquing Rawls' theory, Benhabib (1992, 167) comments: "I do not doubt that respect for the other and their individuality is a central guiding concern of the Rawlsian theory; but the problem is that the Kantian presuppositions also guiding the Rawlsian are so weighty that the equivalence of all selves qua rational agents dominates and stifles any serious acknowledgment of difference, alterity and of the standpoint of the 'concrete other.'" While disability rights are not specifically discussed in Benhabib's analysis, I suggest that Benhabib's argument further demonstrates why it is so important that the original position include identities such as race, gender, and disability. As Benhabib (1992, 4-5, 168) argues in her quest for a postmetaphysical discursive notion of rationality, only through dialogue among people with the relevant identities can one achieve mutual understanding of their struggles and aspirations. I hasten to clarify, however, that my goal is to promote identities in order to secure substantive equality for people with disabilities in the community, rather than to dismiss them as a stigmatized "other." Still, there is no question that Benhabib's intervention, while representing a powerful challenge that enables the transformation of Rawls' framework in a positive direction, is ultimately compatible with Rawls' work. This is because she still seeks to use critical theory to achieve coherent social change, rather than simply dissecting the meaning of identity without any relationship to a larger project of social transformation, or indeed, rejecting entirely the notion of the rationality of self-reflective subjects as a feasible goal.

The debate about piercing the veil of ignorance to include identity raises deeper questions about the legitimacy of Rawls' theory of public reason and deliberative democracy. As noted above, Rawls' theory of public reason seeks to articulate a principled framework for addressing appropriate constraints on democratic governance (Rawls 1997). However, as critical theorists such as Benhabib (1992, 102) have suggested, the Rawlsian analysis of public reason, for all its very real accomplishments, is too limited in its scope because it confines its analysis to a critique of what legislative committees and other official government agencies do. While the legislature is unquestionably an important locus of political struggle, disability rights advocates need what Benhabib, influenced by Habermas, aptly calls a discursive model of public space in order to promote will formation around the issues of the day wherever they may arise. In Benhabib's model, participation in society is not limited to a narrow political realm but is expanded to include the social and cultural spheres (Benhabib 1992, 102). Having adopted a Habermasian sense of discourse ethics but going beyond it to challenge the boundary between publicly shared standards and privately held values through the lens of feminist praxis (Benhabib 1992, 111), Benhabib formulates a powerful approach that has much to offer theorists of disability rights. Therefore, the lack of wheelchair access at a university or a workplace, or degrading depictions of people with disabilities in the media, would be regarded as valid a political issue as a parliamentary report, and, consequently, foster the development of a far richer deliberative democracy. Taking to heart the feminist motto that the personal is political, the Benhabibian discursive model of public space permits the politicization of all manner of issues faced by people with disabilities, whether they relate to a government service or the workplace.

Consequently, my arguments, while retaining the commitment to redistributionist equality in the Rawlsian paradigm, would dramatically reconfigure and transform Rawls' principles of justice. I argue that first, Rawls' arbitrary distinction between natural primary goods and social primary goods ought to be rejected. Second, a duty to accommodate people with disabilities in the workplace, subject only to significant hardship to an employer, ought to be required. Since a priority rule mandating the priority of justice over efficiency and welfare already exists, this fits well with Rawls' model even as it suggests a significantly broader scope. Third, the veil of ignorance ought to be pierced to allow contracting parties in the original position to have full knowledge of their own identities and of each other, including the existence of a disability. This allows those with disabilities to derive a set of principles based on their actual circumstances while retaining sufficient generality in the economic sphere to permit a consensus of principles for a just society to be achieved. Finally, and most dramatically, I propose that Rawlsian public reason ought to apply discursively to all spheres of social life, not simply to the government or to the basic structure of society.

Such significant changes may well mean that this transformed Rawlsian model has been unrecognizably altered by its encounter with critical theory and the social model of disablement. I would, in response, note the redistributionist dynamic that is unmistakably Rawlsian, and the fact that Rawlsian theory has become such a cornerstone for social theorists in the English-speaking world. Accordingly, a convincing alternative must challenge orthodox Rawlsian theory on its own terrain. At the same time, I openly acknowledge the contribution of critical theorists such as Benhabib, and observe that the engagement with, and incorporation of, critical theory can only be of benefit to those seeking social justice for people with disabilities. I turn now in the final section to applying this transformed Rawlsian framework in order to analyze the state of anti-discrimination jurisprudence for people with disabilities in Canada.

A Transformed Rawlsian Analysis of Employment Law in Canada
In Canada, the duty to accommodate workers with disabilities up to the point of undue hardship exists under provincial and federal human rights statutes as well as jurisprudence. Recent decisions of the Supreme Court of Canada have made clear that this is a significant duty that is not easily

discharged by merely perfunctory or token efforts of an employer. Rather, in the *Meiorin* case, the Supreme Court held that an employer had to make significant efforts before it would be allowed to claim that an accommodation constitutes undue hardship. Moreover, the court has mandated employers and unions to make efforts to transform the workplace to better suit minorities, rather than simply to make token attempts. An employee must, on the other hand, be able to perform the essential functions of the position, as the employer has the right to operate a productive workplace (*BCGSEU* 1999; *Stelco* 2001, 236).

Let us again examine the fictional case of Joanna, the quadriplegic lawyer working for an employer, the provincial government, which, at least theoretically, has significant resources at its disposal. It would not be unreasonable to expect the employer in this case to accommodate Joanna by allowing her flexible hours or working at home to accommodate the unpredictability of the wheelchair accessible transportation system. Such flexibility would be comparable to what should be expected for employees with childcare responsibilities – mostly women. Just as pregnancy has been denaturalized from a female role for which she ought to bear the accommodation costs to a social responsibility, the same principle could clearly apply to people with disabilities. The employer could also reassign some of the clerical duties that an articling student is expected to do to support staff, since these tasks are clearly not essential functions of the job. In Canada, I believe that these kinds of flexible accommodations, such as offering modified duties, can be realized under current jurisprudence (Lynk 2002, 86-88). The Canadian jurisprudence mandates employers to provide significant accommodations before they may claim undue hardship, and this would particularly be the case in the context of a huge employer such as the provincial government (Lynk 2002, 67). However, there remain significant environmental barriers, such as inaccessible transportation, with the undesirable consequence of dependence on an unreliable paratransit system; the provision of attendant care services in only a finite number of locations and with long waiting lists; and the enormous barriers for Joanna in acquiring a post-secondary education in the first place, when many universities are still inaccessible to wheelchair users and tuition fees are sharply escalating. These must be regarded as socially constructed barriers and not a natural part of the environment that cannot be politically contested.

I suggest therefore that while the Canadian jurisprudence on disability accommodation in the workplace has positive aspects that some commentators have correctly emphasized (Lynk 2002), the outcome for people with disabilities remains troubling in terms of labour force participation rates and poverty levels. This outcome certainly does not meet the high standards set by the Difference Principle. On the one hand, the ruling in the *Meiorin* case is emblematic of the best redistributive impulses of the Difference Principle in setting a very high bar for an employer before it may claim that a requested accommodation is simply undue hardship. Having said that, there are, unquestionably, improvements that need to be made, such as ensuring that overloaded and underfunded human rights tribunals deal with complaints promptly without dismissing cases with merit simply to reduce their caseloads (Etherington 2000, 56-57). Even by the modest standards of Rawls' theory of public reason, one can make a strong case that the perfunctory way in which many human rights commissions in Canada deal with discrimination cases is profoundly unsatisfactory. Addressing the systemic nature of disability discrimination in all spheres of society (from transportation to health care and beyond) is another enormous challenge because clearly achieving substantive equality for workers with disabilities cannot be done solely through interventions in labour and employment law.

Conclusion

In his compelling book about John Rawls' philosophical legacy, Thomas Pogge (1989, 2) comments that "there is a widespread sense that Rawls's work is in shambles." In this chapter, I have tried to show that the Rawlsian goal to seek a more equitable society remains a viable perspective for critical disability scholars, but only once one thoroughly transforms the theory through a sincere engagement with critical theory and the social model of disablement. I have therefore proposed four modifications that I feel would radicalize Rawls' two principles of justice to better respond to the circumstances of people with disabilities. Having then applied my transformed Rawlsian approach to the Canadian context, including through the use of a fictional example that suggests many of the barriers faced by workers with disabilities, I conclude that while the Canadian jurisprudence after *Meiorin* in labour and employment law is a positive first step, far more must be done to challenge disability discrimination in all spheres of life. A reading of Rawls, enriched by the insights of critical theory, demands such a thorough transformation of current practices in society as a whole to ensure substantive equality for people with disabilities.

References
Adler v. Ontario (1994), 19 O.R. (3d) 1 (C.A.).
Barnes, Colin, Geof Mercer, and Tom Shakespeare. 1999. *Exploring disability: A sociological introduction.* Cambridge, UK: Polity Press.
Barry, Brian. 1989. *Theories of justice: A treatise on social justice.* Vol. 1. Berkeley: University of California Press.
[BCGSEU]. *British Columbia (Public Service Employee Relations Commission) v. BCGSEU,* [1999] 3 S.C.R. 3 *(Re Meiorin)* [BCGSEU].
Benhabib, Seyla. 1992. *Situating the self: Gender, community and postmodernism in contemporary ethics.* New York: Routledge.
Bickenbach, Jerome E. 1993. *Physical disability and social policy.* Toronto: University of Toronto Press.

Brighouse, Harry. 2001. Can justice as fairness accommodate the disabled? *Social Theory and Practice* 27: 537-60.

Canada. 2002. *Advancing the inclusion of persons with disabilities: A Government of Canada report December 2002*. Hull: Human Resources Development Canada.

Canadian Charter of Rights and Freedoms, Part I of the *Constitution Act, 1982,* being Schedule B to the *Canada Act 1982* (U.K.), 1982, c. 11 [Charter].

Drake, Robert F. 1999. *Understanding disability policies*. London: Macmillan.

Etherington, Brian. 2000. Promises, promises: Notes on diversity and access to justice. *Queen's Law Journal* 26: 43-65.

Fisk, Milton. 1975. History and reason in Rawls' moral theory. In *Reading Rawls: Critical studies on Rawls'* A theory of justice, ed. Norman Daniels, 53-80. Oxford: Blackwell.

Fudge, Judy. 2002. From segregation to privatization: Equality, the law, and women public servants, 1908-2001. In *Privatization, law and the challenge of feminism,* ed. Brenda Cossman and Judy Fudge, 86-127. Toronto: University of Toronto Press.

Jhappan, Radha. 2002. The equality pit or the rehabilitation of justice? In *Women's legal strategies in Canada,* ed. Radha Jhappan, 175-234. Toronto: University of Toronto Press.

Lynk, Michael. 2002. Disability and the duty to accommodate: An arbitrator's perspective. In *Labour arbitration yearbook 2001-2002.* Vol. 1, 51-122. Toronto: Lancaster House.

Martin, Rex. 1985. *Rawls and rights*. Lawrence: University Press of Kansas.

Nagel, Thomas. 1975. Rawls on justice. In *Reading Rawls: Critical studies on Rawls'* A theory of justice, ed. Norman Daniels, 1-16. Oxford: Blackwell.

Nozick, Robert. 1974. *Anarchy, state and utopia*. New York: Basic Books.

Oliver, Michael. 1990. *The politics of disablement: A sociological approach*. London: Macmillan.

Pendo, Elizabeth A. 2003. Substantially limited justice: The possibilities and limits of a new Rawlsian analysis of disability-based discrimination. *St. John's Law Review* 77: 225-76.

Pfeiffer, David, Anna A. Sam, Martha Guinan, Katherine Ratliffe, Nancy Robinson, and Norma J. Stodden. 2003. Attitudes toward disability in the helping professions. *Disability Studies Quarterly* 23, 2: 132-49.

Pogge, Thomas W. 1989. *Realizing Rawls*. Ithaca, NY: Cornell University Press.

Pothier, Dianne. 1999. BCGSEU: Turning a page in Canadian human rights law. *Constitutional Forum* 11, 1: 19-29.

Rawls, John. 1997. The idea of public reason revisited. *University of Chicago Law Review* 64: 765-807.

–. 1999. *A theory of justice*. Rev. ed. Cambridge, MA: Belknap Press of Harvard University Press.

[*Renaud*]. *Central Okanagan School District No. 23 v. Renaud,* [1992] 2 S.C.R. 970.

Schwartz, Justin. 1997. Relativism, reflective equilibrium and justice. *Legal Studies* 17, 1: 128-68.

Sheppard, Colleen. 2001. Of forest fires and systemic discrimination: A review of *British Columbia (Public Service Employee Relations Commission) v. BCGSEU. McGill Law Journal* 46: 533-59.

Stein, Mark S. 1998. Rawls on redistribution to the disabled. *George Mason Law Review* 6: 997-1012.

Stelco Inc., Hilton Works and U.S.W.A., Local 1005 (2001), 99 L.A.C. (4th) 230 (Carrier).

Torjman, Sherri. 2001. Canada's federal regime and persons with disabilities. In *Disability and federalism: Comparing different approaches to full participation,* ed. David Cameron and Fraser Valentine, 151-96. Montreal and Kingston: McGill-Queen's University Press.

Tremain, Shelley. 1996. Dworkin on disablement and resources. *Canadian Journal of Law and Jurisprudence* 9: 343-59.

Weber, Mark C. 2000. Disability and the law of welfare: A post-integrationist examination. *University of Illinois Law Review* 2000: 889-956.

Wilton, R. 2005. Working at the margins: Disabled people and the growth of precarious employment. Chapter 6, this volume.

Wolff, Robert P. 1977. *Understanding Rawls: A reconstruction and critique of* A Theory of Justice. Princeton, NJ: Princeton University Press.

4

Multicultural Citizenship: The Case of the Disabled

Theresa Man Ling Lee

Disability is not an issue that draws much attention from contemporary political theorists and philosophers. Since the end of the Cold War, they have been predominantly preoccupied by what are regarded as new challenges to the Western world. These challenges are considered under the rubric of nationalism, cosmopolitanism, citizenship, and multiculturalism. Closely connected to these issues are concepts such as identity, group representation, minority rights, civil society, and civic engagement. As a political theorist, I became interested in the subject of disability only because of personal circumstances.

In the winter of 2001, I began to develop difficulty with movements of my tongue. It turned out that I have a localized degenerative nerve palsy, a complication arising from the treatment of a previous major illness. At this point, there is no known cure for the condition. The concrete manifestations of this condition are slurred speech and difficulty swallowing. Although these symptoms are intermittent and vary in their intensity, they do have the general effect of causing impairment of vital activities – speaking and eating.[1] Given my job as an academic, the latter is clearly my own business but the former does have a direct and major impact on my capacity to carry out my professional responsibilities, including teaching and engaging in intellectual exchanges in conferences.

Thus in the spring and summer of 2001, I embarked on a negotiation process with my employer, the University of Guelph, on workplace accommodation. It was this process that prompted my initial research on the subject. In the meantime, as I learned to live with my impairments, I also began to develop a new sense of identity that incorporates these impairments. Being already a woman of visible minority background (I am an ethnic Han-Chinese), I am now a person with disabilities as well.[2] I also happen to be a citizen of Canada – a society that is committed to an official policy of multiculturalism on the one hand, and on the other, a state that is constitutionally bound by the *Canadian Charter of Rights and Freedoms*.

It is obvious that the Charter, in particular the principle of equality rights as articulated in section 15, is highly relevant to my situation, as I am someone who is at the crossroads where race, ethnicity, gender, and disability meet. I want to focus for the moment on disability. By guaranteeing the disabled equality when the Charter was adopted in 1982, Canada became the first country to "accord persons with disabilities constitutional recognition and protection" (Goundry and Peters 1994, 10, note 25).[3] Since then, one major development in the area of disability rights is workplace accommodation. It is clear from the legal literature that the Supreme Court has played an active role in the last decade or so in making workplace accommodation a fundamental legal obligation on human rights grounds. As noted by Michael Lynk (2002, 56), "At the heart of the accommodation duty is the recognition that employment is central to an individual's aspirations and self-esteem." Put differently, workplace accommodation is the right of an individual *qua* individual. However, in contrast to the legal approach, there is a growing grassroots movement of the disabled to consider themselves as a cultural minority. What this entails, among other things, is an approach to disability rights as group rights.[4]

In light of these different approaches, I want to raise the following questions: (1) Can the disabled be considered a cultural minority group in the same way that ethnic groups are? (2) Is the policy of multiculturalism relevant to the struggle of the disabled for equality? In what follows I shall outline the grounds put forth by those who maintain that the disabled are a cultural group. Against this conceptualization of the disabled as a cultural group, I argue that the association between disability and culture is problematic in tackling practical equality issues such as workplace accommodation, especially in situations where other recognized grounds of discrimination, such as race and ethnicity, come into play.[5] However, I am by no means suggesting that disability is simply a biological fact for a given individual. Indeed, the issue of workplace accommodation shows precisely that disability is a social condition impaired individuals inevitably find themselves in as much as it is a biological fact.

Persons with Disabilities as a Cultural Group

In the 2002 fall issue of the journal *Disability Studies Quarterly*, an article by Lawrence Shapiro (2002, 1) begins with the premise that "Ontarians with disabilities" are a "cultural minority" and are therefore no different from "other minority groups such as People of Colour, Jews, Muslims and Gays and Lesbians." These disparate groups all share the same experience of struggling for their "rights to be equal citizens of society" as enshrined in the *Ontario Human Rights Code*. In this case, Shapiro sets out to defend the sexual rights of Ontarians with disabilities on the ground that "sexuality is an inherent aspect of being human and the opportunity to express that sexuality is a right of all people" (5). However, there is a widespread misperception, even among the medical professionals, that people with disabilities are "asexual and poorly socialized." Consequently, the disabled are often denied their sexuality, especially if they become disabled while they are single. Against this background, Shapiro argues that people with disabilities should have access to government-funded sexual surrogacy as a "therapeutic mechanism" in order to develop their much-needed "sexual self-esteem" (3).

At issue here are two interrelated but separate claims. The first is the assertion that the right to sexuality is a human right. The second is that the right to sexuality as a human right can be readily translated into a group right of the disabled on cultural grounds. Leaving aside the validity of the first claim,[6] I want to focus on Shapiro's assertion that Ontarians with disabilities are a "legitimate and recognized cultural minority" when the official policy of multiculturalism is explicitly and exclusively about racial and ethnic diversities.

To begin, Shapiro is by no means alone in regarding people with disabilities as a cultural group. The political backdrop to such a claim is the proliferation of identity-based politics in the last decade or so as citizens of the Western world become more and more disillusioned and critical of the universalistic ideals of liberalism. On the intellectual front, there is a parallel movement against universalism. Under the rubric of postmodernism, a spectrum of intellectual perspectives that share between them a general "incredulity toward metanarratives" started to question the philosophical foundation of the Enlightenment and its ideals of universality, rationality, objectivity, and progress (Lyotard 1984, xxiv). Drawing from the original feminist insight that the politically marginalized is also epistemologically excluded, new areas of studies began to emerge in the 1980s and gathered considerable momentum throughout the 1990s. In addition to women's studies, gender studies, ethnic studies, and cultural studies are now well-established academic programs in institutions of higher learning in both North America and Europe. These disciplines are distinct from the traditional ones, which are informed by the modernist vision of the Enlightenment. This vision is perhaps best captured by Francis Bacon's dictum that "knowledge is power," in which the empowering capacity of knowledge lies in its capacity to liberate us from ignorance by way of reason.[7] In contrast, the new generation of scholarship informed by postmodernism subscribes to the idea that the struggle for power is, at least in part, a struggle for knowledge. In short, postmodernism facilitates a new equation between knowledge and power by asserting that to be known as a cognitive subject in one's own terms is to be empowered.

Hence, when the *New York Times* reported in 1997 that Hunter College of the City University of New York was planning to be the first American college to offer an undergraduate program in disability studies (Ramirez 1997), it was regarded as a logical step for a well-recognized marginalized group to take (Thomson 1998). In establishing disability studies as a discipline in the humanities and the social sciences, the pioneers in the field maintain that disability, like gender, race, or ethnicity, should be "seen as an 'ordinary human variation'" and as such disability is a "constant state" (Ramirez 1997). As a constant state, disability, again like gender, race, and ethnicity, becomes part of one's identity. The emerging field of disability studies therefore borrows from its immediate predecessors, including cultural studies, women's and gender studies, and ethnic studies (Monaghan 1998).[8] Concerned with "the political content of scholarship and pedagogy," the pioneers of disability studies are committed to the empowerment of disabled individuals by ensuring that the "under-represented" have a say in knowledge about themselves (Thomson 1998). Simi Linton, the co-director of the Disabilities Studies project at Hunter College, professed, "One of our rallying cries is, 'Nothing about us without us'" (Monaghan 1998).

At the core of this politicized approach to disability studies is "the shift from a medical model to a minority model in studying disability" (Thomson 1998). On behalf of people with disabilities, Linton (1998) proclaims that "we are all bound together, not by this list of our collective symptoms, but by the social and political circumstances that have forged us as a group." However, the postulation of the socio-political model of disability is in fact not an original move. The World Programme of Action Concerning Disabled Persons adopted by the United Nations (UN) in 1982 already put forth such a view (United Nations 1982). As one critic notes, this UN document marked the beginning of a systematic adoption of the socio-political model of disability in contrast to the biomedical model (McKenna 1997-98, 163-64).[9] The key concept in this approach is "handicap," which is defined by the World Health Organization as "a disadvantage for a given individual, resulting from an impairment or disability that limits or prevents the fulfillment of a role that is normal, depending on age, sex, social and cultural factors, for that individual" (United Nations 1982). The UN, in adopting this definition, provides the following interpretation: "Handicap is therefore *a function of the relationship between disabled persons and their environment.* It occurs when they encounter cultural, physical, or social barriers that prevent their access to the various systems of society that are available to other citizens. Thus, handicap is the loss or limitation of opportunities to take part in the life of the community on an equal level with others" (United Nations 1982 [emphasis added]). In other words, the World Programme recognizes that the handicap experienced by a disabled person is as much a social condition created as a result of the constraint as it is a physiological constraint. As noted by Rioux and Valentine in Chapter 2, the resolution was instrumental to the advent of a rights-based disability movement that revolutionizes the way the disabled interact with society and vice versa.

However, whether we attribute the current change in thinking about disability to activists or to the United Nations, one fact remains constant. This fact is that individuals always have impairments. It is part of being human. We are not born perfect. Moreover, individuals are vulnerable to illnesses and accidents that may render an otherwise functional part of their bodies dysfunctional. Yet, it is only recently that the disabled have come to consider themselves a distinctive cultural minority group. What then are we to make of this assertion?

To answer the question, we need to first ascertain what constitutes "disability culture." In the article "What Is Disability Culture?" Steven E. Brown of the Institute of Disability Culture in New Mexico provides a global survey of the concept and concludes with the following thought:

> First ... disability culture is a set of artifacts, beliefs, expressions created by disabled people ourselves to describe our own life experiences. *It is not primarily how we are treated, but what we have created.* Second, we recognize that disability culture is not the only culture to which most of us belong. We are also members of different nationalities, religions, colors, professional groups, and so on. Disability culture is no more exclusive than any other cultural tag. Third, no matter what the disability or location of the person with the disability *we have all encountered oppression because of our disabilities.* Fourth, disability culture in the southwest of the U.S. may be very different than in the northeast U.S. or Europe or Africa, but all of us have the similarities described in the first three points. (Brown 2002, 10 [emphasis added])

Having identified the common elements that bind the disabled as a cross-cultural "cultural" group, Brown then immediately takes apart this shared identity by reminding his readers that disability is no more than a social construct. Hence, Brown (2002, 10) recognizes that the differences between disabled individuals may be so large that it is perhaps "more accurate to say that there are 'cultures of disabilities.'" In the end, for Brown, whether there is one disability culture or more, the issue at stake is integration. But integration is not about the disabled trying "to fit in with mainstream society," which Brown regards as a "backward perspective." Rather, "mainstream society needs to figure not how we fit in, but how we can be of benefit exactly the way we are" (10).

Based on Brown's analysis, it appears that those on the frontline of the disability rights movement are ready to regard themselves as an oppressed cultural minority group complete with its own "set of artifacts, beliefs, [and] expressions." More importantly, group identification is seen as an act of empowerment that enables the disabled to redefine the terms of their relationship with society. In a contemporary pluralistic democratic society such as Canada, this negotiation between different cultural groups takes place under the rubric of multiculturalism, which adheres to the ideal that differences between groups should be accommodated rather than eliminated. It thus makes sense to find out whether a multicultural society such as Canada is ready to take on the disabled as a distinctive cultural group with specific group rights.

Multiculturalism and Cultural Minorities

By adopting the *Multiculturalism Act* in 1988, Canada became "the first country in the world to pass a national multiculturalism law" (Leman 1999, 6). Not surprisingly, Canadian political theorists such as Charles Taylor (1992), Will Kymlicka (1995), and James Tully (1995) have all made distinctive contributions to the current thinking on the subject. However, in examining these theorists' works, I can only identify one discussion by Kymlicka that addresses specifically the issue of the disabled and multiculturalism. The discussion is in his 1998 book, where Kymlicka uses people with disabilities, along with gays and lesbians, as test cases for whether multiculturalism should be extended to non-ethnic groups.[10] These groups are chosen because they represent the "new social movements" that are rooted in a "common identity" rather than a "common interest." However, unlike traditional ethnic and racial groups, membership in these new social movements is not determined by one's lineage. Rather, members in these groups see themselves as parts of a community with a shared "history" and "way of life" (Kymlicka 1998, 91).

More importantly, the choice of gays and lesbians and the disabled is by no means random; they share "a similar shift from a medical category to a cultural identity" (93). Specifically, Kymlicka uses "the Deaf" as a case in point. Like homosexuality, deafness used to be seen "as an affliction or a disease." But increasingly the deaf are being considered as "a people with a distinctive language, sensibility, and culture of their own" (93). As Kymlicka continues with the analysis, we have a better understanding as to why he focuses on the deaf. It turns out that the key lies in the fact that the deaf have their own language (sign languages). Moreover, like many other minority languages, sign languages have had a history of being suppressed and dismissed as not being languages complete with the capacity to express "sophisticated thoughts or artistic creativity" (94). In short, the historical assault on sign languages is nothing less than the persecution of a cultural minority when Kymlicka says that "for the Deaf as a cultural group ... Sign is not only their mother tongue: it is also what unites them as a culture" (95).[11]

That the deaf have their own language is crucial.[12] It means that the deaf have in effect a "greater" claim to a distinct cultural identity than do gays (93). Yet, in the end, Kymlicka returns to what the two have in common, which is that they are both "genuine subcultures, with significant degrees of residential concentration, institutional complexity, and cultural distinctiveness, as well as a sense of history" (95). Hence, to Kymlicka, while the deaf and the gay/lesbian community are not "ethnic" as "defined by a common ethnic descent," "they are certainly 'cultural'" (95).

Having established the point that these groups are cultural groups, Kymlicka moves on to address what is to him a central question: whether these groups are more like immigrant groups or national minorities. The distinction is important, as the two categories represent very different goals, with profound implications on the question of nation building and national unity. National minorities aspire to nothing short of "separatist self-government," whereas immigrant groups seek integration rather than assimilation (97, 100).[13] Integration is the proper goal of multiculturalism, which, for immigrants, "will involve both a strong sense of identity and an affective bond with their subgroup, together with concerted efforts to reform institutions and public perceptions within the larger society" (100).

Analogizing the distinction, Kymlicka regards gays and lesbians as akin to an immigrant group, whereas the deaf are more like a national minority. This is because "Deaf people were raised in a Deaf culture, and indeed this is the only culture they are effectively able to participate in" (102). On the other hand, gays and lesbians are predominantly socialized in the mainstream culture as children (98). Accordingly, the goal for gays and lesbians ought to be integration, while the deaf should be pursuing separatism. Yet, despite the argument that the deaf have a strong claim to "national minority" status, in the end, Kymlicka dismisses the case on what appears to be practical considerations. He notes that the deaf will simply "have a difficult time developing and maintaining a complete societal culture" and can only be "at best a quasi-national group." However, "the cultural nationalist aspirations of the Deaf must be respected, and accommodated as far as possible." This is because for the deaf, "the obstacles to integration in the mainstream are enormous – much greater than for immigrant groups, or even for more traditional 'national' minorities" (102).

Given that Kymlicka is first and foremost a thinker rather than a statesman, I believe that what matters most is what he is prepared to defend in principle, as opposed to what is feasible. Kymlicka is no postmodernist. To appreciate why he ventures into the debate on whether the deaf constitute a cultural group, we need to consider his earlier works on cultural minority rights (Kymlicka 1989; 1995).[14] One of the challenges that Kymlicka embraces is to make a case for cultural minority rights on liberal grounds. He duly notes that to defend such rights, one needs to have some notion of collective rights or group rights. However, such an idea appears to be incompatible with liberalism because its "moral ontology" is predicated on individualism. In Kymlicka's words: "Liberalism, as I have presented it, is characterized both by a certain kind of *individualism* – that is, individuals are viewed as the ultimate units of moral worth, as having moral standing as ends in themselves, as 'self-originating sources of valid claims;' and by a certain kind of *egalitarianism* – that is, every individual has an equal moral status, and hence is to be treated as an equal by the government, with equal concern and respect" (Kymlicka 1989, 140 [emphasis in original; references omitted]).

Consequently, to defend "minority rights within liberalism," two points need to be demonstrated. The first is the recognition that individuals are not simply members of a state, that is, citizens. Rather, individuals are importantly "members of a particular cultural community, for whom cultural membership is an important good." Yet, liberal thought has consistently failed to address the significance of cultural membership (Kymlicka 1989, 162). Building on Rawls' notion of the primary goods, Kymlicka maintains that cultural membership should be considered a primary good because it is essential to self-respect (164). Citing Rawls, Kymlicka defines self-respect as "'the sense that one's plan of life is worth carrying out'" (Kymlicka 1989, 164). For this sense of self-respect to develop, one must have the freedom to choose for oneself what is worthy of pursuit. However, as Kymlicka points out, individuals do not make their choices in a vacuum. There is always *"a context of choice,"* which he calls culture (166 [emphasis in original]). Such a conception of culture is fluid and does not reify culture. Consequently:

> The notion of respect for persons *qua* members of cultures, based on the recognition of the importance of the primary good of cultural membership, is not, therefore, an illiberal one. It doesn't say that the community is more important than the individuals who compose it, or that the state should impose ... the best conception of the good life on its citizens in order to preserve the purity of the culture, or any such thing. The argument simply says that cultural membership is important in pursuing our essential interest in leading a good life, and so consideration of that membership is an important part of having equal consideration for the interests of each member of the community. (167-68)

The second point is related to the question of justice once the primacy of cultural membership is established. This entails the recognition that members of a minority cultural group may be denied the full benefits of their respective cultural membership because the group as a whole may face "particular kinds of disadvantages" vis-à-vis the larger society (162). Kymlicka notes that liberals have always maintained that differences which arise from individuals' choices are their own responsibility, provided that these choices are made freely, but "differences which arise from people's circumstances – their social environment or natural endowments – are clearly not their own responsibility" (186). Hence, it is vital for a liberal "to know whether a request for special rights or resources is grounded in differential choices or unequal circumstances" (186). This distinction is at the core of a liberal case for affirmative action programs. Since no one gets to choose which cultural community one is born into, no individual should be left alone to bear the consequences of his or her inherited cultural membership. Hence, minority rights are justified if they help ensure that "the members of minority cultures have access to a secure cultural structure from which to make such choices for themselves" (192). The provision of minority rights, by rectifying disadvantages arising from circumstances beyond individuals' control, is in keeping with a liberal notion of justice.

In sum, Kymlicka's theory of minority rights maintains that if the preservation of group identity can foster the context within which individuals make choices, then in the end, group rights are by no means antithetical to liberalism. Although these special rights are rights that individuals have as members of a group, they are meant to enhance rather than suppress individual autonomy. Culture, then, is treated as a necessary component of positive identification for individuals. Specifically, in the context of a multi-ethnic state, minority rights support the claim to self-government by national minorities, while immigrants are entitled to what Kymlicka refers to as "polyethnic rights." The latter are "group-specific measures" that are "intended to help ethnic groups and religious minorities express their cultural particularity and pride without it hampering their success in the economic and political institutions of the dominant society" (Kymlicka 1995, 31). However, unlike self-government rights of national minorities, polyethnic rights of immigrants are "usually intended to promote integration into the larger society, not self-government" (31). Accordingly, multiculturalism is the outcome of this model of integration. My identity as a Canadian is only to be reinforced by my Chinese identity. The two sets of identity are considered to be constantly enriching one another.

Multiculturalism and Disability
Is Kymlicka's liberal multiculturalist vision for protecting the rights of cultural minorities relevant to the disabled? It appears that the current disability movement is not just about gaining equality rights for the disabled but also about the fostering of a positive identity, namely, that there is nothing wrong with a disabled person. Hence, the onus is on the non-disabled to adjust to the disabled, not the other way around.

One concrete venue in which this change is manifested is workplace accommodation, especially as it pertains to disability.[15] As defined by Shelagh Day and Gwen Brodsky (1996, 435), "accommodation is the adjustment of a rule, practice, condition or requirement to take into account the specific needs of an individual or group." The duty to accommodate as a legal principle supported by human rights legislation was first developed by the Supreme Court of Canada with respect to religious discrimination (Day and Brodsky 1996, 435). In a speech to the Canadian Bar Association in 1995, Madame Justice Beverley McLachlin articulated the principle of accommodation as follows: "It starts from the premise of each individual's worth and dignity and entitlement to equal treatment and benefit. It operates by requiring that the powerful and the majority adapt their own rules and practices, within the limits of reason and short of undue hardship, to permit realization of these ends" (434). Day and Brodsky note that accommodation thus conceptualized is inherently "flawed by its implicit acceptance that social norms should be determined by more powerful groups in the society, with manageable concessions being made to those who are 'different'" (435). As such, accommodation fails to challenge "the power of the powerful and the majority" and therefore leaves intact "power imbalances among groups" (473).

Much has happened since this critique was made. Indeed, the critique itself was cited by McLachlin as she delivered the judgment of the court in the *Meiorin* case, in which she concluded that "formal equality undermines substantive equality" (*BCGSEU* 1999, para. 41). The significance of the case lies in its adoption of a "unified approach" that aims at ending the "problematic distinction between direct and adverse effect discrimination" (para. 50). From here on employers are required to "accommodate as much as reasonably possible the characteristics of individual employees when setting the workplace standard (para. 50). The court will take "a strict approach to exemptions from duty not to discriminate, while permitting exemptions where they are reasonably necessary to the achievement of legitimate work-related objectives (para. 50). To meet these requirements, the court developed the "three-step test for determining whether a *prima facie* discriminatory standard is a BFOR," that is, a bona fide occupational requirement (para. 54).

Although the case itself dealt with a work standard held to be discriminatory against women, the general principles articulated are applicable to other workplace accommodation issues. As Lynk (2002, 61) notes, "The essence of the new approach in *Meiorin* is to require employers to accommodate the characteristics of individual employees as much as reasonably possible, while taking a strict approach to exceptions." More importantly, the rationale behind the ruling signalled "a much bigger, more transformative version of accommodation; a version that defines accommodation as a central feature of substantive equality" (Peters 2004, 19). McLachlin (2003, 1), speaking in her current position as the chief justice of Canada, articulated this new vision of accommodation as follows: "Accommodation ... means more than grudging concessions. Accommodation, in the strong sense in which I wish to use it, means ending exclusion, encouraging and nourishing the identity of the other, and celebrating the gifts of difference."

In accordance with this explicit commitment to accommodation as the venue for achieving substantive equality, the rulings of the Supreme Court of Canada in recent years establish that once an employee has demonstrated a *"prima facie* case that she or he has a mental or physical disability that requires accommodation, the burden shifts to the employer to prove that every reasonable effort was made to accommodate the disability" (Lynk 2002, 59). What is reasonable is determined by whether such an adjustment will lead to undue hardship.[16] However, while the threshold for undue hardship is high, employers are by no means "obligated to create an unproductive position" (76). Moreover, "in any permanent accommodation arrangement, an employee has to be able to perform the *essential* duties of the existing, restructured or newly-assigned position" (76 [emphasis in original]). These stipulations are important because they highlight the primacy of dignity for those who are in need of accommodation.[17] In short, workplace accommodation should not be misconstrued as an entitlement to guaranteed employment, regardless of job performance.

Being someone who needs accommodation in order to carry out one of my essential duties, which is to be a teacher at the university, I can say that my need is met. If this reinforces a positive sense of self-identity, then one can say that the ideal of accommodation is reached. However, it is important to note that this positive identity is in fact based on *dis-identification*. For the whole point of accommodation is that I am no longer a handicapped person as defined by the World Health Organization. On the other hand, multiculturalism is about enhancing my identity precisely because I can identify, rather than dis-identify, myself as a Chinese.

So perhaps the basis of a positive identity as envisioned by multiculturalism is different from that of workplace accommodation. But the idea of culture as the context of choice for individuals may still be relevant. Within Kymlicka's framework, workplace accommodation can be seen as ensuring that the context of choice be retained for disabled individuals who may otherwise be completely shut off from work because of circumstances beyond their control. By this, I do not simply mean that individuals do not usually wish for their own impairment. Rather, workplace accommodation demonstrates that, among other things, handicap is indeed a result of a disabled person interacting with the society. In my case, for example, class size was the major thorny issue because of the reality of Canadian campuses, especially in Ontario these days. During negotiation, I could not help but wonder whether my speech impairment would not have been a handicap that needed to be accommodated by way of reduced class size if I were teaching in a well-endowed liberal arts college in the United States. I recall my visit to the Department of Political Science at Swarthmore College in Philadelphia in 1998 (before the development of my impairment), to deliver a guest lecture. My audience was the combined class of two undergraduate courses with a grand total of twenty or so students. I was told at the time that these classes were large by Swarthmore standards. Similarly, as noted earlier, my other impairment, swallowing, is not a workplace issue. However, if I were a taste-tester for a food manufacturer, this impairment would become a handicap that needs accommodation from my employer.

I can therefore understand from my own case how disability is a social construct. Our inability to perform certain tasks is by no means an absolute fact. Rather, the incapacity often results from the convergence of a number of factors and circumstances. However, do these observations warrant the claim that the disabled constitute a cultural minority? Commenting on disability and human rights legislation, Michael Lynk (2002; 53-54) notes that in contrast to the "various protected grounds" under the Charter, disability is unique for "three distinct reasons." First, "persons with a disability are characterized by greater heterogeneity than virtually any other group covered by the legislation." Second, "unlike the predominantly fixed character of most other protected grounds, such as race or gender, the condition of disability is potentially quite mutable."[18] Third, because of the heterogeneous nature of disabling conditions, "the modes of accommodation" that are needed "to extend equality to persons with disabilities" are "invariably broader and more complex than those required by other protected grounds."

I agree with Lynk that the accommodation of the disabled in the workplace constitutes a special case. While society has one category to refer to individuals who are impaired – that is, the disabled – current legal thinking in effect recognizes that the disabled are not a group. Workplace accommodation demonstrates that it is simply not enough to state that the disabled cannot be discriminated against, though this is clearly an important step in dismantling prejudices and stereotypes. Indeed, it is precisely prejudices and stereotypes that lump individuals with impairments into a group with no individual identity. In contrast, workplace accommodation suggests that beyond their shared identity as a disadvantaged group, impaired individuals are first and foremost distinctive individuals who want to be able, rather than unable, to participate as "active member[s] in the productive processes of [their] society" (Kavka 1992, 264). However, each case of disability is unique (it is, as noted above, a condition created by different variables, which can have varying implications). For example, the Ontario *Policy and Guidelines on Disability and the Duty to Accommodate* states as one of its guiding principles that "there is no set formula for accommodation – each person has unique needs and it is important to consult with the person involved." This principle is a recognition that "individual accommodation has grown in significance as a central principle of human rights law" (Ontario Human Rights Commission 2000, 6-7).

The question that confronts us at this point is whether the legal approach can coexist with the multicultural approach. One obvious advantage of the latter is, of course, its ability to rally the disabled as a group in a positive way. Hence, while the two approaches represent very different perspectives on disability, it seems strategically advantageous to maintain both. This is indeed an attractive conclusion. But it also looks suspiciously too good to be true.

Here again I want to use my own case as an illustration. In general, I do warn people of my speech disability ahead of time, except when it is just a brief exchange in which no important information needs to be conveyed. I recall an incident at a local dollar store in the fall of 2002 when I attempted to purchase cheesecloth for cooking. As I asked for help from two sales staff at the front desk to locate the material, they insisted that they could not understand me even after I spelled the word. They just simply stared at me as if I were an alien. I did not disclose my disability in this instance, as my speech was relatively clear. Given that I am the only visible minority in this encounter, I could only conclude that racism was at work. In another occasion, a Toronto cab driver of South Asian background said to me that he could not understand "the accent of you people." The interesting dynamic here is that my race is visible but my disability is not. I suppose people draw what they see as the obvious conclusion based on what is visible. Even in instances where I disclose my speech impairment, I cannot help but wonder if people think that my speech does not sound right because English is not my mother tongue rather than because of my impairment. In fact, I have been asked more than once if my speech is clearer when I speak in my mother tongue, which is Chinese.

As part of the accommodation plan, I now have an instructional aid in the classroom. The aid's responsibility is to take over the class when my speech becomes too slurred to be understood or when my tongue is completely immobile. This aid has access to all my lecture notes. Hence, the aid acts more as my surrogate when I am disabled by my impairment. Given that I am a visible minority who is not a native speaker of English, I had insisted that the rationale for the measure be made clear to students.[19] This accommodation measure, which was first suggested by my speech pathologist, turns out to be enormously important in restoring my sense of dignity and confidence. The awkwardness of staring at students without being able to speak is no longer there to haunt me. Of course, it is conceivable that the same provision could be used to compensate for my accent rather than my impairment. But in such a case, I would regard the provision a racist measure because there would be no other reason to question my proficiency in the English language.

My point in relating my own experience with workplace accommodation is this: the disabled are not a cultural group, and the rights of disabled

individuals ought not be conflated with cultural rights. The cultural boundary, once crossed, can be only detrimental to impaired individuals who also
happen to be members of a visible minority in a multi-ethnic society. For
whatever the impairment may be, it can easily feed into common racist
assumptions such as, "these people are simply inferior," "these people are
simply troublemakers," "these people are taking advantage of our system."
A case in point is the SARS outbreak in the winter of 2003 in Toronto. Dr.
Colin D'Cunha, then Ontario's commissioner of public health, responded
to reports of racism against members of the Asian community with the
following words: "I want to stress that SARS is a challenge for all of society
and it is not a disease of ethnicity ... SARS may have emerged in Asia, but a
person of any race or colour is capable of being a carrier of this disease. It is
both wrong and prejudicial to fear or shun any or all people in the Asian
community based on the assumption that they must have SARS" (Wharry
2003). In documenting the impact of SARS, the Chinese Canadian National
Council reported numerous examples of heightened racism against Chinese and Southeast Asians during the crisis (Leung 2004, 16-21). This particular crisis was a powerful reminder of the kind of disturbing outcome
that may develop when the line between one's medical condition and one's
ethnicity is blurred.

To illustrate how this hybrid form of discrimination can set back the equality claim of both ethnic minorities and the disabled, I'll use the following
hypothetical scenario based on the SARS outbreak in Toronto. A Chinese-
Canadian respiratory therapist, being a frontline health-care worker, contracted a severe case of SARS from working intensely with a patient who is
also a Chinese-Canadian. The therapist is fully recovered, but her respiratory system has endured permanent damage. As a result of her condition,
she no longer has the physical strength needed to carry out the full range of
patient care. She is now in the midst of working out an accommodation
plan with her employer, but she is also in a work environment that ostra-
cizes the "ethnic" carriers of SARS. In this scenario, when more than one
form of discrimination is at play, I can see how workplace accommodation
construed as cultural compensation can easily be turned around to support
the idea that "even though these people (Chinese-Canadians) deserve what
they get (SARS), we still try to accommodate them." Here one form of compensation is construed as fixing two forms of discrimination.

A critic of my position may concede to the above observation and yet
argue that it is still advantageous for the disabled to be under the policy of
multiculturalism. Returning to Kymlicka at this point is illuminating. Having concluded that gays and lesbians as well as the deaf are in effect closer
to immigrant groups, Kymlicka subscribes to multiculturalism as the normative framework within which these non-ethnic cultural groups can negotiate their place in the larger society. For multiculturalism is about "defining

fair terms of integration into mainstream society for newly arriving or previously disadvantaged groups" (Kymlicka 1998, 102). Yet Kymlicka refrains
from advocating for the amendment of official multiculturalism policies to
include these identity groups. The reasons that he gives are as follows:

> There may be good administrative and jurisdictional reasons why gays and
> the Deaf should continue to be served by different government agencies
> and policies. In addition, to extend the notion of multiculturalism to in-
> clude all issues of identity and cultural difference might create unnecessary
> confusion. Multiculturalism in Canada has, to date, provided a more or less
> coherent framework for debate over the fair terms of integration for immi-
> grant groups. Extending this debate to include all issues of diversity and
> pluralism might simply invite misunderstandings and false analogies. We
> can see this problem in the American literature on "multiculturalism." Be-
> cause in the United States all issues of pluralism – not just questions con-
> cerning immigrants and national minorities, but even feminism and gay
> rights – are discussed under the heading of "multiculturalism," the latter
> has ceased to have any coherent meaning. It has become a vague label for a
> vast range of disparate issues, with the result that important differences
> among groups are often ignored or downplayed in the American debate.
> (103)

Kymlicka then moves on to say that even if immigrant integration remains
the only focus of multiculturalism in Canada, multiculturalism "should be
seen as one part of a larger struggle to build a more tolerant and inclusive
society, working together with policies to promote the integration of gays
and people with disabilities" (103).[20]

Kymlicka's conclusion is rather disappointing. By considering the disabled
as a cultural group, he himself has extended the multiculturalism debate to
include "all issues of diversity and pluralism" that may indeed simply "in-
vite misunderstandings and false analogies." Among the problems is
Kymlicka's privileging of the deaf over gays and lesbians when he notes
specifically that the former have a language of their own and therefore have
a stronger claim to be "a distinct quasi-ethnic culture" (93). There is no
doubt that language plays an important role in Kymlicka's definition of
culture. In his words, "The sort of culture that I will focus on ... is a *societal
culture* – that is, a culture which provides its members with meaningful
ways of life across the full range of human activities, including social, educational, religious, recreational, and economic life, encompassing both public
and private spheres. *These cultures tend to be territorially concentrated, and
based on a shared language*" (Kymlicka 1995, 76 [first emphasis in original,
second emphasis added]).[21] Moreover, Kymlicka makes the observation that
unlike those who are born deaf, individuals who have become deaf in the

course of their lives are more inclined to identify themselves with those who can hear (Kymlicka 1998, 95). Does this mean that those who are not "naturally" deaf are less-worthy members of this cultural group? What about all the other disabled individuals who simply do not have a language of their own? These questions suggest that Kymlicka's attempt to extend the inclusivity of multiculturalism to non-ethnic-based identity groups is ill-considered. At its worst, Kymlicka's characterization of the deaf as a "quasi-ethnic" group can generate unproductive and potentially divisive hierarchical differentiation within an already disparate group of disabled persons.

The goal of integration of differences is indeed crucial to creating "a more tolerant and inclusive society." However, this does not entail labelling all differences as cultural differences and then somehow making the ethnic-based cultural groups more properly "cultural" and therefore deserving of the policy of multiculturalism.[22] The disabled are not a cultural group, second class or otherwise. In this regard, it is significant that the Supreme Court, in the *Eldridge* case, rejected precisely the proposition that providing sign-language interpreters to deaf persons to facilitate their equal access to medical service is analogous to providing interpreters to "other non-official language speakers" (*Eldridge* 1997, paras. 88, 89, 90).

Conclusion

Who then are the disabled? The answer, I suggest, lies in recognizing the full implication of the socio-political model of disability. The most significant legal contribution of this model is the fostering of a formal partnership between impaired individuals and society to jointly address the social consequences of impairments, as demonstrated through workplace accommodation.[23] Within the framework of integration, if there is one thing that identity-based disability activists and the courts share, it is the obligation to ensure that individuals are no longer marginalized by society because of their impairments. This objective, if and when realized, has a paradoxical outcome, for to recognize that disability is a socio-political construct is precisely to destabilize disability as the essential basis for identity. Ideally, an accommodating society should not have in its midst a distinctive group of impaired individuals whose identity is fostered by the shared condition of disability. I have argued that workplace accommodation is one concrete venue in which this paradoxical goal of recognition and dis-identification can be achieved.[24] A multicultural society, on the other hand, is about sustaining, rather than eradicating, cultural groups.

Acknowledgments
I wish to thank Richard Devlin, Peter Goddard, Win-Chiat Lee, Ravi Malhotra, Dianne Pothier, Troy Riddell, Sarah Song, and especially Michael Lynk. These individuals have contributed in different ways to various stages of the manuscript, including its inception.

Notes

1 Here I am using the word "impairment" as defined by the World Health Organization and adopted by the UN in 1982. The word means "any loss or abnormality of psychological, physiological, or anatomical structure or function" (United Nations 1982).

2 In the same document referred to in note 1, the word "disability" is defined as "any restriction or lack (resulting from an impairment) of ability to perform an activity in the manner or within the range considered normal for a human being."

3 However, the inclusion of the disabled in section 15 was not without a major struggle from disability rights advocacy groups, represented by the Coalition of Provincial Organizations of the Handicapped, now renamed as the Council of Canadians with Disabilities (Peters 2004, 3-12).

4 For a helpful discussion on the concept of group rights as human rights, see Peter Jones, "Human Rights, Group Rights, and Peoples' Rights," *Human Rights Quarterly* 21, 1 (1999): 80-107.

5 Sampson addresses, in Chapter 12, the issue of multiple identity by focusing on women and disabilities.

6 While the right to marriage is recognized internationally as a human right, it is not to be conflated with the right to sexuality (United Nations 1948, article 16). There are clearly cases of otherwise able-bodied people who have been denied sexuality despite their desire to be sexually engaged. Should these people be entitled to government-funded sexual surrogacy program in order to enhance their self-esteem?

7 M. Horkheimer and T. Adorno begin their famous work, *Dialectic of Enlightenment* (New York: Continuum, 1972), with a discussion of these words by Bacon.

8 *The Disability Studies Reader,* edited by Lennard Davis (New York: Routledge, 1997), is considered a collection of groundbreaking scholarship on disability studies. This new trend in disability studies clearly crosses paths with cultural studies. See Snyder and Mitchell 2001, 367. Articles in *Disability Studies Quarterly,* published by the Society for Disability Studies, are reflective of this general trend.

9 Rioux and Valentine provide in Chapter 2 an extensive analysis of these two basic models of disability.

10 This appears to be a reversal of the position laid out in *Multicultural Citizenship* (1995). Here Kymlicka states clearly that he does not consider these groups to be cultural groups. As such, multiculturalism does not address the issues raised by these movements (Kymlicka 1995, 19). I thank Shelley Tremain for raising this point.

11 For an alternate account of the deaf culture, see Jones 2002, 51.

12 In the United States, there has been sustained effort to make American Sign Language a recognized foreign language in undergraduate programs. See Lennard J. Davis, "The Linguistic Turf Battles over American Sign Language," in *Chronicle of Higher Education,* 5 June 1998, A60.

13 For a more detailed analysis of the differences between national minorities and immigrant groups, see Kymlicka 1995, chapter 5.

14 The book, *Multicultural Citizenship* (1995), is where Kymlicka develops a full-blown theory of multiculturalism within the framework of liberalism. However, I think that the philosophical groundwork for the theory is laid in his first book, *Liberalism, Community and Culture* (1989).

15 As Lynk (2002, 56) notes, in recent years disability has consistently been "the leading ground of [discrimination] complaint" filed with the Canadian and Ontario Human Rights Commissions. In *Policy and Guidelines on Disability and the Duty to Accommodate,* the Ontario Human Rights Commission begins with the following observation: "Almost one-third of complaints filed with the Ontario Human Rights Commission are on the ground of disability. Most are in the area of employment ... For this reason, this Policy focuses in the workplace" (Ontario Human Rights Commission 2000, 5). For the most current statistics, which indicate a continuation of this trend, see Table 1, *Annual Report 2003-2004* (Ontario Human Rights Commission 2004, 16).

16 As noted by Lynk (2002, 64-65), in *Central Alberta Dairy Pool v. Alberta (Human Rights Commission)* (1990), 72 D.L.R. (4th) 417 (S.C.C.), the Supreme Court identifies six factors

applicable to the determination of undue hardship: "(1) financial cost; (2) impact on collective agreement; (3) problems of employee morale; (4) interchangeability of the workforce and facilities; (5) size of the employer's operations; and (6) safety." Of these factors, cost, safety, and the size of the employer's operations are given the highest priority in subsequent case law, while employee morale is given the lowest.

17 In providing a moral defence for the right to work by the disabled, Gregory Kavka uses the Rawlsian concept of self-respect as a primary good. As Kavka (1992, 272 [emphasis in original]) notes, "because of the way the psychology of self-respect interacts with the work ethic present in modern advanced societies ["employment, earnings, and professional success"], this disadvantage *cannot be rectified by transfer payments,* but (sometimes) can be rectified by training and employment opportunities." In contrast, Malhotra in Chapter 3 of this book argues that the Rawlsian theory of distributive justice fails to address the structural barriers faced by disabled workers in Canada.

18 Specifically, what Lynk has in mind is disability as a biological condition that can change as a result of a number of factors, including a person's health, medical advancement, technology, and aging. Lynk's claim, however, can still be challenged in that race and gender as biological markers (as opposed to socio-cultural constructs) are also potentially mutable given modern medical technology. In these instances, however, we are likely to be dealing with conscious choices made by individuals and probably a one-time challenge.

19 To help students understand the rationale behind the provision, they are reminded that the accommodation of my disabilities provided by the university is informed by the same principle that regulates academic accommodation for students with disabilities. For a Foucauldian analysis of the dynamics of power involved in this latter form of accommodation, see Hibbs and Pothier, Chapter 9.

20 These concluding thoughts are more consistent with his 1995 position. See note 14 above. Kymlicka's more recent book, *Politics in the Vernacular: Nationalism, Multiculturalism, and Citizenship* (Oxford: Oxford University Press, 2001) focuses exclusively on ethnocultural groups.

21 In *Liberalism, Community and Culture,* Kymlicka (1989, 165 [emphasis added]) notes that culture is what enables us to attribute "significance" to "options and choices." He then continues to say that "the processes by which options and choices become significant for us are *linguistic* and historical processes."

22 As David Scott (2003, 111) notes, culture has become "a sort of general-purpose concept" in Anglo-American political theory.

23 In Chapter 8, Baker examines the working of this partnership in the area of public policy by focusing on autism.

24 Wilton demonstrates in Chapter 6 that we are far from the ideal of integrating the disabled into the workforce. Moreover, as a multicultural society built on immigration, Canada has contributed to the exclusion, rather than the inclusion, of disabled individuals through its immigration policy. The basic assumption is that disabled individuals are a burden to society, and are therefore by definition unproductive members.

References

[BCGSEU]. *British Columbia (Public Service Employee Relations Commission) v. BCGSEU,* [1999] 3 S.C.R. 3 *(Re Meiorin)* [BCGSEU].

Brown, Steven E. 2002. What is disability culture? *Disability Studies Quarterly* 22, 2 (Spring): 34-50. http://www.dsq-sds.org/2002_spring_toc.html.

Canadian Charter of Rights and Freedoms, Part I of the *Constitution Act, 1982,* being Schedule B to the *Canada Act 1982* (U.K.), 1982, c. 11 [Charter].

Canadian Multiculturalism Act, 1988, S.C. 1988, 36-37 Eliz. II, vol. I, c. 31.

Day, Shelagh, and Gwen Brodsky. 1996. The duty to accommodate: Who will benefit? *Canadian Bar Review* 75, 3: 433-73.

Eldridge v. British Columbia (A.G.), [1997] 3 S.C.R. 624 [*Eldridge*].

Goundry, Sandra A., and Yvonne Peters. 1994. *Litigating for disability equality rights: The promises and the pitfalls.* Winnipeg: Council of Canadians with Disabilities.

Jones, Megan A. 2002. Deafness as culture: A psychosocial perspective. *Disability Studies Quarterly* 22, 2 (Spring): 51-60. http://www.cds.hawaii.edu.

Kavka, Gregory S. 1992. Disability and the right to work. *Social Philosophy and Policy* 9, 1: 262-90.

Kymlicka, Will. 1989. *Liberalism, community and culture*. Oxford: Clarendon Press.

–. 1995. *Multicultural citizenship: A liberal theory of minority rights*. Oxford: Clarendon Press.

–. 1998. *Finding our way: Rethinking ethnocultural relations in Canada*. Toronto: Oxford University Press.

Leman, Marc. 1999. Canadian multiculturalism. *Current Issue Review* (93-6E). Ottawa: Library of Parliament.

Leung, Carrianne. 2004. *Yellow peril revisited: Impact of SARS on the Chinese and Southeast Asian Canadian communities*. Toronto: Chinese Canadian National Council. http://www.ccnc.ca/sars/SARSReport.pdf.

Linton, Simi. 1998. *Claiming disability: Knowledge and identity*. New York: New York University Press. An Excerpt. Posted in Society for Disability Studies, "Articles about disability studies."

Lynk, Michael. 2002. Disability and the duty to accommodate: An arbitrator's perspective. In *Labour arbitration yearbook 2001-2002*. Vol. 1, 51-122. Toronto: Lancaster House.

Lyotard, Jean-François. 1984. *The postmodern condition: A report on knowledge*. Trans. G. Bennington and B. Massumi. Minneapolis: University of Minnesota Press.

McKenna, Ian B. 1997-98. Legal rights for persons with disabilities in Canada: Can the impasse be resolved? *Ottawa Law Review* 29, 1: 153-214.

McLachlin, Beverley. 2003. The civilization of differences. LaFontaine-Baldwin Symposium Lecture, Halifax. http://www.operation-dialogue.com/lafontaine-baldwin.

Monaghan, Peter. 1998. Pioneering field of disability studies challenges established approaches and attitudes. *Chronicle of Higher Education*, 23 January. Posted under "Articles about Disability Studies," http://www.uic.edu/orgs/sds/articles/html.

Ontario Human Rights Code. R.S.O. 1990, c. H. 19.

Ontario Human Rights Commission. 2000. *Policy and guidelines on disability and the duty to accommodate*. Toronto: Government of Ontario.

–. 2004. *Annual report 2003-2004*. Toronto: Government of Ontario.

Peters, Yvonne. 2004. *Twenty years of litigating for disability equality rights: Has it made a difference?* Winnipeg: Council of Canadians with Disabilities.

Ramirez, Anthony. 1997. Disability as field of study? *New York Times*, 21 December. Posted under "Articles about Disability Studies," http://www.uic.edu/orgs/sds/articles/html.

Scott, David. 2003. Culture in political theory. *Political Theory* 31, 1: 92-115.

Shapiro, Lawrence. 2002. Incorporating sexual surrogacy into the Ontario Direct Funding Program. *Disability Studies Quarterly* 22, 4 (Fall): 72-81. Page references in text are based on html format. http://www.dsq-sds.org/2002_fall_toc.html.

Snyder, Sharon L., and David T. Mitchell. 2001. Re-engaging the body: Disability studies and the resistance to embodiment. *Public Culture* 13, 3: 367-89.

Taylor, Charles. 1992. *Multiculturalism and "the politics of recognition": An essay*. Princeton, NJ: Princeton University Press.

Thomson, Rosemarie G. 1998. Incorporating disability studies into American studies. http://www.georgetown.edu/crossroads/interests/ds-hum/thomson.html.

Tully, James. 1995. *Strange multiplicity: Constitutionalism in an age of diversity*. Cambridge: Cambridge University Press.

United Nations. 1982. General Assembly Resolution 37/52 (3 December). http://www.un.org/esa/socdev/enable/diswpa00.htm.

–. 1948. *Universal Declaration of Human Rights*. GA Res 217(III), UN GAOR, 3d Sess., Supp. No. 13, UN Doc. A/811 (1948). Reprinted in Ian Brownlie, *Basic documents in human rights*, 21-27. Oxford: Clarendon Press, 1992.

Wharry, Steve. 2003. Health officials warn against SARS racism. *eCMAJ* (Canadian Medical Association Journal) 4 April. http://www.cmaj.ca/news/04_04_03.shtml.

5
Ghosts in the Machine: Civil Rights Laws and the Hybrid "Invisible Other"
Carolyn Tyjewski

> We boast of the freedom enjoyed by our people above all other
> peoples. But it is difficult to reconcile that boast with a state of the
> law which, practically, puts the brand of servitude and degradation
> upon a large class of our fellow citizens, – our equals before the
> law. The thin disguise of "equal" accommodations for passengers
> in railroad coaches will not mislead any one, nor atone for the
> wrong this day done.
> – Justice Harlan (*Plessy* 1896, 562, Dissenting)

In *Ghostly Matters: Haunting and the Sociological Imagination,* Avery Gordon
states that the case of a ghost is the case of starting with the "other" – what
we normally exclude, deny, or ignore – and the difference that starting point
makes in our analysis (1997). What has frequently been ignored in the examination of *Sutton et al. v. United Air Lines, Inc.* (1999) has been its relationship to decisions by US courts concerning other minority communities and
their respective civil rights. The question of who should and should not be
protected by civil rights law is not new for the US court system. In the past,
this question was primarily posed about race. However, recently, it has
branched out to discuss the legal rights of people who are queer and/or
disabled. Yet, analysis of decisions concerning disability has remained almost exclusively focused on impairment and "reasonable" accommodations
and not on the law or historical precedence of civil rights cases. Gordon
(1997, 164) states: "To get to the ghost story, it is necessary to understand
how something as simple as a hat can be profoundly and profanely illuminating, if you know how to read the signs. To get to the ghost and the
ghost's story, it is necessary to understand how the past, even if it is just the
past that flickered by a moment before, can be seized in an instant, or how
it might seize you first." In this chapter, I discuss a particular ghost, the
invisible other, and how the US court system has used our collective unwill-

ingness and/or inability to read the signs of the past to deny people with disabilities equal protection under the law. Specifically, I compare three legal decisions – *Sutton et al. v. United Air Lines, Inc.* (1999), *Equality Foundation of Greater Cincinnati, Inc. v. City of Cincinnati* (1995), and *Plessy v. Ferguson* (1896) – and explore how the persons who argued for the protection of their individual civil rights were used by the court system to perpetuate stereotypes about and the status quo for the minority communities these persons purportedly represented.

This chapter is an examination of how the US court system has historically used societal stereotypes, rather than the law or legal definitions, to deny civil rights when faced with cases dealing with hybridity in terms of disability, gender, sex, race, and sexual orientation. While different definitions of hybridity exist in various fields, in this context "hybridity" refers to people who, according to society, do not exist. For example, African-Americans who are of pale complexion, blind people who see, walking quadriplegics, and intersexuals fall under the notion of hybridity because they do not conform to mainstream societal stereotypes. Although the three cases examined in this chapter happened over a period of approximately one hundred years and address four purportedly separate and distinct identity categories, I demonstrate the common theme running through the logic of the courts' decisions.[1] In so doing, I show how approaching a specific problem from a cross-cultural perspective may illuminate the problem far more than if one focuses on one specific problematized group.

In doing this type of analysis, one must be conscious of the differences in particular political moments and of other historical factors. For example, while *Plessy* occurred at the end of Reconstruction and at the beginning of the Industrial Revolution in the United States, both *Equality Foundation* and *Sutton* occurred after the decline of industrial manufacturing in the United States and within a neo-liberal political climate. The neo-liberal ideological emphasis on individualism and the capitalist construction of the worker are also key aspects in understanding the *Sutton* decision. Evelyn Nakano Glenn (2002) notes in *Unequal Freedom: How Race and Gender Shaped American Citizenship and Labor* that gender, race, and the ability to freely sell one's labour have always been intertwined in the definition of citizen in the United States. The creation of a so-called normal worker during the Industrial Revolution left people with disabilities almost completely outside the discourse of labour and, consequently, citizenship. The *Americans with Disabilities Act of 1990 (ADA)* may have been an attempt to bring disabled people back into the discourse; however, the language used to construct the law was a neo-liberal language. This language, unlike that of the liberal language used to create the *Civil Rights Act,* for example, ultimately undermined the purpose and intent of the act when placed in a dialectical relationship with the United States' definition of citizenship and the court's history with hybrids.

In other words, the combination of the court's history of civil rights decisions concerning hybrids, the definition of citizenship within the United States, and the neo-liberal language of the *ADA* culminated in the *Sutton* case to undermine the intent and purpose of the act. While this culmination is not the focus of this chapter, I will conclude with a discussion of how neo-liberalism and the United States' notion of "citizenship" have also informed the *Sutton* decision.

According to most US disability rights activists and scholars, *Sutton* marked the beginning of the dismantling of the *Americans with Disabilities Act.*[2] While the *Canadian Charter of Rights and Freedoms* has not been attacked in the same fashion, there is the potential for similar decisions within the Canadian court system that could lead to the dismantling of the Charter. Therefore, I will also conclude by discussing how this analysis may inform Canadian civil rights discourse. To have a clear understanding of how I approach the problem, one must first have a basic background of the three cases being discussed and an understanding of the methods used to examine the decisions.

Background and Methods

Plessy v. Ferguson

Most people tend to associate *Plessy v. Ferguson* with the upholding of Jim Crow laws in the South or the phrase "separate but equal."[3] However, *Plessy v. Ferguson* also dealt with identity politics or, more specifically, the question of colour. In 1892, Homer Plessy bought a first-class ticket on the East Louisiana Railway to travel from New Orleans to Covington, Louisiana. At that time, Louisiana's statutes mandated racial segregation. Because Mr. Plessy considered himself white, he took a seat in the car reserved for white passengers. When the conductor identified him as being of African descent, Mr. Plessy refused to move to the car reserved for people of colour and was forcibly removed from the train and imprisoned. His case was taken to the United States Supreme Court to question the constitutionality of racial segregation in Louisiana and elsewhere by arguing that the state law went against the Thirteenth and Fourteenth Amendments to the US Constitution. It also attempted to call into question the arbitrariness of legal racial definitions (F. Davis 1991, 8-9, 52-53, 68). In the end, the court upheld the state statute by contending that, because being told to sit in a separate car was not reinstating slavery nor was it denying people of colour any rights or privileges they were accorded by law, the Thirteenth and Fourteenth Amendments were not being violated.

Equality Foundation of Greater Cincinnati, Inc. v. City of Cincinnati

Almost one hundred years later, in November of 1992, the city council of

Cincinnati, Ohio, passed a human rights ordinance, Ordinance No. 490-1992, prohibiting discrimination based on race, gender, age, colour, religion, disability, sexual orientation, marital status, or ethnic, national, or Appalachian regional origin in employment, housing, and public accommodations. An immediate backlash occurred and the organization Equal Rights Not Special Rights was created. Its goal was to pass a ballot initiative that would invalidate the Human Rights Ordinance's protections for homosexuals and bisexuals. The initiative passed and became Amendment XII to the *Charter of the City of Cincinnati*. In response, the Equality Foundation of Greater Cincinnati took its case to the Sixth Circuit Court of Appeals, claiming that the Cincinnati city charter was unconstitutional because it prohibited legislation protecting bisexuals or homosexuals from discrimination.[4] The Sixth Circuit Court decided the case in favour of the city, stating that no law could be created or enforced that protected a group or class of individuals who had no visually discernible characteristics.

Sutton et al. v. United Air Lines, Inc.

Sutton et al. v. United Air Lines, Inc. involved the issue of employment discrimination based on a disability or a perceived disability under the *Americans with Disabilities Act (ADA)*. The case involved two sisters, Karen Sutton and Kimberly Hinton. In 1992, they applied for, and were asked to interview for, the position of commercial airline pilot. Upon arriving at their respective interviews, they were informed that they should never have been asked to interview because of the company's policy of not hiring anyone with uncorrected visual acuity of 20/100 or worse. The sisters filed a suit claiming they were being denied employment because of an arbitrary company policy that denied employment based on a physical characteristic that would not affect one's ability to do the job. In other words, Sutton and Hinton contended that because their eyesight was correctable, their eyesight would not prevent them from performing the job. However, United Airlines claimed they could not pilot a plane because, although their eyesight was correctable, their uncorrected vision fell below a company-set unit of measure. The sisters eventually lost their case in the US Supreme Court. The court contended that because their eyesight could be corrected, they could not have a disability according to the *ADA*.

Commonalities

On the surface, the three cases have little in common. However, beneath the surface issues of race, gender, sex, sexual orientation, and disability are common themes. Each of these cases deals with an individual or individuals who are, for lack of a better term, invisible. People who possess pale skin, for example, are presumed to be white. Most people are presumed to be heterosexual and either male or female and non-disabled unless one bears some stereotypical characteristic, such as carrying a white cane or having a "limp wrist." What each of these cases raises, and the courts face, is the problem with the arbitrariness of definitions involving identity categories.

Each of these categories (disability, gender, race, sex, and sexuality) is considered fixed by society and, given the courts' decisions, the courts as well. Like the surveys McColl and colleagues discuss in Chapter 1, the US courts (like the larger society) have created a norm of other that is based on stereotypes of what disabled, raced, sexualized, gendered, and sexed bodies are thought to look like. One is presumed to either be one thing or another based on a stringent and limited understanding and definition of the particular category. As Frazee, Gilmour, and Mykitiuk note in Chapter 10, there is "a complex sequence of interactive rules" that a body is presumed to fit within to be considered disabled, and the same is true of race, gender, sex, and sexuality.

None of these categories is fixed, and anyone can become disabled, raced, gendered, sexed, or sexualized depending on the time, space, place, and moment of any given experience. For example, I can be (and frequently am) considered male one moment and female the next. I have been referred to as both white and black – frequently within the same sentence. I am blind and continually referred to as sighted, and my sexuality has been publicly debated since the age of five. I bring these personal experiences to this discussion not to navel gaze but to point out the utter lack of fixity of identity categories and society's insistence on their fixity. Like those of the women Frazee, Gilmour, and Mykitiuk discuss in Chapter 10, my body does not fit the definition of "disabled" or "woman," but it also does not fit the social definition of race or sex or sexuality. Like the individuals discussed in the court decisions I am analyzing, I am hybrid – neither this nor that. My non-conformity with societal notions of what I "should be" wreaks havoc on every societal encounter I have in one form or another.

The belief in the fixity of these categories creates problems not only for society at large but for public policy and law as well. When faced with the existence of hybrids, public policy makers and the courts become befuddled and confused by the evidence before them. Courts hit a proverbial brick wall with cases dealing with hybrids because the social definitions come into direct conflict with the legal definitions of disability, gender, sex, race, and sexual orientation. I would suggest that to get to the heart of an issue, one must first examine the problem and how it manifests itself across community lines, looking for the commonalities within the differences.

Some may question the rationale of this approach – an examination of civil rights decisions across apparently divergent and disparate communities. However, this is not an examination of minority communities. Rather, it is an analysis of how a particular power structure has historically used stereotypes of minority communities to perpetuate the status quo. This type of analysis is also not without precedence. Ruth Colker (1996), for example, discusses race, gender, sexuality, and disability and each community's relationship to civil rights law in her creation of a bi-jurisprudence in *Hybrid: Bisexuals, Multiracials, and Other Misfits under American Law*. Judy Scales-Trent (1995) discusses her personal experience with the law, inclusion and exclusion, and the commonalities across community lines in *Notes of a White Black Woman: Race, Color, and Community*. This approach is not a one-for-one comparison of identical cultural experiences but, rather, recognition of the similarities of oppression and struggle each community faces within a particular societal construct, for example, education or employment.

To use Avery Gordon's (1997, 24-25) terminology, I am simply looking at a type of haunting. "It is a case of the difference it makes to start with the marginal, with what we normally exclude or banish, or, more commonly, with what we never even notice." What do we not notice by examining a societal problem from only a particular stereotyped version of a given community? What do we miss, for example, when we do not include white black women or walking quadriplegics or intersexuals? And, what else do we miss when we do not compare notes on similar societal problems across community lines?

Various scholars have begun asking these questions. For example, in their introduction to *The Nature and Context of Minority Discourse*, Abdul JanMohamed and David Lloyd define the central task of minority discourse theory as:

> drawing out solidarities in the form of similarities between modes of repression and struggle that all minorities experience separately but experience precisely as minorities. "Becoming minor" is not a question of essence (as the stereotypes of minorities in dominant ideology would want us to believe) but a question of position: a subject-position that in the final analysis can be defined only in "political" terms – that is, in terms of the effects of economic exploitation, political disenfranchisement, social manipulation, and ideological domination on the cultural formation of minority subjects and discourses. (JanMohamed and Lloyd 1990, 9)

As alluded to above and discussed below, the problematic positioning of hybrids creates a particular mode of repression for most, if not all, minority communities. This brief chapter is by no means an exhaustive analysis of this topic. It is merely a starting point for a larger, broader discussion of the confusion that occurs in a given society over identity politics, the law, and hybridity.

I have chosen to use the term "hybrid" for several reasons. Although all the communities discussed have various names for those who can pass, each of these names tends to speak to only one specific identification category. For example, the term "mulatto" is most often associated with people who are of multiple ethnicities but look white, and the term "partial" often refers to someone who is blind but looks sighted. Using just one of these terms, for example, would focus the reader's attention, consciously or not, on the one group associated with that particular term. To use more than one term would be problematic because doing so tends to create an unnecessary separation among these identity categories when looking at a mode of repression that affects all of them. This is not to suggest that these identity categories do not have differences among them that need to be acknowledged. Rather, it is a means of focusing on the mode of repression instead of on particular marginalized groups. As bell hooks (2000), Lennard Davis (1995), and others have noted, ableism, homophobia, racism, and sexism are interconnected and inextricably entangled in the United States. Although the term "hybrid" has its own problematic positioning in the United States,[5] I am using this term because it is not associated with one specific identity category, and in terms of definition, is closest to clearly naming the group of people being described. By examining the common experiences of people who can pass as the norm, one can begin to understand how society utilizes notions of exoticism, abhorrence, and invisibility to control or negate the existence of hybrids and, in doing so, retain control of the predominant image of specific minority groups.

Talking to Ghosts
The construction of hybrids and the offshoot issues surrounding hybrids within minority communities, specifically in terms of disability, gender, sex, race, and sexual orientation, are not coincidental. Lennard Davis (1995, 4) points out in *Enforcing Normalcy: Disability, Deafness and the Body* that "binarism [disabled/nondisabled], like so many others – straight/gay, male/female, black/white, rich/poor – is part of an ideology of containment and a politics of power and fear." Given the extremes of this society's binaries, the construction of hybrids becomes a stop-gap that explains away the supposed exceptions. In other words, the construction of hybrids is a necessary gesture, if these dichotomies are to retain the status quo. To the extent that the creation and perpetuation of hybrids as anomalies promotes the binary society we live in and that the promotion of dichotomies perpetuates discrimination, prejudice, misrepresentation, and general miseducation, examination of this phenomenon may help in deconstructing society's identity politics.

In the *Sutton* case, for example, the two sisters' applications were rejected because the women did not meet the company's minimum requirement of uncorrected visual acuity of 20/100 – they both had uncorrected visual acuity of 20/200 or worse. Like Plessy, neither Sutton nor Hinton self-identified as being a member of a minority community.[6] Plessy identified as white. As the US Supreme Court noted: "That petitioner was ... of mixed descent, in the proportion of seven-eighths Caucasian and one-eighth African blood; that the mixture of colored blood was not discernible in him, and [he claimed] that he was entitled to every recognition, right, privilege, and immunity secured to the citizens of the United States of the white race" (*Plessy* 1896, 538 [headnote]). According to the court's documents, Plessy was not visually discernible as being of African descent and, as Mr. Plessy contended in his plea to the court, considered himself to be white. He also contended that state statutes enforcing "separate but equal" violated the Fourteenth Amendment. The court, however, refused to accept his self-identification or his interpretation of the Fourteenth Amendment. While the majority of the court was willing to acknowledge that his complexion was pale and that having the reputation of belonging to the "dominant" race could be construed as "property,"[7] it was not willing to concede that the act of separate but supposedly equal situations was neither equal nor reasonable accommodation (549). The court was also unwilling to consider Louisiana's state law a violation of the Fourteenth Amendment to the US Constitution (550-51).[8] According to the court, the state law in question was constitutionally sound because it did not reinstate involuntary servitude or slavery, nor did it take away any right or privilege accorded people of colour (543, 548). The court's decision ignored both ocular evidence and Plessy's self-identification and came up with its own definition that was not based on the intent of the Fourteenth Amendment. This was much the same way as the court made its decision about two sisters more than one hundred years later.

Sutton and Hinton filed their suit under the *ADA,* a civil rights law prohibiting discrimination based on disability or a perceived disability. According to court records, the sisters not only met the basic job qualifications but were both invited to interview for the position. It was at these interviews that both women were informed that someone had made a mistake in inviting them, because of their uncorrected visual acuity. In other words, Sutton and Hinton were told that they could not interview for the position because they were disabled and not because they were not qualified to be commercial airline pilots.

According to the *ADA,* one has a disability if one has "a physical or mental impairment that substantially limits one or more major life activities ... has a history of such an impairment ... or being regarded as having such an impairment" (*ADA* (2)(A)). Further, the *ADA* states, in establishing whether a person is a qualified individual with a disability, "the term 'qualified individual with a disability' means an individual with a disability who, with or without reasonable accommodation, can perform the essential functions of the employment position that such individual holds or desires" (*ADA* (101)(8)). Therefore, the sisters needed to be considered based on their qualifications and whether or not they could fulfill the essential job functions.

According to United Airlines' own admission, Ms. Sutton and Ms. Hinton were both qualified for the position. United Airlines simply claimed that the sisters did not meet their visual acuity criteria, which it claimed was essential to job function (*Sutton* 1999).

According to the *ADA,* an employer's judgment is taken into account when considering the essential functions of a position. However, the law also states: "The term 'discriminate' includes – ... (3) utilizing standards, criteria, or methods of administration – (A) that have the effect of discrimination on the basis of disability" (*ADA* (102)(3A)). Therefore, one must consider whether a criterion such as having 20/100 vision before correction is an essential job function. The criterion created by United Airlines appears to have no reason for existing beyond eliminating a percentage of the qualified applicants based on a perception of people who possess a particular physical trait. That is, the effect of the criterion is not necessarily to establish a safe pool of pilots or anything related to actual job function,[9] but rather to exclude individuals based on group affiliation or perceived affiliation. Like Plessy, Sutton and Hinton were singled out because of a perception of a group to which they were believed to belong. As Justice Stevens notes in his dissenting decision: "If the Act were just concerned with their present ability to participate in society, many of these individuals' physical impairments would not be viewed as disabilities. Similarly, if the statute were solely concerned with whether these individuals viewed themselves as disabled – or with whether a majority of employers regarded them as unable to perform most jobs – many of these individuals would lack statutory protection from discrimination based on their prostheses" (*Sutton* 1999, 497-98). In other words, Justice Stevens was pointing out that looking at the intent of the particular employer's criteria for employment and whether it was being used to exclude whole groups of people based on perceptions of that group as disabled should be considered under the act. Unfortunately, the majority of the court did not agree. According to the majority decision,

> The agency guidelines' directive that persons be judged in their uncorrected or unmitigated state runs directly counter to the individualized inquiry mandated by the ADA ... Thus, the guidelines approach would create a system in which persons often must be treated as members of a group of people with similar impairments, rather than as individuals ... The guidelines approach could also lead to the anomalous result that ... courts and employers could not consider any negative side effects suffered by the individual resulting from the use of mitigating measures, even when those side effects are very severe ... Congress did not intend to bring under the ADA's protection all those whose uncorrected conditions amount to disabilities. (*Sutton* 1999, 483-84)

The US Supreme Court felt that the court system and employers should be allowed to decide whether an accommodation would cause any negative side effects to the individual with the disability. The court also felt that Congress did not intend to cover all persons with disabilities and that to consider each individual's impairment, prior to mitigation, was to treat the individuals as members of a specific group.

A counter-intuitive logic lies at the heart of this decision. Such logic denies how discrimination is legally defined in the United States. Discrimination is based on how one is treated or regarded because of an individual's affiliation or perceived affiliation with a protected class. The only way to test for discrimination with this type of legal definition is to see if the individual is, at least, perceived to be a member of a protected class. This system, by default, requires individuals to be looked at in terms of their group affiliation or perceived group affiliation. The individual inquiry to which the court refers asks how one should apply the law so as not to discriminate, not how to test whether one is discriminating. As Justice Stevens points out:

> When it enacted the Americans with Disabilities Act of 1990 ... Congress certainly did not intend to require United Airlines to hire unsafe or unqualified pilots ... Nevertheless, if we apply customary tools of statutory construction, it is quite clear that the threshold question whether an individual is "disabled" within the meaning of the Act and, therefore, is entitled to the basic assurances that the Act affords focuses on her past or present physical condition without regard to mitigation that has resulted from rehabilitation, self-improvement, prosthetic devices, or medication. (*Sutton* 1999, 495)

The majority decision's argument reinforces discrimination rather than ameliorating disabling practices.

Definition or, more specifically, who is defined as what, is key in these cases. In both of the cases mentioned above, the lines drawn between this and that are quite clear. Or, at least, the court would like to presume that disability and race are clearly marked on the body – even when the picture is a bit fuzzy. In other words, the court presumes that stereotypical visible traits are noticeable on the body, even when faced with an individual who does not display those traits. The court is no less presumptuous about sexuality or gender. For example, in the *City of Cincinnati* decision, the court was deciding whether a section of the Human Rights Ordinance could be rescinded so that gays, lesbians, and bisexuals would no longer be covered.[10] In its decision to uphold the anti-queer initiative,[11] the court stated: "The reality remains that no law can successfully be drafted that is calculated to burden or penalize, or to benefit or protect, an unidentifiable group or class of individuals whose identity is defined by subjective and unapparent characteristics" (*Equality Foundation* 1995, 267). In essence, the court was suggesting that the law could not protect individuals who could not be seen. However, in other contexts, US law has recognized that the invisible other can be a victim of discrimination. For example, the *ADA* was written with the intent of protecting not only a class of individuals whose disability is visually unidentifiable but also those who have a history of such an impairment and those perceived to have a disability – whether or not one actually does. Given that the Sixth Circuit Court of Appeals had heard at least three cases involving the *ADA* within a year of this case, the comment made by the court in *City of Cincinnati* seems to be rather peculiar.[12] After all, it should have read the *ADA* sometime prior to deciding cases concerning that law. Given that the *ADA* was designed to do exactly what the court said could not be done, to protect individuals who were identified by subjective and possibly unapparent characteristics, the court appears to be making decisions without knowing the law – or suffers from amnesia. As Ruth Colker (1996, 5) notes, the court also seemed to be ignorant of the more historical case of *Plessy v. Ferguson*.

In her discussion of the Sixth Circuit Court's decision, Colker (1996, 43-45) points out that the decision suggests not only that homosexuals are invisible but that bisexuals are also non-existent. The court did so by not mentioning bisexuals in its decision even though bisexuals are specifically mentioned in the initiative and the complaint. In her words: "Such reasoning causes monogamous bisexuals to be labeled as heterosexual or homosexual, depending on the sex of their current partner. Under the court's reasoning, it would not be possible for a woman, like myself, who is married to a man (thereby meeting the 'public display of heterosexual affection' test) to hold myself out as bisexual. The court assumes that public displays of affection and self-proclamations will be consistent along bipolar categories of heterosexual and homosexual" (44). The court takes an either-or approach to sexuality that renders non-existent those who do not fit easily (or at all) within the two acknowledged categories. At the same time, the court assumes that the sexual orientation of a person is identifiable only by public displays of affection, and that most homosexuals and bisexuals are closeted (42-43). Therefore, according to the court's logic, homosexuals and bisexuals "do not need or deserve nondiscrimination protection because they have the choice of remaining closeted or, in the case of bisexuals, heterosexual" (45). As with the US Supreme Court's decisions, it would seem that the Sixth Circuit Court felt it more expedient to simplify the situation than deal with the already complex issue of sexuality. The court chose to ignore that no one should have to hide who they are in order to live without fear of bigotry and prejudice. It chose to ignore that the legal and social definitions of race, sexuality, gender, sex, and disability are arbitrary.

Although the case concerned itself only with sexual orientation discrimination, the bipolarity of sex in the United States also comes into play in the Sixth Circuit Court's decision. More specifically, how would someone who is intersexed fit in this ruling if that person refused to remain in the closet about being neither male nor female?[13] Given that female and male are the only two legally recognized sexes in the United States, how would one's relationships be defined, within a court system that denies this possibility, if one is intersexed? What about someone who is transgendered?[14] Although neither intersexuals nor transgenders were specifically mentioned in the Human Rights Ordinance or the initiative, these questions need to be addressed because individuals who are intersexed or transgendered do exist and, right or wrong, the United States does proscribe how people should interact sexually. Like the exclusion of bisexuals from the court's decision, the invisibility of bisexuals within these documents is quite telling of the societal beliefs in the United States about the bipolarity of sex.

Because the Cincinnati Human Rights Ordinance was designed to be an all-inclusive non-discrimination policy but the initiative did not choose to invalidate all non-discrimination policies within the ordinance based on sexual orientation, a very peculiar and rather amusing result occurs from the passing of this initiative and the court's decision.[15] Technically, anyone who does not fit within the identity categories of bisexual (being sexually attracted to both males and females) or homosexual (being sexually attracted to members of the same sex) is still covered by the city charter. As a result, the Human Rights Ordinance covers heterosexuals and intersexuals or transgenders who are attracted to either males or females. It also covers males and females who are attracted to intersexuals or transgenders. Given the initiative's specific list of sexual orientations that would no longer be covered by the ordinance and the societal assumption that there are only two sexes, it is relatively safe to conclude that the creators of the initiative did not intend this outcome. Like the writers of the law that instituted separate but equal railroad cars in Louisiana in the 1800s, they had a specific agenda of exclusion in mind. To echo Justice Harlan in his dissenting opinion in *Plessy,* everyone knows "the thing to accomplish was ... to compel [non-heterosexuals] to keep to themselves" (1896, 557).

In all three cases, the arbitrariness of the definitions of each minority community is ignored. In *Sutton* (1999), the US Supreme Court ponders endlessly over who is covered by the law, given the some 43 million US citizens who, according to the *ADA,* have disabilities, in much the same way that the earlier court meandered around the idea of who is "of colored blood" (*Plessy* 1896). The problem for both US Supreme Courts is similar to the Sixth Circuit Court's problem with sexuality and sex. All three courts are, on some level, conscious of a problem with the definition they have chosen to use for a given community. But at the same time, they refuse to acknowledge the various myths they have chosen to perpetuate. For example, Justice Brown, in rendering the decision of the Supreme Court in 1896, states:

> While we think the enforced separation of the races, as applied to the internal commerce of the State, neither abridges the privileges or immunities of the colored man, deprives him of his property without due process of the law, nor denies him the equal protection of the laws ... we are not prepared to say that the conductor, in assigning passengers to the coaches according to their race, does not act at his peril ... The power to assign to a particular coach obviously implies the power to determine to which race the passenger belongs, as well as the power to determine who, under the laws of the particular State, is to be deemed a white, and who a colored, person. (*Plessy* 1896, 548, 549)

Having previously acknowledged that Plessy identified as white, the court continually insists that Plessy is not white without ever stating it and continues to act as if this case were brought to them to discuss a coloured man's rights and privileges rather than a citizen's rights and privileges. In doing so, the court attempts to explain away its prejudice just as the Sixth Circuit Court attempts to hide its homophobia by feigning ignorance of the law and legal history of race and disability. In *Sutton,* although Justice O'Connor and her cohort utilize another set of examples to excuse their rationale, it is essentially the same technique as that employed by both the previous US Supreme Court and the Sixth Circuit Court of Appeals. All three courts attempt to deny their prejudice, and that of society, while justifying its continuation.

As alluded to previously in *Sutton,* the court had a preoccupation with the population figure for people said to have disabilities as cited in the *ADA*. Given that the forty-three million figure was already dated, the court's fixation with this particular number (*Sutton* 1999, 484-87) seems questionable logic at best. Regardless, based on who was involved in drafting and sponsoring the *ADA* and which organizations pushed for its passage, it is clear that those involved intended to include all people with disabilities, including hybrids (Shapiro 1993, 105-41; Burgdorf 2002).[16] As Shapiro (1993, 7) notes in *No Pity: People with Disabilities Forging a New Civil Rights Movement:* "But even this figure [the forty-three million used in the *ADA*] did not include people with learning disabilities, some mental illnesses, those with AIDS, or people who are HIV positive and have other conditions covered under the civil rights legislation." Further, the only exclusionary clause within the *ADA* was added at the insistence of Senator Helms (Colker 1996,

163). This "morality" clause was added to exclude sexuality and "other sexual behavior disorders" (*ADA* 1990) creating, as Ruth Colker (1996, 163) notes, "a new class of untouchables." Although this clause does require further analysis of how it reifies the bipolar categories of disabled/non-disabled, homosexual/heterosexual, and female/male, it does not apply to the *Sutton* case directly and, therefore, it will not be dealt with here other than to note it as the only exclusionary passage within the *ADA*. Because it is the sole exclusionary clause within the *ADA,* and because the legislative history sur-rounding the *ADA* is rife with examples of why and how hybrids would be covered under this legislation, it appears the court disregarded the evidence of the intent of the act so that it could continue to ignore that disabled could look/be able just as, in *Plessy v. Ferguson,* the court disregarded the intent of the Fourteenth Amendment so it could continue to ignore that black could look/be white.

Another error in *Sutton* is the court's belief – reflected in its use of the phrase "substantially limiting" – that disability concerns only an individual's impairment and not how society is constructed. The court felt it was the inability to see normally, for example, that made one substantially limited and not that society had created an environment hostile toward those whose visual acuity was not considered the norm (*Sutton* 1999, 489-94, *passim*). Had the court examined the legislative history of the *ADA*, it would have found that the testimony involved account after account of the experience of living within a hostile environment in the United States, due to the fact that people were seen as disabled and not in terms of how their individual impairments did or did not limit their present major life activities (Shapiro 1993, 105-41).[17] Had the court taken these testimonies or previous court decisions into account when determining what the *ADA* meant by its defi-nition of disability, it may have come to the same conclusion that Justices Stevens and Breyer came to in their respective dissenting remarks. Justice Stevens stated: "In my view, when an employer refuses to hire the indi-vidual 'because of' his prosthesis, and the prosthesis in no way affects his ability to do the job, that employer has unquestionably discriminated against the individual in violation of the Act" (*Sutton* 1999, 498). As Justice Stevens noted, the court's majority decision creates a situation that penalizes any-one with a disability who can and does use ameliorative accommodations that simply make it possible to live in a hostile environment and, in terms of the *Sutton* case, more employable. Like Justice Harlan, the dissenting voice in *Plessy,* Justice Stevens in essence states that the United States has no caste system, that the US Constitution does not know or tolerate class distinc-tions. Both concluded a century apart that it is regrettable that the US Su-preme Court determined that it is permissible and competent for the state to deny individuals their civil rights by regulating those rights based on a particular physical trait whether it is visible or not. On the surface, in *Plessy v. Ferguson* the court was deciding the validity of a state law to regulate separate-but-equal standards of civil rights based on race, and *Sutton* was a decision on whether a company was discriminating against two women based on a disability. However, both courts assumed that being minor in the United States is a matter of essence and presented their respective cases in similar fashion. Both dissenting views identified these assumptions.

The final misconception in *Sutton* was based on a belief in the inherent inferiority of the suspect class. According to Justice O'Connor,

> The dissents suggest that viewing individuals in their corrected state will exclude from the definition of "disab[led]" those who use prosthetic limbs ... or take medicine for epilepsy or high blood pressure ... This suggestion is incorrect. The use of a corrective device does not, by itself, relieve one's disability. Rather, one has a disability under subsection (A) if, notwithstanding the use of a corrective device, that individual is substantially limited in a major life activity. For example, individuals who use prosthetic limbs or wheelchairs may be mobile and capable of functioning in society but still be disabled because of a substantial limitation on their ability to walk or run. The same may be true of individuals who take medicine to lessen the symptoms of an impairment so that they can function but nevertheless remain substantially limited ... The use or nonuse of a corrective device does not determine whether an individual is disabled; that determination depends on whether the limitations an individual with an impairment *actually* faces are in fact substantially limiting. (*Sutton* 1999, 487-88 [emphasis in original])

Based on Justice O'Connor's insightful examples, one can reasonably conclude that the court believes that the only people who should be covered by this civil rights law are people who are incapable of competing equally for employment, even though the act clearly states that one must be "otherwise qualified." In essence, the *ADA,* according to the professed beliefs of the court, is not a civil rights law at all. For it to be a civil rights law, it would have to address a social injustice against an individual or group of individuals who belong to a protected class, rather than addressing an inherent flaw in the individual or individuals being defined. The court saw no injustice because, like the courts before it, it saw no harm in confirming separate and unequal status within the United States.

According to the court's assessment, a continuous unemployment rate of approximately 70 percent among employable disabled people in the United States (Bush 2001) has nothing to do with prejudice in society and everything to do with a proverbial limp. By drawing this subjective line between those who use accommodations that supposedly cure the impairment – thereby denying disability – and those people with disabilities that, according to the court, cannot be accommodated, the court attempts to make these bipolar legal categories neat and clean by suggesting that there can never be an equal playing field. As the court justices of 1896 proclaimed: "The object of the amendment was undoubtedly to enforce the absolute equality of the two races before the law, but, in the nature of things, it could not have been intended to abolish distinctions based upon color" (*Plessy* 1896, 544). Or, as it was put by the Sixth Circuit Court, "the constitutional guarantee of equal protection insulates citizens only from unlawfully discriminatory *state action;* it constructs no barrier against *private* discrimination, irrespective of the degree of wrongfulness of such private discrimination" (*Equality Foundation* 1995, 265-66 [emphasis added]). Paralleling the *Plessy* and *Equality Foundation* cases, the US Supreme Court in *Sutton* ignored the societal construction of minority status that created the need for these civil rights laws.

Conclusion: Putting It into a Canadian Context

In all three cases, the courts based their decisions on the stereotypical notion that being a minority in the United States is a matter of essence, rather than on the evidence, which clearly shows that being minor is a socially and politically created phenomenon. To put it another way, these decisions were based on societal stereotypes and definitions and not on the law or legal definitions. In the process, the courts presumed the visibility and discreteness of these categories (black/white, disabled/non-disabled, female/male, and homosexual/heterosexual), even when faced with evidence that these categories were not insular or necessarily visible. In all three cases, the courts appear to be attempting to prescribe the legal rights of a minority group by proscribing the actions of hybrids within that group.

This tendency is important to note for a Canadian context. While my analysis does foreground the historicity of these decisions, the more recent decisions are premised on a neo-liberal ideology as well as historical notions of citizenship and stereotypes of protected classes. As Rioux and Valentine state in Chapter 2, neo-liberalism tends to posit disability as an individual pathology. Within the neo-liberal discourse of the judiciary, "see the individual not the disability" becomes a rationale for denying difference and discrimination.

While there has not been a decision in the Canadian courts that compares to *Sutton* in terms of the definition of disability, there is the potential for a similar dismantling of the Charter. Beyond the definition of disability, there are other elements of a section 15 analysis that can undermine equality claims. If "secure and meaningful employment" is one of the building blocks for full citizenship, as Wilton states in Chapter 6, then Canada, like the United States, already excludes a large portion of its population from full citizenship. This exclusion from the citizenry, in combination with the neo-liberal discourse, could create a similar scenario: a Canadian court could conclude from a case that one is not disabled enough to be covered by the Charter and, therefore, not discriminated against. Or, it could decide that one is disabled enough to be covered by the Charter but is not being discriminated against because one cannot compete with non-disabled peers because of one's individual problem. Reliance on stereotypes of "truly" disabled people as always and already outside the realm of labour (thereby, not citizens) provides the opportunity for a neo-liberal discourse to appear unbiased in its most discriminating moment. However, this stereotyping of the "truly" disabled also makes invisible masses of people who do not fit the norm of other, thereby making them both legally non-disabled and discriminated against because of disability.

This problem, contrary to what many disability scholars insist, is not unique to disability. Disability is not the only category one can suddenly fall within and certainly not the only group of people in jeopardy within a neo-liberal capitalist discourse. As demonstrated above, disability, gender, race, sexuality, and sex are not fixed categories, and yet, all are essentialized by the court and, arguably, by society. As Siobhan B. Somerville (2000, 5) notes, "The challenge is to recognize the instability of multiple categories of difference simultaneously rather than to assume the fixity of one to establish the complexity of another." I agree with Sampson, who writes in Chapter 12 that, "if equality is understood as the right of historically disadvantaged groups to have subordinating barriers removed, it makes sense that the historical disadvantage experienced by the group and its connection to the barrier being challenged must be clearly articulated as part of the claim." However, I also feel that doing this contextualized analysis with tunnel vision limits one's ability to see the pitfalls others have fallen prey to, pitfalls that can be avoided.

The similarities among the three decisions analyzed in this chapter are not coincidental. As Gordon (1997, 166 [emphasis in original]) puts it: "You have bumped into somebody else's memory; you have encountered haunting and the picture of it the ghost imprints. Not only because this memory that is sociality is out there in the world, playing havoc with the normal security historical context provides, but because *it will happen again; it will be there for you. It is waiting for you. We were expected.*" In this chapter, I have consciously taken historical events out of their familiar contexts to expose a pattern, to play with a ghost. As those concerned with law and public policy, we have an obligation to think not just outside the box but beyond it. To do that effectively, we need to be aware of our ghosts, *all* of our ghosts, and how their memory plays havoc with the present. As clichéd as it may sound, history does tend to repeat itself, while at the same time morphing into something different, something new. Beyond the similar phrases and excuses, there is still something seething beneath this surface. There is a ghost in the proverbial machine. History tells a tale both in and out of context. So the question becomes: How does one read the signs? Once read, how will one respond?

Notes

1 Although I do not address the complexities of the interactions of multiple identity categories in this chapter, it should be noted that all people, at all times, belong to multiple identity categories regardless of where one falls on the so-called normal curve of identity, and that one's experiences are inflected, at all times, by these multiple identities, whether one is aware of the interplay or not. As Lee notes in Chapter 4, society frequently misidentifies what it sees because of a variety of factors. When examining society with regards to hybrids, the lack of vision becomes more apparent.

2 The *ADA* has not been rescinded. What I and others are referring to when we discuss the dismantling of the act is its ineffectiveness as civil rights law since *Sutton*. As I discuss later in this chapter, in terms of employment protections, the ADA covers no one because of how the Supreme Court ruled.

3 A Jim Crow law is "a law enacted or purposely interpreted to discriminate against blacks, such as requiring separate restrooms for blacks and whites," according to *Black's law dictionary*, 7th ed., ed. Bryan A. Garner (St. Paul, MN: West Group, 1999), 840. For an in-depth discussion of Jim Crow laws and analysis of legal racial definitions in the United States, see F. James Davis, *Who is black? One nation's definition* (University Park: Pennsylvania State University Press, 1991).

4 At the time of these court proceedings, the decision in *Bowers v. Hardwick*, 478 U.S. 186 (1986), made it legal to regulate and discriminate based on conduct. Therefore, the case was brought based on status and perception rather than conduct.

5 As a term, "hybrid" is most often associated with the mixing of two species, breeds, varieties, or genera of plants or animals. It is not associated with people because, on a scientific level, we recognize the social construction of race, due to the lack of enough variability among the various "races" to actually have separate and distinct groups/races. Although this term is most often associated with genetically mixed breeds of plants and animals, and, in this sense, perpetuates the misconception that these binaries are genetically created, Colker (1996, xi-xii) points out that these binaries are socially constructed, and in turn, their construction creates hybrids by virtue of the gap that exists between the two points.

6 Plessy admitted to having African ancestry (*Plessy* 1896) and Sutton and Hinton admitted that, without correction, they would be disabled (*Sutton* 1999).

7 By acknowledging that "whiteness" could be construed as property, the court demonstrated its belief that the "dominant race" was better because the court would not afford the same propertied rights to a person of colour. In effect, the court was admitting that the accommodations and the individuals assigned to those accommodations were not considered equal under the law.

8 The Fourteenth Amendment deals with the equal protection of a US citizen's rights and privileges under the law. It does not deal with slavery or involuntary servitude, which are covered under the Thirteenth Amendment.

9 Coverage under the *ADA* would have provided an opportunity for any purported safety rationale to be evaluated. The conclusion of the US Supreme Court that there was no disability within the meaning of the *ADA* precluded such external evaluation of the airline's policy.

10 The original Human Rights Ordinance covered all sexual orientations. The initiative, however, specifically targeted gays, lesbians, and bisexuals (*Equality Foundation* 1995).

11 Although the court ignored that the initiative also referred to bisexuals, its decision affected bisexuals as well. Because the initiative includes more than just homosexuals, describing this initiative as an anti-queer initiative seems more appropriate and expedient.

12 In 1995, the Sixth Circuit Court of Appeals heard the following cases: *Stoutenbororugh et al.*

v. National Football League, Inc. et al. (1995); *Maddox v. University of Tennessee* (1995); and *Sandison v. Michigan High School Athletic Association* (1995). All three involved aspects of the *ADA* and, therefore, it would be reasonable to conclude that the court would be familiar with the *Americans with Disabilities Act* and its wording.

13 The term "intersexed" means to be born with a combination of primary and secondary sex characteristics of both sexes, or to be born with neither sex's physical characteristics.

14 The term "transgendered" is used here to refer to people who feel they were born with the physical characteristics of one sex but are or believe they are another sex.

15 The Human Rights Ordinance states that it prohibits discrimination based, among other things, on gender and sexual orientation. Because the ordinance does not state specific gender or sexual orientation identities, all possible gender and sexuality identities are covered under this ordinance. Unlike the Human Rights Ordinance, the initiative stated only that it would eliminate the section protecting the rights of homosexuals and bisexuals (*Equality Foundation* 1996).

16 Many of the individuals involved in the writing of the *ADA* had "hidden" disabilities that did not affect their daily life activities but did affect how they were perceived by society, employers, and so on; namely, as being incapable. Many of the organizations pushing for the passage of the *ADA* had a majority of constituents with invisible disabilities such as diabetes and asthma.

17 For example, during the writing of the *ADA*, Justin Dart Jr. conducted town meetings with disabled people in all fifty states; "Sometimes Dart would bring along members of the council, who would be surprised to find people defining protection of rights – not, say, government welfare or health benefits – as their most pressing issue" (Shapiro 1993, 108). Also, Lisa Carl testified in front of the US Senate that she was denied a ticket to a movie theatre because she had cerebral palsy (105). These meetings, as well as testimony like that of Lisa Carl, provided the evidence that demonstrated the intent of the *ADA*.

References

Americans with Disabilities Act of 1990. Pub. L. 101-336. 42 U.S.C., ss. 12102 and 12211 (b)(1) [*ADA*].

Burgdorf, Robert L. Jr. 2002. Significance of the ADA finding that some 43 million Americans have disabilities. In *The Americans with Disabilities Act policy brief series: Righting the ADA*. No. 3. National Council on Disability, http://www.ncd.gov/newsroom/publications/43million.html.

Bush, George W. 2001. *Freedom Initiative*. Executive Summary, http://www.whitehouse.gov.news/freedominitiative/freedominitiative.html.

Civil Rights Act of 1964, Pub. L. No. 88352, 78 Stat. 241.

Colker, Ruth. 1996. *Hybrid: Bisexuals, multiracials, and other misfits under American law*. New York: New York University Press.

Davis, F. James. 1991. *Who is black: One nation's definition*. University Park, PA: Pennsylvania State University Press.

Davis, Lennard J. 1995. *Enforcing normalcy: Disability, deafness and the body*. New York: Verso.

Equality Foundation of Greater Cincinnati, Inc. v. City of Cincinnati, 54 F.3d 261 (6th Cir. 1995) [*Equality Foundation*].

Glenn, Evelyn Nakano. 2002. *Unequal freedom: How race and gender shaped American citizenship and labor*. Cambridge, MA: Harvard University Press.

Gordon, Avery F. 1997. *Ghostly matters: Haunting and the sociological imagination*. Minneapolis: University of Minnesota Press.

hooks, bell. 2000. *Feminist theory: From margin to center*. 2nd ed. Cambridge: South End Press Classics.

JanMohamed, Abdul R., and David Lloyd, eds. 1990. *The nature and context of minority discourse*. New York: Oxford University Press.

Minow, Martha. 1990. *Making all the difference: Inclusion, exclusion, and American law*. Ithaca, NY: Cornell University Press.

Plessy v. Ferguson, 163 U.S. 537 (US Supreme Court, 1896) [*Plessy*].

Scales-Trent, Judy. 1995. *Notes of a white black woman: Race, color, and community*. University Park: Pennsylvania State University Press.

Shapiro, Joseph P. 1993. *No pity: People with disabilities forging a new civil rights movement*. New York: Times Books.

Somerville, Siobhan B. 2000. *Queering the color line: Race and the invention of homosexuality in American culture*. Durham, NC: Duke University Press.

Sutton et al. v. United Air Lines, Inc., 527 U.S. 471 (1999) [*Sutton*].

Part 3
Policy Analyses

6
Working at the Margins: Disabled People and the Growth of Precarious Employment
Robert D. Wilton

In 1998, federal, provincial, and territorial ministers responsible for social services published *In Unison* (Canada 1998). This report articulates a vision of full participation for persons with disabilities in Canadian society, with secure and meaningful employment identified as one of three building blocks necessary for full citizenship. In reality, however, people with disabilities continue to be poorly represented in formal employment in Canada and other countries (Fawcett 1996; Gleeson, 1999; Canada 2002). Their relative absence from paid employment is a primary reason for continued dependency on the state and high rates of poverty. There is evidence to suggest that when they are able to secure employment, people with disabilities are disproportionately concentrated in poorly paid positions (Barnes, Mercer, and Shakespeare 1999), less likely to occupy visible positions involving contact with the customers (Oliver 1990), less likely to be promoted (Drum 1998), and paid less than non-disabled coworkers (Canada, HRDC 1999).

Broadly, exclusion and marginalization within paid employment can be linked to the undervaluing of disabled people in capitalist labour markets (Oliver 1990; Gleeson 1999) and to ongoing social and cultural devaluation of impairment in Western societies. In a more immediate sense, multiple factors are implicated in the reproduction of this problem. Marginalization of disabled students in the education system places them at a disadvantage when entering the labour market (Barnes, Mercer, and Shakespeare 1999). Lack of accessible public transportation may make it difficult to get to and from a place of work (Kitchin, Shirlow, and Shuttleworth 1998). Public assistance programs that do not permit additional earned income also act as a barrier to employment (Turton 2001). In recent decades, considerable attention has also been paid to employer attitudes as a key barrier to paid employment for persons with disabilities (e.g., Ravaud, Madiot, and Ville 1992; Gooding 1994).

However, as Bickenbach (1999) and others have argued, overemphasizing the role of employer attitudes may obfuscate the role of institutional and structural conditions that contribute to the marginalization and exclusion of people with disabilities in the labour force. This is an important critique, as economic restructuring and policy developments hold important implications for persons seeking paid work. Changes in the nature of the employment relationship and in the labour process, for example, have the potential to facilitate or frustrate efforts to find secure, living wage work. The increasing use of short-term contracts and part-time work in recent decades may hold particular implications for women and men with disabilities, especially if the sectors and occupations most affected by this trend are those in which people with disabilities are disproportionately located (Barnes, Mercer, and Shakespeare 1999; Baron, Riddell, and Wilkinson 1998). At the same time, welfare state restructuring has placed greater emphasis on work for those receiving social assistance, including disabled people (Roulstone 2000).

In addition, a focus on structures and institutions draws attention to the ways in which the marginalization of disabled people in paid work is produced and reproduced systematically through relations of domination and resistance that characterize contemporary capitalist economies. Adopting such a critical perspective, this chapter is concerned specifically with the ways in which recent changes to the structure and organization of paid work, and in particular the growth of more precarious forms of employment such as part-time work and short-term contracts, impact people with disabilities. To achieve this end, I use a combination of quantitative and qualitative data from a project in Hamilton, Ontario, to examine the experiences of disabled people in paid work and to relate these experiences to ongoing restructuring in the organization of paid work. The chapter is divided into three major sections. The first outlines recent changes in the nature of paid work. The second and third present quantitative and qualitative findings on the experience of disabled workers in the Hamilton paid workforce. Together, these data point to the ways in which changes in the nature of employment confront individuals with work and workplaces that are increasingly disabling. This is true not only in terms of the wages paid and the job (in)security offered, but also in terms of work environments and labour processes geared to provide flexibility to employers at the expense of individual workers.

The Changing Nature of Paid Work

Non-Standard and Precarious Work

Economic restructuring and the search for lower labour costs in recent decades has led to a growth in non-standard work arrangements – jobs that differ from the postwar standard of full-time permanent employment

(Cranford et al., 2003). The most common form of non-standard work is part-time work, but scholars also include other arrangements, such as multiple-job holding, own-account self-employment, and temporary (contract) positions (Vosko 2000). Estimates suggest that these four categories of non-standard work accounted for about one-third of all employed working-age Canadians in 1998 (Krahn and Lowe 2002).

The growth of non-standard work is subject to a range of interpretations. For some, non-standard jobs provide greater flexibility for both employer and employee. Thus, while companies save money through outsourcing, subcontracting, and downsizing, workers also exercise choice to work part-time, hold multiple jobs, or become self-employed. However, critical scholars have noted that while workers make choices, these are made under conditions not of their own choosing. Analyses of non-standard work indicate that such work typically pays lower wages, provides fewer benefits, comes with less security, and is less likely to be covered by existing labour laws (Krahn and Lowe 2002; Cranford, Vosko, and Zukewicz 2003). It is precisely these trends that have led some scholars to characterize forms of non-standard employment as precarious work.

In an important discussion, Rodgers (1989) argues that while there is a wide range of employment forms that differ from the postwar standard of full-time, permanent, paid work, four dimensions can be used to conceptualize precarious work. The first of these is the degree of certainty of continuing work. Positions that have short time horizons or where the risk of losing the job is high can be characterized as insecure. Second, the precariousness of work is influenced by the extent to which workers have control over the work they perform. Work is more insecure if the worker has less control (individually or collectively) over the working conditions or pace of work (Smith 1994; Reiter 1996). Third, the issue of worker protection is important: the extent to which workers are protected by law or collective organization in the workplace and, more broadly, in the sense of having access to unemployment benefits and social services. Finally, the level of income influences the precariousness of work. Rodgers (1989, 3) argues that low-income jobs can be conceptualized as precarious if they are associated with poverty and "insecure social insertion."

Precariousness can be understood as involving all these elements in some combination. This multi-dimensional approach recognizes that not all forms of non-standard work are necessarily precarious. Some contract work for professionals, for example, may involve substantial income and control over work, while other forms of contract work may be extremely precarious. The incidence of precarious work varies considerably across sectors of the economy. Lower-tier service industries are key sources of precarious employment, in part because of their relative size in the economy (Krahn and

Lowe 2002). There is also considerable variation in the likelihood of some-one being employed in this type of work. Inequalities along dimensions of gender, race or ethnicity, citizenship, and age mean that women, visible mi-norities, recent immigrants, youth, and older people are more likely to be in non-standard jobs (Rodgers 1989; Cranford 1998; Smith 1998; Acker 2000; Vosko 2000). This has prompted efforts to theorize the ways in which these dimensions of inequality intersect within, and are reproduced by, the chang-ing organization of work. While this scholarship raises interesting and im-portant questions, the literature on the changing nature of work has not paid much attention to disability as a dimension of inequality in the context of paid work or to the impact of recent changes on disabled workers.

Disability: Implications and Questions

Among disability scholars, some attention has been paid to the impacts of recent economic restructuring on disabled people's access to paid work. Early analyses argued that the changing nature of work in the post-industrial or post-Fordist economy might offer new jobs and opportunities for disabled people (Cornes 1984; Saddler 1984), a perspective that can be linked con-ceptually to Finkelstein's (1980) argument that a post-industrial economy characterized by new technologies would facilitate the economic liberation of disabled people.

More recent analysis, however, has tended to be less optimistic. Barnes, Mercer, and Shakespeare (1999, 116) contend that "optimism has been ex-pressed that the changing nature of work in advanced capitalist society offers particular opportunities for some groups within the disabled population, most notably, the younger, better-educated minority. But in the absence of policies aimed at the creation of a barrier-free work environment, the out-look for the majority of disabled people of working age remains bleak." Studies suggest that employment opportunities for disabled people offer low wages, many workplaces remain inaccessible, and the quality of training is often poor (e.g., Roulstone 2000). While recent welfare state restructuring has emphasized the importance of paid work for people with disabilities, many employers remain reluctant to hire disabled people (Hyde 2000). As Hendriks (1999) argues, from employers' perspectives, disabled workers may be conceived as lacking flexibility – a product of both recent changes to the structure and organization of paid work and enduring stereotypes about disability.

As a result of the changing nature of work, several issues come to the fore. For example, the prospect of more part-time work opportunities may ap-pear opportune for women and men whose disabilities make full-time work less feasible, but the dimensions of precariousness outlined above prompt questions about the nature of such work, as well as the associated wages, benefits, and level of security. Questions about the extent to which part-time work compensates financially for loss of access to social assistance are also pertinent. In addition, the increase in short-term contract and temporary work raises questions about the extent to which people will be able to build long-term relationships with supportive employers. Likewise, contract and temporary work may impact employers' willingness to accommodate precisely because these employment arrangements are designed to externalize companies' labour costs. An increase in short-term contract work could also limit the effectiveness of disability discrimination legislation (Jackson, Furnham, and Willen 2000).

Emerging from this discussion, the analysis in this chapter is concerned with the ways in which an increase in precarious work may impact people with disabilities. Three questions guide this inquiry. First, to what extent are people with disabilities disproportionately concentrated in precarious work? Second, to what extent and in what ways does the structure and organization of precarious work impact these workers? Third, how does disability intersect with other dimensions of inequality such as gender and race to shape individuals' experiences within the context of paid work? The data presented here point to the disproportionate concentration of women and men with disabilities in occupations subject to increasing precariousness. This concentration has immediate consequences in terms of job security and income, especially for women workers, while the character of precarious work – in terms of diminished control over the labour process and workplace – places people with disabilities at a particular disadvantage.

Quantitative Overview

Research for this chapter is part of a larger study of disabled people's paid-work experiences in Hamilton, Ontario. Like many cities, Hamilton experienced significant economic restructuring in recent decades. Long known as "steel town," Hamilton saw substantial contraction of the steel industry and the loss of unionized jobs in heavy manufacturing through the 1980s. By the late 1990s, manufacturing was the still the largest single industry sector for employment (with 21 percent of all employees), but service industries, including retail, health and social services, and educational services accounted for more than 70 percent of all employees (Canada, HRDC, n.d.). Relative and absolute declines in secure, skilled blue-collar manufacturing work and the growth of service sector employment and low-end manufacturing are at the core of the restructuring and have had multiple social and economic consequences (Luxton and Corman 2001).

Research was undertaken in collaboration with a non-profit employment service for disabled people. The service, which has been active in Hamilton for three decades, is funded principally by Human Resources Development Canada. It serves a diverse population of disabled people, including individuals with workplace injuries, learning-disabled youth with little or no employment experience, and psychiatric consumers re-entering the labour market. As a result, it offers a wide range of services tailored to individual needs. These include career counselling, resumé preparation, job-search skills, assistance with training and education, and employment referral. In the first stage of the research, data from the agency's client database was examined to establish the types of paid work found by people who had used the agency between 1997 and 2001. In this period, approximately 650 people found roughly 900 jobs through the agency (some people were clients of the agency more than once during the period). Missing data meant approximately 150 of the job records had to be removed from the analysis. As gaps were not a product of non-response, it was assumed that they did not reflect a bias for or against any particular group of clients or occupations.

Comparing the client population with the provincial disabled population revealed notable differences.[1] Clients were more likely to have psychiatric and cognitive or learning disabilities. One explanation may be that people with these disabilities face additional challenges in finding paid work, and are more likely to use an employment service. On average, clients were also markedly younger than the larger disabled population – not surprising, given that clients were actively looking for work, while the latter included a substantial number of older people with disabilities who were retired. More than half of all clients had a post-secondary certificate or diploma, a much larger percentage than in the provincial disabled population. One consequence of recent economic restructuring has been higher standards of academic or technical qualifications for many jobs (Baron, Riddell, and Wilkinson 1998). Given existing barriers, disabled people may feel particular pressure to take additional training, though this is no guarantee that they will find work (Kitchin, Shirlow, and Shuttleworth 1998). The following discussion provides an overview of the jobs people found. Data from the 2000 Labour Force Survey (LFS) for all employees in Ontario (disabled and non-disabled) provides a comparison.

Occupations
Jobs found by clients were coded according to the LFS classification scheme for "occupation at main job." Table 6.1 shows those occupations most commonly occupied by women and men clients. For both groups, comparable figures for all Ontario employees are also shown. In general, clients were tightly concentrated in a small number of occupations when compared with the employee population as a whole. This is particularly the case for the agency's male clients. Few management and professional occupations were reported, something that was not surprising, as these positions were unlikely to be accessed through an employment agency of this type. However, clients were also under-represented in skilled trades and supervisory roles.

Table 6.1

Occupations most commonly occupied by clients, by disability (%)

Occupation	Female clients	Physical	Psychiatric	Sensory	Cognitive/ learning	Female employees (Ontario)
Female clients						
Sales and service occupations	23.4	29.6	21.4	13.8	31	8.2
Retail salespersons and sales clerks	17.5	16.3	9.2	27.6	20.7	5.5
Clerical occupations	10.5	10.7	11.2	6.9	13.8	15.9
Occupations in food and beverage services	5.9	–	10.2	10.3	10.3	2.5
Secretaries	5.1	4.6	–	–	–	3.4
Trades helpers, construction, transportation labourers	–	5.1	8.2	–	–	0.5
Assisting occupations in support of health services	–	–	–	–	6.9	2.6
Machine operators in manufacturing	–	–	–	6.9	–	3.6

Source: Client database (1997-2001) and *Statistics Canada Labour Force Survey* (2000)

Occupation	Male clients	Physical	Psychiatric	Sensory	Cognitive/ learning	Male employees (Ontario)
Male clients						
Sales and service occupations	25.6	25.3	24.1	35.8	28.6	7.0
Trades helpers, construction, transportation labourers	22.3	21.3	22.8	22.6	26.8	3.5
Retail salespersons and sales clerks	7.8	8.6	10.1	–	5.4	2.6
Occupations in protective services	5.8	–	6.3	–	5.4	2.4
Occupations in food and beverage services	4.3	–	–	3.8	5.4	0.8
Clerical occupations	–	5.7	3.8	5.7	–	6.3
Transportation equipment operators and related	–	5.7	–	–	–	5.0
Paralegals, social services workers	–	–	–	3.8	–	0.6

Source: Client database (1997-2001) and *Statistics Canada Labour Force Survey* (2000)

Considering gender, important similarities and differences emerge. A significant number of jobs held by women clients were concentrated in so-called feminized occupations such as clerical work, while jobs held by men were concentrated in occupations such as trades helpers and protective services. At the same time, both men and women were concentrated in sales and service, retail sales, and food and beverage service. Sales and service is a broad occupational category, so these figures do not necessarily indicate that men and women were in the *same* jobs, but they do point to similarities in overall occupational concentration.

Considering occupation by disability, positions held by people with physical and sensory disabilities were the most widely dispersed. Despite heavy concentrations in a small number of occupations, positions were also found in management and professional occupations, and in some skilled trades. The narrowing of employment opportunities was most pronounced for jobs held by women and men with cognitive or learning disabilities.

Salaries and Hours
The average wages and hours per week worked for jobs found by clients are shown in Table 6.2. Wages and hours worked are significantly below the provincial average for all employees. When gender is considered, there are marked differences in the number of hours worked by men and women clients, with women working significantly fewer hours. This difference mir-

Table 6.2

Mean hours and salaries by gender and disability

		Hours per week	Wages per hour ($)
Ontario employees	Male	38.5	19.41
	Female	33.2	15.61
	Mean	36.0	17.58
Clients	Male	33.4	9.29
	Female	28.2	8.59
	Mean	30.9	8.94
Physical	Male	34.2	9.83
	Female	27.5	8.78
Psychiatric	Male	31.7	8.67
	Female	27.9	8.73
Sensory	Male	35.4	9.74
	Female	25.6	8.65
Cognitive/Learning	Male	33.3	8.90
	Female	28.4	7.86

Source: Client database (1997-2001) and *Statistics Canada Labour Force Survey* (2000)

rors the gender difference in the larger employee population, but the wage gap is less pronounced among clients. The narrower wage gap may be a function of the similar occupational concentrations for men and women clients, suggesting that disability as a dimension of inequality was acting to depress the privilege of masculinity in paid work.

Considering disability, some differences emerged, though few were statistically significant. On average, jobs held by men with physical and sensory disabilities offered the highest hourly wages and the most hours. Interestingly, jobs held by women with physical and psychiatric disabilities paid average wages *above* those held by men with psychiatric disabilities. Positions held by women with cognitive or learning disabilities offered the lowest hourly wages on average.

Full-Time vs. Part-Time Work
For all jobs found by clients, a little under two-thirds were full-time, but there were significant differences on the basis of gender (Table 6.3). Gender differences for jobs held by all clients, and among the groups with different disabilities, were significant at or above the 95 percent level. Compared with all provincial employees, men and women clients were much less likely to have full-time work, suggesting greater precariousness among clients.

Length of Employment
Increases in short-term contract and temporary work have been documented in the labour market, raising concerns about the growing precariousness of work. In 2000, just fewer than 10 percent of jobs held by men employees in Ontario were temporary, compared with 11.4 percent for women employees. No comparable figures were available for the client population. However, analysis of employment counsellors' written comments in the client database showed frequent reference to temporary and seasonal work. Two employment counsellors interviewed about clients' experiences also mentioned a growing incidence of temporary positions. As one counsellor commented,

Table 6.3

Percentage of jobs full-time by gender and disability

	Male	Female	Total
Ontario employees	89.8	75.0	82.7
Clients	74.6	52.2	63.8
Physical	75.9	51.6	63.1
Psychiatric	71.9	52.1	60.8
Sensory	82.6	42.9	70.1
Cognitive/Learning	77.6	50.0	68.5

Source: Client database (1997-2001) and *Statistics Canada Labour Force Survey* (2000)

"There's such a push toward contract work, temporary work, part-time work, right, because it's cheaper for companies to do it that way, make less of a commitment to people. That really impacts people with disabilities because if they're looking for an entry-level job, the job isn't as attractive anymore. It puts them into a cycle. We got a lot of the same clients coming back to us within the same year [or] over multiple years, not because they lost their job, but because their job ended."

Taken together, these data suggest that, on average, agency clients are disproportionately concentrated in precarious work – jobs that offer lower wages, fewer hours, and less security – in comparison with the provincial population of employees. This concentration is reflected in clients' low average salaries and in the fact that women in particular were much more likely to be in part-time jobs, placing them at a material disadvantage. Data on length of employment were limited but suggest that clients' jobs were more precarious than those held by provincial employees in general.

Work Histories

The preceding figures provide a snapshot of the jobs people secured with varying degrees of assistance from the employment service. Subsequent to the quantitative analysis, a sample of sixty-two clients participated in semi-structured interviews to further explore the paid work experiences of disabled people. The people had a diversity of physical, psychiatric, sensory, and cognitive or learning disabilities. They were roughly half women and ranged in age from twenty to sixty-two. They spoke on a variety of topics, including the nature of the work, their relationships with employers and co-workers, and the process of negotiating disclosure and accommodation in the workplace. This chapter draws on work histories of respondents to illustrate the ways in which people's labour force trajectories are set within, and shaped by, broader trends in the structure of the economy and the organization of paid work.

The value of life histories as a data collection method in the social sciences has received greater recognition in recent years (Babbie and Benaquisto 2002; Bryman 2004). There are at least two reasons for this. First, documenting the complex and "messy" nature of individual experiences can provide insight to broader processes of social change. Connell (1995, 85) argues that an individual's experiences over time can be conceptualized as a project constituted by "the relation between the social conditions that determine practice and the future social world that practice brings into being." Second, life histories foreground the agency of people, particularly marginalized populations, and help to enliven the understandings of social life provided by statistical analyses. For example, Li (1985) uses life histories to explore employment experiences of Chinese-Canadians in the early twentieth century. He argues that while official data showed a marked increase of this group in restaurant-related occupations, statistics said little about how "racism restricted their economic opportunities, and how the ethnic business provided a niche for survival in a hostile labour market" (1985, 69). As with all methods, tradeoffs are involved. Life histories offer considerable depth at the expense of breadth. However, where analysis of data from life histories is theoretically informed, it can offer findings of broader relevance (Li 1985).

In this chapter, analysis draws from four specific work histories.[2] While it is difficult to argue that these are typical cases, given the diversity of experiences reported, the histories presented have much in common with experiences reported by other participants, as evidenced in a broader thematic analysis of all sixty-two respondents (Wilton 2004). In addition, the experiences described relate directly to, and elaborate on, information contained in the preceding quantitative overview.

Work History 1: Gordon

Gordon is a white man in his mid-forties. He is married and has adult children. In the mid-1980s he had a brain tumour that affected his memory, hearing, and ability to process information. It also caused a drooping of one eyelid, a visible difference that he thought was important in later hiring decisions. At the time of his injury, Gordon was in a full-time permanent job as a machine operator for a large company that prefabricated steel products. After almost a year off work, Gordon returned to the company and was moved into a position crating finished products, a job he enjoyed. That the company was a union shop made a substantial difference to his post-injury experience in terms of job security and salary. During this period, he felt that he was watched closely by management and wondered if he would have been let go if the company had been non-union. He commented: "A lot of times they were watching me a little bit tighter than they were watching somebody else, so I felt discriminated against, if you will, it's a very broad term, but that's the way I felt. You know, like if I, the slightest little cut on my fingers, they come rushing up and say: 'Well, we want to know from your neurologist that you're okay.'"

Although the position worked out well, the company closed in the early 1990s for financial reasons. Gordon then decided to retrain with support from the federal government's Human Resources Department, enrolling in a three-year apprenticeship as an industrial mechanic at a technical college. After one year at college, Gordon tried unsuccessfully to find a placement for on-the-job training. Although he was hired on at several companies, he was let go for what was labelled performance problems. Gordon expressed frustrations about employers' expectations of training: "A lot of employers nowadays want somebody that can walk in, do the job, and go home, okay? Where in my case I couldn't do that. I have to walk in, I need some coaching.

Number one, I'm older than most of the guys in the class, which had a bit of a bearing on it. [And] they didn't have any disabilities, I did." Gordon left the apprenticeship and went back to manual labour with a large food manufacturer. The company was non-union, and Gordon started at a rate of $10/hour. Although he worked forty hours per week, he was considered permanent part-time and did not qualify for benefits. He worked there for two years before being let go when the company restructured.

At this point, Gordon completed another course in machine shop and welding skills and was hired at a small machine shop, earning $12/hour. He worked there for two years, until he was fired by a new manager who cited performance concerns and Gordon's requests for help calibrating the machines. Gordon continued to apply for similar positions but was unsuccessful. He thought that his age and the visibility of his disability worked against him. Subsequent to this, Gordon worked as a delivery driver for a local grocery wholesaler ($7.50/hour) and detailing cars at a local showroom ($9.00/hour). Both jobs were full-time, but neither provided benefits or much job satisfaction. At the time of the interview, Gordon had left the labour market and was in the process of being approved for Canada Pension Plan (CPP) disability benefits.

Analysis

Before his injury, Gordon was in a relatively privileged position as a white, working-class man with a skilled position in a unionized shop. Although the injury and impairment prompted increased scrutiny from management, the presence of the union diminished the degree of precariousness he experienced on his return to work. Economic restructuring eroded this protection. His efforts to retrain for a skilled trade were countered by employers' attitudes about hiring an older candidate with a visible disability and by performance-related concerns that can be interpreted, at least in part, as a product of non-accommodation by management. Over a period of ten years, Gordon experienced downward mobility, working jobs that paid less, offered fewer benefits, and over which he had less control. His response – what might be read as his effort to resist this trajectory – was to exchange paid employment for CPP benefits, a strategy made possible by his having worked long enough to qualify for the federal plan.

Work History 2: Henry

Henry, in his early forties, emigrated from Southeast Asia in 1990. He is married and has a young daughter. He developed juvenile rheumatoid arthritis when he was three years old. While his arthritis is no longer active, the joint deformities caused by the disease mean that Henry uses crutches to get around and has limited manual dexterity. Before coming to Canada, Henry had a permanent, full-time job as an accountant for a public auditor.

In Canada, he looked for similar work. While he has been successful, all his jobs have been contractual. The longest job he had was with a bank shortly after he emigrated. He worked for two years on a direct contract. During this period, restructuring caused him to be transferred to Toronto – an hour's commute away. As a contract worker, he received no benefits except sick leave after six months.

Since then, Henry has had a series of temporary positions, interspersed with periods of unemployment. He has also had seasonal work as a tax accountant with a small company. In 1999, he signed up with a work agency specializing in temporary accounting jobs. The longest period of employment he has had with the agency is two months. His wages have ranged from $11/hour to $14/hour, significantly below what he would earn in a full-time permanent job.

Henry's experiences with the agency highlight a number of issues that have broader relevance for thinking about the impact of precarious employment forms on disabled workers. First, on the issue of training, Henry noted: "Companies are really relying so much on employment agencies and for every company that you're assigned to, they will expect you to really have a master knowledge or a great knowledge of the job. Because, basically, when they hire you and put you there ... you really are required to keep on top of it in such a short span of time." The speed with which companies and supervisors expect all employees, but especially temporary employees, to train may have particular consequences for disabled people who require accommodation. At the same time, asking for help or accommodation may reproduce stereotypes of disabled people as less productive or unreliable.

Second, Henry noted that many companies expect temporary workers to engage in multiple work tasks. For him, this included filing and organizing paperwork in addition to accounting tasks. He explained: "[Filing] brings me discomfort and so that's why as much as possible I avoid those kinds of work. But with the trend now, it's multi-tasking, you are expected to do everything, from doing your work in your desk and your filing them and at the end of the year putting them in boxes. Nobody will help you to do it." Expectations of multi-tasking or cross-training were mentioned by people with a range of disabilities. At the same time, the use of temporary and contract positions may increase employers' reluctance to accommodate disabled people in the workplace. Working in an accounts payable department, for example, Henry had asked for a hands-free telephone headset like the one used by the non-disabled women training him. He was told there was no money left in that month's budget. The use of non-standard work, including temporary help, as a strategy for capital to reduce labour costs indicates that companies may be even more reluctant to spend money on accommodation for part-time, temporary, or contract employees.

Lastly, Henry's experiences raised concerns about employer accountability. Henry had recently been given a two-week position at a company, only to be called after one day of training and told not to report back. Because the position was brokered through the temporary work agency, he had little opportunity to obtain an explanation for his dismissal, though he felt sure it was due in part to his trainer's discomfort with his disability. At the time of the interview, Henry was considering self-employment as a certified financial planner, believing that this would provide greater control over his work and reduce the ongoing stress of negotiating his disability in new workplaces.

Analysis
Inequalities along lines of immigrant status and disability are evident in Henry's labour market experiences. Recent immigrants, particularly visible minorities, experience downward mobility due to racism and a lack of recognition of credentials (Hiebert 1999). At the same time, Henry's precariousness is exacerbated by the disabling nature of available temporary and contract positions. These jobs pay less than permanent positions while demanding that temps adapt rapidly to multiple work tasks in settings that may offer little accommodation – something that may be problematic for disabled people. The absence of a clear relationship with a single employer also raises concerns about accountability (Vosko 2000). Henry's efforts to move into self-employment reflect a desire to gain additional control over the nature of the work, and to avoid repeated efforts to negotiate his impairment in the workplace. However, Rodgers (1989) and others note that own-account self-employment (i.e., working alone) is also often a precarious form of paid work.

Work History 3: Janice
Janice is in her early fifties and has a cognitive disability. She described it in the following way: "Well, I don't have the speed. Ah, comprehension has a lot to do with it. Ah, I seem to, ah, don't pick up things, ah, as fast as other people do." Janice has three children and, while they were young, she was a stay-at-home mom. After her children left home, she decided to go back to paid work full-time.

One of the first jobs she got was at a local college cleaning residence halls. She enjoyed the job, getting on well with coworkers and her supervisor. She earned $9/hour without benefits. After three years, however, organizational changes were implemented, with efforts to exert greater control over the labour process in order to speed up the work. A new supervisor dramatically changed the working environment, requiring employees to time their work. Janice commented: "We do a student's room; we'd have to be timed for that ... Then you had to time each room, and then you had to hand it in at the end of the shift. Ah, we got the work done, but it was, you couldn't please, you couldn't please them, you know. It didn't matter what you did. First I think, well, is it me?" Janice stayed at the college for more than a year after the restructuring efforts began, but eventually left, saying that she couldn't tolerate the demands for greater speed.

Janice then got a job as a housekeeper at a hotel. Again, she encountered problems with the pace of work. She explained that she was supposed to spend only twenty minutes in each room, but that she sometimes needed longer to get everything done. After several months, Janice fell at work while changing the curtains in a room and was subsequently fired after requesting time to go to a physiotherapist. Her experiences point to the links between speed-up and health and safety, which may be exacerbated for people with learning disabilities. After recovering from her fall, Janice was hired by a small cleaning contractor to help clean a department store at $7.50/hour for twenty hours per week. Again, she initially liked the job: "I was on my own, and I had a really, really nice supervisor. He, ah, as long as you showed up for work, as long as you did the job and at first, it was only four hours." However, after about twelve months, the contractor added more work to the workload, with no increase in hours.

Janice left, taking a cleaning job at a condominium complex for seniors in a neighbouring city. The job paid $9/hour and offered more hours per week, though still no benefits. The job was demanding in that the contractor provided for only one hour per condo but residents sometimes asked Janice to do extra work, which put her behind. She was at first reluctant to refuse residents' requests, but co-workers persuaded her to tell residents that she must leave after an hour. While she likes the job, Janice said there had been some "gimmick" with the wages recently, as she was working six hours a day but only being paid for five. At the time of the interview, Janice was still working at the condo job. She also worked Saturdays cleaning the department store at $7.50/hour and had a contract with a local grocery store to collect trash in the parking lot, for which she was paid $90/week. Although Janice wants a single full-time job, she thinks there are few out there for her.

Analysis

The gendered division of labour meant Janice was primarily occupied with unpaid domestic work until her children left home. Entering the labour market in her forties, with a grade 12 education and no recent work experience, meant Janice's options were limited. However, she enjoyed the cleaning job at the college for several years until the supervisor exerted additional control over the labour process in order to reduce costs through speed-up. For Janice, the effect was disabling – a job she had previously performed effectively was transformed to the extent that she could no longer meet employer demands. De-skilling and intensification of service work such as janitorial and cleaning services are common (Cranford 1998) and, as Rodgers (1989) notes, diminishing control over the labour process is one dimension of increasing precariousness. For people with cognitive or learning disabilities, speed-up may present particular problems. As Janice and other respondents noted, supervisors were often intolerant of workers who could not pick up the pace. Janice encountered similar pressures in other jobs that also paid poorly and offered few benefits. Although searching for a full-time permanent job, Janice was working multiple part-time jobs to make ends meet.

Work History 4: Tina
Tina is a white woman in her late twenties. She is married with no children. She has had diabetes for about eighteen years, and in recent years the disease has contributed to ongoing problems with her eyesight. After high school, Tina decided to pursue a career in nursing home care. She enrolled at a local college in a course dealing with care work for the elderly but couldn't afford to complete the course. Without the diploma, Tina worked in two nursing homes doing laundry and cleaning work. Both jobs were part-time and paid minimum wage. She had a number of other short-term low-wage jobs and then was hired at a video store, where she worked for four years. The job started at minimum wage and was full-time shift work. After two years, Tina was earning $9/hour as a shift supervisor. Two years later, Tina and her partner moved to Alberta, but, unable to find work, they returned to Ontario a year later. On her return, Tina got a job with a private home care agency, starting at $9.15/hour with no benefits. As is standard in that field, Tina was paid only for the hours she spent at clients' homes and not for travel time between. Because of her visual impairment, she did not have a driver's licence and so used the bus to travel between clients.

After several months, Tina experienced bleeding from her eyes. A doctor informed Tina that she needed laser treatment and additional surgery. She was also advised to not do heavy lifting, something that was necessary with some of her home care clients. The surgery stabilized Tina's vision and she started using a magnifying glass to read. After the surgery, Tina asked the agency supervisor if she could be assigned clients who did not need to be lifted. Her supervisor said the agency could not guarantee specific assignments, and also told Tina that she could not use a magnifying glass in front of clients, as it might "worry them" about her capacity to provide care.

Tina quit the agency, and the manager at the video store hired her back. Tina explained she would have trouble doing cash with the computer screens and was assigned to floor service, restocking rentals and helping customers. She explained: "It was hard because even with the floor service, people would ask you about movies and stuff, so I was having to go and check the computers so it would take me a while to try and you know, focus on the com-

puter or, I would have to get somebody who's on cash to read it for me."
Tina talked repeatedly about the speed with which the employees were expected to respond to customer inquiries, particularly on weekend evenings.
The expectation of speed and customer satisfaction is a common feature of
service and retail work (Reiter 1996). Conscious of this, Tina approached
the manager to ask about accommodation, but, she said, "my manager wasn't
willing to get a special computer in or something like that, where I would
be able to do cash maybe ... or get a special program that could, you know,
would magnify the screen or something, so I don't know. I had mentioned
it but I don't think it really sunk in to him, because they think: 'Well we're
gonna get this one computer in for this one employee, you know, and who
knows how long she's gonna be here?'" Tina's experience, like Henry's, points
to the ways in which the growth in precarious work and the expectation of
high turnover reduce employers' willingness to accommodate. Tina was later
surprised to find out that her employer was on a Canadian National Institute for the Blind (CNIB) list of companies open to hiring visually impaired
people. In reality, the lack of any modifications to the sales computer meant
Tina continued to face pressure from customers, as well as from co-workers
who expected her to take turns at the cash desk. Frustrated, Tina left the
video store and spent three months unemployed, until a friend offered her
casual cleaning work. She wants permanent full-time care work but is not
optimistic, given her recent experience.

Analysis

Tina's pursuit of care work – a feminized occupation – was hindered by
material constraints that prevented her from completing a college diploma.
As a result, she found herself in cleaning work, rather than direct care. While
her job at the video store was full-time permanent, there were few opportunities for promotion or pay raises. Her experiences at the home care agency
were shaped by the restructuring of care work and the growing use of private
agencies to provide home care (Aronson and Neysmith 1997). While private agencies provide little consistency for clients, Tina's experience points
to lack of consistency for workers, something that may have particular implications for people who require accommodation. In addition, her supervisor's
comments about using a magnifying glass reinforce the conception of disabled people as care recipients, rather than as care workers. While Tina was
rehired at the video store, the employer's reluctance to accommodate in a
job where high turnover is the norm (even though Tina was known to the
manager as a potentially long-term employee) placed her under increased
pressure from co-workers and customers. Organizational change in recent
decades has facilitated new forms of control over workers. Rather than direct
control from managers and supervisors, co-workers and customers are increasingly involved in the disciplining of workers (Smith 1998; Acker 2000).

The experiences of Tina and other respondents suggest that these new forms of control may hold particular implications for disabled people.

Conclusion

This chapter is concerned with the fortunes of disabled workers in an economy characterized by increasing rates of non-standard or precarious employment. The experiences of disabled people seeking work with the assistance of a non-profit employment service in the Hamilton regional labour market provided the empirical basis for the study. Quantitative analysis of the service's client database offered a snapshot of the employment opportunities available to disabled people in Hamilton in recent years. Analysis indicated that the jobs found by clients were strongly concentrated in a small number of occupations (primarily in service work and unskilled and semi-skilled manufacturing work). This concentration was slightly less pronounced for jobs held by people with physical or sensory disabilities and more pronounced for those held by clients with psychiatric or cognitive or learning disabilities. Reflecting this concentration in specific occupations, average salaries for clients were half that received by all Ontario employees, and jobs were much more likely to be part-time.

Analysis also revealed important differences by gender. On average, jobs held by women provided significantly fewer hours and lower hourly wages than those held by men. That the gendered wage gap is considerably smaller among clients than among all workers can be explained in part by the similarities in jobs found by men and women clients. It also points to the way in which disability counters but does not eliminate the privilege of masculinity – the gendered division of labour was still clearly visible in the differential rates of full- and part-time work, which means men on average are significantly better off materially. Data on length of employment was limited but suggested that positions held by clients are more precarious than those held by all employees.

The overall picture from the quantitative analysis, then, is one in which disabled people on average appear disproportionately concentrated in precarious work – those jobs that offer lower wages, fewer hours, and less job security – in comparison with the provincial population of employees. This is not to suggest that all persons with disabilities are working in precarious low-wage jobs. Indeed, a limitation of a study using data from an employment service is that people with disabilities who are seeking managerial and professional occupations are unlikely to use such a resource. Nevertheless, a concern with the implications of precarious work for disabled people made a focus on those occupations found through the agency appropriate.

Complementing the quantitative analysis, the work histories provide some sense of the ways in which ongoing changes in the nature of paid work contribute to the reproduction of disability as a basis of inequality in individuals' lives. This is true in a number of ways. First, people's experiences point to the difficulties of finding paid work that offers sufficient hours, adequate wages, and desired security, mirroring the findings of the quantitative work. Moreover, different people experience this growing precariousness in different ways. A middle-aged white man such as Gordon, who experiences an accident or illness, may find that disability as a dimension of inequality exacerbates his precariousness in a structural context already characterized by a diminishing supply of secure, unionized employment opportunities to which he previously had access. In contrast, a young woman graduating from high school with an existing impairment, such as Tina, confronts a range of service sector job opportunities in which low wages, few benefits, part-time status, and high turnover are the norm. For a recent immigrant with an existing condition, such as Henry, racism and the devaluation of existing qualifications and experience in Canadian labour markets narrow job opportunities to temporary and contract positions that offer little security and are predisposed against effective accommodation. For a middle-aged woman with a learning disability returning to paid work, such as Janice, opportunities may be restricted to low-wage service jobs and manual labour, few of which are full-time and many of which are subject to speed-up. In these and other instances, disability intersects with race, gender, immigrant status, and age to shape labour market experiences in complex ways.

In addition, the work histories show how reorganization of the labour process in different occupations contributes to an increasingly disabling work environment. The shortening of time horizons – either through the use of temporary contracts or the expectation of high turnover among interchangeable and increasingly disposable workers – is one strategy used to cut labour costs. This strategy may have particular consequences for disabled workers who require some form of accommodation. The frequency of moves between jobs may also pose particular problems for disabled people in terms of social integration and acceptance. Organization of work and strategies of control, including minimal training, multi-tasking, speed-up, and teamwork, are geared to achieve flexibility for employers at the expense of flexibility for workers. The work histories demonstrate the ways in which the implementation of these strategies reproduces, indeed intensifies, disability inequality in the workplace. Lastly, disabled women and men face ongoing challenges for material survival, caught as they are between social assistance reforms that encourage greater economic independence and a shortage of living-wage jobs. For disabled women in particular, this situation may necessitate holding multiple precarious jobs in addition to undertaking unpaid work in the home.

Despite the small number of people who had found what they considered to be good jobs, clients' experiences raise important questions about

the nature of work in the contemporary capitalist economy, questions that
have implications not only for disabled people but for all workers. In policy
terms, several implications can be identified. First, the experience of clients
points to the urgent need for an increase in the minimum wage. Their strong
concentration in a small number of precarious occupations and sectors means
that many clients, and especially women, struggle to survive on poverty-
level wages. Second, the material circumstances of some clients would also
be improved through an increase in the earned income allowance of provincial social assistance programs. Currently, the general welfare program
provides little opportunity to supplement social assistance with earned income, while the provincial disability support program allows people to earn
up to $160/month without penalty. Third, recent literature on the chang-
ing nature of paid work and the labour process has argued for the revision
of current labour laws designed to regulate the postwar standard of full-
time, permanent employment (duRivage, Carre, and Tilly 1998; Vosko 2000).
A key focus of this scholarship is the way in which revised labour laws could
facilitate collective organizing among precarious workers in order to counter
the instability, lack of benefits, and low wages they currently face. While
such a call is timely and important, the lack of attention to disabled workers in this scholarship raises concerns that the collective organizing and
unionization that it informs will not be fully inclusive. The relationship
between labour unions and disabled people – as both patients/clients/
consumers and workers – has historically been problematic (Oliver 1990).
Explicit recognition of the presence of disabled people in the labour force,
and efforts to facilitate their participation in collective organizing, are vital
to the success of these endeavours, not least because the insight and experiences of disabled people can be used to articulate an alternative to precarious employment that would meet the needs of all workers.

Acknowledgments
The research reported in this chapter is supported by a grant from the Social Sciences and
Humanities Research Council (Grant No. 410-2001-0786). Thanks to Cynthia Cranford for
insightful comments on drafts of this work, to staff at PATH employment services, and to
the people who took time to participate in this study.

Notes
1 Data from Statistics Canada's Health and Activity Limitation Survey (1991) were used for
   this comparison. At the time, data from the 2001 Participation and Activity Limitation
   Survey (PALS) were not available.
2 The names given to workers in this qualitative analysis are fictitious. In addition, specific
   details about individuals and their experiences in the labour market have been altered
   and/or omitted to safeguard confidentiality.

References
Acker, J. 2000. Revisiting class: Thinking from gender, race and organizations. *Social Politics*
   7, 2: 192-214.

Aronson, J., and S. Neysmith. 1997. The retreat of the state and long-term care provision: Implications for frail elderly people, unpaid family carers and paid home care workers. *Studies in Political Economy* 53 (Summer): 37-66.

Babbie, E., and L. Benaquisto. 2002. *Fundamentals of social research.* Scarborough, ON: Nelson.

Barnes, C., G. Mercer, and T. Shakespeare. 1999. *Exploring disability: A sociological introduction.* Malden, MA: Polity Press.

Baron, S., S. Riddell, and H. Wilkinson. 1998. The best burgers? The person with learning difficulties as worker. In *The disability reader: Social science perspectives,* ed. T. Shakespeare, 94-109. London: Cassell.

Bickenbach, J. 1999. Minority rights or universal participation: The politics of disablement. In *Disability, divers-ability and legal change,* ed. M. Jones and L. Basser Marks, 101-15. The Hague: Martinus Nijhoff.

Bryman, A. 2004. *Social Research Methods.* Oxford: Oxford University Press.

Canada. Federal, Provincial, and Territorial Ministers Responsible for Social Services. 2000. *In unison: A Canadian approach to disability issues.* Hull: Human Resources Development Canada.

Canada. HRDC (Human Resources Development Canada). 1999. *Employment Equity Act: Annual report.* Hull: Human Resources Development Canada.

–. 2002. *Advancing the inclusion of persons with disabilities: A Government of Canada report December 2002.* Hull: Human Resources Development Canada.

–. N.d. Industrial structure of the Hamilton labour market. http://www.on.hrdc-drhc.gc.ca/english/offices/hamilton/lmi/content.

Connell, R.W. 1995. *Masculinities.* Berkeley: University of California Press.

Cornes, P. 1984. *The future of work for people with disabilities: A view from Great Britain.* New York: World Rehabilitation Fund.

Cranford, C. 1998. Gender and citizenship in the restructuring of janitorial work in Los Angeles. *Gender Issues* 16, 4: 25-51.

Cranford, C.J., L.F. Vosko, and N. Zukewicz. 2003. The gender of precarious employment in Canada. *Relations Industrielles/Industrial Relations* 53, 3: 454-82.

Drum, C. 1998. The social construction of personnel policy: Implications for people with disabilities. *Journal of Disability Policy Studies* 9, 2: 125-50.

duRivage, V., F. Carre, and C. Tilly. 1998. Making labor law work for part-time and contingent workers. In *Contingent work: American employment relations in transition,* ed. K. Barker and K. Christensen, 263-80. Ithaca, NY: Cornell University Press.

Fawcett, G. 1996. *Living with disability in Canada: An economic portrait.* Hull: Human Resources Development Canada, Office for Disability Issues.

Finkelstein, V. 1980. *Attitudes and disabled people.* New York: World Rehabilitation Fund.

Gleeson, B. 1999. *Geographies of disability.* New York: Routledge.

Gooding, C. 1994. *Disabling laws, enabling acts: Disability rights in Britain and America.* London: Pluto Press.

Hendriks, A. 1999. From social (in)security to equal employment opportunities: A report from the Netherlands. In *Disability, divers-ability and legal change,* ed. M. Jones and L. Basser Marks, 153-69. The Hague: Martinus Nijhoff.

Hiebert, D. 1999. Local geographies of labor market segmentation: Montreal, Toronto and Vancouver, 1991. *Economic Geography* 75, 4: 339-69.

Hyde, M. 2000. From welfare to work? Social policy for disabled people of working age in the United Kingdom in the 1990s. *Disability and Society* 15, 2: 327-41.

Jackson, C., A. Furnham, and K. Willen. 2000. Employer willingness to comply with the Disability Discrimination Act regarding staff selection in the UK. *Journal of Occupational and Organizational Psychology* 73, 1: 119-29.

Kitchin, R., P. Shirlow, and I. Shuttleworth. 1998. On the margins: Disabled people's experience of employment in Donegal, West Ireland. *Disability and Society* 13, 5: 785-806.

Krahn, H.J., and Graham S. Lowe. 2002. *Work, industry and Canadian society.* Scarborough, ON: Thomson/Nelson.

Li, P. 1985. The use of oral history in studying elderly Chinese-Canadians. *Canadian Ethnic Studies* 17, 1: 67-77.

Luxton, M., and J. Corman. 2001. *Getting by in hard times: Gendered labour at home and on the job.* Toronto: University of Toronto Press.

Oliver, M. 1990. *The politics of disablement: A sociological approach.* New York: St. Martin's Press.

Ravaud, J.F., B. Madiot, and I. Ville. 1992. Discrimination towards disabled people seeking employment. *Social Science and Medicine* 35, 8: 951-58.

Reiter, E. 1996. *Making fast food: From the frying pan into the fryer.* Montreal and Kingston: McGill-Queen's University Press.

Rodgers, G. 1989. Precarious work in Western Europe: The state of the debate. In *Precarious jobs in labour market regulation: The growth of atypical employment in Western Europe,* ed. G. Rodgers and J. Rodgers, 1-16. Brussels: International Institute for Labour Studies.

Roulstone, A. 2000. Disability, dependency and the New Deal for disabled people. *Disability and Society* 15, 3: 427-43.

Saddler, J. 1984. Home work. *Wall Street Journal* 203, 1: F7.

Smith, V. 1994. Braverman's legacy: The labor process tradition at 20. *Work and Occupations* 21, 4: 403-21.

–. 1998. The fractured world of the temporary worker: Power, participation and fragmentation in the contemporary workplace. *Social Problems* 45, 3: 411-30.

Statistics Canada. 2001. *Essential labour market data resource: Labour force survey products and services, 2000-2001.* Ottawa: Statistics Canada.

Turton, N. 2001. Welfare benefits and work disincentives. *Journal of Mental Health* 10, 3: 285-300.

Vosko, L. 2000. *Temporary work: The gendered rise of a precarious employment relationship.* Toronto: University of Toronto Press.

Wilton, R. 2004. From flexibility to accommodation: Disabled people and the reinvention of paid work. *Transactions of the Institute of British Geographers* 29, 4: 420-32.

7

A Life without Living: Challenging Medical and Economic Reductionism in Home Support Policy for People with Disabilities

Kari Krogh and Jon Johnson

The current neo-liberal political climate in British Columbia and much of the rest of Canada has encouraged the development of policies that restrict the provision of government-subsidized home support services for people with disabilities. Rather than facilitating the inclusion of people with disabilities as citizens within the public sphere, the policies and administration governing home support service provision reinforce disempowering definitions of disability as well as the power relations that have historically prevented people with disabilities from participating fully as citizens. Home support service policies in regions such as the Capital Health Region of British Columbia suppress the citizenship rights of people with disabilities, impede their ability to participate in policy-making decisions that directly affect their lives, and put serious constraints on their ability to define themselves in ways that resist limiting notions of disability and impairment.

Home support, also known as home care or personal assistance, as we are defining it, is non-medical support to aid disabled people in undertaking activities of daily living such as bathing, dressing, eating, basic mobility, meal preparation, house cleaning, and errands. When people who live with impairments receive quality home support, they are enabled to participate in the social, economic, and political activities of community life in ways that many able-bodied citizens take for granted (see Krogh 2001a).

In this chapter, we examine the administrative organization of home support services in Victoria, British Columbia, and its impact on the lives of people who live with impairments. We begin by outlining how recent neo-liberal trends in British Columbia's Capital Health Region (CHR) have undermined the funding and quality of home support services in the region, and some of the negative effects these changes have had on the lives of people with disabilities.

The recent changes to home support in the CHR highlight the need for more democratic and equitable policies and for policy making to be informed by the perspectives of people with disabilities, since they are directly affected by these policies. To this end, the methodology section describes how the first author collaborated with the Home Support Action Group (HSAG) – a community coalition comprising individuals, community advocates, and representatives of disability, family caregiver, and First Nations disability organizations – to conduct research that contributes to the understanding of the perspectives of people with disabilities on home support and to theorize how these understandings could be mobilized to positively affect home support policy in the CHR. The data include videotaped interviews with recipients of home support service who live with impairments, as well as a series of audiotaped analytic discussions with HSAG members. Researchers also systematically gathered data over a two-year period (1999-2001) to document the efforts of the HSAG to participate in home support policy making in the CHR.

We then outline our theoretical framework and how it can be used to contextualize and explain the findings and implications of the data collected during the study. To explore how particular definitions of disability are reflected in, and reinforced by, home support policies, we draw on the work of disability and feminist theorists (Morris 1993; Oliver 1992; Rioux 1997; Wendell 2001). In addition, we examine the application of Michel Foucault's notion of the reifying and controlling "gaze" as it relates to people with disabilities who request home support. Pierre Bourdieu's "theory of practice" is also used to build an understanding of how home support policies and administration maintain the interests of dominant groups through the use of symbolic violence. These concepts are particularly helpful in explaining the frustrated attempts of the HSAG to influence home support policy.

We apply the above-mentioned theoretical framework to the data to illustrate how the narrowing of definitions of disability, home support, and citizenship are being reinforced through the rhetoric of medical certification, economic efficiency, charity, and employability. We demonstrate how individualistic medical conceptualizations of disability are reified in home support policy and its administrative structures and practices in ways that ultimately limit disabled people's expectations and opportunities to participate in a range of community activities, including policy making. The efforts of the HSAG to influence policy making are documented, as are the many barriers it faced while trying to achieve its goals. We argue that community participation in policy making is a precondition for the design and implementation of equitable and democratic policies.[1] We conclude that, economically, reductionistic home support policies that emphasize the medical model of disability must be replaced by policies emphasizing the social model of disability and the role of home support in enabling citizenship for people with disabilities. However, the relations of power that structure home support service and policy making in the CHR and that effectively exclude people with disabilities from policy making must be recognized and challenged before the perspectives of people with disabilities will be acknowledged by policy makers.

Home Support and Policy Context

People who live with impairments consider home support's non-medical nature and its location both within and outside of a home setting to be essential characteristics of the service. Although a connection between health and citizenship is acknowledged, many disabled people consider this service a requirement for enabling full citizenship, rather than simply a health service.

People interviewed for the study were asked to describe how they envisioned home support in their lives. One participant, Maria, made a point of describing how sufficient levels and quality of home support enabled her to have a life with choices rather than feeling institutionalized within the four walls of her bedroom: "Everything that we want to do outside our own home and to be up and about in your own home, to have people in – you need home care in order to do that ... How would you feel if you were stuck in bed and couldn't get out and all you could do was not get out the door ... get up to turn on the radio or, go to the fridge and get yourself a drink whenever you wanted to?" (Krogh 2001a).[2]

Home support is administered at the provincial level and is not protected under the federal *Canada Health Act* (Canada 2003). As a result, home support policy is particularly vulnerable to provincial initiatives founded on the rhetoric and principles of economic restraint. The current neo-liberal political climate in Canada has supported a revision of home support policies in ways that have reduced life opportunities and options for people who rely on the service. Over the past decade, changes to home support policy have resulted in fewer people being eligible for services, a reduction in the types of service available, and wider implementation of user fees (Canada 1999; Krogh et al. 2005).[3]

For example, the Province of British Columbia responded to the introduction of the Canada Health and Social Transfers in 1994 by introducing a regionalized health-care administrative system that promised to improve health care by bringing care "closer to home." In accordance with an emphasis on economic efficiency throughout this period, CHR and Ministry of Health officials implemented a number of cost-cutting measures aimed at streamlining the delivery of health services. Restrictive eligibility criteria for home support were introduced and a tighter definition of health was adopted such that the hygiene of the home environment and bodily sustenance through meal preparation were no longer considered legitimate health services.[4] Home support, in many instances, became restricted to those services considered medically necessary that were predominantly delivered within the home. However, such an approach ignores the relevance of community participation for disabled people. It also fails to consider that even services that are not labelled medically necessary, if not adequately provided over time, can lead to the declining health of home support users. Together, these changes essentially limited the federal government's role in funding and monitoring health services, and significantly reduced the level and quality of home support services within the province of British Columbia for people with disabilities. The subsequent reorganization of services created accountability problems among the regional, provincial, and federal levels of government, leaving those who had their services eliminated or significantly reduced with no clear recourse (see also Vogel 2000).

Furthermore, because each province or territory has responded to these changes differently, variations in home support service have been exacerbated among the provinces and territories. The variations in home support services across Canada have made it difficult for home support users to move within and between provinces and territories in Canada. A move frequently triggers a reassessment process (using newer, more restrictive criteria) that is likely to result in a reduction or elimination of home support services. Many home support users and their representative organizations believe that these regional variations in home support service impinge on their mobility rights as outlined in section 6(2)(a) of the *Canadian Charter of Rights and Freedoms*.[5]

Those relying on home support were hit hard by these cost-cutting measures. Between 1994 and 1997, the number of BC residents receiving home support was cut by almost 20 percent at a time when many claimed that the need for these services should have risen, given the demographics of the population (Sanford 2000). In 2000, a reassessment process was introduced, resulting in a reduction or elimination of home support for individuals, with no access to a formal appeal mechanism. In place of government-subsidized home support services, people with disabilities were handed a list of charities and pay-for-service agencies (Krogh 2001a).[6]

The administrative confusion resulting from the reorganization and dispersal of home support services presented particular challenges to people with disabilities who wished to participate in home support policy making. In response to its lobbying of the government to improve home support policy and service delivery, the HSAG was redirected between regional and provincial authorities for six months – what HSAG members came to refer to as being given the "runaround." Ironically, HSAG members frequently worked from their beds at home or in the hospital and clearly felt they had no choice but to sacrifice their personal health in order to participate in influencing health policy.

Methodology

We attempt to ground our theoretical explorations and policy recommendations in the descriptions, experiences, and understandings of home support presented by those who consider home support integral to their lives. In this chapter we will draw on findings from a study conducted by the first author in collaboration with the HSAG. The primary purpose of the study was to understand home support from the perspectives of disabled people. A secondary goal was to explore how the collection, review, and dissemination of videotape-based interview data might methodologically facilitate the participation of home support users in research, analysis, and policy activities (see Krogh 2001b). We argue that collaborative research on home support that meaningfully involves people with disabilities in the collection and analysis of the data is an important step toward enabling the participation of people with disabilities in policy making; such research provides an opportunity for their perspectives to be heard by a wider audience.

A foundational source of information for this study was four two-hour interviews with disabled people who received home support services. These were supplemented by video of the interviewees (Krogh 2001a) demonstrating how their home support services facilitate household tasks as well as their inclusion within the workplace and larger community. These materials were reviewed in several cycles of analysis: first, the interviewees reviewed content to omit anything they did not want to share publicly and then identified what they believed to be the most important ideas expressed; second, the videographer and principal researcher (using transcribed interviews and the N6 qualitative data analysis software) conducted a comparative thematic analysis of issues; and finally the analysis team, consisting of ten people who were either home support users or advocates, reviewed the tapes, layering and integrating their own narratives to give further depth or breadth to the ideas presented on tape. Recorded analytic discussions that drew on these three sources of information led to the identification of central themes, a determination of the appropriate sequence of themes, and, eventually, the central argument of citizenship reflected in the resulting videotape, entitled *Beyond Four Walls: The Impact of Home Support on Health, Work and Citizenship for People with Disabilities*. The discussions that emerged from this process formed the basis for the design and implementation of new home support lobbying strategies. The Home Support Action Group's efforts to participate in policy making were carefully documented over a two-year period. Data were gathered through participant observation of HSAG activities, minutes from its biweekly meetings, written correspondence with decision makers, presentations to policy makers, and public speeches. In addition to thematic analysis of transcripts and field notes, a discourse analysis was applied to home support policy documents and media coverage.

In order to contextualize and understand the systematically documented experiences described by study participants, we drew on the arguments of several disability and feminist authors, as well as the theoretical insights of Foucault and Bourdieu. The remainder of this chapter explores how a synthesis of these authors' arguments can help us understand and contextualize the recent changes to home support policy and service in the Capital Health Region of British Columbia and the actions of the HSAG to improve home support policy and service for people with disabilities. The application of this theoretical framework to the data has contributed significantly to our critical discussion of the relations of power that characterize the field of home support, of the implications these relations have for people with disabilities, and, subsequently, of the changes to home support policy that must be made before it can enable people with disabilities in Canada to enjoy a wider range of life opportunities and to contribute to society through their participation.

Bourdieu's Theory of Practice

Bourdieu's theory of practice examines social phenomena simultaneously as the product of large-scale political, economic, and social structures and the actions of individuals or groups in local contexts. Bourdieu emphasized the importance of understanding social practices in terms of the larger sociopolitical context in which they occur. He conceptualized social practices as operating within specific social fields, which he defined as competitive systems of social relations among groups of actors that function according to their own specific logic or rules (Lash 1993, 197-98). For instance, the CHR can be considered a social field composed of various groups of actors – government officials, administrators, physicians, nurses, patients, and people with disabilities – that act in relation to each other according to a set of rules, values, and assumptions specific to that field. The CHR, for instance is largely structured by an emphasis on physiological health, individual treatment, and medical technology. Its administrative structures are informed by an emphasis on efficiency and the authority of doctors and other medical professionals. The main objective of individuals or groups of actors within the field is to ensure their interests are satisfied by attaining the power to confer or withhold legitimacy from other participants. Such legitimacy is obtained through the accumulation and strategic mobilization of symbolic capital, which is Bourdieu's term for the prestige and power associated with the possession of various forms of socially recognized wealth and prestige that are valued within the field (Bourdieu 1990, 112-21; Lash 1993, 200-1).

Symbolic capital is itself derived from three other forms of capital: social, cultural, and economic capital. Social capital involves the number of culturally, economically, or politically useful relations accumulated by a given person and can involve such social networks as family, friends, acquaintances, or other potentially strategic contacts (Bourdieu 1990, 35). Economic capital includes that which is directly convertible to economic wealth such as money, property, goods, or labour (132-33). Finally, cultural capital consists of culturally specific or specialized knowledge – for example, artistic knowledge, educational credentials, verbal facility, or aesthetic tastes that are considered prestigious or advantageous within the field (125). Key to Bourdieu's notion of capital is the idea that the various forms of capital are mutually convertible. For instance, a home support user might be able to use his or her knowledge of the home support system (cultural capital) to gain more home support service hours (economic capital). These home support hours can then be used for employment training (cultural capital) or for participating more fully as a citizen in community activities such as socializing or political letter writing that might result in the individual's developing socially useful contacts (social capital). By contrast, physicians might use their economic and social capital to lobby the government for increased funding for medical research or imaging technologies, which could be used to increase their knowledge of physiology and pathology (cultural capital).

In their struggle for various forms of capital, individuals or groups of actors in a social field adopt strategies that are in part shaped by the rules (laws, policies, norms, social mores) governing that field. Over time, these strategies become general dispositions acquired through practical experience in the field, and eventually become embodied practices.[7] For instance, in an effort to restrict home support funding, home support staff might try to make home support users feel guilty for requesting new services (or old services that were eliminated). Insofar as this strategy works, it may become a reflexive strategy used by home support staff. This gradual embodiment of social rules (structure), combined with actors' own choices of how those rules should be interpreted or practised (agency) within a particular field, form what Bourdieu (1990, 53) calls the "habitus." Although the habitus is a set of durable dispositions that endure over time, it is not entirely static. Through social interaction, the habitus changes slowly over time in ways that reflect changes in a given social field as well as ways in which individuals continually reinterpret their position within the field and the strategies they use to negotiate that field. Every individual or group within the field possesses a particular habitus that reflects their position within the field, as well as their specific articulation of structure and agency.

The symbolic capital of the dominant group gives it the authority to define and confer legitimacy within a particular social field: its members are able to interpret, define, or change the rules or laws that structure the field to further their interests and goals. By mobilizing various forms of capital in strategic ways, dominant groups are able to maintain their dominance over other groups of actors within a given field. Through its ability to define what is and is not legitimate within a social field, a dominant group can subvert challenges to its authority by convincing dissenting groups to adopt the values of the dominant group. In this way, dominant groups are able to convince subordinates to willingly act according to rules that virtually ensure that the dominant group will retain its dominance. This process, similar to Gramsci's notion of hegemony (Edgar and Sedgwick 2002, 88), is what Bourdieu called symbolic violence – it is a means of imposing the symbolic system of one group on another group (Krais 1993, 172).

When the symbolic representations of the dominant group become inscribed within the habitus of other individuals or groups, the strategic actions of these individuals or groups often unwittingly reflect and legitimate the prevailing relations of power in a given field. However, one's habitus can also involve strategies that resist or challenge those power relations (Edgar and Sedgwick 2002, 30-31). For instance, the HSAG members initially emphasized economic arguments in their analytic discussions of the data, but then consciously resisted this strategy once they recognized that there was no way of engaging in such discussions without leaving out some people, such as those with impairments who were unable to earn an income yet were still deserving of home support.

In summary, Bourdieu's theory of practice is invaluable for conceptualizing the relationships between actors within a social field that simultaneously describes how power relations structure and constrain the actions of actors within a particular field, the ability of actors to manoeuvre within those constraints, and how the interplay between structure and agency informs the creation of embodied dispositions that endure over time. It illustrates how specific policy decisions are influenced by the prevailing relations of power and how policies are designed to satisfy the interests of particular powerful groups to the exclusion of others. This theoretical framework also explains how power relations can be maintained through the strategic mobilization of capital and demonstrates the effects of this power on subordinate groups within the field.

Understanding CHR as a Social Field
Burke (2000, 180) argued that the discourse of efficiency has been used to justify a neo-liberal argument for the increased role of the private sector in the provision and administration of health services: "The dominant meaning of efficiency emerges from a powerful coalescence of political forces, including governments at all levels, which are consumed with the need to control deficits and pay down debt by containing social policy costs; the medical profession, which has long argued for the injection of additional private funds into the health-care system; and the business sector, whose concerns with flexibility, lower tax burdens and enhanced global competitiveness point directly to a minimal social role for the state." In this formulation, the state is characterized as inefficient and the free market is upheld

as the natural alternative. However, Burke rightly points out that although better care for less money is implied in the term "efficiency," the neo-liberal practices justified under this term may result in compromised care for more money (Burke 2000, 181; see also Browne 2000). Another related side effect of the discourse of efficiency has been a tightening of the definitions of health and disability in the CHR. By redefining more restrictively what constitutes health, CHR officials reduced or eliminated services not considered medically necessary, including meal preparation. Such a side effect is especially problematic for home support users, who often rely on home support for tasks they have difficulty performing alone but that are not immediately medically necessary. In such a political and economic climate, only those home support service areas deemed efficient and medically necessary are likely to escape reduction or outright elimination.

As upper-level administrators and politicians, CHR executives have been trained to synthesize large amounts of data pertaining to the administration of the region, and to decide how these data translate into fiscal and policy requirements. However, they lack the cultural capital to make informed choices about the day-to-day delivery of health services, which they view as the domain of health professionals.[8] CHR executives rely on the input of those staff members who are connected to the on-the-ground administration of health services (Capital Health Region 2000). Among the thousands of health professionals employed in the CHR, physicians possess the most symbolic capital. Home support workers may feel economically vulnerable if they voice a dissenting opinion, and service recipients may believe that they risk losing services if they speak out. The doctor's position of influence, on the other hand, is based on academic and legal credentials (cultural capital), affiliation with powerful institutions such as the Canadian Medical Association and the Ministry of Health, proximity to other health professionals by virtue of his or her prominence within hospitals (social capital), and the ability to garner health service, technology, and research dollars (economic capital). As such, physicians constitute the most influential group in terms of their ability to advise government officials on the needs of patients and hospitals and, thus, their ability to influence the funding priorities of the CHR board and executive. Because home support is the only service within the CHR that is not directly under the supervision of physicians, they are more likely to emphasize the need for funding other areas within the CHR over home support.

Foucault's Notions of Discipline and Surveillance through the Gaze

An understanding of how home support policy affects its users requires an analysis of social relations involving policy makers and recipients of service. In particular, we examine the power relations that exist between home support administrators and users who live with impairments. Foucault (1973,

1977) has written extensively about the power relations within institutions such as prisons, medical clinics, and hospitals; his arguments are equally applicable to the social organization of government-subsidized home support.

According to Foucault (1977, 27), power and knowledge are inextricably connected: "Power and knowledge directly imply one another ... there is no power relation without the correlative constitution of a field of knowledge, nor any knowledge that does not presuppose and constitute at the same time power relations." Power can define what constitutes legitimate knowledge, and knowledge often legitimizes the use of power; as such, all knowledge is necessarily political. This power-knowledge nexus is particularly evident in the medical encounter, during which the physician uses a highly codified system of measurement to associate particular groups of symptoms with particular classes of diseases. Foucault (1973) calls this system of abstraction, measurement, and classification the medical gaze. The medical gaze involves a normalizing judgment that categorizes human bodily variation as either normal or aberrant. Medical knowledge, in turn, legitimizes the application of medical power onto patients' bodies. The prestigious cultural capital of physicians in the field of health care gives them the authority to classify bodies as normal or aberrant, and the "discovery" of aberrant bodies legitimizes further medical investigation and intervention on those bodies. People with disabilities experience the medical gaze in everyday life, for example, in accessing post-secondary education, medical services, or employment training.

Home support policy and delivery are likewise informed by particular ways of understanding disability. Because of the economic strain that has been placed on the home support system, home support policies in the CHR have been rigidly redefined to restrict home support services to those individuals deemed most in need by home care administrators.[9] In this way, home support largely becomes focused on providing only those services that are viewed by administrators as essential for physical survival, rather than those that facilitate community involvement and full citizenship. Home support policies often tend to define disability in terms of dependency and to instruct home support administrators and service providers to understand disability in these terms (Tighe 2001).

The equation of disability with dependence is mobilized during the assessment process in ways that reflect the power of home support administrators. The power of home support administrators in the field of home support comes from their ability to confer or withhold economic capital in the form of home support service hours. Assessment tools are designed to classify potential home support recipients as either dependent and thus worthy of assistance, or as independent and therefore unworthy of assistance. Such categorizations undermine the potential of home support to enable independence, interdependence, and full citizenship for disabled people. Similar to the medical gaze, this administrative gaze is a system of abstraction, measurement, and classification that reduces disabled people to impairments that are either worthy or unworthy of home support service. When disabled people defy the notion that disability involves dependence, they are subjected to disciplinary power or consequences through the denial of adequate home support service and, even when they are deemed worthy of home support service, they remain the objects of surveillance. When they attempt to access services such as home care within a welfare framework, people with disabilities are expected to give up their right to freedom from interference and their right to privacy (Orme 2001). Furthermore, it is possible that among administrators there is a belief that disabled people may deliberately exaggerate the severity of their disabilities. Such actions would serve to attain or retain home support services in a manner that legitimizes administrative surveillance and disciplinary action on home support users. Through this constant system of surveillance and the persistent threat of disciplinary action, whether real or imagined, home support users learn to discipline themselves and their bodies in ways that accommodate the administrative gaze. They construct themselves in ways that demonstrate their dependency, and thereby legitimize the ongoing application of administrative intervention, surveillance, and control in their lives. These identity constructions and the power relations they reflect then become embodied dispositions that are enscribed in the habitus.

Defining Disability: Who Has the Power to Define Bodies as Worthy of Supports?

Delegitimizing Embodied Expertise and Erasing the Body

When interviewees spoke about home support, they communicated a clear understanding of home support in relation to who they were, their needs, and their goals. For example, one recipient of home support, Amber, stated: "Having somebody come in, cook me food so I don't burn my feet [again], help me get dressed so I don't fall in the shower, help me maintain my [mobility/security] dog so I have access to independence, and also being around at times because you don't have the energy to go and find social support ... There's a lot more to home support than just the physical aspects of it" (Krogh 2001a). A medical model of disability, informed by the medical gaze, emphasizes individual incapacity and medical authority, leaving little room for the expertise derived from a disabled person's embodied experience.[10] By refusing to recognize the value of embodied knowledge, the current structure severely hampers disabled peoples' efforts to contribute to the design, organization, and monitoring of home support services. Some policy makers in the CHR commented that the personal stories used in the video were unscientific, and therefore unworthy of their attention. One stated, for example, that this research-based video "lacked supporting evidence for claims" (Krogh 2002). The cultural capital of medical professionals is reinforced, while delegitimizing the cultural capital of people with disabilities. By defining what does or does not constitute legitimate knowledge, medical professionals and administrators can ensure their dominant position within the field of home support.

Although home support is, currently, administratively organized under the auspices of health maintenance or health promotion, we found examples where the body was totally disregarded in home support administrative policy and practice. For instance, Maria described how home support was reorganized in her region so that the lowest bidding agency would be awarded the government contract to deliver the service. Maria's description illustrates how her body was erased by the primacy of economic efficiency:

> When they changed the system around, they changed those hours on me too which meant that I had to retrain my body to go to the bathroom at a slightly different timeframe ... I had had those hours for about 14 years and overnight ... they were gone ... I was glad I got the hours back to the way I wanted ... but to wait six months is a long time and the only reason that it really went through, at all, was that the person [home support worker] that was willing to make those changes kept saying to the agency, well you took me out of here, now I can go back to Maria from 1 to 3 ... If they have somebody that's going to stick to their ... rules and laws to the letter and not bend one little inch, then ... you may as well be in a jail or an army camp. (Krogh 2001a)

This neglect of the body indicates that despite the CHR's claim to promote and maintain health, it is economic restraint that largely determines the design and administration of home support services, rather than the health of home support users. Good health is a precondition for enacting citizenship. However, given the failure of home support administrators to take into account even basic biological requirements when allocating home support services, it is unlikely that community involvement and the citizenship rights of home support users are even considered. This example illustrates how, despite the strong service commitment of some home support workers, in the face of budgetary cuts, people with disabilities can come to feel trapped within a system that sees recipients of service as objects of expenditure.

Meeting Expectations: Who Has the Power to Define Disability?
Disempowering notions of impairment and disability are derived from, and reinforced by, dominant notions of disability that are themselves a product

of larger social relations. These notions have become inscribed into home support policy, service organization, and administrative practices. When disability is understood as a medical condition located within the individual, there is little recognition of the ways in which the environment, including physical space, attitudes, and policy, create oppressive barriers. The aberrant body remains the focus of attention, rather than social policy or dominant social values (see Rioux 1997; Rioux and Valentine 2005). The medical gaze legitimates the notion that it is the impaired individual who is problematic, not the system of knowledge that maintains existing power relations by defining people with disabilities as inadequate.

The idea that disability is socially constructed has been written about extensively by disability scholars (see Barnes, Mercer, and Shakespeare 1999; Oliver 1996). One could argue that when people with disabilities are constructed as incompetent, unworthy, child-like, charity cases, or drains on the system, with little acknowledgment of their social, cultural, or economic capital, we can expect that policy will not consider the level and quality of home support required to enable disabled people to engage in a range of activities within social, economic, or political spheres of society. People with disabilities are in an impossible situation when those determining the service levels do not even anticipate that some people will want to, for example, hold a full-time job, go to school, engage in regular exercise, or socialize in the community. One participant described how she was once offered employment but was unable to accept the position because her home support services could not be reorganized to enable her to be up and ready for work by 8 a.m. Another woman spoke about how she was considering giving up her full-time job because she was having difficulty affording the income-dependent user fees for home support services after covering other disability-related expenses. There is an assumption that people with disabilities are not and cannot be productive members of society, and this assumption is perpetuated and legitimized through home support policy when home support users are restricted to services that are deemed medically necessary. HSAG chairman Gordon Argyle offered the following on how home support policy could foster the citizenship of people with disabilities: "Policy makers should first reflect upon ... what it is they themselves do [in a given day] and ask how can that policy be shaped so that people with disabilities can achieve that same level of activity? If you're falling short of that, then there's a flaw in the policy" (Krogh 2001a). The HSAG initially believed that a central reason why its concerns were not addressed was a lack of awareness of home support and disability among home support policy makers and administrators. As a result, the coalition made public education a central part of its stated mandate. Coalition members attempted to describe their desires in life, and the precise ways that their life goals could be achieved with adequate home support services. To this end, the HSAG produced the aforementioned research-based video, highlighting the role of home support in their lives, and showed it to home support policy makers, administrators, and others. A survey was used to ascertain the audience's response to this video. The findings indicated that, while this video was found by most subgroups to be educational, it appeared to have little effect on the policy makers and administrators surveyed.[11] Therefore, HSAG members began to realize that lack of education was not the most significant factor involved in the persistence of disabling home support policies, and they changed their lobbying strategies accordingly. The persistence of disabling policies is largely explained by the need of powerful groups within the field of home support to maintain existing relations of power and subordination. The authors have learned that attempts to change home support policy must first identify and challenge the political and economic interests of these powerful groups in maintaining home support policy and service as is.

Medical Surveillance

Physicians have the authority to diagnose legitimate impairments and, along with policy administrators, interpret which level and forms of impairment warrant government-subsidized supports. Assessments by physicians of individual impairment frequently determine whether a person is deemed a worthy candidate for home support service. Foucault (1973), however, would argue that "worthy" impairments are defined according to what is visible to the medical gaze, namely, those that are empirically measurable through medical technology. Just as physicians do, home support administrators use the assessment process to measure and rank people with various forms of impairment. As such, it is during the assessment encounter that administrators often apply techniques of surveillance and discipline. This medicalized assessment erases the social, political, and environmental dimensions of disability, and disregards the expertise that a person with a disability comes to develop about how to live with(in) a particular mind/body.

The Council of Canadians with Disabilities, a national advocacy organization for people with disabilities in Canada, articulated in its 2002 report *Consumers with Disabilities Speak Out on Health Issues* that the most common reason people with disabilities go to a physician is not to receive medical care but to have their impairment documented so as to enable them to receive the disability supports they require (Council of Canadians with Disabilities 2002).[12] Thus, health care for people with disabilities is largely about social control. Without a consideration of socio-political context and personal life goals, such a narrow medical approach to defining disability reinforces the notion that the barriers to community participation exist exclusively because of bodies or minds that differ from the norm.

Home support needs are increasingly defined on the basis of empirically measurable impairments, which tends to reduce the legitimacy of non-visible mental or physical impairments (Krogh 2003). The DisAbled Women's Network Canada has clearly stated that this increasingly medical involvement in assessments of eligibility for disability-related supports is particularly problematic for women with disabilities, who, for example, more frequently than men experience non-visible impairments, such as pain and fatigue, which are associated with chronic illness and are difficult to measure (Masuda 1998; Trypuc 1994; Wendell 2001). This administrative strengthening of the medical gaze not only marginalizes people with non-visible impairments but also serves to increase medical control and individualistic medical definitions of disability, thereby removing or decreasing emphasis on issues such as participatory policy development, government accountability, and home support as a form of mediated citizenship.

Symbolic Violence: Imposing Notions of Disabled and Disabled Enough
People with disabilities may learn to accommodate medical definitions of their impairments and may begin to embody these definitions, essentially using the medical gaze to monitor themselves and inscribe medical power onto the habitus.[13] When people with disabilities adopt medical definitions of their impairments, a situation is created in which medical power can function continuously, regardless of whether a physician is present, because people with disabilities discipline themselves into thinking that it is the impairment that is the problem, rather than the social construction of impairment. Here again, we find correspondence between Foucault's notion of discipline and Bourdieu's notion of symbolic violence.

The CHR introduced a new assessment tool called the Home Care MDS-HC 8 Nursing Discipline Specific Assessment Tool that was effective in reaching its publicly stated goal of increasing the proportion of clients with high care needs receiving home support.[14] Because the focus was on proportion, it appeared that the CHR was able to retain some level of service for many people who had the highest level of need and associated visible impairments, while reducing or eliminating services for those with lower levels of need and non-visible impairments.[15] In this way, it was able to reduce expenditures for home support, while avoiding some public criticism by not removing service from those, for example, with multiple visible impairments. This acted as an instrument of subtle self-discipline, in that disabled people were told that their services were being removed because there were others who were in greater need. When some disabled people in British Columbia were able to retain their services with relatively minor reductions, they were simultaneously informed that as a result of receiving services, several senior citizens would no longer receive home support (P. Gauthier, British Columbia Coalition of People with Disabilities, pers. comm.). This use of guilt by home support administrators can be understood as a method of disciplining or coercing people with disabilities to accept a lower standard of care for themselves by positing greed at the individual level, rather than admitting to socio-political factors such as budget cuts to home support services. This guilt is then internalized as part of the habitus of people with disabilities.

As currently conceived, home support policy and service delivery legitimize the application of administrative power on the bodies of home care recipients. Disabled people seeking home support assistance are enmeshed in a system of ongoing surveillance that puts serious constraints on their ability to represent themselves in ways that defy the categories of the administrative gaze or disrupt the functioning of administrative power upon them (Foucault 1977). This administrative control can become embodied as a part of the habitus of home support users (Bourdieu 1990, 53-55). The equation of disability with dependency and the implementation of assessment tools designed to measure home support recipients in terms of their degrees of perceived dependency place the onus on disabled individuals to demonstrate their desperation for, and dependence on, home support services. By prompting the disabled person to list all the reasons why home support is necessary according to the system's assessment criteria, the disabled person accommodates and reinforces the equation of disability with dependency. Restricting home support services to those with the most immediate perceived need is repressive in its application, because it requires that people with disabilities become complicit with the notion of disability that views dependence as a precondition for receiving home support service. This subverts potential resistance by rendering people with disabilities docile (see Foucault 1977, 136-38). In this way, disempowering notions of disability are rarely challenged, and existing configurations of power are maintained. For instance, one home support administrator, quoted in a local newspaper, infantilized people with disabilities by comparing adults with disabilities to able-bodied youth (Krogh 2001a; Watts 1999). Infantilizing people with disabilities is a common form of symbolic violence that forces adults with disabilities to enact dependent roles. This performance of disability as dependency also carries implications for one's conception of self.

It is clear that disempowering conceptions of disabled persons are embedded within home support policy and program development. This becomes especially difficult when citizens have developed certain expectations related to a more empowered vision of themselves, their child, or friend, only to discover that such identities need to be supplanted with that of a passive and grateful recipient of charitable assistance.[16] When disabled persons are not successful in becoming socially or economically integrated into the community, personal limitations or impairments are quickly blamed, further reinforcing an individualistic medical model of disability.

Symbolic violence occurred when Maria came to internalize home support administrators' perception that physical exercise was not a worthy use
of home support service hours and that providing service should function
to reduce overall financial costs of care. At one point in the interview, Maria
described herself in medical terms as a mature woman with high blood
pressure who had concerns related to weight and lack of circulation because of sitting in a wheelchair all day. At another point, she stated that she
used her scant "extra hours" to go swimming once a week: "The only time
I have an extra bit of time is once a week to go swimming so that my muscles
will have some exercise and some energy ... which keeps me more mobile
so that when I do transfer in and out of bed, I have the strength to help the
worker so that it makes a smooth transfer. Otherwise, if I don't keep my
strength up ... I'll need hospitalization which will cost the government
more money and my quality of life will go out the window" (Krogh 2001a).
People with disabilities assume a passive and dependent role, coming to believe, as they are told, that they are financial burdens and unworthy of the
assistance they are requesting. By virtue of their power to independently
decide who does and does not get home support services, and according to
which criteria, home support administrators can exercise a coercive form of
symbolic violence on people with disabilities. In this way, people with disabilities are instructed to remain complicit with administrators' conceptions
of them. Thus, the assessment process, as currently conceived, puts serious
constraints on people's right to self-determination.

Home Support and Citizenship: Life, Death, or Life without Living?

Who Has the Power to Define Home Support?
In interviews, home support recipients referred to the essential needs that
are met through the service. For example, Maria commented, "I cannot go
to the bathroom without help ... I need people to come in at least three
times a day because otherwise I can't go to the bathroom. How much more
basic in life is that?" (Krogh 2001a).

At least one local home support policy administrator repeatedly and publicly presented notions of home support that countered the understandings of home support held by recipients and that acted to garner public
support for cuts to services. This administrator spoke in official meetings
with the HSAG about how she, too, would like to get her windows cleaned
or have a visitor for tea, but that the CHR could not afford such luxuries
(Krogh 2001a). Her comments enraged disabled people who relied on the
service. One activist responded directly in a public health rally speech when
she said: "Home support [is] not tea and companionship but [is] wiping
butts, bathing, brushing teeth, blowing noses, etc. Home support is my

line to life – without it I'd be in some facility. It enables me to take my rightful and equal place as a citizen in this country, a member of society, community and my family ... With good [home support] employees my life is interesting, full and even fun" (Tammy, HSAG member, public speech, May 2000). Two opposing notions of home support are presented: one views home support as an expensive and luxurious service that the state can no longer afford, while the other attempts to highlight the services as both a necessity for living and a citizenship right. When those in power are able to impose the former notion at the expense of the latter, the consequences are limited life opportunities and symbolic violence in the form of reduced expectations for home support among people with disabilities. We wish to counter this economically reductionistic view of home support by emphasizing the latter view of home support as a necessary citizenship service for people with disabilities.

Home Support as a Citizenship Service

Home support should be understood as a material or technical mediator to citizenship for people who live with impairments, because it offers avenues for participation in the larger community. Several people contacted for this study discussed how home support services can enable individuals with disabilities to live their lives as full and active citizens. One participant, whom we will call Joe, described it in this way:

> The way I look at it is this: home support is no more and no less significant to my daily life than is food – as long as it's there, my health is maintained and I don't give it any more thought day to day than breathing. When my home support is stable, I can focus on the everyday things that everyone else focuses on: maintaining a home, working, learning, social interaction, leisure activities, community development, family, planning a future, independence. But like when food is cut off, my health will deteriorate and I will eventually die ... When my home support is threatened, the majority of the focus in my life becomes fear; in these situations my first fear is not for my health but for the other focuses in life [such as losing my job]. My fear works backwards through the list, distracting my focus and removing my hope in each area. (Joe, HSAG member, public speech, May 2000)

Citizenship, in the form of active participation within the realms of health, work, socialization, education, and spiritual practice, is mediated through home support for many people with disabilities (see Krogh 2001a). We need, therefore, to re-examine dominant notions of who is a citizen,[17] how citizenship rights can be exercised (i.e., via home support service), and the government's role in ensuring equity in terms of citizens' rights to equal opportunities.

Home support for people with impairments exemplifies what it can mean to live fully and interdependently. It can also present a deep-rooted challenge to dominant notions of citizenship and the range of ways in which citizenship can be enacted, particularly in the context of a Western society, where independence is so highly valued. Disabled people experience such disjunctures as problematic. Home support can be understood as a technology, that is, as a tool or instrument used to accomplish a task. Similar to other assistive technologies, such as ventilators or wheelchairs, home support for some people with disabilities may become integrated into one's life, lifestyle, and identity, and may enable a recipient to self-direct or otherwise engage in the act of living. Like pulling the plug on a ventilator, or not providing wheelchairs to those who need them, removing or failing to provide home support can have dire emotional and physical consequences. Withdrawal of such technologies can clearly be viewed as abusive, not only because it is neglectful and disallows opportunity but because it may in fact be removing one integrated element of habitus or self-identity – and identity is essential to life itself.[18] While a person without home support or a wheelchair may be kept alive physically, that person will not be enabled to live his or her life. Gordon Argyle, HSAG chairman, described what he has observed in others who are facing cuts to home support services: "[For] a lot of people [it] is the stress of not knowing how secure their home support is ... people [are] giving up, and not looking for work and not bothering to get involved in school, giving up their community activities."

Symbolic Violence: Imposed Notions of Home Support and Citizenship
In the midst of a wave of reassessments for home support, Gordon Argyle stated: "[Administrators are] taking away the hours of home support and not taking into account any of the expectations [people with disabilities] have of participating as citizens in the community." People with disabilities expect to participate in society. In their interviews, some study participants referred to the influence of parental philosophies and the dominant rhetoric of independence. For many, the inability to participate in community life is especially painful after years of building up expectations for participation and exposure to popular rhetoric about inclusion. Patrick described how his parents raised him to expect to participate in society: "When I was growing up my father was a very strong advocate ... He encouraged me [to be] as independent as I could be." Another participant spoke of how community efforts to increase accessibility in a wide range of areas, such as municipal transit, educational institutions, and workplaces, are useless if people with disabilities are not provided with sufficient home support to get out of bed and out the door. Telling disabled people that their expectations of engaging in society and envisioning a full life in a manner that incorporates home support are not only unrealistic but an unreasonable burden on society can

be considered a form of symbolic violence, since it is a method of coercing people with disabilities to accept the symbolic system of the dominant group. People are expected to accept that they are burdens to the system and to unquestioningly readjust their expectations.

Work without Choice: Fighting for the Right to Live

Numerous people interviewed or otherwise involved in the project spoke about the work they undertook to try to retain their hours of home support service. Because this was work requiring immediate attention without consideration of negative personal health or lifestyle consequences, Krogh came to refer to this as "work without choice." One home support recipient, Maria, commented, "If you're wasting your time fighting an issue ... it's just very, very difficult to spend all your energy [this way]; you feel so narrow, whereas there's so much in life to enjoy." Gordon Argyle described the impact of fighting home support cuts on health and life opportunities of HSAG members specifically when he stated: "[There are] only so many hours in the day, so you have to start giving up, so you make that conscious decision and they're not always the healthiest decisions. I'm sure that members of the [HSAG] group who can't always make the meetings ... working from bed ... or hospital, sometimes you ... have to work yourself a little harder and basically put your health at risk to achieve goals – it's the cost that's involved." During the course of the study, Dwayne Gough, a resident of the CHR who lived with paraplegia and who had his hours of home support eliminated, died.[19] The HSAG believes that Gough would not have died if his home support had been retained. However, the group's request for an inquiry into the matter was not acted on.

Barriers to Policy Participation

HSAG's Strategies to Influence Policy

To influence policy, the HSAG used many strategies based on its social, cultural, and economic capital. One of the strategies was letter writing, in an attempt to garner support from socially and politically useful contacts. The HSAG sent correspondence to the premier of British Columbia, the BC minister of health, MLAs for all parties, and the Capital Health Region board of directors, as well as disability organizations, unions, and Canadian celebrities. The HSAG considered that, although time-consuming, letters would be strategically effective because they often prompt a response from the recipients. In its letters to organizations and unions, the HSAG requested moral, political, and financial support (all forms of capital) for its lobbying activities aimed to stop the cuts to home support services. The HSAG attempted to assail provincial and regional health boards with letters outlining the unacceptability of the current situation, giving personal examples of impacts of the cuts and proposing possible solutions. The HSAG also held meetings with provincial and regional government officials, making presentations to groups such as the CHR Advisory Committee. The HSAG would often follow up these meetings with a letter to summarize statements and commitments made.

The group was successful in receiving limited financial support from disability organizations such as the British Columbia Coalition of Persons with Disabilities and from the British Columbia Government Employees' Union, with which the HSAG established strategic working partnerships. More recently, it has increased its collaboration with the Council of Canadians with Disabilities to become part of a national effort to bring attention to the issue of home support for people with disabilities. Thus, the HSAG managed modest increases to its social and economic capital, and raised public awareness about the effects of home support cuts.

HSAG's letter-writing and meeting strategies had limited success in influencing home support policy and administration. Letters to celebrities and a national citizen's coalition went unanswered. Although there was talk among CHR officials of increased user participation, the demonstration of real participation in decision making was lacking. Shortly after a meeting with the HSAG in March 2000, the CHR board of directors decided to modify its structure to make it more participatory. An advisory group composed of community members was established to promote community participation in the development of an appeal mechanism. However, contrary to the advisory group's wishes, the CHR did not include any impartial members on the appeal committee, thereby reducing its utility and legitimacy in the minds of the HSAG members (G. Argyle, HSAG, pers. comm.).

The effectiveness of meetings with BC's minister of health was also limited, especially given that the minister was replaced in May 2001 after an election. The jurisdictions of ministries were subsequently reorganized, and many ministry policies were internally reviewed. The resulting administrative confusion may have contributed to the result – that none of the issues raised by the HSAG at the meeting with the BC minister of health was addressed. The CHR said it wanted to work in collaboration with the HSAG to communicate to the province about the need for resources to fund home support services. However, when large infusions of funding occurred in 1999 and 2000, the CHR did not increase home support service levels in the region; instead, the funds were diverted to pay down the deficit. The chief executive officer of the CHR board informed HSAG members that although these funds existed, they should be ignored, and that there were no anticipated increases in the level of services to those who had had their services cut (G. Argyle, HSAG, pers. comm.).

The efforts of the HSAG to influence home support policy in the CHR need to be assessed in the context of the dominant discourses of economic efficiency and medical necessity that have structured this social field, and the relative symbolic capital of the HSAG needs to be compared with that of other groups of actors in the field of health, particularly physicians. The HSAG lacked the social and economic capital to effectively lobby the government for policy change in the CHR. Although members of this community coalition had much knowledge of the home support system and the effects that budget cuts were having on people with disabilities, their cultural capital was not highly valued by CHR officials, who were focused on the bottom line. It was difficult to sustain the pressure required to effectively lobby the government for policy and service changes, and some individuals had to devote their diminishing home support hours to performing this particular "work without choice," which often resulted in declining health. From this perspective, it is easy to understand why the efforts of the HSAG to participate in home support policy making were frustrated.

Conclusion

Individualistic medical conceptualizations of disability reinforce the notion that the oppressive nature of disability begins and ends within the body, leaving governments unaccountable for the impact of the home support policies they develop and administer. An individualistic model of disability that views and constructs disability as a medical phenomenon needs to be challenged. The systems that keep it in place need to be recognized as a source of symbolic violence imposed on people with impairments, especially when their contextual and embodied knowledge is disregarded, and when opportunities to enact their identities are restricted. It is important that home support be reframed as a citizenship-rights issue worthy of government accountability.

In certain respects, home support services are ambiguously placed within the administrative structures of health. Home support services provide people with disabilities the assistance necessary to maintain their health and their day-to-day lives. However, CHR officials have been able to justify cuts to home support services on the basis of their being not medically necessary. Furthermore, the neo-liberal emphasis on economic efficiency exacerbates damaging attitudes toward people with disabilities, who are seen as unproductive burdens on the system; indeed, new policies such as income-dependent user fees require some home support recipients to give up their jobs. In such circumstances, the contradictory efforts of various government departments becomes apparent.

Tremendous differences in symbolic capital exist among the actors in the health field, and dominant discourses play a significant role in shaping definitions of health, disability, home support, and citizenship. Therefore, disabled people requiring home support will face significant barriers in their attempts to have their perspectives represented within home support administration systems as they are currently structured. One solution would be to redefine home care as a citizenship service instead of primarily a health service. This might necessitate relocating responsibility for home support provision away from administrative bodies, such as the CHR, into a more appropriate field, or perhaps to a partially independent field that receives funding from provincial ministries of health as well as other government departments, given that home support affects many other areas, including employment and citizenship. Relocating home support within a field that emphasizes citizenship rather than medicalization would at least prevent government officials from cutting home support services on the basis that they are not "medically necessary." We recommend that home support be included as part of a large group of disability support services, including, for example, American Sign Language for people who are deaf, and be reframed as citizenship supports. We recognize, given the complexity of the issues involved, that these could be first steps among many and, ultimately, that fundamental shifts would need to take place in how disability is understood and responded to. Current home support service, policy, and administration, because they are informed by disempowering definitions of disability, severely limit the potential for full citizenship for people with disabilities in Canada. We argue that home support policy making must be informed by those who live with impairment in order for the Canadian government to offer disabled people opportunities for full democratic citizenship. Our research contributes to this goal by involving people with disabilities in the production of knowledge, acknowledging the value of their perspectives on home support, and providing avenues for the expression of their perspectives and dissent. Nothing short of full democratic citizenship will enable those living with impairments to move beyond a life without living.

Acknowledgments
We would like to acknowledge personnel and grant support provided to Kari Krogh from the Social Science and Humanities Research Council and the Canadian Institutes of Health Research. In addition, we wish to acknowledge the contributions to the referenced project of the many people involved, including the Home Support Action Group (HSAG); Sally Kimpson, the original coordinator of the HSAG; and research assistant Victoria Bowman.

Notes
1 Participatory policy making refers to the involvement of people whose lives are intimately affected by a policy in the design, implementation, and evaluation of the policy. People with disabilities often require home support to be able to express their ideas, take action, and participate in analytic exchanges that lead to proposed solutions. Cuts to home support reduce opportunities for such engagement. Removal of home support is a powerful force that operates to constrict individual and collective voice, circumvent resistance, and limit opportunities for our society to benefit from contributions from all its members.

2   With the exception of the chairperson of the HSAG, Gordon Argyle, the names of the participants of this study have been changed to protect their privacy.

3   This national study funded by the Social Sciences and Humanities Research Council, Canadian Institutes of Health Research, and Human Resources and Skills Development Canada, examines home care policy as it affects people with disabilities in each province and territory in Canada.

4   McColl and colleagues report in Chapter 1 that housework and meal preparation are the most commonly reported activity limitations.

5   A discussion of whether this would actually be successful in the courts, and whether this is the most relevant section of the Charter, is beyond the scope of this chapter. It is included because it represents the current analysis from the perspective of disability organizations such as the Council of Canadians with Disabilities, the British Columbia Coalition of People with Disabilities, and the Home Support Action Group.

6   This is problematic not only because those who rely on government-subsidized home care find it difficult to pay for services but also because people with disabilities are then forced to return to a system of charity that necessarily characterizes them as pitiful, passive, and eternally grateful.

7   Here we are using "embodied" to refer to knowledge and practices that are simultaneously the outcome of individual positioning within the larger field of social structures, and how one understands these structures. From this perspective, all knowledge is subjective because it originates from individuals who are differentially positioned within social fields with corresponding knowledge, values, and understandings that are heavily influenced by that positioning. All knowledge comes from somewhere, and the term "embodied" is explicitly used to recognize that "somewhere" is an individual person with a physical body that is marked by class, ethnicity, gender, age, stigma, and so on. See, for example, Thomas J. Csordas, "Words from the Holy People: A Case Study in Cultural Phenomenology," in *Embodiment and Experience: The Existential Ground of Culture and Self*, ed. Thomas J. Csordas, 269-90 (Cambridge: Cambridge University Press, 1994).

8   Despite the fact that many disabled people have considerable knowledge of home support and the effects of policy on people with impairments, this form of cultural capital is not highly valued by CHR executives. As such, the perspectives of disabled recipients are rarely sought on home support policy decisions that directly affect them.

9   See Home Care MDS-HC 8 Nursing Discipline Specific Assessment Tool, Vancouver Island Health Authority.

10 See Dorothy Smith, *Writing the Social: Critique, Theory, and Investigations* (Toronto: University of Toronto Press, 1999), writing about situated embodied knowledge.

11 Subgroups of people who viewed the videotape included people with disabilities receiving home care, those who provide paid or unpaid care, students in human services, the general public, and policy decision makers. Of all subgroups, a quantitative and qualitative analysis of the findings was that the CHR policy decision makers were the least likely to indicate that they learned a lot from the video about the role of home support from the perspective of people with disabilities. The number of people included in this subgroup was small, so this should be considered a trend, rather than a statistically significant finding.

12 The Council of Canadians with Disabilities emphasized that this surveillance through medical documentation is a poor use of medical services and health resources (Council of Canadians with Disabilities 2002).

13 By "accommodate," we mean that people come to think of impairments using medical frames of reference, so they, in a sense, believe and accept medical definitions of impairment.

14 This goal was openly communicated to members of the HSAG and posted on the CHR website at the time it was introduced.

15 Considering those with lower care needs as less worthy of home support is problematic. These individuals typically require smaller amounts of assistance in order to participate in society. However, when no service is provided, they experience significant barriers.

16 For a discussion of the passive role that people who live with impairments are expected to adopt, see, for example, Morris 1993.

17 For example, feminist scholars have written about the dominant notion of citizen as white male. See Helen Meekosha and Leanne Dowse, "Enabling Citizenship: Gender, Disability and Citizenship in Australia," *Feminist Review* 57 (Autumn 1997): 49-72; Nira Yuval-Davis, "Women, Citizenship and Difference," *Feminist Review* 57 (1997): 4-27.
18 Such understandings of the role of home support in disabled people's lives can be supported by the writings of Donna Haraway, *Simians, Cyborgs and Women: The Reinvention of Nature* (New York: Routledge, 1991) (on the cyborg self); Pierre Bourdieu, *The Logic of Practice*, trans. R. Nice (Stanford, CA: Stanford University Press, 1990) (on the theory of the body); and Merleau-Ponty's phenomenological explorations of living in Maurice Merleau-Ponty, *The Phenomenology of Perception*, trans. Colin Smith (London: Routledge and Kegan Paul, 1962).
19 See Gerard Young, "Board Tight Lipped on Death of Paraplegic," *Times Colonist*, 18 January 2001. The full article is also available as a link from the Krogh 2001a multimedia report.

References
Barnes, Colin, Geof Mercer, and Tom Shakespeare. 1999. *Exploring disability: A sociological introduction*. Malden, MA: Polity Press.
Bourdieu, Pierre. 1990. *The logic of practice*. Trans. R. Nice. Stanford, CA: Stanford University Press.
Browne, Paul Leduc. 2000. *Unsafe practices: Restructuring and privatization in Ontario health care*. Ottawa: Canadian Centre for Policy Alternatives.
Burke, Mike. 2000. Efficiency and the erosion of health care in Canada. In *Restructuring and resistance: Canadian public policy in an age of global capitalism*, ed. Mike Burke, Colin Mooers, and John Shields, 178-93. Halifax: Fernwood Publishing.
Canada. Health Canada. 1999. *Provincial and territorial home care programs: A synthesis for Canada*. http://www.hc-sc.gc.ca.
–. 2003. *Canada Health Act – Overview*. http://www.hc-sc.gc.ca/medicare/chaover.htm.
Canada Health Act, 1984, c. 6, R.S.C. 1985, vol. 1, c. C-6.
Canadian Charter of Rights and Freedoms, Part I of the *Constitution Act, 1982*, being Schedule B to the *Canada Act 1982* (U.K.), 1982, c. 11 [Charter].
Capital Health Region. 2000. http://www.caphealth.org.
Council of Canadians with Disabilities. 2002. *Consumers with disabilities speak out on health issues*. Submission to the Romanow Commission on the Future of Health Care in Canada. Winnipeg: Council of Canadians with Disabilities.
Edgar, Andrew, and Peter Sedgwick. 2002. *Cultural theory: The key thinkers*. New York: Routledge.
Foucault, Michel. 1973. *The birth of the clinic: An archaeology of medical perception*. Trans. A.M.S. Smith. New York: Vintage Books.
–. 1977. *Discipline and punish: The birth of the prison*. Trans. A. Sheridan. New York: Pantheon Books.
Krais, Beate. 1993. Gender and symbolic violence: Female oppression in the light of Pierre Bourdieu's theory of social practice. In *Pierre Bourdieu: Critical perspectives*, ed. Craig Calhoun, Edward LiPuma, and Moishe Postone, 156-77. Chicago: University of Chicago Press.
Krogh, Kari. 2001a. *Beyond four walls: The impact of home support on health, work and citizenship for people with disabilities*. Multimedia research report distributed at the World Health Organization's Rethinking Care from the Perspectives of People with Disabilities: A Global Congress. http://www.ryerson.ca/~kkrogh.
–. 2001b. Video action research: Possibilities as an emancipatory research methodology and reflections on a health policy study for people with disabilities. Paper presented at the 14th annual conference of the Society of Disability Studies, Winnipeg. http://www.ryerson.ca/~kkrogh.
–. 2002. Using video in emancipatory disability research to facilitate community participation in health care policy making. Paper presented at the 6th annual Research Conference of the Nordic Network on Disability Research, Reykjavik, Iceland.
–. 2003. Redefining home care for women with disabilities: A call for citizenship. In *Caring for/caring about: Women, home care and unpaid caregiving*, ed. Karen R. Grant, Carol

Amaratunga, Pat Armstrong, Madeline Boscoe, Ann Pederson, and Kay Willson, 115-46. Aurora, ON: Garamond Press.

Krogh, K., M. Ennis, J. Johnson, and T. Bowman. 2005. A national snapshot of home support from the consumer perspective: Enabling people with disabilities to participate in policy analysis and community development. Final Research Report. http://www.ccdonline.ca/publications/index.htm.

Lash, Scott. 1993. Pierre Bourdieu: Cultural economy and social change. In *Pierre Bourdieu: Critical perspectives,* ed. Craig Calhoun, Edward LiPuma, and Moishe Postone, 193-211. Chicago: University of Chicago Press.

Masuda, Shirley. 1998. *The impact of block funding on women with disabilities.* Ottawa: Status of Women Canada.

Morris, Jenny. 1993. *Independent lives? Community care and disabled people.* Basingstoke, England: Macmillan.

Oliver, Michael. 1992. Changing the social relations of research 'production.' *Disability, Handicap and Society* 7, 2: 101-14.

–. 1996. *Understanding disability: From theory to practice.* Basingstoke, England: Macmillan.

Orme, Joan. 2001. *Gender and community care: Social work and social care perspectives.* Basingstoke, UK: Palgrave.

Rioux, Marcia. 1997. Disability: The place of judgment in a world of fact. *Journal of Intellectual Disability Research* 41, 2: 102-11.

Rioux, Marcia, and Fraser Valentine. 2005. Does theory matter? Exploring the nexus between disability, human rights, and public policy. Chapter 2, this volume.

Sanford, Glenn. 2000. Anger and frustration transform into campaign. *Transitions magazine,* July/August: 4-7.

Tighe, C.A. 2001. "Working at disability": A qualitative study of the meaning of health and disability for women with physical impairments. *Disability and Society* 16, 4: 511-29.

Trypuc, Joann. 1994. Gender based mortality and morbidity patterns and health risks. In *Women, medicine, and health,* ed. B. Singh Bolaria and Rosemary Bolaria, 73-88. Halifax: Fernwood Publishing.

Vogel, Donna. 2000. Unfulfilled promise: How health care reforms of the 1990s are failing community and continuing care in BC. In *Without foundation: How Medicare is undermined by gaps and privatization in community and continuing care,* ed. Donna Vogel, Michael Rachlis, and Nancy Pollak, 17-54. Vancouver: Canadian Centre for Policy Alternatives.

Watts, Richard. 1999. Health region eyes home care cuts. *Times Colonist,* 15 October.

Wendell, Susan. 2001. Unhealthy disabled: Treating chronic illnesses as disabilities. *Hypatia* 16, 4: 17-33.

8

Autism as Public Policy

Dana Lee Baker

Disability policy has recently come into its own. Policies targeting disabilities have existed in Western countries for over a hundred years. However, early policy was based on the equation of disability with a disadvantage. The individual was considered liable for the disadvantage(s), while the society sought to occasionally mediate the effect of this disadvantage through charitable services. This essentialist understanding of disability prevailed until late in the twentieth century, when the conceived locus of responsibility for disability began to shift away from the individual and toward society at large. At the extreme, this constructivist understanding of disability defines all disability as solely the result of created social exclusion varying tremendously by time and space (Stroman 2003). At a minimum, it holds society responsible for the prevention of handicap; that is, it provides a critique of a society that does not provide enough accommodation to allow individuals with disabilities to participate as fully as possible.

Modern disability policy seeks a balance between the extremes of individual or social responsibility for disability. This chapter compares the expression of this balance in the formulation of modern disability policy in Canada and the United States by examining the case of autism-related policy prior to the Supreme Court of Canada's decision on *Auton v. British Columbia* (2004).[1] This examination demonstrates that although the theoretical basis of modern disability policy is close to the constructivist end of the continuum, current policy tends to retain limited essentialist elements. Somewhat paradoxically, in order to ensure that disability does not become a cause for complete social dependence, the constructivist understanding of disability requires a level of personal responsibility for the disability, on the part of the individual with the disability.

The three predominant forms of disability policy are civic education policy, rights policy, and service provision policy. The balance of responsibility is negotiated in each of these categories. The balance between individual and social responsibility is especially interesting in the case of developmental disabilities because of the urgency of decisions made before the individual reaches an age of personal responsibility. Failing to provide adequately for a child with a developmental disability leads to costly deterioration of potential. The case of autism and related conditions (hereafter referred to as autism) is particularly compelling because of the surge in observed incidence (Baker 2004).

Three Forms of Modern Disability Policy

According to John Kingdon (1997), public policy formulation takes place at a confluence of three streams: problems, politics, and policy. Issues gain access to public agendas as a result of either a crisis or the invention of a crisis around a transcendent condition or compelling anecdote. Autism's place on policy agendas is the result of the autism baby boom originating in the early 1990s. Despite initial arguments of construction of crisis, by the early 2000s there was a multinational feeling that the observed rise in incidence from 1 in 10,000 to approximately 1 in 250 constitutes a genuine public challenge (Bertrand et al. 2001; Chakrabarti and Fombonne 2001).

The policy stream contains generic policy solutions preferred by players in a policy arena. Three archetypical disability policy solutions exist: civic education, rights, and public services. As discussed by Rioux and Valentine in Chapter 2, changes in the conception of disability push researchers and policy makers to consider political aspects of the creation of disability as constructed inequality. Furthermore, as Malhotra describes in Chapter 3, disability has been historically equated with victimhood and the inability to work. The conception of people with disabilities as patients or paupers drove North American disability policy development until the last third of the twentieth century. The transition toward an understanding encompassing both the constructivist and essentialist paradigms (Stroman 2003) is expected to have a strong shaping influence on all forms of public disability policy, as suggested by autism's policy presence.

Civic Education Policy

The constructivist understanding of disability requires an ever more active civic education policy. Governmental (as a proxy for societal) responsibility includes the education of targeted groups as well as universal education. Civic education policies are designed to either directly communicate or facilitate the distribution of information.

Most information is norm oriented. As a result, disability is expected to involve a quest for specialized information. This has grown easier, yet more complex, over the past decade. For example, as Judy Singer explains, "thanks to the Internet, autistics are taking diagnosis, scientific speculation, experimentation with self-medication into their own hands" (Corker and French

1999, 65). However, increased access to information increases the transferability of "bad" information. A growing aspect of the government response to disability is the promotion of "good" information.

Rights Policy

Rights-based policy is the workhorse of modern disability policy. Many types of infrastructure, including attitudinal, physical, economic, and fiscal, have historically been constructed with handicapping elements. According to Colin Barnes, "'disability' represents a complex system of social constraints imposed upon people with impairments in a highly discriminatory society" (Taylor 1996, 96). Whether the absence of constraints is conceived as a civil right – an essentially negative right belonging to the individual – or a human right – an essentially positive right belonging to humanity as a whole – this rights-based approach is a recent innovation. The concept of rights for individuals with disabilities is not entirely new, however. Social rehabilitationists sought to change attitudes toward disability at the beginning of the twentieth century (Longmore and Umansky 2001, 143). The rights-based approach strives to extend well beyond compassion to the ultimate reconstruction of the social contract of societies at large.

There is residual resentment of the inclusion of disability alongside other discrimination experiences. Part of the reason for this is that the allegation of disability, such as the supposed medical fragility of women or the imagined lack of mental capacity of those of African descent, was a common justification for discrimination. Groups deliberately distanced themselves from disability, thereby tacitly acknowledging disability as a justifiable target of discrimination (Longmore and Umanksy 2001, 51). The extension of rights policy to include disability requires an ever more resilient definition of diversity. In the case of autism, for instance, "the key significance of the 'autistic spectrum' lies in its call for, and anticipation of a politics of, neurological diversity, or neurodiversity. The 'neurologically different' represent a new addition to the familiar political categories of class/gender/race" (Corker and French 1999, 64).

Furthermore, rights-based disability policy presumes a flexibility of the social contract that has proven difficult in related policy arenas. As can be seen by the conflict surrounding affirmative action policies, some contest the positive construction of rights (Thernstrom 1996, 767; Schuck 2002, 24). While they agree that the negative civil right should be protected, they object to so-called special provisions to ensure that citizens are actually involved. The exercise of disability rights requires radical and often individualized reconstructions of infrastructures. Perceiving society at large as the benefactor of these changes in infrastructure involves a revision of the social contract.

Policies of Public Services

At first glance, public services policies present a challenge from the perspective of a constructivist understanding of disability. If disability is a consequence of violation of rights, then presumably the only policy challenge is fixing the rights. Services up to full-time institutional care were the hallmark of society's old response to disability. However, the social policy safety net – though often insufficient – is an indelible infrastructure of modern nations.

The focus of publicly provided services is shifting. One shift is a diffusion of the location of services. Ingstad and Whyte (1995, 4) explain: "Studies of disability require us to move away from the clinic toward the community." Service goals are also changing. For example, the generally preferred form of public services has moved away from public assistance toward including obligations such as work requirements. Finally, there is a shift away from a set package of services distributed at the discretion of the professionals toward more individually coordinated services.

Why Autism?

Developmental disabilities pervade all arenas of disability policy (Stroman 2003, 9). In recent years, this has been especially true for autism. While the identification of autism had begun by the 1940s, during the 1990s, autism changed dramatically from its origins as an extremely low incidence disability generally coincident with mental retardation (Gabbard 2001).

The emergence of autism in the late twentieth century implies that much of its policy presence will reflect of the ongoing negotiation of the essentialist and constructivist understandings of disability. As John Swain and Colin Cameron explain, "as befits a disability emerging for the first time in the postmodern era, the autistic spectrum has fuzzy boundaries" (Corker and French 1999, 63). To take this argument a step farther, since autism emerged alongside (post)modern disability policy, the role of autism in modern disability policy formulation reflects and is defined by this transition, arguably to a greater extent than is possible for more traditional categories of disability.

Policy initiatives occur in a more or less differentiable set of interdependent policy stages. While it is expected that the other stages of policy – its implementation and evaluation for instance – will have important shaping effects on the outcome of policy, the concern in this chapter is intent, that is, policy formulation. The policies discussed are neither settled nor stable. Policy formulation in the disability policy arena has unique characteristics. For example, "there is generally no organized opposition to disability groups, no competing advocacy coalition that would challenge their message and complicate the decision-making processes of governments" (Puttee 2002,

65). This does not mean that the arena is without controversy – only that there is not the dichotomous opposition that one might find in policies about abortion or capital punishment. The formulation of policy addressing autism's emergence onto the policy agenda clearly reflects the balance of disability paradigms rather than an open warfare of outwardly motivated moral positions.

Public Policy and Autism

Disability policy is created throughout Canada's federalist structure. As Puttee (2002, 1) explains, "Like many of Canada's social programs, the jurisdiction over the bundle of public programs directed at people with disabilities is divided: each order of government, federal and provincial, plays important roles in program governance." Similarly, disability policy in the United States is developed at all levels of government. While the specifics of autism-related policy vary, there is a prevailing policy tenor that makes it tenable to discuss both Canada's and the United States' policies as single cases.

Examples of Civic Education Policy in Canada

Civic education policy balances the responsibilities of individuals and society by seeking to ensure (1) that the disability is as uniformly understood across policy arena stakeholder groups as possible, and (2) that all of the players understand their expected roles in addressing needs associated with the disability. Such policy deliberately privileges chosen information and articulates discussion boundaries about a particular topic. This type of policy is often dominated by non-legislative policy makers.

Education policy can be both indirect (ensuring the accessibility of information) and direct (ensuring the delivery of education). For example, the Division of Student Support Services of Newfoundland and Labrador reported that "during the fall of 2001, the provincial consultants for autism spectrum disorders visited districts to provide professional development and consultations to teachers who work with students diagnosed with autism spectrum disorders (ASDs)" (Newfoundland and Labrador 2001). This directed policy was followed by an indirect policy specific to the same audience. According to the Division, "a handbook has been developed, entitled 'Teaching Students with Autism Spectrum Disorders.' This handbook will be available during the winter of 2002" (Newfoundland and Labrador 2001). Similarly, the government of Saskatchewan's Special Education Unit produced in January 1997 an issue of *Challenges, Choices and Changes* dedicated to autism. Perhaps the most advanced type of civic education policy in Canada is the building of government websites that gather together information and links about autism in one virtual location (Mavromatis 2001, 9; Battey 2001, 59).

Another type of civic education policy formulated around autism is the creation of specific times to commemorate autism. Health Canada advertises October as autism month, which both promotes general awareness of autism by highlighting the Autism Society of Canada and encourages the learning of roles in the public management of autism. Several provinces have followed suit. For example, the Attorney General of British Columbia proclaimed October 2002 as autism awareness month because "the Autism Society of British Columbia together with their branches wishes to raise the awareness of the public and practicing professionals and to provide information on autism spectrum disorder" (Plant 2002). The balance between individual and social responsibility is asserted most forcefully (though with a paucity of details) within these types of proclamations. These proclamations tend to delineate responsibility for disability between broadly cast stakeholder categories without discussion of specific roles in the management of disability-related challenges.

Examples of Civic Education Policy in the United States
Civic education policy in the United States has a tradition dating back to the *Federalist Papers* (Rossiter 1961). Promotion of autism awareness is a common type of civic education in which many who are governing are actively involved. For example, on 6 February 2003, a Republican congressman, Richard Baker, "introduced a resolution in Congress ... calling for a postage stamp to promote autism awareness" (Louisiana's Sixth District 2003). A wide variety of state agencies, including agencies with missions that do not directly involve individuals with autism, formulated civic education policies. For example, in Virginia, the Department of Motor Vehicles has special "unlocking autism" licence plates available for purchase. It is perhaps somewhat ironic that the key message of many of these basic education policies is that autism is largely a mystery.

As in Canada, the designation of specific periods as being dedicated to autism education is a common civic education policy. The United States Department of Health and Human Services recognizes April as autism awareness month. According to its website, "Autism Awareness Month, celebrated every year in April, provides an opportunity for families, friends, and local communities to raise public awareness about autism" (United States 2003). Many lower levels of government have also proclaimed policies designating April autism month. For example, the governor of California proclaimed April 2003 autism awareness month. Among the reasons given was that "it is important to continue research and advocacy efforts to find a cure and to improve understanding of autism" (Davis 2003).

As Alexis de Tocqueville first pointed out, Americans are forever forming associations (DeLeon 1997, 27). In the public sector, these associations are often vehicles of civic education policy. Autism-related civic education policy is no exception. For example, in 2001, the Congressional Coalition for Autism Research and Education (CARE) was founded within Congress. Representative Baker describes the effort: "This bipartisan, bicameral congressional membership organization grew to 180 members of the House and Senate from over forty states by the end of the 107th Congress" (Louisiana's Sixth District 2003). Bipartisan efforts, though not rare, retain novelty value. They are often focused on civic education policy because of wider party divides in the preferred implementation processes of other types of public policy.

A similar type of civic education policy directed at autism is demonstrated in efforts of those who are governing to lobby one another to work toward a better understanding of autism. For example, in November 2002, a Republican member of the House of Representatives, Dan Burton, wrote to President Bush "urging him to host a White House conference on autism ... to begin a national effort to determine why autism has reached epidemic proportions" (Burton 2002).

Another key component to civic education policy is the message of inadequacy of current services. For example, in Alaska, according to the Governor's Council on Disabilities and Special Education, "a great deal of technical expertise is needed to serve these individuals effectively in the community. This expertise does not exist in Alaska other than with the specific and targeted Intensive Early Intervention program" (Alaska 2003). In a nation that is historically less than comfortable with a social safety net for those with the presumed ability to pull themselves up by their bootstraps, the argument for community-based services requires a significant shift in civic education policy. Americans have traditionally been conditioned to support paternalistic public services for those in need of institutionalization (or quasi-institutionalization) in the name of compassion. Publicly provided community-based services for those who are believed to be able to live independently is not a traditional understanding of the social contract and is one toward which citizens need to be educated.

Examples of Civil or Human Rights Policy in Canada

In 1982, Canada became the first country in the world to constitutionally specify rights of individuals with disabilities (Puttee 2002, 18). Policy in Canada leans toward the positive, human rights position. The specifics of the definition of disability vary within rights-based policy in Canada but tend to be inclusive. For example, "the British Columbia Human Rights Commission has interpreted the concept of disability very broadly ... many health conditions such as heart disease, learning disabilities, asthma, HIV/AIDS and depression have been considered to be a disability" (Vancouver Island Dog Guide Society 2003).

The balance of the individual versus social responsibility in rights-based policy is challenging in the case of autism. First of all, early diagnosis of autism is connected in the minds of many with an immediate service need for intensive interventions such as Applied Behavior Analysis (ABA). Effective treatment in this genre involves dozens of hours of therapy each week, best begun well before a child enters kindergarten. Obviously, this service involves significant cost. Quite apart from the expense issue, however, the therapy is designed so as to radically force the extant personality, thought processes, activity patterns, and communication style of the child toward conventional social norms. The hope is that the autistic personality will be trained out of the child so that he or she is able to pass for neurologically typical within society.

A learned ability to function within society is an asset for a developing human being. Nevertheless, since the children in need of this therapy are young and often unable to communicate effectively, an unusual balance is struck in policies mandating this therapy. The balance between the individual and social responsibility is realized by defining the right of the child as a right of the family. The characterization of the family as the holder of the child's civil rights is not unique to children with disabilities. However, the role that must be played in the exercise of this right is often more demanding for the parents of children with disabilities. The family, rather than the child, is assigned the responsibility to ask for, and participate in, the therapy, and society is assigned the responsibility of ensuring that this cutting-edge therapy is available and accessible. As the Tracy Latimer case – which involved a father killing his disabled daughter, purportedly in the name of compassion – demonstrated, the equation of the child's rights with that of the family is not clear-cut (Derksen 1995; Kunc 2001). In less extreme situations, policy formulation in Canada also reflects this concern that a family will be incapable (or differently capable from other families) to exercise the right. For example, in an October 2002 submission to the Ontario Human Rights Commission on Education and Disabilities, the Autism Society Ontario argued:

> Children with disabilities are not accommodated in the same degree as disabled adults ... If the code applies to children then the Ministry of Education must be made to comply. The Ministry of Education is failing to meet the standards of the code and the decisions from the Supreme Court of Canada. The OHRC has standards in place and must ensure that the school boards and Ministry are meeting the code in all current legislation. It is not acceptable to place the burden on families to prove their child needs specific services or accommodations. (Autism Society Ontario 2002)

One of the implicit reasons for public involvement in the raising of children – from public schools to public health care to a variety of other social services – is to compensate for some of the disparity between families so that the civil rights of children are not overly compromised as an accident of birth.

Type of service is also becoming an aspect of rights as the balance between individuals and society is renegotiated under the more constructivist understanding of disability. Access to a specific type of therapy for autism is sometimes defined as a civil right in Canada. This of course is a different conception of self-determination, which is considered the basis of more traditional civil rights. For example, in a debate occurring in Newfoundland, "Adjudicator Marshall noted that she was not making a finding that all waitlists for medical services are discriminatory. The factors which distinguish the case of autistic children include the nature of autism, the critical necessity for early intervention, the negative impact on prognosis caused by delaying treatment and the fact that autism is not a disability conducive to the department's usual practices regarding waitlisting" (Newfoundland and Labrador 2002). The characterization of access to a particular service as a right has been addressed with different outcomes in other provinces. For example, in Quebec in *Théroux (tuteur à) c. Commission Scolaire Lester B. Pearson* (2000), "the school board refused to provide a particular accommodative program that the parents preferred (Giant Steps), rather than the Board's usual program. The court found that there was no discrimination" (Learning Disabilities Association of Canada 2003). The expression of autism in this dimension of civil rights-based policy in Canadian courts questions the positive right of parents to pick a particular type of service that they have deemed most appropriate for the child, while more universally supporting the negative right of not being kept from services through mechanisms such as wait lists.

The case of *Auton v. British Columbia* (2004) asked the Supreme Court of Canada to determine whether specific services for autism are a constitutional right. The court's decision to reject the constitutional claim puts the issue into the realm of public policy, that is, in the political rather than the judicial arena. The specific therapy addressed in this particular case is Applied Behavior Analysis, championed by the parents. Proponents of the ABA intimate that ultimately it can set a balance between the individual and society that makes it the individual's (or family's) responsibility to limit autistic tendencies whenever possible. However, this is in spite of the fact that therapies such as ABA are far from being universally accepted by stakeholders (including parents) as the most appropriate treatment for autism. Parents who choose not to have their child undergo ABA therapy despite its availability, and individuals with autism for whom the treatment does not make a difference, could be perceived as not only making an anti-social choice but also failing to fulfill social responsibility. The constructivist understanding of disability largely depends on the reality that disability is forced rather than elective difference.

Civil or Human Rights Policy in the United States

The rights of individuals with disabilities are not specifically constitutionally mandated in the United States. There is, however, a strong tradition of
civil rights-based disability policy beginning with section 504 of the *Rehabilitation Act of 1973* (29 U.S.C. 701 (1973)). The most encompassing of
these policies is the *Americans with Disabilities Act of 1990* (ADA) (Pub. L.
101-336. 42 U.S.C., section 12102), which was particularly innovative because it did not assign (or limit) rights to specific activities. According to
Longmore and Umansky (2001, 1), "while hardly a panacea, the ADA proposes to ensure the right of Americans with disabilities to move from the
margins of society into the mainstream."

The discussion of rights in the formulation of disability policy in the United
States is almost entirely in terms of the negative right of a prevention of
discrimination. Although the *Individuals with Disabilities Education Act* (IDEA)
(20 U.S.C.A. s. 1400ff.), which grants rights to education to children with
disabilities beyond those granted to children without disabilities, might seem
at first glance to be more of a positive right, the debate surrounding IDEA is
almost entirely focused on civil rights. The Office of Civil Rights of the
federal Department of Education is in charge of investigating accusations of
violations of individuals' civil rights within the schools. The Individuals
Education Plan process is the gateway to a civil right to special education
and, operationally, the parent's rights are considered in the place of the
child's. Although the child is presumed to be included in the process, the
parent is assigned the right and responsibility to advocate for the child's
rights, often in direct opposition to the public education system's efforts to
contain the education rights of children with disabilities in the face of system constraints.

There is also a long history of policies formulated to specifically protect
the civil rights of people with autism. In Iowa, for example, "in July, 1977,
Governor Ray designed the Iowa Civil Rights Commission to implement a
system that would advocate for and protect the rights of people who are
developmentally disabled" (Iowa Civil Rights Commission 1978). Autism
was one of the six types of developmental disabilities specifically mentioned.
Furthermore, even at this early time, inappropriate institutionalization
(though not any institutionalization) was mentioned as one of the common violations of the rights of individuals with developmental disabilities.
Despite this, however, the specific definition of a positive right to community inclusion did not become widely articulated in policy until the Supreme Court case of *Olmstead v. L.C.* in 1999. In this decision, the court held
that institutionalization of individuals who might be served in the community is a violation of their civil rights and that a lack of available community services can not be used as a reason for "undue isolation" (*Olmstead v.
L.C.* 1999).

After this case, there was formulation of community inclusion civil rights policies through Olmstead committees and commissions.[2] For example, the legislature of Oklahoma mandated the creation of the Olmstead Strategic Planning Committee. Its mission is "to develop a plan for ensuring all Oklahomans with disabilities have access to and informed choice of services in the most integrated settings" (Oklahoma Olmstead Committee 2002). Olmstead policy often includes specific discussion of autism. Similarly, in Georgia, the Olmstead committee discussed "the supports a family or other caretaker needs to continue caring for an individual with mental retardation, autism or other developmental disability. The Governor's Council on Developmental Disabilities is working with the Department of Human Resources to develop a statewide network of family support services" (Georgia Olmstead Planning Committee 2002). The prevalence of organized activity addressing *Olmstead* is such that states without such committees provide public justification. For example: "The state of Minnesota does not have an official *Olmstead* task force, due to the fact that the Minnesota Department of Human Services (DHS) already 1) offered many options to support people with disabilities, the chronically ill, and the elderly in the community; 2) was working on several initiatives to expand community-based and self-directed services; and 3) has several established stakeholder committees involved in these areas. Minnesota chose to use existing feedback mechanisms and to focus and build on the work that was under way related to the expansion of community-based services" (Fox-Grage, Folkemer, and Lewis 2003).

Another dimension of discussion in civil rights-based policy related to autism is the distinction between entitlements and non-entitlements (Hirschl 2000, 1060). Entitlements are those services that are articulated components of civil rights from which no individual with a defined set of characteristics may be excluded. Since 1990, autism has been one of thirteen categories of disability that invokes an entitlement to a free and appropriate public education under IDEA. Through policy exceptions such as Medicaid waivers, much of the policy directed specifically at people with autism (and adults with autism in particular) is being deliberately constructed as non-entitlements (Serafini 2003; LeBlanc, Tonner, and Harrington 2000). Many advocates perceive this as a violation of the civil rights of individuals since access to services becomes a matter of privileged selection rather than a guarantee. It also places the onus of responsibility more on the individual than entitlement programs do, since individuals must not only prove they need the service but must also keep abreast of often less than well-publicized opportunities. As with much of civil rights-based policy in the United States, entitlement programs are well in keeping with a negative construction of rights but, by their very structure, serve to work against a more positive construction of rights related to disability.

Examples of Programs and Services Policy in Canada

Policies for the provision of public programs and services are the oldest type of disability policy. Given bureaucratic entrenchment, it might be expected that a balance of individual and social responsibility would be difficult to establish under a new disability paradigm. There is also incredible disparity in public services for individuals with disabilities in Canada. As Puttee (2002, 139) explains, "The policy problems are serious: the wide variation in the availability of disability supports and services in the current system significantly compromises equity, both vertical and horizontal; the same variation drastically reduces both economic and geographic mobility." This disparity further complicates the creation of a stable balance in any given province and in Canada as a whole.

A number of autism services policies have been created in recent years. A primary motivation for this is the fiscal constraints of the public sector. Successful services for children with autism are intensive and expensive. This, combined with the rise in services demand driven by the rise in autism incidence, opens a window of opportunity for autism service policies. A frequent policy response in the last few years is to publicly increase government funding for autism. For example, in November 2002, Ontario's Ministry of Community, Family and Children Services announced that it was "investing an additional $58.6 million for services for children with autism, bringing the total commitment to almost $100 million by 2006/ 07" (Ontario 2002). The ministry quickly earmarked these funds. The same news release states: "New programs and services for older children include transition coordinators who will help families with the transition to alternative programs. Elementary school-age children will also have new out-of-class programs available to them that are focused on developing and improving social interaction, behavior and communication. Additionally, the Ministry of Education will pilot its Autism Program Standards in the 2003/04 school year and will host forums to help teachers learn about new approaches being used to educate children with autism" (Ontario 2002). Similarly, on 14 February 2003, Newfoundland and Labrador's Health and Community Services minister announced an increase in fiscal effort directed specifically toward autism in the amount of $1.88 million over three years. The spending plan is outlined in the press release: "With this increased funding, early intensive intervention services will be offered to pre-school aged children who are currently waiting for the service, as well as address the anticipated demand for all new referrals to the program as they arise" (Newfoundland and Labrador 2003).

Beyond heightened fiscal commitment lies the reformation of services as a mechanism of acknowledging the new understanding of disability. According to Puttee (2002, 140), "the goal of policy reform is a system of disability supports and services that contributes to greater participation of people with disabilities in all aspects of Canadian society." The autism case has been interesting because of the focus on early childhood services. Because the autism baby boom began only recently, young children with autism have been the focal point of most innovations in services policy. For example, in British Columbia, the Ministry of Children and Family Development reported in 2002 that "the number of B.C. children with autism receiving early intervention therapies through government has increased seven-fold in the past year" (British Columbia 2002). The ministry attributed the increase to a new policy with options including "an individualized funding program to help families with the cost of behavioral treatments and interventions of their choice. Other families can use contracted services under the Ministry's early intensive behaviour intervention program." In this case, the line between individual (that is, family) responsibility and the responsibility of the government was deliberately created so as to be flexible. That the *Auton* case was being fought in a province in which flexibility is permitted is either the result of a lack of communication between agencies, brought on by the enormity of social responsibility for assuring the rights of individuals with autism, or the result of an effort to make an end run around the case's potential implications.

In the past few years, more attention has been paid to the creation of autism service policy for older individuals. For example, in British Columbia, "beginning April 1, 2003 eligible families of children and youth with autism spectrum disorder (ASD), over the age of 6 and under the age of 19, can receive direct funding of up to $6,000/year to assist with the cost of autism intervention services for out-of-school hours" (British Columbia 2003). The services are still focused on independence as an ultimate rather than immediate goal. As the Alberta's Ministry of Children's Services explained:

> One problem with the current status of children "on extension," as families and service agencies point out, is that there are few appropriate community supports into which their children can effectively transfer. In addition, sufficient resources do not exist to support children and their families in the transition from Intensive Behavioral Intervention (IBI) services to school programs at the end of the three years of programming provided for in policy. Therefore, the perception is that there are not alternatives to Intensive Behavioral Intervention ... Even so, the Child Welfare Appeal panel has been confirming the director's decision not to provide Intensive Behavioral Intervention services to school aged children, stating that these cases fall within the jurisdiction of Alberta Learning. (Alberta 2002, 12)

The borders of agency responsibility are often debated. Not only does this debate reflect self-protective behaviour of cash-strapped agencies, but it also speaks to a lack of resolution on the social responsibility for services policies for people with autism beyond the earliest years of life. Today's children with autism are different from those of the past, who were generally institutionalized and diagnosed with mental retardation (whether as a result of essential mental retardation or as an effect of inappropriate treatment). Without a firm concept of the self-actualized adult with autism, and with an agency structure that tends to divide social responsibility by need rather than group, it is difficult to reach consensus on the division of individual and social responsibility for service-related policy for adults with autism.

Programs and Services Policy in the United States

The United States tends to have more difficulty with accepting the notion of a social safety net (at least at the formulation stage of policy) than do other Western democracies. Despite this, state paternalism directed at people with disabilities was widely accepted up until the late twentieth century. As discussed above, the shift toward an understanding of disability that balances essentialist and constructivist perspectives necessitates a reconstruction of the services policy infrastructure.

Public education is a uniquely accepted services policy in the United States. Except for those involved in the Republican revolution of the early 1990s, who called for the dismantling of the Department of Education and the proliferation of charter schools, the public provision of primary and secondary education has been basically uncontested. In the case of autism, it is therefore not surprising that a favoured mechanism of new services policy formulation has been the extension of public education. During the last decade, there has been a growing trend of earlier intervention provided through IDEA, with origins in the Treatment and Education for Autistic Communication and Handicapped Children, begun in North Carolina in the 1960s (Gabbard 2001). In a political environment that tends to be services policy resistant, it makes sense that one way in which to create new aspects of social responsibility for disability is by using mechanisms within a less questioned arena of services policy.

As mentioned previously, health care is a far more conflicted arena of services policy than is education. Medicaid, the federal-state health-care program for the very poor, is an optional entitlement program. Once states have agreed to set up a Medicaid system, they receive federal matching of Medicaid expenses, but must provide health-care services to all who meet the defined eligibility criteria. As a component of this entitlement, the state must ensure that services provided through Medicaid are available on a statewide basis. Waivers are limited exceptions to these entitlement restrictions for which states can apply in order to meet specific or unique needs on a usually experimental basis. Waivers are also a way of ensuring that a particular group has access to special services. Participation in waiver programs can be limited. Because preferred treatments for autism are largely experimental, often expensive, and hotly contested, waivers are a popular form of autism-related services policies. For example, Maryland applied for an Autism Waiver in 1998. According to Maryland's Department of Federal and State programs, "the Autism Waiver through Medical Assistance allows eligible children with Autism Spectrum Disorder to receive specific services to support these very high-needs children in their homes, educational settings, and communities in an effort to keep them from being institutionalized" (Maryland 2003). Similarly, in 2002, the Connecticut legislature also forced the application of an autism waiver with the following: "Be it enacted by the Senate and House of Representatives in General Assembly convened: That the general statutes be amended to require the Commissioner of Social Services to seek a waiver from federal law to establish Medicaid-financed home and community based programs for children with autism" (Connecticut 2002). Waivers reintroduce an element of luck into the balance between individual and social responsibility for disability that is more limited in entitlement programs. If the established number of waiver slots is less than the number of qualifying individuals, there is reduced horizontal equity in the services policy. Interestingly, autism-related waivers often include specific provisions for assistance in coordinating services. Because the effort associated with negotiating services from multiple agencies often strains the ability of individuals to fulfill their responsibility of securing services for which they qualify, this dimension can further privilege individuals with a waiver slot over those on the waiting list or those who are unaware of the program.

A newly evolving area of autism-related services policies focuses specifically on adults. As is the case in Canada, services for people with autism traditionally tend to be situation rather than diagnosis specific. For example, as the Connecticut General Assembly (2002) explained: "The state does not provide services specifically for adults with autism or any form of pervasive developmental disorder ... Individuals with such diagnoses display a wide range of intellectual and communicative abilities. Those who are able to work and live on their own can avail themselves of several Department of Social Services (DSS) programs and services, including vocational rehabilitation and employment services through the Bureau of Rehabilitation Services (BRS) and, if they are income-eligible, community-based 'essential services' and rent assistance." Some of the newest services policies related to autism are diagnosis specific, however. For example, in Illinois, adults (as well as children) with severe autism can apply to participate in the Home-Based Support Services Program, which pays for services to help adults (age eighteen and older) become more independent living on their own or with their families. Participating adults are entitled to goods and services worth up to 300 percent of their Federal Supplemental Security Income (SSI) payment level (Illinois 2002). Similarly, Arkansas has a $500 Developmentally

Disabled Individual Credit, for which individuals with autism are eligible to apply after receiving an official diagnosis from a physician, psychologist, or psychological examiner (Arkansas 2005).

Return to Function: Removing Society's Disability

Changing paradigms can take a long time to become manifest in public policy. In the transition toward a more constructivist understanding of disability, much of the necessary work in public policy takes place in the articulation of a revised balance between the individual and the society's responsibility for the prevention of handicap. Under the modern understanding of disability, if a society fails to uphold its responsibilities in this arena, then society itself experiences disability because one of its major life functions (the protection of its citizens) becomes compromised. Looking at examples of how autism is addressed in civic education, rights-based and services policies demonstrate that creation of a new balance is a work in progress in North America. Although the policies found in Canada and the United States include expected national differences, there are important commonalities. The dominant generic policy solutions of civic education, rights-based and services policies drawn in both countries from Kingdon's policy stream are identical. Furthermore, the promotion of basic awareness, the alteration of the social contract to accommodate rights-based policy, and the expansion and reconstruction of services are the chief themes of changing intent of disability policy, as demonstrated through the case of autism.

As would be expected in a period of transition, the policy arena is far from settled or stable, and implementation lags farther behind intent than it might in other policy arenas. Nevertheless, as the autism case demonstrates, the balance being struck between individual and society responsibilities is potentially quite revolutionary. The new flexibility in the social contract that results from the move toward the constructivist understanding of disability allows for a negotiation between two loci of power, rights, and responsibilities. This new balance eliminates charitable action of government or society as a preferred and stagnant response to disability and instead involves all stakeholders in the governance of disability policy.

Notes

1 The case involved the claim by parents of autistic children that section 15 of the *Canadian Charter of Rights and Freedoms* placed an obligation on government to fund Applied Behavioral Analysis for autistic children. Given the decision of the Supreme Court of Canada to reject the constitutional challenge, the court's ruling does not mandate policy change so as to fundamentally alter the analysis that follows. See, further, the Appendix to this book.

2 After the Supreme Court decision, "Olmstead" became a generic tag both for efforts to comply with the decision's implications and, to a certain degree, community inclusion more generally.

References

Alaska. Governor's Council on Disability and Special Education. 2003. Unserved and underserved groups. http://www.hss.state.ak.us.

Alberta. Ministry of Children's Services. 2002. A system of care for children with autism: Expert panel report. http://www.child.gov.ab.ca/whatwedo/disabilities/pdf/autism_ expert_report.pdf.

Arkansas. Department of Finance and Administration. Certificate for Developmentally Disabled Individual. 2005. http://www.accessarkansas.org/dfa/taxes/ind_tax.

Autism Society Ontario. 2002. Submission to Ontario Human Rights Commission on education and disabilities. http://www.autismsociety.on.ca/news/ASOhumanrights.pdf.

Auton (Guardian ad litem of) v. British Columbia (Attorney General), [2004] 3 S.C.R. 657 [*Auton v. British Columbia*].

Baker, Dana Lee. March 2004. Public policy and the shaping of disability: Incidence growth in educational autism. *Education Policy Analysis Archives* 12, 11. http://epaa.asu.edu/epaa

Battey, Jim. 2001. Governing with e-speed. *InfoWorld* 23, 13: 59-62.

Bertrand, J., A. Mars, C. Boyle, F. Bove, M. Yeargin-Allsopp, and P. DeCoufle. 2001. Prevalence of autism in a United States population: The Brick Township, New Jersey, investigation. *Pediatrics* 108, 5: 1155-61.

British Columbia. 2002. Autism month celebrates improved services for children. News release. http://www2.news.gov.bc.ca/nrm_news_releases/2002MCF0018-000830.htm.

–. 2003. Autism spectrum disorder. Informational website. http://www.mcf.gov.bc.ca/ autism/index.htm.

Burton, Dan. 2002. Dan Burton speech before Congress. http://www.whale.to/a/burton6. html.

Chakrabarti, S., and E. Fombonne. (2001). Pervasive developmental disorders in preschool children. *JAMA* 285, 24: 3093-99.

Connecticut. Connecticut General Assembly. 2002. An act concerning services for children with autism. http://www.cga.ct.gov/.

Corker, Mairian, and Sally French, eds. 1999. *Disability discourse.* Buckingham: Open University Press.

Davis, Gray. 2003. Proclamation by the Governor of the State of California. http://www. ca.gov/state/portal/myca_homepage.jsp.

DeLeon, Peter. 1997. *Democracy and the policy sciences.* Albany: State University of New York Press.

Derksen, Jim. 1995. Deadly compassion – fearsome kindness: Murdered in the name of kindness. http://www.normemma.com/areut_derksen01.htm.

Fox-Grage, Wendy, Donna Folkemer, and Jordan Lewis. 2003. The States' response to the *Olmstead* decision: How are states complying? http://www.ncsl.org/programs/health/ forum/olmsreport.htm.

Gabbard, Glen O., ed. 2001. *Treatments of psychiatric disorders.* 3rd ed. Washington, DC: American Psychiatric Press.

Georgia. Olmstead Planning Committee. 2002. Summary of Olmstead meeting with Governor Barnes, 2 July 2002. http://www.gcdd.org/pi/olmstead.

Hirschl, Ran. 2000. "Negative" rights vs. "positive" entitlements: A comparative study of judicial interpretations of right in an emerging neo-liberal economic order. *Human Rights Quarterly* 22, 4: 1060-98.

Illinois. Department of Human Services. 2002. Home-based support services. http://www. dhs.state.il.us/mhdd/dd/homebasedsupportservices.asp.

Ingstad, Benedicte, and Susan Reynolds Whyte. 1995. *Disability and culture.* Berkeley: University of California Press.

Iowa Civil Rights Commission. Biennial report. 1978. Developmental Disabilities Protection and Advocacy Division. http://www.state.ia.us/government/crc/annual78 developmentaldisabilities.html.

Kingdon, John W. 1997. *Agendas, alternatives and public policies.* New York: Longman.

Kunc, Norman. 2001. Robert Latimer and the dread of disability. http://www.normemma. com/ar_eutkunc01.htm.

Learning Disabilities Association of Canada. 2003. LD and the law: Case summaries. http://www.ldac-taac.ca/ld-law/casesumm/notfully.htm.

LeBlanc, Allen J., M. Christine Tonner, and Charles Harrington. 2000. Medicaid 1925(c) home and community-based services waivers across the States. *Health Care Financing Review* 22, 2: 159-74.

Longmore, Paul K., and Lauri Umansky, eds. 2001. *The new disability history: American perspectives*. New York: New York University Press.

Louisiana's Sixth District. Baker introduces resolution for commemorative postage stamp to raise autism awareness. http://baker.house.gov/html/release.cfm?id=65.

Maryland. Baltimore County Public Schools. Department of Federal and State Programs. 2003. Autism waiver. http://www.bcps.org/offices/dfsp/special_ed_autism_waiver.html.

Mavromatis, K. Alexa. 2001. E-Government sites should be portals, not potholes. *Providence Business News* 16, 117: 9-10.

Newfoundland and Labrador. Division of Student Support Services. 2001. Newsletter no. 10, October. http://www.gov.nf.ca/edu/k12/sss/no_10a.htm.

–. Human Rights Commission. 2002. http://www.gov.nf.ca/releases/2002/just/1220n01.htm.

–. Health and Community Services. 2003. Province enhances autism services. Press release, 14 February 2003. http://www.gov.nf.ca/releases/2003/health/0214n18.htm.

Oklahoma Olmstead Committee. 2002. Notices and notes for Oklahoma's legislated Olmstead strategic planning committee. http://www.csctulsa.org/olmstead.htm.

Olmstead v. L.C., 527 U.S. 581 (1999).

Ontario. Ministry of Community, Family and Children's Services. 2002. Eves government makes landmark investment for children with autism. http://www.cfcs.gov.on.ca.

Plant, P. Geoffrey. 2002. Order in Council 823. http://www.qp.gov.bc.ca/stratreg/oic/2002/procs/oic_823.htm.

Puttee, Alan, ed. 2002. *Federalism, democracy and disability policy in Canada*. Montreal: McGill-Queen's University Press.

Rossiter, Clinton, ed. *The federalist papers: Alexander Hamilton, James Madison, John Jay*. New York: New American Library, 1961.

Schuck, Peter H. 2002. Affirmative action: Don't mend it or end it – bend it. *Brookings Review* 20, 1: 1, 24-27.

Serafini, M.W. 2003. Waiving red flags. *National Journal* 35, 14: 1072-78.

Stroman, Duane F. 2003. *The disability rights movement: For deinstitutionalization to self-determination*. New York: University Press of America.

Taylor, David, ed. 1996. *Critical social policy: A reader: Social policy and social relations*. Thousand Oaks, CA: Sage Publications.

Thernstrom, Abigail. 1996. The real problem. *Harvard Journal of Law and Public Policy* 19, 3: 767-72.

Théroux (tuteur à) c. Commission scolaire Lester B. Pearson (2000). J.Q. no 2881, (2001) C.C.S. 7485. Quebec Court of Appeal, July 3, 2000.

United States. Department of Health and Human Services. 2003. Autism awareness month, April 2003. http://mentalhealth.samhsa.gov/highlights/April2003/autism/default.asp.

Vancouver Island Dog Guide Society. 2003. Disability and human rights. http://victoria.tc.ca/Community/Vidgs/rights.htm.

9

Post-Secondary Education and Disabled Students: Mining a Level Playing Field or Playing in a Minefield?

Teri Hibbs and Dianne Pothier

> So first of all, I went to the Grad Advisor and appealed to her on the basis of my disability. What I said was – I have a chronic illness. I'm older than most of the other students. I have a disability of pace, and I need you to recognize that and treat me equitably. And what I got back was a line about – well, we need to create a level playing field for all of the students. And I said to her – when you live with a disability, there is no level playing field, most of the time we're not even on the field – and I said – I don't want fairness, I want equity. And she didn't understand the difference. She kept falling back on – we have to treat everyone the same, we have to be fair to the other students as well. (Jung 2000, 105)

Most universities in Canada provide academic accommodations (course or program modifications, extension of assignment due dates, alternate testing procedures), as well as access to adaptive technology and structural modifications to buildings (e.g., ramps) to facilitate access to education for disabled students. While these policies, practices, and modifications can make it possible, or at least less arduous, for disabled students to earn degrees or diplomas, they are based on the assumption that they are sufficient to create equitable access to "level the field," so that students can compete on merit. They also exist so that universities meet their legal obligations not to discriminate under human rights legislation or the equality provisions in the *Canadian Charter of Rights and Freedoms*.[1]

Balanced against these objectives are the interests of universities in protecting academic (and other) standards and in managing resources and restricted budgets, especially given the potentially high costs associated with the provision of some accommodations or modifications.[2] The tensions between these objectives and interests are often played out in the language of policy which, on its face, may be seen as fulfilling the legal requirements for access and accommodation but can fall far short of achieving equity, especially on examination of the assumptions about disability that underlie the policies and the means by which equity – in the form of academic accommodation – is administered and disputes are resolved. The concept of equity in law manifests in the duty to accommodate to the point of undue hardship, which is what is required by most human rights legislation (*BCGSEU* 1999). In the context of practices that have historically excluded disabled people, equity is seen as a goal that ensures not only an equal opportunity to access and participate in post-secondary education but an opportunity that does not create or result in disadvantage for the person seeking access and accommodation.

In this chapter, I critically examine the process that disabled students are required to undertake to be granted academic accommodation at the University of Victoria, in British Columbia. On the basis of an external review of the university's equity policies and programs, I discuss the way the university approaches its commitment to accessible education. I contextualize this analysis by examining the manner in which power is conceptualized as either a characteristic of the individual or of the social structure. Further, I maintain that seeing power as a "thing" that can be possessed and manipulated inappropriately assumes that a balance of power exists (or can be made to exist) between the instructor and the disabled student with whom he or she is negotiating. Instead, I suggest that Michel Foucault's concept of disciplinary power provides an accurate picture of the interaction, specifically in terms of the role of choice or agency. Disciplinary power requires not only participation; it invokes an aspect of complicity within the hegemony (i.e., the dominant discourse as represented through university policies and practices) and operates invisibly as a self-regulated activity carried out by disabled students.

In light of this understanding of the disciplinary nature of power, I look at how disability is defined in the university's policy on *Providing Accommodation for Students with a Disability* and describe the process through which accommodation is reached. I argue that the biomedical conceptualization of disability represented in the policy individualizes and shapes the accommodation process such that the substantive evidentiary requirements (e.g., medical or psychological documentation from a recognized professional) and the steps involved in reaching accommodation (i.e., self-identifying as disabled, proving need through documentation, and negotiating the actual accommodation with each course instructor) signifies, in effect, a process of appeal based on an assumption that students are non-disabled and are not entitled to accommodation unless they prove otherwise. What is more, the policy language places the onus on disabled students to initiate and maintain the process through to completion, despite the university's recognition of its responsibility to "provide reasonable accommodation, up to the point of undue hardship, to otherwise qualified students with a disability" (Accommodation Policy, section 6.2(a)). The university will act only on a student's request for accommodation; it does not, in practice, see itself as having a positive obligation to initiate proactive solutions or to create equitable access to programs and courses.[3]

This places disabled students in an adversarial position vis-à-vis the university, such that their objective – to complete a course, to win a scholarship, or to earn a degree – may be thwarted if they are unable or unwilling to identify themselves as disabled, if they cannot provide acceptable documentation that proves the legitimacy of their claim, or if they are unable to reach agreement with an instructor over an accommodation. I look specifically at the requirement that disabled students negotiate with each of their instructors to come to an agreement on the accommodation needed.[4]

Throughout this analysis, I refer to and draw on the reported experiences of disabled students at the University of Victoria as recorded in various studies undertaken between 1994 and 2002. As well, I include examples from my own experience as the graduate student representative on the Advisory Committee on Issues Affecting Students with a Disability and as a disabled student to illustrate the application of policies and practices and the way power operates in these interactions.

Approaching Equity at the University of Victoria

How universities approach their commitment to accessible education has been described as either proactive or reactive. Those institutions that are seen to be proactive generally initiate action independent of demands or requests for change by those who are most affected. Institutions that are seen as reactive operate as passive agents of change in response to demands or requests for access or accommodation (Roberts 1996, 6-7). Because the *nature* of access (i.e., how universities go about implementing equity measures for disabled students) is not guaranteed in legislation or in most provincial policies, funding cuts, rising tuition rates, and financial pressures can undermine the commitment to full access and limit available accommodation services (Killean and Hubka 1999, 5). As Rioux and Valentine point out in Chapter 2, the fixation by governments on deficit and debt control that gained momentum in the 1990s (and continues to grow) has coincided with losses of civil and social rights for disabled people. They describe a resurgence in patterns of policy development based on assumptions of disability as an individual, biomedically based deficit which depicts disabled people as passive, sick, asexual, and apolitical. And they observe that, despite the enshrinement of formal citizenship rights in the Charter and in human rights legislation, substantive citizenship rights found in programs and services do not fully extend to most disabled people. In their view, this has to do with tension over the interpretation of whether the guarantee of equality is seen as full access to government programs and services, or as a discretionary benefit subject to the need for governments to contain spending. Even in those post-secondary institutions that see equitable access as a worthy goal and have dedicated services to facilitate access and accommodation for disabled students, the theoretical framework of disability under which they operate significantly impacts how policies and practices advance the goal of equitable access.

In an effort to demonstrate its commitment to equity and diversity, the University of Victoria underwent an external review of its equity policies, programs, and services.[5] The review was designed to determine "if structures, mandates, and policies respecting equity and fairness could be improved to advance the university's goal to 'recruit and retain a diverse group of exceptionally talented students, faculty, and staff and to support them in ways that allow them to meet their highest potential'" (Bujara, Scholefield, and Trehearne 2003, 3). The review panel found that, in general, equity services and policies have developed in a reactive and piecemeal fashion at the University of Victoria (21). Specifically, equity programs, policies, and services at the university, including those relating to access and accommodation for disabled students, were brought into being primarily by members of equity-seeking groups, in contrast to other public institutions, which have taken more of a leadership role (21). The review panel found little evidence of conscious concern for educational equity by the university, highlighting, for example, the lack of formal policy relating to and equity services provided for students from particular equity-seeking groups (9). The review panel commented that even though there is a policy on accommodation for disabled students and an office for students with disabilities, the overall approach of the university is reactive, requiring the student to initiate action for the purpose of receiving accommodation. They recommended that the university "assess the ability of the current Students with Disabilities Office to provide effective services to students with visible and invisible disabilities" (27).

An important issue raised in the report is the belief of some university administrators that equity-seeking groups, such as disabled people, Aboriginal people, and other under-represented groups, are special interest groups. This belief, the review panel noted, may explain the view held by some that existing equity policies and programs are the result of pressure from these groups rather than a genuine commitment to equity by the university (20-21). The review panel was concerned that such language is needlessly divisive and that "it fails to comprehend Canadian law and jurisprudence as it has developed over the last twenty years. It conveys to members of designated groups a sense that they must lobby for the opportunities to which they are entitled under law. It suggests strongly that a few administrators have yet to see that the onus for action falls to the University" (20).

This finding was confirmed for the panel by the submissions of disabled students who "discussed the extra effort they must sometimes undertake to achieve an accommodation that would appear to be nothing more or less than what the University is legally obliged to provide" (20).

Accommodation can be conceptualized in two broad forms: accommodation within the general standard (i.e., flexibility for all), and accommodation by means of individual exceptions to the general standard. The University of Victoria's accommodation policy for disabled students is geared almost entirely to the latter, which is a large part of why the burden of enforcing the policy falls so heavily on individual disabled students themselves. If accommodation is already built into the general academic standard, thus avoiding the need to create exceptions, there is no need for a process to consider exceptions. For example, if examinations are normally written under limited time constraints, a significant number of students with particular kinds of disabilities would need to make an exceptional request for extra time. If, however, the examination is normally done as a take-home with extended time, many disabled students would have no need for additional accommodation. Moreover, many non-disabled students would find such flexibility more conducive to demonstrating their academic capabilities. Nothing in the University of Victoria's accommodation policy mandates or even encourages reassessment of general academic standards to determine whether accommodation of disability within the general academic standard is feasible or appropriate. This is so despite pronouncements from the Supreme Court of Canada that accommodation within the standard should be the starting point for compliance with human rights legislation (*BCGSEU* 1999, paras. 65, 68).[6]

Even where accommodation needs to be addressed via exceptions, the manner of doing so is crucial. If exceptions are treated as within the realm of expectation, requests for exceptions will be treated very differently than if requests for exceptions are treated as presumptively illegitimate. Whereas equality under human rights legislation demands the former (*BCGSEU* 1999, para. 68), as I will elaborate below, the University of Victoria's accommodation policy exemplifies the latter.

Power and the Accommodation Process

Birkhoff (1996, 7), in a review of perspectives on power in the conflict resolution literature, argues that many of the different views of power generally reflect one of two underlying ontological frameworks: agency or structure. Definitions of power are seen as falling along a continuum that ranges from an emphasis on individual attributes (agency) to an emphasis on the social structure. The accommodation policy's focus on an individualized biomedical concept of disability is consistent with an agency conception of power, given that students are expected to take the initiative and act independently to obtain the accommodations they require. There is little recognition of structural or systemic barriers to access, particularly in the reactive environment of the university, where the responsibility for the amelioration of difference lies with the disabled student. And, even in those post-secondary institutions that have adopted a social/political definition of disability, the onus remains with the student to bring a human rights (or similar) complaint should he or she experience barriers to access. Within these frameworks, legal and alternative dispute resolution processes are aimed at balancing power and, in cases of "equity" disputes, they rely on identity as a key determinant of how the power will be balanced.

The idea that power *can* be balanced – as if it is a commodity, a thing that can be divided up, weighed, or measured – means also that it can be attained and possessed as property. This is the hegemony of power, the dominant discourse of policies and practices that function as though power is a thing that can be manipulated. In the accommodation policy, power is seen to be reasonably balanced by the process of accommodation: the documentation requirements purportedly take discretion regarding the nature of the accommodation out of the hands of the instructor and balance it against the opportunity for the student to have a role in suggesting appropriate accommodations. But how can there ever be a genuine balance of power when the student is ultimately dependent on the professor as evaluator? How can there ever be a genuine balance of power between an individual student and a university bureaucracy, especially a resistant one? As indicated in the following passages, some students are aware of issues of power that affect them in their attempts to access disability-related services:

> You get this feeling of being taken advantage of because of the power differences. You get almost to the place that you give them what they want and you don't rock the boat. (Turner et al. 2002, 33)

> There is a lack of understanding of what the consequences are of so many things. I mean tiny, little things. Like I fought for three years to get my own handicapped spot for parking because, I mean, you can't see my disability so it can't possibly be there. They treat each situation as if it was the first time they've heard of it and there is nothing you can do. Can't you just go home: because it is not going to change. Go away! (Turner et al. 2002, 27)

This "thingness" of power as represented in processes such as interest-based negotiation characterizes power as inherent to the individual. As mentioned earlier, this implies that individual agency is the driving force in the negotiations and that a failure to negotiate an acceptable accommodation is a failure of communication or lack of ability to develop the most satisfactory arrangement. This view, however, does not conceive of the *relationship* between the student and the professor, or between the student and an administrative body such as the Resource Centre for Students with Disabilities that has a hand in facilitating accommodation. In this conceptualization, power, rather than being an inherent characteristic, is a fluid network of relations in which an individual's self-perceptions and behaviours are based on their role or classification in a system of relationships (Foucault 1995, 145-46). In the university context, the identification of students as disabled, based on a biomedical classification, provides an avenue through which they attain a sense of legitimacy and entitlement to services. By voluntarily adopting their role as disabled, students maintain and perpetuate their distribution in a network of relations.

Foucault (1995, 177), for example, discusses disciplinary techniques of power that are intended to produce a "docile" body. These practices of disciplinary power presuppose agency by the individual but not on the basis of power as a thing or as property. Disciplinary power is not the same as physical force or violence; to operate, individuals must be free to act or to have a choice in their response. The actions of individuals in these disciplinary practices reinforce and recreate the disciplinary power. But the legitimizing and normalizing influence of these practices comes through their seeming invisibility, the voluntary adoption of the role that makes the power structure possible: "Disciplinary power ... is exercised through its invisibility; at the same time it imposes on those whom it subjects a principle of compulsory visibility. In discipline, it is the subjects who have to be seen. Their visibility assures the hold of the power that is exercised over them" (187).

The operation of disciplinary power is exemplified in the following two passages, in which disabled students voluntarily or freely take on a role that supports existing structures of power and demonstrates their willingness to self-regulate by accepting responsibility for that which is rightly the province of the university:

Professors often feel a bit threatened, probably because they know that if they mistreat a disabled student they could be in a lot of trouble. I do not think it could be worth the extra training to rectify this misperception; rather, I find it helps if the disabled student approaches the professor on the most informal level possible, has his/her documentation ready, and helps the professor with all the questions that may arise (when do I write the exams, who will invigilate, etc.). (University of Victoria Accommodation and Accessibility Survey 1994, 27)

I approach all of my instructors via a telephone call before each semester begins. I inform them of my deafness and let them know I will be attending class with an interpreter (this is done to avoid the element of surprise on the first day). I provide all of my profs with a list of suggestions regarding deafness and speech reading. I approach each instructor during the first class to introduce myself, and my interpreter to give them the info I am providing them with and to explain the audio equipment I use (FM system) as they must agree to wear the microphone (a few have been very reluctant). On the second day I ask that my plea for a note taker be read. This is not a problem in the last few years as I know most of my classmates and they approach me. I did however, in my second year, have to wait 3 weeks without a note taker before the instructor was willing to pursue the matter. Some of my instructors attended the inservice for instruction of the deaf conducted through [the coordinator's] office. (I have found that those attending are usually the ones who are already knowledgeable and accepting). (University of Victoria Accommodation and Accessibility Survey 1994, 28-29)

Although these particular comments predate the current accommodation policy, they are still pertinent given the current policy's primary reliance on student negotiation with individual professors.

For disciplinary power to operate, it requires not only participation; it invokes in students an aspect of complicity illustrated by their acceptance of responsibility for initiating and following through on the accommodation process described in the passages above. Defining disability from a biomedical perspective, which individualizes the process and makes students responsible for instituting their own "equity," illustrates the disciplinary nature of power in its self-regulating and productive aspects, especially when contrasted with other explanations of power that see it as a thing that can be possessed and manipulated.

Foucault (1995) refers to "power-knowledge," a term that reflects his belief that the two are intimately connected and embedded in each other. Knowledge, seen as a social product, has within it the power to influence what is seen as relevant and not relevant in particular social practices. In the case of documentation requirements, biomedical discourse is the method of legitimating and "normalizing" the experience of students seeking accommodation. It constructs the nature of disability in the policy, places students in a field of surveillance, and situates them in a "network of writing; ... a whole mass of documents that capture and fix them" (189). Practices that are consistent with this construction of disability constitute, and are given legitimacy in, the discourse. Perceptions that are different or radical and that do not fit within the existing constructions are rejected, and behaviours are redefined as inappropriate or deviant and are constrained by social practices that marginalize and exclude. Foucault does not separate the concepts of knowledge-power; he sees both as interactive and dependent on each other.

What is so insidious, however, about the operation of disciplinary power is the process of normalization that follows from individualized practices of accommodation based on one's identity as disabled. Although no one is immune to the techniques of normalization that exist in our culture on a day-to-day basis, disabled people are particularly vulnerable because of the greater "deviation" from the norm that they present and the pressure to make themselves fit in, especially in a university environment from which they have historically been excluded. Foucault (1995, 184) writes about the establishment of "The Normal" as a principle of coercion in teaching (with the introduction of standardized education), in the organization of medical systems, and in the standardization of industrial processes. He explains that normalization, as an instrument of power, not only indicates one's membership in a homogenous group; it also plays a part in the classification, hierarchization, and distribution of rank. He states: "It is easy to understand how the power of the norm functions within a system of formal equality, since within a homogeneity that is the rule, the norm introduces, as a useful imperative and as a result of measurement, all the shading of individual differences" (184). The biomedical conceptualization of disability exemplifies the classificatory and measured indices of difference among students with disabilities. Their membership in the so-called homogenous group of students is demarcated by their identification with, and description of, themselves as disabled. Individualized accommodations, which attempt to create a level field, are based on this concept of normalization and, because all in the policy flows from a biomedically defined disabled identity, strengthen and validate the existing reactive processes.

It is against this backdrop of the disciplinary nature of power that I turn to a more detailed examination of the University of Victoria accommodation policy.

Individualized Policy: Representation of Disability in the Policy
Much of what is written about disability is from either a biomedical or a socio-political perspective. The dominance of a biomedical interpretation of disability has been criticized for keeping disabled people under the direction of the medical profession and for individualizing disability by emphasizing treatment of the condition or the person with the condition (Linton 1998). This medicalized version of disability "casts human variation as deviance from the norm, as pathological condition, as deficit, and, significantly, as an individual burden and personal tragedy" (Linton 1998, 11). A biomedical understanding of disability assumes it to be inferior to "normalcy" (Corker and Shakespeare 2002, 2), and practices to "rehabilitate" or include people with disabilities are generally directed at normalizing them, that is, engaging in activities that will help them fit as closely to the concept of normal as possible.

A socio-political approach sees disability as a political category, an identity through which people with a wide range of physical, emotional, cognitive, and sensory conditions are bound by common social and political experiences (Linton 1998). This approach generally makes a conceptual distinction between impairment and disability such that disability is seen as a social construction on top of a pre-existing impairment (e.g., Wendell 1989). From this perspective, disability is not in the person; it is in the social environment and in the social practices that restrict the participation of people with so-called impairments. Not all social models of disability exclude the individual's experience, but the emphasis is on emancipation from restrictive social practices. The idea behind the social model is to demedicalize disability but, as Shelley Tremain (2002, 33) points out, citing Hughes and Paterson (1997), the split between impairment and disability still renders the impaired body the exclusive jurisdiction of medical interpretation.

The accommodation policy at the University of Victoria embraces a biomedical definition of disability. This forms the foundation on which the rest of the policy is constructed. Section 4.2 states:

A disability results from a physical or mental impairment arising from an anatomical, physiological, neurological and/or psychiatric condition. The impairment is such that it results in:
(a) limited access to *regular* university facilities;
(b) need for modifications in the way that instructional materials are *typically* presented/accessed; and/or
(c) limitations in the ability to demonstrate knowledge or skills in the manner in which they are *typically* evaluated. (emphasis added)

This explanation of disability focuses on individual incapacity and relies on medical or psychological authority for verification. As can be seen in the language of this section, the assumption is that the limitation or need is within the person and that it results from impairment. Notice also how the limitation or need is seen in relation to what is regular or typical. This implies that disabled students are expected to conform as much as possible to what is considered normal by the university's standards. The policy is not based on any questioning of what is regular or typical, or of the privilege attached to what is regular or typical.[7] Support for this can be found in the section of the accommodation policy dealing with the responsibilities of students with a disability:

5.1 Every student who seeks accommodation due to disability has a responsibility to ...

(c) receive or be receiving appropriate treatment for, or remediation where appropriate of, his or her disability (e.g., will be wearing glasses or hearing aids, if prescribed, to enhance their visual or hearing functional level).

This language individualizes the disability, making it the student's responsibility to ameliorate the difference, with the goal of moving toward what is considered normal. While many students probably will indeed use technologies such as hearing aids and glasses to enhance their ability to fit with the dominant methods of learning, the policy does not take into account that alternative forms of communication – American Sign Language, large print, audiotape, or Braille – are also valid. The problem is that they are not *typical* or *regularly* used in an academic setting.[8] This section of the policy also conveys the potential for coercion. Not only must the students be receiving treatment or remediation for their disability, but their choices are limited even further by the requirement that the treatment be prescribed. The university can potentially deny accommodation should the student opt for an alternative treatment or remediation, especially if it requires the expenditure of additional resources for accommodation by the university.[9]

The Accommodation Process
Because biomedicine views disability as an individualized limitation or deficit, it follows that equity processes designed on this model also focus on the individual as the starting point for action. This is clearly represented in sections 7-10 of the accommodation policy, which set out three main elements requiring positive action by students: self-identifying as disabled, supplying appropriate and verifiable documentation, and negotiating and arranging the actual accommodation with their instructors and other appropriate university officials.

Although presented in the accommodation policy as linear, the process – especially those aspects that are not visible and which the student carries out individually to satisfy the policy requirements in order to be granted accommodation – can be complex, time-consuming, and, in some cases, too costly or overwhelming for students to pursue. For example, students who suspect they may have a learning disability but are unable to pay the cost of a psycho-educational assessment would not be eligible for services of the Resource Centre for Students with a Disability (RCSD) or for academic accommodations through that office. Since neither the university nor the province will bear the cost of such testing, economic class intersects with disability as a barrier to education.[10] True educational equality for students with learning disabilities would entail public responsibility for the costs of testing.

Although many requests for accommodation are routine, they can become quite arduous for the student, even if ultimately successful.[11] Furthermore, time and effort devoted to negotiating accommodation can take away from study time. Also, an often-ignored issue is the impact of the nature of disability on one's ability to successfully carry out the steps in the accommodation process. If the process becomes an onerous one, the disability may become a barrier to negotiating the accommodation, precluding the demonstration of the need for accommodation. Nevertheless, disabled students must take the initiative to engage with, and carry to completion, the accommodation process.

Self-Identifying as Disabled and Timely Requests

Section 7.1(a) of the accommodation policy states: "New students are encouraged to self-identify at the time of application (e.g., by indicating the presence of a disability on the University of Victoria Application Form). Delays in notifying RCSD staff may result in accommodation requests not being processed in time for the term/course in which the accommodation is sought." The 2004-5 Undergraduate Application for Admission includes a section at the end of the form allowing students from four designated groups (Aboriginal, disabled, visible minority, and minority sexual orientation/ transgender) to self-identify.[12] In addition, there is an extra box that can be checked regarding disability: "Because of my circumstances, I may need assistance in order to participate in my program. Please forward this information to appropriate services available to students with disabilities." If the student checks the box identifying that he or she has a need for assistance, it triggers a letter of introduction from the RCSD. However, on the original application form, there is no explanation of the kinds of assistance available to disabled students, or how and by whom the information will be used.[13]

There is no requirement to self-identify; that is, a disabled student is not required to request individualized accommodation. However, if a disabled student wants individualized accommodation, the invitation to self-identify ultimately turns into a requirement, even if the student does not share the policy's biomedical understanding of disability (i.e., that the need or deficit is within them). As noted earlier, the accommodation policy nowhere encourages accommodation within the general standards, thereby enabling a decrease in the need for individualized accommodation. There is no prompting to build into academic standards the flexibility that would move away from a single "typical" or "normal" standard geared to those who are nondisabled. Thus, a high proportion of disabled students will ultimately be required to self-identify in order to make the necessary requests for individualized accommodation. This involves self-identification not only to the staff in the RCSD but, repeatedly, to all of one's instructors or other university officials who have a role in the accommodation process. The disadvantages associated with openly taking on a disabled identity for the purpose of academic accommodation can manifest in "blatant discrimination, lowered expectation for success, and being actively discouraged from applying for certain programs by administrative and teaching staff" (BCEADS 1995).[14] Self-identification brings disabled students under the potential scrutiny of university officials; it allows for surveillance of their activities as they are singled out in the process of accommodation.

The policy's encouragement to self-identify as disabled at the time of application ignores the legitimate concerns that self-identification as disabled may lead to a discriminatory refusal to admit. As documented throughout this book, disability is commonly viewed as a limitation, deviance, or pathology; thus, self-identification as disabled has a potentially stigmatizing impact. In this climate, it is understandable that some students are reluctant to self-identify as disabled, especially given the paradox that the biomedical or psychological evidence required for accommodation points to and emphasizes the individual's particular physical, emotional, sensory, or cognitive limitations or deficits – in other words, what one *cannot* do – in a university environment that thrives on and rewards stamina, ability, independence, and mental fitness – what one *can* do.

A disabled student needing individualized accommodation does have the option of waiting until after admission to self-identify. However, he or she runs the risk of being told that the request is too late to be met for the term or course requested (Accommodation Policy, section 7.1(a)). While requirements for timely requests (sections 1.3 and 5.1(a)) may at first glance seem necessary from the university's perspective, the question of the amount of lead time required is very much dependent on the university's overall approach to accommodating disability. When the university is well-prepared for the kinds of accommodation requests that can be anticipated, a lot of lead time may not be required to accede to the request. For example, if course materials are already in electronic format, the production of alternate format versions can be done quickly. Although self-identification may still be required, providing the student with the alternate format version will likely be a hassle-free process for all concerned. In contrast, when course materials are not available in electronic format, the production of an alternate format version can be a laborious and time-consuming process. Similar comments can be made about other types of accommodation. The general point is that only if the university is ill-prepared is there usually a need for a lot of advance notice. If the university's approach is essentially reactive, problems with a timely response to accommodation requests can be expected. Conversely, in adopting a proactive approach, the university anticipates and plans for various accommodations that will be needed (based on input and involvement of disabled students and faculty members). The likely outcome is a more efficient process with fewer delays.

As noted above, the accommodation policy does not seriously address accommodation within the general standard that would avoid the need for individualized accommodation, and hence self-identification. There is thus an overreliance on self-identification that is linked to the biomedical model. Nevertheless, some level of individualized accommodation is inevitable and will require self-identification. In that context, however, the expectations of the fact and timing of self-identification need to take account of the power dynamics underlying students' reluctance to self-identify.

Documentation

Self-identification as disabled for the purpose of academic accommodation involves more than simply announcing this to RCSD staff. All claims must be supported with documented proof "acceptable to the University" from "medical doctors, psychologists, and/or other appropriate clinicians ... [who] must be appropriately certified and/or licensed to practice in their professions" and "the disabling condition must be demonstrable by medically accepted clinical or laboratory diagnostic procedures" (Accommodation Policy, section 8.2). As well, according to section 9, if the university does not find the documentation acceptable, it is not bound by professional opinions and has the right to obtain further opinions, which may also mean referring the student for a further independent assessment by a professional of the university's choice. The use of documentation to justify the provision of services and accommodations to disabled students is contentious. Not only can obtaining documentation be onerous, costly, and time-consuming for the student, but there are inconsistencies across departments and faculties as to how information is handled (BCEADS 1995). There are also concerns about the dissemination of documentation, despite the accommodation policy's acknowledgment of privacy protection rights (section 2.3). Students are frequently required to provide documentation not only to the RCSD but also to individual departments in order to be accommodated, which creates a network of writing, as referred to above (Foucault 1995, 189). This gives the university access to detailed information about the student, in some cases widely dispersed across different offices on campus.

The rigidity of this requirement of "medically accepted clinical or laboratory diagnostic procedures" (Accommodation Policy, section 8.2) has been confirmed in an audit of access policies at BC post-secondary institutions. Roberts (1996) found that the University of Victoria has instituted rigid and narrow documentation requirements that give medical professionals and psychologists authority over the academic prospects of disabled students. Such rigidity in documentation is likely discriminatory and in violation of the Charter in light of the recent Supreme Court of Canada decision in *Martin v. Nova Scotia (Workers' Compensation Board)*. *Martin* (2003) ruled that excluding chronic pain from regular workers' compensation coverage, and limiting workers' compensation benefits for those with chronic pain to a four-week functional restoration program, is discriminatory under section 15(1) of the Charter and is not saved by section 1. The court held that distinguishing injured workers with chronic pain (which is characterized by the lack of "objective" evidence) from those with other more easily documented disabilities is still disability-based discrimination. Further, the court held that the blanket denial of compensation benefits that were available to other injured workers went too far in pursuing the objective of preventing fraudulent claims and abuse of the compensation system, because it more than minimally impaired the rights of injured workers with chronic pain. In other words, the absence of objective evidence of the condition is not a sufficient reason to exclude a subgroup of disabled people from the benefits accorded to other disabled people.

As *Martin* applies to disabled students who wish to access accommodation, the lack of a medically accepted diagnostic procedure should not prevent students from accessing accommodation services. There needs to be flexibility in the documentation requirements that enables professionals to confirm a disability, even in the absence of "objective" evidence, on an evaluation of what the person reports. The diagnosis of some conditions, such as fibromyalgia or myalgic encephalomyelitis, is arrived at through the elimination of other illnesses as the cause of the symptoms. There are no medically accepted clinical or laboratory diagnostic procedures to determine the presence of either of these conditions, yet they are often chronic and debilitating and would require academic accommodations in order for students to manage their programs. While the university has an interest in some validation beyond self-reporting to guard against fraudulent claims, rigid documentation requirements are an overreaction that will work hardship on many disabled students.

The accommodation policy also demands that the documentation be "current" (section 8.5). Where a condition is variable or changing, the university's interest in current documentation may be legitimate, depending on the individual's particular circumstances. But for a permanent condition, why is current documentation necessary? The requirement of currency assumes that disabled students have ongoing contact with physicians and other medical professionals about their disability and its impact on day-to-day activities. But as Krogh and Johnson point out in Chapter 7, a 2002 report by the Council of Canadians with Disabilities reveals that the most common reason people with disabilities go to a doctor is not to receive medical care but to have their impairment documented so they may receive the disability supports they require.

The accommodation policy sets out the university's expectation of documented information:

> Documentation should outline the nature of the disability and provide a detailed explanation of the functional impact of the disability on the pursuit of post-secondary education. When possible, the documentation should give explicit recommendations for remedial and/or coping strategies that will assist the student in his or her pursuit of a program or post-secondary education. (Accommodation Policy, section 8.3)

The policy advises further that "a diagnosis alone ... is not sufficient to support a request for accommodation." It must be accompanied by information about the functional impact so that the university is able to determine the appropriate accommodation. It is not clear why a diagnosis alone cannot be sufficient documentation. For example, if a student is diagnosed as visually impaired, what more is needed to entitle the student to large-print materials? There is no conceivable academic advantage to the visually impaired student over non-disabled students. Moreover, it is hard to imagine that anyone who did not a have a genuine need would put up with the bulkiness of large-print materials. The administrative time and cost of producing the alternate format may explain the requirement of documented need, but there is no necessity for an onerous documentation requirement.

Even where the appropriate academic accommodation is less obvious, the proposal that medical documentation include recommended accommodation raises serious concerns. What is problematic about this practice is the assumption that medical professionals are best suited to speak to issues of academic accommodation, that is, that they are knowledgeable about and can recommend specific academic adjustments and so-called coping strategies for the student. As Moss and Dyck (1999, 378) point out, the power and legitimacy attributed to biomedical knowledge is utilized to legitimate and justify unrelated, and sometimes competing, practices, such as those involved in reaching academic accommodation in a university setting. Expertise in identifying an impairment and in identifying appropriate academic accommodation can be quite different. Once a disability is acknowledged, the student's input as to what works for him or her may be the most important expert opinion.

A rigid medicalized documentation process puts professional opinion above the experience and knowledge of students about their own bodies and their learning or evaluation needs. And, although it is indicated in the same section (8.3) that "students should be consulted by the instructor and the RCSD as to the most appropriate accommodations in their specific case," the language, in the context of the whole policy, appears to be advisory rather than mandatory. The authority clearly lies with the professional to decide whether the student is entitled to accommodation based on the diagnosis and its associated functional limitations.

While the university does have an interest in documentation, both to justify resources devoted to accommodation and to guard against fraudulent claims, the documentation requirements cannot be allowed to trump everything else. Although fraudulent claims are a legitimate concern, such concerns should not be determinative; policy should not be based on a presumption of fraud that needs to be rebutted. Rigid and onerous documentation requirements risk defeating the very purpose of the accommodation policy, namely, to make education accessible to disabled students.

Negotiating Equity

Once the documentation requirements have been satisfied, students are eligible to register with the RCSD for disability-related services and will usually have met with a service provider in the RCSD office. To reach accommodation, however, the student is expected to take the lead role in initiating and working out the details of the accommodation with the instructor or professor. The RCSD will provide a letter to the instructor *at the student's request,* outlining the student's functional limitations, and may also include recommended accommodations based on the documentation received. Generally, however, the RCSD will not intervene unless asked to do so by either the instructor or the student.[15]

Most requests for accommodation appear to be relatively uneventful. Yet, many students report difficulties in coming to an acceptable accommodation with some professors. Section 10 of the Accommodation Policy deals with "Reaching Accommodation." Section 10.1 of the accommodation policy directs students and instructors to "discuss the appropriate accommodation in light of the nature and requirements of the particular course." If the instructor rejects any RCSD recommendation and the instructor and the student cannot agree on an accommodation, the instructor is required to explain in writing the reasons for rejecting the requested accommodation (Accommodation Policy, section 10.4). If the student is not satisfied, he or she may request that the chairperson or director of the instructors' academic unit make a recommendation. If either the student or the instructor is dissatisfied with that recommendation, the dean can be asked to review it. If the dean's decision is in favour of the requested accommodation, it will be implemented. If the dean's decision is against the requested accommodation, the student can appeal to the Senate Committee on Appeals. Notice the entire absence of the RCSD in these processes. The onus is entirely on the student to negotiate with or challenge the instructor.

The rationale behind the practice of the instructor and student negotiating accommodation between themselves is that disabled students know what they need and are, therefore, in the best position to communicate this to their instructors. As a process of coming to agreement, negotiation relies on the capacities and strengths of the individuals involved, and takes place only if the student initiates the process. In this context, the policy is imbued with assumptions about power that focus on the autonomy of individuals as agents of their own destiny and as the source of knowledge and action (Thomas and Corker 2002, 28). In other words, it assumes that both parties are starting from a place of equal strength and capacity. This is not to say that disabled students do not have the capacity to act on their own behalf; it is the assumption that they are in an equal bargaining position that is problematic.

From this perspective, successful negotiation relies on one's skill or negotiation power – popularly defined as "the ability to persuade someone to do something" – usually something they would not otherwise do (Fisher, Ury, and Patton 1991, 178). Power is assumed to be relatively balanced between the student and instructor on the basis of the involvement of the RCSD – usually in the form of a letter with recommendations for accommodation – and the right of review and appeal that exists for both parties in the negotiation. However, as I argue above, conceiving power as something that resides in individuals limits the way a conflict over an accommodation can be understood and explained. The conflict itself is individualized as a problem between the student and the instructor, but because the student is ultimately dependent on the professor for a grade, the prospect of a refusal of accommodation by the professor can be daunting.

A 1994 University of Victoria Accommodation and Accessibility Survey reported students' experiences with faculty around disability. Although this survey predates the current policy, the fact that the current policy gives a primary role to the individual professor makes the survey results still relevant. One student stated: "There is always, initially, an uneasy feeling when I approach a prof with the issue of my needs. It depends on the professor's attitude whether this feeling goes away or increases. I feel on the defensive and get angry inside. I don't want to have to defend the fact that I have special needs. It is hard to be dependent on other people's kindness and understanding" (University of Victoria Accommodation and Accessibility Survey 1994, 31). Students may be successful with one instructor and unsuccessful with another depending on the instructor's knowledge and awareness of disability and accommodation issues. For example, Karen Jung (2000) looked at the accommodation policy as it was experienced by women with chronic illness at the University of Victoria and found reports of inconsistencies between instructors in what they deemed to be acceptable accommodations. One woman recalled: "The problem was that I was having a hard time typing ... So the only thing I could come up with was taping, for me to tape my assignments ... And that worked for one course ... And then

I came up against the next professor who just said, flat out – No! No to the taping. It's not fair to the other students" (Jung 2000, 105). This reflects a lack of awareness among faculty of the concept of equity. It also shows that the training provided to them of what it means to provide academic accommodation for students is inadequate. As well, this example indicates that it is not a matter of asking for and receiving – or discussing – accommodation. The process of negotiating can be fraught with many obstacles for students, the most salient being the impact of power on the negotiation (and its outcome) between the student and the instructor (or other university official).[16] Students who are unwilling or unable to approach their instructors, or who do not want to have a conflict with an instructor who is resistant to the accommodation, may suffer the consequences of a dropped course, compromised health, lower grades, or even complete withdrawal from school (BCEADS 1995).[17]

In this climate – which some disabled students have described as hostile – there is little recourse except to notify the RCSD of the problems or, as a last resort, to appeal to the campus ombudsperson for assistance (Turner et al. 2002). However, this does not acknowledge the risks that students take in reporting an instructor, particularly if the course is mandatory and the instructor is responsible for evaluating the student's progress in the course and in grading work. A recent research project about conflict and its resolution at the University of Victoria canvassed the experiences of students identified on the basis of their membership in a marginalized group. One disabled student reported: "In my class, someone had to use the ombudsperson with an instructor. And I saw how negative that turned out. You want to get a good grade and you don't want to alienate the instructor" (30). Another stated: "Well I find that I'm not really getting a lot of help from the university ... passing the buck thing; they don't want to take the time to try and help someone with marks or whatever. So you get stuck and you try and go to another person, then another person. Sometimes you just, it's easier to just forget about it, just leave it the way it is. Just try and struggle through on your own" (22). While instructors are encouraged to become familiar with the accommodation policy and participate in an orientation for new faculty that includes training on diversity issues and academic accommodation, it is just one of many pieces of new information to which they are exposed. Accommodation issues are unlikely to become a priority unless instructors are faced with a student who needs accommodation. And even then, there is no certainty that the instructor will consult with the policy or the RCSD before making accommodation decisions. It may be understandable and expected that not all professors will be knowledgeable about, or even supportive of, legal and moral obligations for the accommodation of disability. That premise, however, is incompatible with individual professors's being the primary decision makers about accommodation. Any concerns about academic freedom requiring a primary decision-making role for individual professors are easily met by the dictates of human rights legislation. The sanctity of abstract notions of academic freedom no more trumps human rights legislation than do abstract claims about the sanctity of a collective agreement (*Renaud* 1992).

Appendix I of the accommodation policy, which sets out the guidelines for reasonable accommodation, proposes conditions deemed to be effective for reaching accommodation: "The development and implementation of accommodations are most effective if there is a mutually respectful and trusting relationship between the student and the instructor. Often, the most creative and flexible accommodations are produced mutually by the two parties." The role of the RCSD in this process is to provide guidance, if asked, but it does not take an active role in facilitating a mutually respectful and trusting relationship between the student and the instructor. This is left to the initiative of the student or the instructor. And, given the association of disability with deviance and lowered expectations of success, as well as the view by some that disabled students at the University of Victoria are members of a special interest group, it is difficult to see how mutually respectful relationships can be developed without intervention by the university in some manner.

The hands-off attitude taken by the RCSD in matters of negotiation between the instructor and the student is a manifestation of the university's reactive approach to disability. If the RCSD is not instrumental in administering direct accommodation services, such as providing a private room for an exam, it is unlikely to know whether the student was successful in reaching an appropriate accommodation unless the student reports back to it.[18] The process of obtaining an accommodation through negotiation can be random for the student, especially when the RCSD does minimal follow-through to determine the outcome of a particular negotiation.

An effective accommodation policy needs more proactive involvement by the university as an institution. Effective decision making needs to:

1 move away from a biomedical conceptualization of disability that emphasizes self-identification
2 include disabled students in setting and implementing policy
3 ensure that all university personnel involved in administering the accommodation policy are knowledgeable about, and committed to, creating equitable access for disabled students
4 encourage the reassessment and adjustment of general academic standards to ensure accommodations are in compliance with human rights legislation.

Although there may be dangers in over-centralizing the administration of the accommodation policy in an office that does not appreciate the academic diversity across different programs, more localized involvement could be at the departmental or faculty level, rather than at the level of the individual instructor. In any case, any decentralization still needs to involve knowledgeable and committed people. An effective accommodation policy needs to provide support to disabled students requiring accommodation, not cast them in the role of adversaries of their instructors or the university. The rights of disabled students need to be enhanced by a process that accepts academic accommodation as not only legitimate but also indispensable.

Conclusion

This chapter critically examines the process that disabled students must undergo to access academic accommodations and disability-related services at the University of Victoria. It highlights the need for more flexibility in the way accommodation is approached, with less reliance on one's identity as disabled as a means of instituting equity. It reviews the policy on *Providing Accommodation for Students with a Disability*, which governs the conduct of disabled students, and discusses and critiques some of the assumptions and rationales underlying the policy. Because biomedicine is the predominant theoretical formulation that defines disability in the policy and sets out the requirements and process that students must engage in to access accommodations, the university's approach to equity has been individualized and reactive. I refer to my own experiences and to the experiences of other disabled students through reported studies to illustrate the operation of power in the university's policies and practices.

Each of the steps in the accommodation process serves to strengthen and perpetuate modern relations of power that are based on a biomedical concept of disability and that produce the subjects they subsequently come to represent: self-identification as disabled is sustained through ongoing surveillance and "compulsory visibility" (to use again Foucault's term); documentation requirements individualize and separate students based on a network of writing; and, negotiation to implement equitable accommodations for disabled students fosters the illusion that power is a characteristic that inheres in individuals, who are agents of their own destiny. Looked at from this perspective, the accommodation process at the University of Victoria does little to advance the principles of equity for disabled students. For some the expectation that the accommodation process will ameliorate existing barriers to education has not been met. Consequently, the experience for disabled students at the University of Victoria is more like negotiating a minefield than competing on a level playing field.

Acknowledgments

Teri Hibbs is the primary author of this chapter, which is based on research undertaken as part of her graduate program in dispute resolution at the University of Victoria. The analysis in this chapter draws on her experiences as a disabled student, as a legal advocate for disabled people, and as the graduate student representative on the Advisory Committee on Issues Affecting Students with a Disability. All first-person references in this chapter are hers. Dianne Pothier's supplementary contribution draws on her experience as a (disabled) faculty member of the Dalhousie Law School Studies Committee (which, among other things, deals with the examination of accommodation requests from law students with disabilities), as Dalhousie Law School's Faculty Advisor for Students with Disabilities, and as a faculty member of Dalhousie University's Presidential Advisory Committee on Accessibility for Students with Disabilities (which was involved in the drafting of Dalhousie's accessibility policy in the mid-1990s).

Notes

1 At the University of Victoria, the policy *Providing Accommodation for Students with a Disability* governs the conduct of disabled students who seek accommodation. Section 4.3 states in part: "These accommodations stem from the university's legal and moral duty to take reasonable measures, to the point of undue hardship, to accommodate students with a disability."

   Although in *McKinney et al. v. University of Guelph et al.* (1990), the majority of the Supreme Court of Canada decided, in a case involving employment issues, that universities are not government actors for all purposes regarding Charter application, it is likely that student access to post-secondary education would engage Charter application as per the principles in *Eldridge v. British Columbia (A.G.)* (1997) for effectuating a specific governmental policy or program. It is perhaps worth noting that the University of Victoria's accommodation policy, at Section 2.1, misquotes section 15(1) of the Charter, mistakenly indicating a closed list of grounds.

2 Section 1.2 of the University of Victoria accommodation policy states: "Providing accommodations that permit students with a disability to access courses shall not reduce the standards, academic or otherwise, of the University."

   Budget considerations are expressed through the concepts of reasonableness and undue hardship in the University of Victoria accommodation policy. Section 1.1 of the policy states: "The University of Victoria will provide reasonable academic accommodations, to the point of undue hardship, to all otherwise qualified students who have a disability."

3 This is so despite section 6.2(d) of the accommodation policy, which states that the university has a responsibility to "make their courses or programs accessible to otherwise qualified students with a disability up to the point of undue hardship and, except with respect to the essential course or program requirements, modify any course or program requirements that are discriminatory on the basis of disability. The Resource Centre for Students with a Disability (RCSD) and other University units have been authorized and designated to assist in meeting this responsibility." Even in the case of physical accessibility, the onus remains (at least partially) on students to bring forward concerns about barriers to accessibility, as evidenced by stickers on windows and doors across campus advising those reading them to notify the RCSD of barriers to access.

4 Section 10.1 of the accommodation policy sets out the requirement for disabled students and instructors to negotiate. The remaining subsections, 10.2-10.7 plus section 11, provide the rules and time limits for appeals if agreement on an accommodation cannot be reached.

5 The review panel conducted its review on campus on 10, 11, and 12 February 2003. The report, dated 19 June 2003, was released to the larger university community in early July 2003.

6 The court in *Meiorin* (*BCGSEU* 1999) expressly rejected its previous stance that adverse effects discrimination (which accounts for most disability discrimination) exclusively engages accommodation by means of exceptions to general rules.

7 Recall section 1.2 of the accommodation policy, which cautions that accommodations "shall not reduce the standards, academic or otherwise, of the University." The perceived

threat to academic standards as a rationale for denying accommodation is similar to the argument used not so long ago rationalizing keeping women out of universities. Because academic standards are social creations that can fluctuate depending on such things as curriculum design, changing enrolment patterns, and so on, they can act as a barrier to access for disabled students if accommodation considerations are not built into their design. See, for example, the article "UVic raises admission requirements" in the 5 June 2002 edition of *The Ring: The University of Victoria's Community Newspaper* (p. 3), which describes the rise in GPA (grade point average) cut-off for new admissions from 75 to 81 percent in Arts and Sciences for the 2002-3 year, due to an increase in applications and higher retention rates for returning students.

8 And, I suggest, the association of these technologies with disability in the biomedical sense devalues them as tools for learning or teaching.

9 An example of this might be the denial of a request for sign language interpretation if the student can also use hearing aids, even if the student understands and communicates more effectively using sign language.

10 Current BC legislation and policy changes have drastically cut back on support for disabled persons. This has been accomplished through, among other things, a substantially more restricted definition of disability as the basis for coverage. This impacts on the ability of disabled persons to access university education when all their energy is dedicated to meeting their basic survival needs. See Krogh and Johnson, Chapter 7.

In a draft report prepared in 2001 by Pierre Laliberté, the coordinator of the RCSD, entitled *Issues Facing Students with Cognitive Disabilities at the University of Victoria* (Victoria, BC: University of Victoria Resource Centre for Students with a Disability), the high cost of assessments were discussed in the context of lack of insurance or other funding to cover the costs. It states: "This lack of available funding has resulted in a situation whereby many students with undiagnosed learning disabilities are left without access to much-needed academic accommodation and support services essential to succeed in their program of studies. As reported by RCSD staff, between 5 and 10 students per month contact the center requesting information about testing for potential learning disabilities, many of them referred to the RCSD by their instructors" (3).

11 For example, I recently requested an accommodation that would extend my program end-date and waive the accompanying penalty fees, to compensate for the academic terms during which I was temporarily withdrawn due to disability. Although the accommodation was eventually granted after more than six weeks of intensive and emotionally taxing efforts to negotiate with several departments and administrators, I was, at one point in the process, advised that the university was not certain that my end-date could be extended because "a concern the department might have is use of faculty who, therefore, might not be available to other students" (a university administrator, pers. comm.). As well, process delays by the university (I requested the accommodation a month before classes were scheduled to begin) held up my student loan, requiring that I apply for an emergency loan to purchase essential medical supplies, despite informing the appropriate university administrator of the crisis created by the delay. The university showed no sense of urgency or willingness to expedite the process, leaving me on tenterhooks as to whether the accommodation would be granted while having to deal with financial hardships during the process. Given that a decision to refuse accommodation in this example would not likely meet the legal test of causing undue hardship to the university, it is discriminatory and reflects a lack of awareness of the financial reality of the lives of most disabled people and the adverse impact of being told that one's disability is a drain on the university's resources.

12 The Graduate Application for Admission form does not include this section.

13 At an August 2003 open house for the Society for Students with a Disability (a University of Victoria Student Society constituency group), one student commented that she believed that references to accommodation for disabled students had to do with accessible housing, and because she has an invisible disability, accommodation would not be relevant in her case.

There is a general lack of student awareness of both the existence of and the range of accommodation services and resources offered by the RCSD. The student members of the (now defunct) University of Victoria Advisory Committee on Issues Affecting Students with a Disability brought this issue to the committee, suggesting that accommodation services and resources be publicized more widely to students. This was met with the concern that the high workload of the RCSD and the lack of available resources for learning-disabled students who do not have documentation may send the wrong "message" to students, and that "care should be exercised in how we advertise the services available" (Minutes of the Advisory Committee on Issues Affecting Students with a Disability, University of Victoria, 23 November 2001).

14 Taking on a disabled identity for the purpose of academic accommodation is not to be confused with those who consciously take on a disabled identity as a means to advance the socio-political awareness of disability issues, though they, too, experience the same discriminatory practices.

15 However, the RCSD has been known to intervene in cases where it believes that the requested accommodation is inappropriate or unreasonable, even when students have used the requested accommodation elsewhere (e.g., for high school courses and exams). Section 9 of the accommodation policy allows the RCSD coordinator to convene and chair a panel to review the coordinator's decision to reject the appropriateness of a student's accommodation request. In effect, the policy gives the RCSD authority to review its own decisions by means of a hand-selected panel that reviews the documentation to determine whether the requested accommodation is appropriate. The student is not permitted to be present at the review and, if the requested accommodation is questioned, may be subjected to an involuntary reassessment by an appropriate professional chosen by the university; "if the Review Panel determines that the documentation is not acceptable and/or the requested accommodation is not appropriate ... the student has the option of appealing to the Senate Committee on Appeals" (Accommodation Policy, sections 9.2(b) and 9.3(b)).

16 For example, after I had satisfied the documentation requirements for a request for a temporary withdrawal (for one semester) because of disability, the official considering the information contacted some of my faculty members and department administrative staff to seek further information about my disability, even though this information was irrelevant to the request. And, although the accommodation request was approved, I was advised by letter that I was not entitled to any further temporary withdrawals in my program. When I expressed my concern that others who had nothing to do with my request were contacted in this matter and that the statement regarding no further withdrawals was a preordained denial of further accommodation, I was advised that my request was being considered under the policy on temporary withdrawals, not the accommodation policy, and that the consultation was based on an "ethic of care" to ensure that a semester of withdrawal was appropriate. No rationale was given for the denial of further withdrawals (even the policy on temporary withdrawals does not set a limit on the number of withdrawals that can be requested due to disability) except to say that this statement was on a form letter, and the official encouraged me to permanently withdraw from the university until my health was better, at which time I could reapply for admission. I had to pursue the matter further, seeking support from the RCSD regarding the discrimination on the basis of disability inherent in this statement, and to have a new letter issued that did not include a denial of future accommodation.

17 I am aware of two students who permanently withdrew from the University of Victoria in the fall semester of 2003 because of difficulties they encountered as they were trying to negotiate accommodations, and because of the lack of support or intervention by the university on their behalf.

18 And, in my experience at the University of Victoria, even when a letter is provided with a recommended accommodation, there is no follow-up by the RCSD with the student to determine whether the accommodation actually took place.

References

BCEADS (British Columbia Educational Association of Disabled Student). 1995. "I am all tested out": The problem of documentation requirements for students with disabilities. Position paper, Ministry of Skills, Training, and Labour, Vancouver.

[*BCGSEU*]. *British Columbia (Public Service Employee Relations Commission) v. BCGSEU*, [1999] 3 S.C.R. 3 *(Re Meiorin)* [*BCGSEU*].

Birkhoff, Juliana E. 1996. Conflict and power: An interdisciplinary review and analysis of the literature. Program of Excellence Working Paper, University of Victoria Institute for Dispute Resolution, Victoria, BC.

Bujara, Irène, Wendy Scholefield, and Fran Trehearne. 2003. Equity and fairness at the University of Victoria. Victoria, BC: University of Victoria. Duplicated.

Canadian Charter of Rights and Freedoms, Part I of the *Constitution Act, 1982*, being Schedule B to the *Canada Act 1982* (U.K.) 1982, c. 11 [Charter].

Corker, Mairian, and Tom Shakespeare. 2002. Mapping the terrain. In *Disability/postmodernity: Embodying disability theory*, ed. Mairian Corker and Tom Shakespeare, 1-17. London: Continuum.

Eldridge v. British Columbia (A.G.), [1997] 3 S.C.R. 624.

Fisher, Roger, William Ury, and Bruce Patton. 1991. *Getting to yes: Negotiating agreement without giving in*. New York: Penguin Books.

Foucault, Michel. 1995 [1977]. *Discipline and punish: The birth of the prison*. Trans. Alan Sheridan. New York: Vintage.

Hughes, Bill, and Kevin Paterson. 1997. The social model of disability and the disappearing body: Towards a sociology of impairment. *Disability and Society* 12, 3: 325-40.

Jung, Karen Elizabeth. 2000. The social organization of power in the academy's disability policy: Chronic illness, academic accommodation and "equity." MA thesis, University of Victoria.

Killean, Emer, and David Hubka. 1999. *Working towards a coordinated national approach to services, accommodations and policies for post-secondary students with disabilities*. Ottawa: National Educational Association of Disabled Students.

Linton, Simi. 1998. *Claiming Disability*. New York: New York University Press.

McKinney et al. v. University of Guelph et al., [1990] 3 S.C.R. 229.

Martin v. Nova Scotia (Workers' Compensation Board), [2003] 2 S.C.R. 504 (QL) [*Martin*].

Moss, Pamela, and Isabel Dyck. 1999. Body, corporeal space, and legitimating chronic illness: Women diagnosed with M.E. *Antipode* 31, 4: 372-97.

[*Renaud*]. *Central Okanagan School District No. 23 v. Renaud*, [1992] 2 S.C.R. 970 [*Renaud*].

Resource Centre for Students with a Disability (RCSD) website page on academic accommodation: http://www.stas.uvic.ca/osd/academic_accom.ihtml.

Roberts, Sharon. 1996. *Securing access: Policy and people with disabilities in post secondary education*. British Columbia Educational Association of Disabled Students (BCEADS), Human Resources Development Canada.

Thomas, Carol, and Mairian Corker. 2002. A journey around the social model. In *Disability/postmodernity: Embodying disability theory*, ed. Mairian Corker and Tom Shakespeare, 18-31. London: Continuum.

Tremain, Shelley. 2002. On the subject of impairment. In *Disability/postmodernity: Embodying disability theory*, ed. Mairian Corker and Tom Shakespeare, 32-47. London: Continuum.

Turner, David, Bill Doorschot, Elvira Lopez, Kathy McGeean, Tara Ney, Cathy Rhodes. 2002. Conflict resolution for a diverse campus: The perspective of students. Victoria, BC: University of Victoria Institute for Dispute Resolution. Duplicated.

University of Victoria. University of Victoria accommodation and accessibility survey. 1994. Victoria, BC.

–. 1997. *Providing accommodation for students with a disability*. [Hereafter Accommodation Policy.] Revised 2001. http://web.uvic.ca/uvic-policies/pol-2000/2340DIS.html.

Wendell, Susan. 1989. Toward a feminist theory of disability. *Hypatia* 4, 2: 104-24.

Part 4
Legal Interrogations

10

Now You See Her, Now You Don't: How Law Shapes Disabled Women's Experience of Exposure, Surveillance, and Assessment in the Clinical Encounter

Catherine Frazee, Joan Gilmour, and Roxanne Mykitiuk

> Our very human essence is so damn undignified. And so uncontrollable. We spend most of our life working like fiends to maintain the illusion that we are in control, that we can tame and tidy nature. Let's face it: nature always has the last laugh. Nowhere does the old girl laugh louder than with disability and death. God forbid we human beings should ever have to get up close and personal with our unwieldy, messy, smelly humanness. In every way possible, this culture's rules and values distance us from the realities of our own bodies in all their glorious imperfection.[1]
> – Cheryl Marie Wade, poet, performance artist, and disability activist

In this chapter, which is part of a larger project, we seek to document and analyze the uneasy relationship between that most ubiquitous and unyielding form of social control – the institution of law – and the "unwieldy ... humanness" of women's bodies "in all their glorious imperfection."[2] Our focus is the web of legal regimes superimposed on the embodied experience of women and the regulation of the boundaries of their health. Our overriding objective is to make visible the links between a disabled woman's lived experience of health and the organization of her experience by law.

Our understanding of embodied experience is mediated through elaborate metaphors of system and law. Human reproduction, sustenance, growth, development – even identity – these processes are laid out by medicine as scientifically ordered systems, compliant with a complex sequence of interactive rules and doctrine. The body is read scientifically as living matter organized into structural categories (e.g., the nervous system, the immune system) and performing functions (e.g., respiratory, circulatory, metabolic) in accordance with medical doctrine. Within this paradigm, medicine constructs health normatively, as a state of harmonious compliance with the rules of the body's variously named systems and functions.

Layered over this medical mapping of the body are the social meanings we assign and sustain through formal law, regulation, and policy. Law is a major force in shaping the environment in which women assess risks to health, access health care and health-promoting resources, and make decisions about health. Law mobilizes ideals and assumptions about the nature of bodies in its determinations of what is or is not a health issue, and in its definitions – both explicit and implicit – of health, health care, and rights of access. Interestingly, in this realm, the body tends to lose its materiality, being defined conceptually (e.g., competent, indigent, consenting) and assigned value (e.g., eligible, credible, employable, at risk) in accordance with legal doctrine.

In their form and function, women's bodies express the endless inventions of nature's palette. Bodies that depart from the norm – bodies marked by some condition of impairment – disrupt the rules. Striking their own "bond with the natural order" (Rich 1976), these bodies disrupt the metaphors of science, infuse static notions of health with deeper, richer meanings, and challenge law makers and policy makers who seek to create conditions of justice for all. Mindful of this challenge, our larger project pursues a critique of Canadian health law and policy in an effort to explore the following questions: What is the impact of legal frameworks and forms of legal control that construct disability in women's lives so as to regulate their access to, and interactions with, the health system? What are the ways in which law operates to shape the social and economic policies and institutions that affect the health and well-being of women with disabilities? What are the norms operating through law to circumscribe the concept of health by reference to bodily markers? This chapter has a more particular emphasis: an analysis of aspects of confidentiality and disclosure of personal health-care information.

In this chapter, we introduce the theoretical framework in which this collaborative inquiry is grounded and describe the methods that have guided us along the way. To illustrate our approach, we set out, first, a detailed description and analysis of the legal requirement of confidentiality and disclosure of personal health information, coupled with an account of the experiences of women with disabilities who find themselves having to navigate this terrain. Here we demonstrate that the fundamental legal requirement that personal health information be kept confidential is breached, at times systematically, in the clinical encounter between women with disabilities and their health-care providers. We map out how basic tenets of the law – in particular, those concerning the disclosure of personal health information – are often neglected when the patient has a disability. Second, we analyze the use of personal health information in order to establish entitlements to disability-related income supports, demonstrating how the right to confidentiality is superseded by state interests when determining entitlement to social assistance benefits. What both examples illustrate are the ways in which gender and disability are constructed and regulated by legal rules and practices that shape the encounter between women with disabilities and health-care providers and gatekeepers.

Theoretical Underpinnings

This work seeks to build on contemporary feminist and disability scholarship and activism in local and international fora. To begin, we locate what are often considered the causes of disability within society and social organization, an approach well-established in critical disability scholarship dating back to the work of Michael Oliver: "We define impairment as lacking part of or all of a limb, or having a defective limb, organ or mechanism of the body; and *disability as the disadvantage or restriction of activity caused by a contemporary social organization which takes no or little account of people who have physical impairments and thus excludes them from participation in the mainstream of social activities*. Physical disability is therefore a particular form of social oppression" (Union of Physically Impaired Against Segregation [UPIAS] 1976 in Oliver 1996, 22 [emphasis added]).

We thus begin from the social model of disability, which casts disability as a political rather than medical category, a form of social oppression comparable to sexism, racism, and heterosexism. We adopt as our starting point a definition of disability not as some negative variation in human physiology, psychology, or genotype, but as the manifested outcome of social barriers and deeply entrenched patterns of oppression and discrimination.

Described as a "touchstone of Disability Rights politics and Disability Studies" (Thomas 1999, 16), the social model of disability has served as a central principle for both disability studies discourse and disability rights advocacy. Drawing from a materialist analysis and concerned primarily with issues of economic disadvantage and exclusion, a social model analysis has exposed the many barriers to disabled persons' citizenship, workforce participation, and economic self-determination (for further discussion of this, see the Introduction to this book, Chapter 6, and Chapter 7).

In its efforts to disrupt the pervasive cultural toxins of shame, pity, and charity that mask the social oppression of disabled people, an international community of disability rights activists has drawn from the social model in exposing a collective experience of disadvantage and discrimination. Building from this emancipatory foundation, our intention in this project is to both embrace and expand on the social model. In moving forward from this paradigm, we seek to attend to feminist critiques that the social model may operate to erase women's experience of impairment (French 1993; Crow 1996; Meekosha 2000; Pinder 1996). As Crow (1996, 210) puts it: "External disabling barriers may create social and economic disadvantage but our subjective experience of our bodies is also an integral part of our everyday reality." Drawing on feminist writings, we seek to include the experiences of women with disabilities in our research. By including women's experiences, we, like other feminists, wish to unsettle notions that some areas of life are private and personal, while others are public and political. In addition, our inclusion of women's experiences of impairment challenges the "epistemological foundations of the social sciences," in particular, the view that "there is such a thing as a scientific knowledge of the social which is unconnected to the social conditions ... of its own production" (Thomas 1999, 69). Following Haraway (1991) we work from the position that knowledge is always situated.[3]

To the extent that the social model theory has dichotomized disability as social and impairment as medical, it has been slow to extend critical attention to the subject of impairment, such reluctance apparently stemming from unease about any conciliatory nod toward essentialist medical framings of disablement. As contemporary scholars (Morris 1991; Crow 1996; Hughes 1999; Thomas 1999)[4] press to contest and reclaim the ground of impairment on terms that neither individualize nor pathologize the disability experience, we are persuaded that disabled bodies must not remain unexplored in critical discourse. Our inquiry recognizes that "it is the impaired body that is medically, technologically and culturally disciplined" (Meekosha 2000, 814) and seeks to illuminate the role of law in shaping these disciplinary forces. Moreover, the dominant social model theory, characterized as a disembodied approach to resolving problems (Pinder 1995), has been further criticized for its failure to take account of the experiences of persons with chronic illness and non-stable degenerative conditions. Pinder (1996, 137) reminds us that disability is not "everywhere constituted the same way," and suggests that "the body is embedded in a wider nexus of structure which render[s] a view of disability as social oppression alone over-simplistic."

Our study takes up this invitation to examine impairment as a relational inquiry. We enter into our research rooted in a social model perspective, but at the same time cognizant, as French and Crow have declared, that not every "problem" can be solved by social change. Along with Corker (1999, 639), we seek to examine a "dialogic relationship between disability and impairment," and to avoid totalizing claims about the social model's explanatory power. As Corker and Shakespeare (2002, 15) argue, "The global experience of disabled people is too complex to be rendered within one unitary model or set of ideas." Our framing of disability is both fluid and iterative, embracing both the politics of social and cultural disablement and the material reality of embodied impairment. To this end, we draw significantly from work by Carol Thomas (1999), who argues for a broadening of the social model beyond its primary focus – that focus being one of the social, economic, and political barriers restricting the activity of disabled people in society. Thomas suggests that

> Other dimensions of socially imposed restrictions should move more centre-stage ... [specifically] those which operate to shape personal identity, subjectivity or the landscapes of our interior worlds ... The focus should include not only a concern for what "we *do*" and "how we *act*" (are prevented from doing and acting) as disabled people, *but also a concern for "who we are" (are prevented from being), and how we feel and think about ourselves* ... This "inner world" dimension of disablism is closely bound up with sociocultural processes which generate negative attitudes about impairment and disability, and sustain prejudicial meanings, ideas, discourses, images and stereotypes. These impact upon disabled people in diverse ways and can lodge themselves in their subjectivities, sometimes with profoundly exclusionary consequences by working on their sense of personhood and self-esteem. (Thomas 1999, 46, 47-48 [emphasis added])

Following Thomas, we take up the challenge of identifying a relationship between law and policy on the one hand, and the "inner landscapes of identity," on the other hand. This relationship was writ large in our conversations with disabled women. The stories women shared echoed many of the constructions cited in the literature: disabled women as anxious, devious, and unintelligent (Sherwin 1992); outside the analytic categories of sex and nature (Butler 1990); inclined toward dangerous reproductivity (Meekosha 1998); asexual and unfeminine icons of deviance (Garland-Thomson 1997); socially invisible, without role or gender, childlike, helpless, and victimized (Fine and Asch 1988); abnormal, passive, and needy (Lonsdale 1990); and defective and undesirable as sexual partners or mothers (Kallianes and Rubenfeld 1997).

Garland-Thomson's (1997, 282) commentary on "asserting the body as a cultural text" reinforces our commitment to pursue an embodied discourse of gender and disability, and suggests how this task may be conceptualized without abandoning the social model. Reminding us that impairment – "the particularity of ... embodied experience" (282) – matters, she outlines alternative strategic framings of the body: "*Strategic constructionism* destigmatizes the disabled body (psychologically liberating subjects whose bodies have been narrated to them as defective), locates difference relationally, denaturalizes normalcy and challenges appearance [and functional] hierarchies. *Strategic essentialism* ... validates experience and consciousness, imagines community, authorizes history, and facilitates self-naming" (283 [emphasis added]). Garland-Thomson concludes, and we concur, that "the embodied difference that using a wheelchair or being deaf makes should be claimed, but without casting that difference as lack" (283).

In building from disabled women's narrative accounts of struggle and resistance, we seek to position disabled women not as "different, derivative, inferior and insufficient" (Garland-Thomson 1997, 280), but rather, as knowing agents and competent actors in health promotion and health care. As detailed in the following section, our study begins with the recounted experiences and encounters of individual women, proceeding outward to the broader social, cultural, economic, and political environments in which their experience is shaped. In this way, we have endeavoured to ground our analysis in the disabled women's subjective reality, drawing from narrative accounts both to shape an analytical framework and to develop directions for meaningful response. Such an approach avoids the problem decried by Oliver (1996, 45) that "most social research has tended to privilege methodology above experience and, as a consequence, does not have a very good track record in faithfully documenting that experience."

Methodological Grounding

Voices to Navigate by – Women's Primary Narratives

This study of disability, gender, and the law began with the voices of disabled women. Our objective was to engage women about the laws, policies, regulations, institutions, and actors that shape and order their encounters with health systems and impact on their experience of personal health and well-being. Following Davis (2000, 199), it was our goal to understand the extended institutional processes that organize the daily lives of disabled women and mobilize certain powers in, and over, their lives. Such a method allows us to think clearly about what institutional processes and conditions need to transform in order for women with disabilities to live less encumbered by oppressive rule.

Following a roundtable consultation and our own extensive literature reviews, we initially established three overarching themes of concern about the construction of gender and disability in law and policy:

- health care and the clinical encounter
- sexuality, reproduction, and parenting
- social and economic well-being.

A comprehensive review of legislative and policy frameworks across Canada affecting these concerns in relation to disabled women was clearly beyond the scope of this project. To narrow our purview, as a starting point we chose qualitative analysis of focus groups with women who experience disability so as to attend closely to the most significant aspects of these systems as described by disabled women themselves. These meetings, held at the outset of the project, quite literally focused our research and analysis.

The women's voices formed the boundaries of our discussion, directed our questions and research criteria, and created a critical filter for the wealth of policy and legislative information we gathered. The vividness of the women's stories, their strength, persistence, navigation skills, and clarity of analysis, pervaded every aspect of the project.

Three focus groups with disabled women were then held in Ontario, each concentrating on participants' experiences in relation to one of the overarching themes. Focus group participants were solicited through local disability organizations, key contacts in the disability community, women's community, and racialized women's community, and through community-based service providing organizations in the areas of health, socio-economic support, and reproduction. The groups that formed out of this methodology were each distinct in ways that related in part to the topics under discussion.

The focus group on health issues and the clinical encounter had the most diverse representation in terms of disability, race, ethnicity, socio-economic status, and age. In the group focusing on reproduction, sexuality, and parenting, all participants were mothers or were considering parenthood. A high proportion of the women in this group were white and heterosexual, had professional careers or qualifications, and were active in the disability community. They had a range of impairments, including mobility and sensory impairments and invisible disabilities. By contrast, the discussion group looking at socio-economic concerns included primarily poor women, women of colour, and immigrant women. Many of these women had been diagnosed with psychiatric impairments or had moderate physical disabilities. This group was larger than the others. Many had received services from the same community-based women's drop-in centre, and a number were marginally housed. Most were unemployed.

While the confidentiality of personal health information and its disclosure were raised directly by a number of women in the focus group on health issues and the clinical encounter, each of the three focus groups provided us with information and raised questions relevant to these issues. In our discussions with women in the focus group on socio-economic supports, we deepened our knowledge about the ways in which personal health information (which would otherwise be kept confidential) must be disclosed to government officials in order for one to qualify for access to socio-economic supports, disability tax credits, or assistive devices, for example. Moreover, the focus group on sexuality, reproduction, and family highlighted stereotypical assumptions about the needs and desires of women with disabilities that pervade the assessments of health-care providers and structure their interactions. While such stereotypes are damaging to the relationship between patient and physician within the confines of the clinical encounter, they are more harmful when information that would ordinarily be kept confidential is disclosed to other decision makers who rely on this information in the context of bureaucratic processes.

The differences in focus group composition stem partly from our method of soliciting participants. We targeted certain organizations and key contacts, and participation reflected the composition of those networks and their constituents. The marked differences in race, class, and disability type between the group discussing reproduction and the group discussing socioeconomic issues raises some questions. Certainly, we know from statistical data that, regardless of race, disabled persons are far more likely than non-disabled persons to be living in poverty. It is to some degree chance that more white women living in poverty were not present. Certainly, unintended overrepresentation of women from the same service organization skewed the findings, since this organization serves a particular niche. Yet, the predominance of women of colour in the economic group, and their absence in the group on reproduction, tags the intersection of race and disability. For example, many of the women in the economic group did not qualify for the Ontario Disability Support Program, for various reasons. To what degree does racism come into play here? Many also complained of barriers in getting a diagnosis of physical disability. Was this race linked? Was it because many had diagnoses of mental illness? Did racism and poverty play a part in this diagnosis? The absence of poor women and women of colour in the group concerned with sexuality and their reproductive rights suggests a question of relative privilege. Who in the disabled community can afford to consider having a family and feels entitled enough to fight for these rights? If a professional, middle-class, married, heterosexual woman with relatively adequate support services must fight so hard for this right, what are the chances of a poor, unemployed, single woman or lesbian aspiring mother to access the supports she needs? Finally, the more diverse representation in the focus group on health concerns raises further analytical questions. Is this a matter of chance, or has it something to do with the relationship between the health services system and disabled women? Can this be attributed to the medicalization of disability or the degree to which disabled women use the health system? Does the health system remain a primary juncture in the construction of disability and gender, regardless of disability type, race, age, or other factors? It is difficult at this point to answer these questions. Our sample size was small and intended to provide a lens for analysis rather than a quantitative survey investigating the intersection of disability, gender, race, age, and socio-economic status. Yet the issues are important.

Institutional Mapping and Sharpening our Focus
All three focus group discussions underwent three levels of analysis. First, we clustered issues and drew out common themes from women's own nar-

ratives of their encounters with health and social support systems. Second, we drew on these narratives to map the broad institutional relations structuring and organizing these encounters in an extra-local way. Common themes identified through the initial qualitative analysis were then reanalyzed by the research team, drawing out the policy and legal organization of the health-care system and clinical encounter; social and economic support systems; and sexuality, reproduction, and parenting systems. Issues that emerged as points of concern for women were isolated as discrete policy and legislative areas; these helped to focus the next step in the ethnography, a more detailed analysis of the legislative, common law, and policy review and mechanisms.

In our review of the focus group narratives, we observed the emergence of three key themes, each denoting a distinct phase or constellation of features in women's encounters with the legal and regulatory health system. Reading across the three overarching themes (health care and the clinical encounter; social and economic well-being; and sexuality, reproductive health, and parenting), we discovered recurring threads, ideas, and images – patterns of relationship and meaning cutting through the boundaries of medical, legal, and policy domains. Our focus on the reconstruction of disability and gender status therefore proceeded through an inquiry into three structures through which gender and disability are constructed within the environment of the health system: the gaze, the dialogue and the judgment. Below, we provide a brief description of what we mean in our use of each term. Later in this chapter we return to these three structures in our analysis of confidentiality and disclosure of personal health information.

- *The gaze* – the lens through which consumers of health-care service are observed, assessed, and presumed to be known.

    The gaze can be microscopic, focusing on symptoms, marks, and syndromes, or telescopic, focusing on the broad strokes of a label. In their narrative accounts, focus group participants revealed how meanings were instantaneously attached to their bodies, behaviours, and choices, and how they themselves were variously recognized as equals, lesser beings, or objects. Under the gaze of health-care authority, the disabled women who guided this study reported on how their identities were compromised, transformed, and severed.
- *The dialogue* – the "depth of field" that determines what is, and is not, included in the health transaction, rendering clear definition or suggestive blur.

    Whether it is reciprocal and open or unilateral and discriminatory, the dialogue captures the flow of information that forms the backdrop to every health-care decision. In their reflections on a range of health-related dialogues, focus group participants laid bare the arbitrary underpinnings

that determine the rules of engagement and that govern the selection, interpretation, direction, and exchange of information within the dialogue.
- *The judgment* – the snap of the shutter that brings closure to the dialogue and secures the object of the gaze within her assigned frame.

In the moment of judgment, a woman's role and status are acknowledged, constrained, or denied. With or without their concurrence, the disabled women who contributed to this study were fixed by judgment into positions of relative possibility, entitlement, and eligibility. Their accounts highlighted both permissive and restrictive judgments – some securing freedom and opportunity, others entrenching disadvantage and subjugation.

The information gathered in these ways helps to draw a map of health, social, and economic support, and of reproduction and family systems through which disabled women must manoeuvre. In addition, the data helps to identify the presumptions embedded in law and policy, and in the assumptions held, by those who enact this policy, about the nature of these women's bodies, experiences, needs, and limitations.

Our investigation of the ways in which women's experience of disability is constructed and regulated by systems of law and policy proceeded from an explicit acknowledgment that law and policy are powerful forces in the social construction and regulation of both gender and disability (Albiston, Brito, and Larson 2002, 3). Laws, regulations, and policies mobilize and perpetuate ideals and assumptions about the nature and meaning of both gender and disability. Our aim in this investigation is both descriptive and analytical, involving a mapping of the elements of the regulatory framework that governs encounters between women who experience disability and the health-care system, as well as an inquiry into the manner and extent to which each of these elements advances or restricts their interests. For the purposes of this chapter, we focus on the legal frameworks governing confidentiality and disclosure of health information in two settings: first, when the encounter takes place in a therapeutic context; and second, when the health-care provider is enlisted by both the state and the disabled woman to attest to the existence and degree of disability, in order to determine eligibility for government income-support programs.

Health Information: Confidentiality and Disclosure[5]
In this section we interrogate the ways in which women with disabilities, and the concept of disability itself, are constructed by laws and policies. We also analyze women's experiences within these frameworks, and how these representations of disability and gender condition women's characterization, treatment, and entitlements. Our examination of the first context, the clinical encounter, reveals a troubling pattern of departures from the legal

obligation to maintain confidentiality when people with disabilities seek treatment. By contrasting the requirement that those treating patients keep information about patients' health status and care confidential with women's experiences in the health-care system, we illustrate how clinicians and administrators can, and do, neglect the law and the interests it is meant to protect. Relative to the second context – establishing entitlement to social assistance – we trace the assumptions and implications that underlie the wide-ranging disclosure, collection, assessment, and transmission of intimate health information required when individuals seek disability-related income support. Here, we identify how laws, regulations, and policies shape disabled women's interactions with health systems and health-care providers differently, as the state imposes requirements of surveillance, disclosure, and judgment that supersede the right to confidentiality.

The Clinical Encounter

We were struck by the contrast between the law's strong promise of protection for confidentiality and the experience of women with disabilities in the context of the clinical encounter. Individuals' right to privacy of their health-care information and health status is an important aspect of the right to autonomy and bodily integrity. It grounds the right to control how information about one's health is used, and to whom it is released. The Supreme Court of Canada has recognized that such information "goes to the personal integrity and autonomy of the patient" (*McInerney v. MacDonald* 1992, 422). People will reveal the most intimate aspects of their lives (and of others') to health-care providers in the disclosures they may have to make so that they can be diagnosed accurately and treated appropriately. Health records will chronicle the patient's history, as well as past care, and serve as a direction for the future. Because of the special trust and confidence that patients place in physicians, the court has characterized this aspect of the physician-patient relationship as fiduciary, meaning that the doctor must act with the utmost good faith and loyalty toward the patient (423). The court has also confirmed that individuals have a continuing interest in, and ability to exercise control over, health information, as it "remains in a fundamental sense one's own" (422).

Health-care providers have a legal duty to keep information received from or about a patient confidential. Conversely, they also owe a duty to disclose information about a patient's health status and care to him or her, subject to a very narrow therapeutic exception when there are reasonable grounds to believe that the patient could not cope with the disclosure (*McInerney v. MacDonald* 1992, 426-27). That common law duty has been made explicit in statutes, regulations, and providers' codes of conduct. In Ontario, for instance, according to O. Reg. 856/93, s. 1(1), it is professional misconduct for physicians to give information about a patient's condition, or

any services provided to her, to anyone other than the patient or her authorized representative, unless the patient has consented, or unless the disclosure is required by law. Other health professions are subject to similar
obligations to maintain patient confidentiality (Marshall and von Tigerstrom
2000).

The right to maintain the privacy of one's health information is protected
not just at common law but also under the Canadian constitution. As Justice La Forest noted in *R. v. Dyment* (1988, 431-32), a Supreme Court of
Canada decision addressing the constitutionality of police seizing blood
samples without the consent of an accused suspected of impaired driving:
"The use of a person's body without his consent to obtain information about
him, invades an area of personal privacy essential to the maintenance of his
human dignity." The seizure was held to contravene the *Canadian Charter of
Rights and Freedoms*. Constitutional protection extends beyond the criminal
context to civil lawsuits involving government action (*Canadian AIDS Society v. Ontario* 1995). Even where the Charter does not apply directly (being
limited to government action), courts are still to apply Charter values (*Hill
v. Church of Scientology of Toronto* 1995). Although the right to privacy is not
absolute at common law or under the constitution (*Franco v. White* 2001),
courts do not override it lightly.

In the course of treatment, disclosure of patients' health information to
other health professionals caring for the patient is generally permitted by
both the governing bodies of regulated health professions, and by policy
and practice in hospitals and institutions (see, for example, O. Reg. 856/93,
s.1(2)(a)). Sharing information is considered necessary to ensure safe and
effective care. Disclosure is allowed for instrumental reasons – to benefit, or
at least avoid harming, the patient.

However, for many people with disabilities, disclosure has not been directed toward their health care or their well-being at all. Rather than the
assiduous concern for their privacy interests that the law requires of health-
care providers, the experience of persons with disabilities has often been
quite the opposite. Their privacy interests have routinely been violated.
Sometimes this is from sheer inattention or lack of thought. Sometimes it is
deliberate, out of a paternalistic desire to do what is best, and sometimes,
because the person is an interesting "case" and, consequently, useful for
educating or confounding other health-care providers. As Carol Gill (1997,
105) relates: "Most women with disabilities can recount disturbing experiences of medical exams performed with doors or curtains left ajar, information about our private lives carelessly discussed in public places, or authorities
monitoring and reporting our sexual behavior. Another form of violation
so pervasive and traumatic to us that we have labeled it and categorized it
as abuse is 'public stripping': the practice of being forced to disrobe and
display our different-looking bodies in medical educational settings ...

often before mixed audiences of professionals and non-professionals or photographers." Focus group participants recounted similar experiences. One woman recalled: "I spent half of my life in hospital. I was half the time in the conference room in front of the doctors, bending over so they could see how crooked my back was. When I had my last surgery in 1995 my neurologist was literally drooling over my chart. He was saying, 'This is a wonderful case. I can't believe it!' I thought it was inappropriate. It might be interesting from a scientific point of view, but I don't have to see your pleasure." Another agreed: "You're usually in a state of undress and there are all these people looking at you like you're a science experiment. It screws up your self-image. I've been overweight most of my life and doctors'd always comment on that. I would end up eating more, to comfort myself. I felt very – I felt like I wasn't even human."

For many women with disabilities, the clinical encounter is not an experience of privacy and trust, nor one in which information about their condition and needs is truly heard. Rather, the gaze of the health-care professional is often focused exclusively on the impairment, reinforcing a medical model of disability that locates disablement within the individual. This is not to suggest that the material reality of embodiment should be ignored in the health-care encounter, but, in this context, it needs to be situated and understood within the broader social, economic, and political landscape that constructs disablement. Underpinning the legal requirement of confidentiality in the patient-physician relationship is an assumption about the conditions necessary for a patient to feel secure enough to communicate information relevant to her health and well-being. This is information that health-care professionals are to use in providing assistance to that patient. Stated bluntly, the purpose of the interaction is to benefit that patient. Implicit in this encounter is the need for an open dialogue between physician and patient, one in which patients are consulted, listened to, and heard, and in which their embodied experience forms the basis of clinical assessment.

In our focus groups it became apparent that the women with whom we spoke did not often feel included in the dialogue or judgment about their well-being. Rather, as suggested by the participants above, dialogue was something that took place either between professionals or between health-care professionals and family members, over the body and head of the disabled woman, who was rendered the object at the centre of their gaze but not involved as a participant in the conversation or judgment. As one focus group participant described:

They decided to do experiments on me. They put me in the hospital for a week. They gave me a pill. I have no idea what that pill was. I used to have epileptic seizures, but it didn't have to do [with] that. That one week turned to two, three, four. The pill wasn't even for my seizures. After I was in there four weeks, he called me in and said: "This isn't working because [you're] not walking. So, I would like to operate." My dad said: "What are you going to do?" "Well," [the doctor] said, "We're going to open up her skull and inject some fluid." My father said: "No way." The doctor said: "You know it's my work." My dad said: "No way." The doctor said to my dad: "There's a doctor coming in next week from Switzerland; if he says she's going to benefit, you're not going to have a choice." It's not possible, but my parents didn't know that. The doctor came and I saw him; and it was amazing. *He looked at me and talked at me for two minutes.* He looked over my head at my doctor and said: "You are crazy. The minute you open her head she won't make it." The other doctor said nothing ... He was basically experimenting on me. (emphasis added)

For women with disabilities, the gaze, or look, of health-care profession-als, especially when not accompanied by the reciprocal exchange of infor-mation between them, often affects their self-esteem and self-image. This is exacerbated at the moment of judgment, when they are advised to undergo invasive procedures, the purpose of which is to make their bodies more closely conform to norms of female bodily structure or appearance and Western ideals of feminine beauty. As one participant put it: "It's just us, really; society is just a mirror of what's going on with people. I know with my daughter, [who has] Down's syndrome ... I know of at least one person who had facial reconstruction and tongue surgery for no other reason but aesthetics."

The women involved in the focus groups drew attention to the signifi-cance of gender in these encounters. Gender exacerbates the power differ-ential between doctor and patient, making resistance or refusal to participate more difficult. The exposure imposed on women in displaying their physi-cal condition to a doctor's colleagues and others ignored the effect of this practice on them. It also reinforced their reduction to the status of an inter-esting condition, rather than another human being:

I grew up with a disability, and was in the medical system all my life ... with the view that disability is something very wrong. In the medical field, as a child, you go to appointment after appointment, with them observing your body as an object. Literally stripped down to your underwear. At the time, they would literally make me walk across the room, in my underwear, in front of fifty doctors – men – in front of my dad. My dad felt he was obli-gated to be there. That's just wrong. Nothing ever came out of those "tests." The only reason this happens is for their information. They're curious. It wasn't like I was being fit for a brace. This happened repeatedly. When you are raised that way, you feel like your body is something to be looked at, talked about, and touched by other people.

As another participant remarked: "They say: 'This is medically interesting.' But I'm not there for your medical interest, I'm there for my problems. You feel like a research project. Like a body, not a person." The messages of objectification that imbued these encounters were clear to the women who had been subjected to them. Tellingly, their doctors did not notice, or did not think them significant enough to restructure the experience or rethink the need for it entirely. People with disabilities are not unique in experiencing interactions with health-care providers as sometimes dehumanizing, or in feeling vulnerable in clinical encounters. However, the degree of invasiveness, the frequency of medical scrutiny, and the extent of the disregard that many people with disabilities endure have been of a different and far more onerous order of magnitude.

Disability and Income Support – An Institutionalized End to Confidentiality

For people with disabilities, medical scrutiny may not even notionally be linked to health care meant to benefit them. People with disabilities are more likely to live in poverty than those without disabilities (Fawcett 1996, 130; Ross, Shillington, and Lochhead 2000, 76; Canada 2000, 72, 74; McColl et al. 2005; Wilton 2005). Government transfers and income-support programs are crucially important to many who experience disability, and have become increasingly significant in sustaining low-income households in recent years; indeed, they made up 90 percent of total income for households in the lowest income quintiles in 1997 (Ross, Shillington, and Lochhead 2000, xxiii). By every indicator, women are more severely affected by the harsh economic realities frequently associated with disability than are men and, consequently, are more likely to depend on government income support (Ross, Shillington, and Lochhead 2000, 76).

However, these programs are targeted, and applicants have to establish their eligibility and ongoing entitlement. To do so, people with disabilities must submit to extensive and ongoing medical scrutiny, as well as other forms of evaluation. The otherwise stringent legal protection accorded an individual's right to confidentiality of her health information and described in the preceding section gives way to what are seen as more pressing objectives when an individual seeks disability-based benefits: ensuring the state's ability to learn or confirm information about the person's health status, financial situation, and needs, and to obtain broad access to information about the applicant/recipient in order to detect and prevent deceit. The deep poverty in which many women with disabilities live and their almost total reliance on government support mean that they are particularly vulnerable not only to restrictions and cutbacks in government transfer programs but also to uninformed judgments about them by health professionals and harsh interpretations of the legislation and regulations governing eligibility by the many bureaucratic decision makers involved in administering these programs (Gilmour and Martin 2003).

Examining how eligibility for social assistance is determined highlights the ways in which boundaries between public and private spheres shift, and the role of the state in setting and patrolling that divide. There is a marked contrast in how public and private are determined when one is poor. Not all citizens are entitled to claim private lives free from state scrutiny and control. Those who fit the norm – one that increasingly emphasizes independence and self-reliance – can resist state intrusion, and call on the state to protect their privacy. Yet, for persons or families who need assistance from the state, the assumption of a private realm goes by the board – state surveillance and control is the norm. Feminist writers have long pointed out the state's role in regulating social and economic relations, even in the absence of express laws (Olsen 1983; Boyd 1997, 13). This includes areas that are ostensibly private, notably family life. When individuals and families deviate from the norm of the "self-reliant citizen" (Cossman and Fudge 2002) and turn to the state, their lives are extensively regulated and monitored. The state does not protect their privacy, but rather, does away with it. Social assistance applicants are required to self-report, disclosing intimate details of their lives to the state on an ongoing basis, and also must authorize and even orchestrate reporting by others, including their treating health professionals and family members. Relationships that are otherwise private are enlisted in the service of the state. Access to the limited resources provided under the general and disability income-support regimes is dependent on compliance.

Redrawing the boundary between public and private in these ways affects many disabled people particularly harshly, especially women with disabilities. As noted above, people with disabilities are more likely than non-disabled people to live in poverty, dependent on government transfers and income-support programs. And women are even more economically disadvantaged than men. Consequently, they are more likely to be subject to the regimes of intensified surveillance and control that the law imposes. The impact on how these women organize their lives and see themselves is profound, as the extracts from interviews with focus group participants below make clear.

In Ontario, the provincial government provides both income and employment supports to people with disabilities who meet specified conditions. It does so through the Ontario Disability Support Program (ODSP), an initiative put in place in 1998 together with a companion general welfare program, Ontario Works, as part of a substantial revamping of the social assistance system in the province. The governing legislation, the *Ontario Disability Support Program Act, 1997 (ODSPA)*, sets out a mix of objectives that are marked by tension between benevolence and discipline. First and foremost is the benevolent goal of providing income and employment supports to "eligible persons" with disabilities and "effectively serv[ing] persons with disabilities who need assistance" (*ODSPA*, section 1(a) and (c)). This is an expansive understanding of state responsibilities. However, second, this is tempered by the statutory admonition that communities, families, and individuals share that responsibility with government, a justification for the state limiting and even contracting its role (*ODSPA*, section 1(b); Prince 2001, 19-20). Third, the statute emphasizes the need for cost control and discipline in its requirement that the program must be "accountable to the taxpayers of Ontario" (*ODSPA*, section 1(d)). While one would expect this condition to be so basic an expectation of all government programs as to go without saying (as it generally does), this legislation makes the call for fiscal responsibility explicit, inferentially highlighting fears of overly generous benefit levels, fraud, and recipients' getting "something for nothing."

ODSPA requires that income support be provided to any Ontario resident over the age of eighteen who falls within the statutory definition of a person with a disability or who is a member of a prescribed class (*ODSPA*, sections 3 and 4). The applicant bears the onus of establishing that she qualifies for assistance. Among other requirements, she must make extensive disclosure of and provide access to financial, health, and other personal information and records for herself as well as her dependents. Failure to comply with conditions of eligibility can result in refusal, cancellation, or reduction in the income support payable.

The constant awareness that one's eligibility and abilities are monitored and that one can lose entitlement to benefits is a pervasive source of stress in the lives of the women who participated in the focus groups. As one woman recounted: "What I hate about welfare, they have a lot of investigation on me. I feel like a criminal, but I'm just sick. They want to know how I get money from [the] insurance lawyer. Like I'm a criminal. It hurt me. I did nothing, the only thing I ask is to survive. I ask for a bed; they don't give me a bed. They don't give me for laundry, for telephone. I keep painful in my heart ... So I talk to my friends, who have the same experience. What is the crime? Just because we are poor?" Although ODSP was introduced as an expansive new program formulated in response to what people with disabilities had requested, the enforcement provisions are the same as those in the Ontario Works program (Beatty 1998). *ODSPA* anticipates the same monitoring and surveillance to detect breaches or non-compliance. Sanctions are identical as well (Gilmour and Martin 2003).

ODSPA defines a "person with a disability" as follows:

4(1) A person is a person with a disability for the purposes of this Part if,
(a) the person has a substantial physical or mental impairment that is continuous or recurrent and expected to last one year or more;
(b) the direct and cumulative effect of the impairment on the person's ability to attend to his or her personal care, function in the community and function in a workplace, results in a substantial restriction in one or more of these activities of daily living; and
(c) the impairment and its likely duration and the restriction in the person's activities of daily living have been verified by a person with the prescribed qualifications.

The definition locates both the impairments and any limitations on the person's ability to attend to the activities of daily living squarely within the individual. In that, its adherence to a medical model of disability is clear – it is premised on the assumption that the person cannot participate because he or she is too impaired to do so. The statutory definition states that a person has a disability within the meaning of the act if he or she has a substantial physical or mental impairment expected to last more than a year, and the *effect of the impairment* is to substantially restrict the person's ability to attend to personal care or function in the community or workplace. There is no recognition that barriers built into existing physical, economic, and social structures and arrangements can be the cause of not only substantial limitations on the person's ability to participate but also complete exclusion from what are, as the statute recognizes, "activities of daily living."

The act requires that the nature of the impairment, how long it will last, and how it affects the person's daily life be "verified by a person with the prescribed qualifications" (*ODSPA*, section 4(1)(c)). The categories of health professionals authorized to do so are limited (*ODSPR* 222, section 46). Social assistance programs have long relied on clinical judgment in determining whether a person meets the conditions for eligibility, that is, falls within the program's definition of disabled. This type of clinical encounter – in which the health professional assesses a person's impairments (the gaze), evaluates the extent to which she is prevented from participating in the life of the community (the dialogue), and reports that determination with supporting documentation and reasons to program administrators (the judgment) – is not undertaken for therapeutic reasons. A clinical judgment that the person is substantially disabled is, however, one of the prerequisites to be met before the state will accept that a person is entitled to disability benefits.

ODSP is premised on the assumption that, as Deborah Stone (1984, 148) notes in her study of the American Social Security Disability Insurance program, "most people would prefer to be in the needs-based distribution system (in other words, they don't want to work) and that inability to work is highly subject to deception." Accordingly, to limit the availability of this form of benefit and continue the primacy of a work-based rather than needs-based distribution system, "disability" was made a restricted and narrow category, with what are meant to be objectively ascertainable boundaries. Clinical criteria and clinical methodology applied by health professionals are expected to ensure that the determination is objective. The underlying expectation is that, when applied by experts, these assessment mechanisms accurately identify well-founded claims, and weed out people who do not fall within the statutory definition. Physician certification is widely employed as the "validating device" for disability, and the resulting claim to social aid is legitimized on that basis (Stone 1984, 21). Effectively, verification by a health professional is taken to confirm that the impairment and restrictions on activities are legitimate, and neither contrived nor exaggerated. This is the power of judgment.

However, before such judgment, there is a form of dialogue: the information and assessment ODSP requires from health-care providers is such that, of necessity, it will have to elicit a considerable amount of the information from the applicant. Even though the source of information about the individual's abilities and limitations will often be the applicant herself, her information is considered reliable in the disability determination process only when it is accepted by the health professional and relayed to program administrators. Professional discourse and judgment alone are considered authoritative. In emphasizing this point, we are not suggesting that health providers do not, or cannot, legitimately bring their expertise and independent judgment to bear on these questions. It is troubling, though, that the applicant's knowledge of what her life is like is discounted as uninformed, or disregarded as dissembling, unless and until it is confirmed by a professional. This is particularly so, given that many health-care providers know little about the lives of people experiencing disability. Time and again, studies undertaken by disabled women's organizations and others attuned to disability issues have concluded that health-care providers often do not know about the impact of their patients' impairments, nor do they appropriately assess and meet their needs for health care (Odette 1993; Denham and Gillespie 1994; Masuda 1999; Morrow 2000; DAWN Ontario, n.d.).

Women in the focus group on access to health care confirmed that their experiences in the health-care system clearly demonstrated that health professionals need more education about disability, as well as about the ways in which impairments interact with other factors, such as aging. As one participant put it: "They don't know about disability. They don't have a clue. My doctor will say: 'I don't know why that happened. I have no idea.' She's the only doctor I've ever had who has said that. We often know more [about disability than they do]." Another said: "Usually if it's a doctor that's never seen me, they'll ask what my condition is and write that down. Most doctors don't know about disability. They don't know a lot about aging and disability. Most times you have to explain to them how your disability impacts on what you do." Women with disabilities can be discriminated against because doctors lack information about the effect of their impairment.

The framework and content of the ODSP assessments construct what an applicant has to be like in order to satisfy the authorities that she is disabled and therefore entitled to benefits. People with conditions that are not readily apparent, such as debilitating depression, may not be believed when they recount their experiences or describe how the condition affects their lives. They do not fit the gaze. Some illnesses and conditions can fluctuate; there may be unpredictable periods of remission or reduced severity. Day-to-day variations in ability to function are easily overlooked – a day one can manage to attend a medical appointment is often a good day, though an assessment based on how the applicant performs that day may not accurately reflect what she usually experiences. Nor is there explicit recognition that an individual's impairments may not be serious enough to meet the *ODSPA* definition of disability if assessed individually, but taken together, their cumulative effect is such that the person is substantially restricted in personal care, work, or participation in the community. Throughout the ODSP process, disability is constructed as a fixed condition located in the individual. The *ODSPA* does not lend itself to understanding disability as fluid: contingent on degree of impairment, but also, and importantly, on social, political, and environmental context and the lived experiences of the embodied woman. Rather, the legislation and its administration favour a gaze that fixes disability as a frame of reference and circumscribes its form and content.

A perverse result of the disability determination process is that the limited conception of disability, and of people with disabilities that this conception imposes, spills over beyond the administrative requirements of the social assistance system. Moreover, this conception is incorporated, both generally and by people with disabilities themselves, to become internalized as synonymous with what disability *is*. In the face of the strong emphasis on the person being *un*able to function and being *in*competent, her experiences of ability must be buried or she runs the risk of being disqualified for benefits despite her obvious need for assistance (Doe and Kimpson 1999). A woman in one of the focus groups recounted such an experience: "They said to my daughter, does she cook, and she said she has her own kitchen. And they said, if she can use her kitchen she doesn't need a scooter."

Because of her abilities in one area, she was ineligible for assistance to obtain the mobility device she needed so that she could participate in other areas. Further, as Alfieri (1992) points out, the discursive practices of victimization and helplessness are not only inscribed in the social assistance system's disability determination process but, as a result, also structure the discourse of disability advocacy that challenges denials of benefits. In short, the gaze may be internalized.

The physician's role in the disability determination system is fraught with tension. A physician-patient relationship is built on trust. In recommending treatment, a physician makes determinations meant to advance his or her patient's interests, and certainly not to harm her. The disability determination process requires both the physician and patient to assume different roles and obligations. The patient is now depending on her physician as an applicant to the social assistance system, rather than as a patient requiring treatment. And the physician is assessing the patient and judging the degree of her impairment and its effects, thus functioning in a dual capacity as the filter used by the social assistance program to detect deception and exaggeration by the applicant, and as the validation the patient needs to establish entitlement to benefits. The system relies on the physician to act as gatekeeper not only to ensure cost control but also to prevent fraudulent or otherwise unfounded claims. The patient relies on her physician to support her claim for disability benefits and thus better her circumstances. Professional and societal norms and incentives can pull both ways (Stone 1984, 149-52; Shortell et al. 1998). Health professionals provide important support for patients in this process, and their assessment and advocacy is often essential to convince administrators that the disability claimed is real (*Lalonde v. London Life Insurance Co.* 2001). At the same time, however, health-care providers' general lack of knowledge about the lives of women experiencing disability can lead them to seriously underestimate the extent to which their patients are precluded from carrying out activities of daily living, or to dismiss what their patients tell them, such that they fail to recognize disability, and underestimate the difficulty of functioning with an impairment in a society premised on being able-bodied.

There is something troubling about a process for assessing disability that relies so heavily on evaluations from professionals working within a medicalized frame. Rarely is the understanding of disability demonstrated by health-care professionals informed by a social model of disability that situates impairment in a larger social, economic, and environmental context. To the extent that ODSP is a remedy or program to provide support for disability, it is disability understood through the social model, and not just impairment, that needs to be considered and assessed. A focus on a medical definition of disability (most commonly, impairment) removes from the frame of assessment, evaluation, and judgment the experience of women with disabilities whose lives reside at the intersection of impairment and the social context. In a clinical encounter, both physician and patient have only partial knowledge: the scientific expertise of the physician and the experiential, lived perspective of the patient each interpret only one dimension of their shared concern – the patient's illness or present condition (Komesaroff 1995, 98). Power and authority in that relationship, however, rest with the physician, particularly in questions of the disability determination required to establish entitlement to government transfers and income-support programs. Given health-care providers' circumscribed and often derivative knowledge of life with a disability, acknowledging the distinctive authority of the patient's voice would make for more informed decision making. Such a change would not replace the physician's authority but would alter the current distribution of power in order to augment understanding of the patient's condition. The gaze needs to be expanded, the dialogue opened up, and the judgment cognizant of the complex and hierarchical relationships involved.

Conclusion

To achieve the task mandated for this project, a simple barriers analysis is inadequate. Removing barriers to community, health care, and employment alone offers no assurance that women who experience disability will be valued or will have full opportunity to exercise self-determination. Thus, improving access to health care and other health-related supports for women who experience disability cannot be our exclusive goal.

Instead, we need to deepen the focus of our analysis from barriers to meaning and identity. The central inquiry, as we demonstrate, becomes an exploration of how women who experience disability are compelled to take up predetermined positions and relationships, coupled with an examination of the nature of these constructions and an analysis of their inherent limits and constraints. From this point of departure, we can begin to explore strategies of active resistance to the dominant and oppressive meanings assigned to the status of "disabled woman."

Our first task in this project has been to lay out the systems whereby the status of disability is established – through law, regulation, cultural practice, stereotype, policy, and design. Rather than conducting an inquiry into the nature and extent of discrimination in the encounters between women who experience disability and the health system, we chose to characterize how these systems assign status in their recognition of women whose physical and intellectual characteristics differ from a majoritarian norm. This phase of the project sketches, *from the vantage point of women who experience disability*, the outline and contours of a system reliant on a physician-defined disability status. Its starting point is an examination of the social, relational, and identity positions that women who experience disability are compelled to take up, the meanings of these positions, and the various ways in which they are imposed and enforced.

Notes

1 C.M. Wade, "Thoughts on the 'Right to Die with Dignity,'" in *Electric Edge* (March/April 1997), web ed. *Ragged Edge* (30 November 2003).
2 This chapter is part of a much larger project entitled "The Legal Regulation and Construction of the Gendered Body and of Disability in Canadian Health Law and Policy," undertaken with funding from the National Network on Environments and Women's Health (NNEWH), one of the five Centres of Excellence for Women's Health, which are funded by the Women's Health Bureau of Health Canada.
3 For an excellent and thorough discussion of the epistemological importance of experience in feminist engagement with disability, see Thomas 1999, 69-80.
4 Cited and discussed in Claire Tregaskis, "Social Model Theory: The Story So Far ..." *Disability and Society* 17, 4 (2002): 457.
5 Legislation to expand the protection accorded personal information has been enacted recently: at the federal level, the *Personal Information Protection and Electronic Documents Act*, S.C. 2000, c. 5, and in Ontario, the *Personal Health Information Protection Act, 2004*, S.O. 2004, c. 3. Both legislative initiatives are too recent to have affected the experience of focus group participants and, consequently, are not analyzed further in this chapter.

References

Albiston, Catherine, Tonya Brito, and Jane E. Larson. 2002. Feminism in relation. *Wisconsin Women's Law Journal* 17: 1-21.

Alfieri, Anthony. 1992. Disabled clients, disabling lawyers. *Hastings Law Journal* 43: 769-851.

Beatty, Harry. 1999. Ontario disability support program: Policy and implementation. *Journal of Law and Social Policy* 14: 1-68.

Boyd, Susan. 1997. Introduction: Challenging the public/private divide: An overview. In *Challenging the public/private divide: Feminism, law and public policy*, ed. Susan Boyd, 3-36. Toronto: University of Toronto Press.

Butler, Judith. 1990. *Gender trouble: Feminism and the subversion of identity*. New York: Routledge.

Canada. Federal, Provincial, and Territorial Ministers Responsible for Social Services. 2000. *In unison: Persons with disabilities in Canada*. Hull: Human Resources Development Canada.

Canadian AIDS Society v. Ontario (1995), 25 O.R. (3d) 388 (Gen. Div.); aff'd. (1997), 31 O.R. (3d) 798 (C.A.).

Corker, Mairian. 1999. Differences, conflations and foundations: The limits to "accurate" theoretical representation of disabled people's experience? *Disability and Society* 14, 5: 627-42.

Corker, Mairian, and Tom Shakespeare. 2002. Mapping the terrain. In *Disability/postmodernity: Embodying disability theory*, ed. Mairian Corker and Tom Shakespeare, 1-17. London: Continuum.

Cossman, Brenda, and Judy Fudge. 2002. Introduction: Privatization, law and the challenge to feminism. In *Privatization, law and the challenge to feminism*, ed. Brenda Cossman and Judy Fudge, 3-40. Toronto: University of Toronto Press.

Crow, Liz. 1996. Including all of our lives: Renewing the social model of disability. In *Encounters with strangers: Feminism and disability*, ed. Jenny Morris, 206-29. London: Women's Press.

Davis, John M. 2000. Disability studies as ethnographic research and text: Research strategies and roles for promoting social change? *Disability and Society* 15, 2: 191-206.

DAWN Ontario (DisAbled Women's Network Ontario). N.d. *Women with disabilities: A guide for health care professionals*. Toronto: DAWN Ontario.

Denham, D., and J. Gillespie. 1994. *A process of change: Health and disabled women project 1990-1994: Evaluator's report*. Toronto: DAWN Ontario.

Doe, Tanis, and Sally Kimpson. 1999. *Enabling income: CPP disability benefits and women with disabilities.* Ottawa: Status of Women Canada's Policy Research Fund.

Fawcett, Gail. 1996. *Living with disability in Canada: An economic portrait.* Hull: Human Resources Development Canada, Office for Disability Issues.

Fine, Michelle, and Adrienne Asch. 1988. Introduction: Beyond pedestals. In *Women with disabilities: Essays in psychology, culture, and politics,* ed. Michelle Fine and Adrienne Asch, 1-37. Philadelphia: Temple University Press.

Franco v. White (2001), 53 O.R. (3d) 391, 413 (C.A.).

French, Sally. 1993. Disability, impairment or something in between? In *Disabling barriers– enabling environments,* ed. John Swain, Vic Finkelstein, Sally French, and Mike Oliver, 17-25. London: Sage.

Garland-Thomson, Rosemarie. 1997. Feminist theory, the body, and the disabled figure. In *The disability studies reader,* ed. Lennard Davis, 279-92. London: Cassell.

Gill, Carol. 1997. The last sisters: Health issues of women with disabilities. In *Women's health: Complexities and differences,* ed. S.B. Ruzek, V. Olesen, and A. Clarke, 96-111. Columbus: Ohio State University Press.

Gilmour, Joan, and Dianne Martin. 2003. Women's poverty, women's health: The role of access to justice. In *Head, heart, hand: Partnerships for women's health in Canadian environments,* ed. Penny Van Esterik, 353-81. Toronto: National Network on Environments and Women's Health.

Haraway, Donna. 1991. *Simians, cyborgs and women: The reinvention of nature.* London: Free Association Books.

Hill v. Church of Scientology of Toronto, [1995] 2 S.C.R. 1130.

Hughes, Bill. 1999. The constitution of impairment: Modernity and the aesthetic of oppression. *Disability and Society* 14, 2: 155-72.

Kallianes, Virginia, and Phyllis Rubenfeld. 1997. Disabled women and reproductive rights. *Disability and Society* 12, 2: 203-22.

Komesaroff, Paul. 1995. *Troubled bodies: Critical perspectives on postmodernism, medical ethics and the body.* Durham, NC: Duke University Press.

Lalonde v. London Life Insurance Co. (2001), 55 O.R. (3d) 26 (Sup. Ct.).

Lonsdale, Susan. 1990. *Women and disability: The experience of physical disability among women.* London: Macmillan.

McColl, Mary Ann, Alison James, William Boyce, and Sam Shortt. 2005. Disability policy making: Evaluating the evidence base. Chapter 1, this volume.

McInerney v. MacDonald (1992), 93 D.L.R. (4th) 415 (S.C.C.).

Marshall, Mary, and Barbara von Tigerstrom. 2000. Privacy, confidentiality and the regulation of health information. In *Canadian health law practice manual,* ed. Mary Jane Dykeman, chap. 3. Toronto: Butterworths.

Masuda, Shirley. 1999. *Women with disabilities: We know what we need to be healthy!* Vancouver: BC Centre of Excellence for Women's Health and DAWN Canada.

Meekosha, Helen. 1998. Body battles: Bodies, gender and disability. In *The disability reader: Social science perspectives,* ed. Tom Shakespeare, 163-80. London: Cassell.

–. 2000. A disabled genius in the family: Personal musings on the tale of two sisters. *Disability and Society* 15, 5: 811-15.

Morris, Jenny. 1991. *Pride against prejudice: Transforming attitudes to disability.* London: Women's Press.

Morrow, Mary. 2000. *The challenges of change: The midlife health needs of women with disabilities.* Vancouver: B.C. Centre of Excellence for Women's Health and DAWN Canada.

O. Reg. 856/93, made under the *Medicine Act, 1991,* S.O. 1991, c. 30.

Odette, Fran, ed. 1993. *Staying healthy in the nineties: Women with disabilities talk about healthcare.* Toronto: DAWN Toronto.

[ODSPR 222] O. Reg. 222/98, made under the *Ontario Disability Support Program Act,* being Schedule B to the *Social Assistance Reform Act,* S.O. 1997, c. 25 [*ODSPR 222*].

Oliver, Michael. 1996. *Understanding disability: From theory to practice.* London: Macmillan.

Olsen, Frances. 1983. The family and the market: A study of ideology and legal reform. *Harvard Law Review* 96, 7: 1497-578.

Ontario Disability Support Program Act, 1997, being Schedule B to the *Social Assistance Reform Act,* S.O. 1997, c. 25 [*ODSPA*].

Pinder, Ruth. 1995. Bringing back the body without the blame: The experience of ill and disabled people at work. *Sociology of Health and Illness* 17, 5: 605-31.

–. 1996. Sick-but-fit or fit-but-sick? Ambiguity and identity at the workplace. In *Exploring the divide: Illness and disability,* ed. Colin Barnes and Geof Mercer, 135-56. Leeds: Disability Press.

Prince, Michael. 2001. Governing in an integrated fashion: Lessons from the disability domain. Ottawa: Canadian Policy Research Networks.

R. v. Dyment, [1988] 2 S.C.R. 417.

Rich, Adrienne. 1976. *Of woman born: Motherhood as experience and institution.* New York: W.W. Norton.

Ross, David, E. Richard Shillington, and Clarence Lochhead. 2000. *The Canadian fact book on poverty 2000.* Ottawa: Canadian Council on Social Development.

Sherwin, Susan. 1992. *No longer patient: Feminist ethics and health care.* Philadelphia: Temple University Press.

Shortell, Stephen, Teresa Waters, Kenneth Clarke, and Peter Budetti. 1998. Physicians as double agents: Maintaining trust in an era of multiple accountabilities. *JAMA* 280, 12: 1102-8.

Stone, Deborah. 1984. *The disabled state.* Philadelphia: Temple University Press.

Thomas, Carol. 1999. *Female forms: Experiencing and understanding disability.* Buckingham: Open University Press.

Wilton, Robert. 2005. Working at the margins: Disabled people and the growth of precarious employment. Chapter 6, this volume.

11

Damage Quantification in Tort and Pre-Existing Conditions: Arguments for a Reconceptualization

Darcy L. MacPherson

Tort law is concerned with compensation for personal injuries. For example, if Person A were injured while a passenger in a car which was struck by another vehicle carelessly driven by Person B, tort law says that Person A can demand money from Person B for the injury or loss suffered. But, some plaintiffs *may not appear to have* the same level of physical and/or mental ability as others. Since the reasons for this apparent difference occurred before the car accident (and not because of it), these are called "pre-existing conditions." This chapter considers how tort law deals with plaintiffs with pre-existing conditions. I believe that the law does so inappropriately, and that the law in this area can be improved.

The Supreme Court of Canada has affirmed that the concept of a pre-existing condition is an important element of damage quantification in tort (*Athey* 1996, 473, para. 35). I argue that this idea is in need of reconceptualization, and suggest two reasons why this reconceptualization is particularly desirable and timely. I then argue that there is a specific situation that needs critical reassessment: when someone sells goods designed specifically for a person with a pre-existing condition, and the purchaser is injured by the use of the product. In such a scenario, the concept of a "pre-existing condition" should not apply. Finally, I contend that a more general revision of tort law is necessary. Specifically, I argue that (1) tort law needs to recognize "disability" as being reasonable and that people with "disabilities" fall within the normal range of anticipated plaintiffs, and (2) the underlying assumptions of tort law that support the concept of pre-existing conditions are problematic and should be reformulated. This will entail the recognition of a person's independence as a key value that the law should foster.

Why Now?

There are at least two reasons why a re-examination of this issue is timely. First, "disability" is quite common today. According to Statistics Canada, approximately 12.4 percent of the population lives with some type of "disability" (Canada 2002, 7). With a significant portion of the population being identified as "disabled," the law should, in my view, re-examine the effect such a designation has on a person's rights in tort.

Second, jurisprudential changes make the legal environment more hospitable to the arguments developed below. Two constitutional principles are particularly relevant. First, in its section 15 jurisprudence, the Supreme Court of Canada has held that a key factor to be considered in any discussion of equality under the *Canadian Charter of Rights and Freedoms* is whether there is a violation of "human dignity" (*Law v. Canada* 1999, 529, para. 51). One of the "contextual factors" indicating a violation of human dignity is the presence of pre-existing social disadvantage which the law fails to recognize or, even worse, exacerbates (*Law v. Canada* 1999, 534, para. 63). Without doubt, persons with "disabilities" have historically suffered economic and other social disadvantage by virtue of that status (*Eldridge* 1997, 668-69, paras. 56-57). Clearly, a concept that provides for lower damages to be paid only because the plaintiff happens to be branded as "disabled" is incompatible with the idea of equality advocated by the Supreme Court.

The other principle was put forward in *Hill v. Church of Scientology of Toronto* (1995). There, the Supreme Court of Canada held that Charter values should influence the common law even in the absence of a governmental actor. Justice Cory explained: "Historically, the common law evolved as a result of the courts making those incremental changes which were necessary in order to make the law comply with current societal values. The *Charter* represents a restatement of the fundamental values which guide and shape our democratic society and our legal system. It follows that it is appropriate for the courts to make such incremental revisions to the common law as may be necessary to have it comply with the values enunciated in the *Charter*" (*Hill* 1995, 1169, para. 92). In fact, case law subsequent to *Hill* has arguably strengthened the use of Charter values in litigation between private parties. This later case law has arguably imposed a more stringent standard to justify non-compliance with Charter values, even while purporting to apply *Hill* (1995, 1171, para. 97; *Pepsi* 2002, 174, paras. 36-37).

In my view, these cases establish that, although a tort dispute is a matter between private litigants, if a common law concept is out of step with Charter values, the judiciary must evaluate the appropriateness of the concept. The purpose of this chapter is to suggest that the concept of a pre-existing condition in tort is inconsistent with Charter values and to begin thinking critically about this concept and its application in modern society.

A Special Case
My interest in this area was piqued by a traumatic event. Born with cerebral palsy, a condition that causes tightness in all my limbs, I began to use an

electric wheelchair for mobility at the age of twelve, and my family purchased a van equipped with a wheelchair lift. Months later, the lift fell out
of the van, sending me and my wheelchair crashing to the ground. The
three-foot drop caused three compression fractures in my vertebrae. During
the first week of a two-week hospital stay, I had to remain prone to protect
my spine from further injury.

The manufacturer immediately admitted its liability. However, the quantum of damages, that is, the amount of compensation, was still to be determined. Three and a half years later, it became evident why this lawsuit
would take a long time to resolve. While the words "pre-existing disability"
were never spoken in my presence, it was clear from my examination for
discovery that the defendant contended that I had lost relatively little due
to the accident. The defendant argued that, as I already needed a wheelchair for mobility, the physical ability normally affected by a back injury
(the ability to walk, run, or otherwise enjoy a "normal" lifestyle) had already been lost before the accident. Ultimately, the case settled for just over
$50,000.

This experience put a narrow issue into sharp focus for me. This issue is
the quantum of damages in cases like mine, that is, where a product targeted at the "disabled" malfunctions, causing damage. How should the fact
of "disability" be handled in such a case? My experience also raised a more
general question about the underlying assumptions of tort law regarding
the "disabled." The former I refer to as the "narrow" issue; the latter, the
"broader" issue.

The conventional approach is that a pre-existing condition is properly
considered in damage assessment (*Finbow* 1957, 504-5) as a matter of causation (Cooper-Stephenson 1996, 802-3; Osborne 2000, 88). The argument
runs that no compensation can be achieved for the loss of a "normal" lifestyle
because the loss is attributable not to the injury, but to the pre-existing
condition.

Space does not allow for a full consideration of all issues related to pre-
existing conditions. Therefore, I place aside both the "thin skull" doctrine
and the "crumbling skull" doctrine. The first category involves cases where
the pre-existing condition makes the injuries suffered by the plaintiff more
severe than for a person without the pre-existing condition (Cooper-
Stephenson 1996, 779, note 243; 849). This is a question of liability; when a
plaintiff suffers damage as a result of a tort, the thin skull doctrine stipulates that the defendant cannot claim that the plaintiff *should not* have suffered damage or damage to such an extent (Osborne 2000, 88). The second
category covers cases where the degeneration of a pre-existing condition is
accelerated by a defendant's tortious action (Cooper-Stephenson 1996, 779,
note 243). The crumbling skull doctrine holds that while the defendant is

responsible for losses caused by the tort, the defendant is *not* responsible for the losses that were an inevitable result of the pre-existing condition (*Athey* 1996, 473, para. 35).

A third situation interests me more. A "disabled" person is injured. The injury is not more severe because of the "disability" (the thin skull cases), nor does the injury accelerate the inevitable consequences of the "disability" (the crumbling skull cases). Should the existence of a pre-existing condition reduce damages where neither the "thin skull" nor the "crumbling skull" doctrine applies? Specifically, what is the basis for assessing damages where the tort causes injury to someone previously "impaired" by a "disability"? The current law assumes that a person with a "disability" is not entitled to the same damages, because an injury does not deprive such a person of the same "amenities of life" that an "able-bodied" person would lose (*Haggar* 1972). It also assumes that a person with a pre-existing condition was not in as favourable an "original position" as an "able-bodied" person (*Athey* 1996, 473-74, paras. 35-36).

I turn now to the narrow issue. In the example drawn from my experience, the sale of the lift was entirely dependent on the user's having a "disability." No one without a "disability" requires the lift. Yet, tort law currently maintains for the manufacturer a built-in argument to reduce damages when the product malfunctions. If, on the other hand, the manufacturer had targeted a product to the general public, this argument would not be available against all purchasers of the product. When a company manufactures a product that is targeted to a particular group, that manufacturer makes a choice. By that choice, the manufacturer should forfeit the right to argue that there is something inherent in the entire group that entitles the manufacturer to pay a lower amount of damages. The law, as a policy matter, should disallow those who place a product in the stream of commerce from taking advantage of a lowering of damages for anyone injured by the use of the product because nobody using it could prove a full measure of damages. When a defendant is dealing with a "disabled" plaintiff, it is already recognized that the duty of care is correspondingly higher (*Finbow* 1957, 497). Even though this higher duty exists, the manufacturer, under current law, still has an available argument that the very situation that places a higher duty on it removes the need for as high a compensatory award as would otherwise be the case. The law should not take away with its left hand (through its law of damages) that which it has given with its right (through its conception of duty).

How do we reformulate tort principles to cover the narrow issue? Ultimately, I believe the best way to deal with this problem is through a contextual analysis. I chose the word "contextual" carefully. Originally, I thought the term "functional" analysis captured this idea. "Function," however, contains at least one medical connotation that is unacceptable for my purposes here. One medical dictionary defines it: *"Function:* to perform an activity or to work *properly and normally"* (Anderson 2002, 712 [emphasis added]). If one were to ask medical professionals to assess "function" in my lower limbs, they could easily say the following: "You have 40 percent range of motion, with hypertone in each leg." This means that when I try to move my leg, the leg moves less than the medical "norm," and there is more tension in my tendons and muscles than in those of most other people. But this is a medical perspective of my situation. This is comparative, and I do not favour comparative analysis, as explained below. This biomedical analysis of "disability" is very narrow. I view "disability" from a much broader perspective. Because the term "function" has this biomedical connotation, it is to be avoided.

The term "contextual" has a second advantage. More than anything else, I seek to suggest that the perspective of tort law is fundamentally "ableist" in orientation. As I demonstrate below, the way that the law views pre-existing conditions is very different from the way in which many persons with "disabilities" view their own situations. The law needs to change to be more inclusive and less informed by an ableist view of what is "normal."

I suggest we need to take a broader view of the context in which the plaintiff lived his or her life *before* the defendant's tortious conduct. In terms of the narrow issue posited here, greater context is needed to assess the plaintiff's "loss." This context includes the way the malfunctioning product was supposed to fit into the plaintiff's life on a long-term basis. Tort law must take a panoramic view of both the life of the person with the pre-existing condition and how the product was designed to fit into the totality of that life. In other words, the law needs to understand not only the effect of the pre-existing condition on the person but also how a person with a pre-existing condition is, both by using the product and otherwise, adapting to such circumstances. The law must assess which limitations of the plaintiff were to be assisted by the malfunctioning product. If the defendant relies on certain limitations of the plaintiff to sell the product, the defendant should be required by tort law *not* to use those limitations as a means to reduce compensation when the product malfunctions. The rationale behind this approach is, in my view, simple. The defendant used the fact that the plaintiff has certain limitations in order to earn a profit. In other words, the defendant's profit depends entirely on the plaintiff's limitations. The defendant chooses to take advantage of the plaintiff's limitations. This choice should mean that the defendant waives the right to rely on those limitations at the damages stage. For example, my family purchased the lift to allow me to use my electric wheelchair, a device designed to give me mobility without assistance. The court should treat me as having the abilities that the product was designed to provide. What does this mean? First, it means that the court should ignore that I cannot "walk," in the traditional sense of the word. The manufacturer knows that the product's primary, if not exclusive, users are those with mobility limitations. The law should look beyond the condition that puts the user in the situation that required the lift.

This does not mean that *all* limitations are irrelevant to the negligence committed by the manufacturer of a product targeted to the "disabled." Only those limitations the product was designed to alleviate (or their necessary consequences) can be ignored under the argument made here. I have several pre-existing limitations unrelated to mobility. For example, I cannot write as quickly as others, because of the tension in my hands. The lift was not designed to alleviate this. Therefore, if my hand had been injured in the fall, this argument would not apply. If the manufacturer wishes to rely on those limitations to reduce damages, this would be permissible on the narrow issue I have raised.

In closing this section, I emphasize that this is an alternative suggestion to those made below. The argument made in this section is much more specific than those below, and applies in a much narrower set of circumstances. However, the argument is placed earlier in the chapter because my experience with the narrow issue forced me to consider the broader issues of tort law and pre-existing conditions. It is to these broader issues that I now turn.

The Problems with Tort Law for People with "Disabilities"

In this section, I argue that some of the foundational concepts of tort law (in particular, the law of negligence) do not have a perspective that allows the law to deal equitably with the situation of a person with a pre-existing condition. I then discuss an assumption that tort law implicitly makes about people with "disabilities": the comparison of "disabled" persons with the "able-bodied." This assumption can be divided into two subcategories: the worth of the plaintiff, and the focus on inability. Before turning to those issues, however, I begin with a discussion of the "reasonable person" standard and its potential impact on rights in tort for persons with "disabilities."

The "Reasonable Person" Standard

Earlier, I suggested that the concept of pre-existing conditions was a device to limit recovery for people whom society tags as "disabled." Most writers have dealt with "disability issues" as part of causation. Therefore, it may seem incongruous to start this discussion not with causation but with the standard of the "reasonable person." Such a choice may seem even more

incongruous because this standard is applied to the conduct of the defendant (Osborne 2000, 26-28) in contrast to my focus on the plaintiff. But, as
one author has put it: "Reasonableness is in the lifeblood of our law" (Simester
2000, 85). While reasonableness is explicitly relevant to the actions of the
defendant, the concept also stands behind the outcomes that the law is
prepared to accept (Simester 2000, 85).

Reasonableness is a lens through which the law views its results. Therefore, the law must examine the reasonableness of "disability." The segment
of the population seen as being "disabled" is over 3.6 million Canadians
(Canada 2002, 7). If the law is truly in search of reasonableness, it should be
prepared to reflect the reasonable characteristics that the plaintiff has. Therefore, if a "reasonable person" can have a "disability," it would seem that a
pre-existing condition should not impact the level of damages. Since nearly
one in eight Canadians experiences a "disability," is there really a strong
justification for saying that "disability" removes their situation from the
realm of the "reasonable person"? I think not.

The law seeks a "reasonable person" as its benchmark in determining a
tort plaintiff's rights. Many people are categorized as being "disabled" and
nothing is inherently unreasonable about being such a person. This is an
important point, because if the law begins from the perspective that the
plaintiff is unreasonable, this must affect the outcome that the law is willing to accept. Therefore, the law should be willing to say that having a "disability" is reasonable. This is not to say that the fact that a plaintiff is
"disabled" must be ignored. Rather, the issue becomes one of recognition of
"disability" without attaching legal significance of a kind that deters a possible tort suit by such a person.

This, again, is a matter of perspective. By insisting that a person with a
"disability" is "reasonable," the law would begin to see persons with "disabilities" as just as deserving of compensation as persons who are considered to be "able-bodied," rather than as persons who must be dealt with
separately from, and with lower damage awards than, other plaintiffs. Tort
law focuses on the "disability," which the "normal" plaintiff does not have.
This marginalizes the experiences of a "disabled" person because it unduly
emphasizes the way in which a person is different, and implies that this
difference is what matters. As I will show here, this should not be the case.
A person with a "disability" can be recognized as such without necessarily
concluding that the person is an anomalous plaintiff. The tort system can
still recognize what makes the person different (the "disability") without
making that difference the defining factor in the end result. In other words,
a "disabled" person should not be considered an anomaly in tort law. Instead, a person who comes to the tort system with a pre-existing "disability" should be part of the range of anticipated plaintiffs that tort law seeks
to assist, just like any other anticipated plaintiff.

Comparison between the "Able-Bodied" and the "Disabled"

Worth of the Victim

Another problem with the concept of a pre-existing condition is that whatever its legal basis, at a common-sense level, it indicates that the loss of physical ability by someone whom society has labelled as "disabled" is less worthy of compensation than is a similar loss suffered by an individual labelled as "able-bodied." Put another way, the tort system assumes that there is an "ideal" candidate for recompense. Everyone who comes to the tort system is judged against that ideal. Since a pre-existing condition necessarily means that a plaintiff does not meet that ideal, the amount of compensation will necessarily be lowered. Few courts articulate this in their judgments. However, despite their indirectness, in my view, this is a necessary consequence of their reasoning.

For example, in one English case, *Haggar v. De Placido* (1972), the judge valued damages for what was termed "tetraplegia" (paralysis of all four limbs) of a twenty-nine-year-old plaintiff at only £13,500 for "amenity damages," because the plaintiff suffered from arthritis of the spine (*Haggar* 1972, 718). The plaintiff was not compensated with the same amount of damages as another plaintiff because of the pre-existing condition (Kemp 1986, 11001, para. 11-002). In a second English case, *Gateson v. Kiln Park Estates Ltd.* (1980), the facts were described in a leading damages text as: "Boy, aged 10 at date of accident and 13 at date of trial. Pre-existing disability in left eye. Hit in that eye by golf club. Eye retained but complete loss of vision in it. Agreed discount of 25 per cent. [sic] in respect of pre-existing disability" (Kemp 1986, 11006, para. 11-012). In my view, the practical reality of the concept of pre-existing "disability" remains inherently comparative. In any comparison with the "average" or ideal plaintiff, it would be rare that the person who is labelled as "disabled" would measure up. I believe that, even if this comparison is not specifically stated by the court, the comparison is indeed being made by our judiciary.

This comparison does not reflect the fact that the life of a "disabled" person is their *entire* life, despite any challenges associated with that life. Put another way, challenges associated with a "disability" change the way in which a person does things. But does this mean that the life of a person with a "disability" is only a fraction as "full" as the life of a person who is not so categorized? I hope this is not the case. It may be argued that a "disabled" person has a more tenuous grip on a "normal" lifestyle than does an "able-bodied" person. But it *is* possible for "disabled" individuals to use their skills to adapt their lifestyles so that they end up with the lives they want, even if that desire is not fulfilled in the "normal" way.

Perhaps a better way to illustrate this concept is through the analogy of a toolbox. Imagine that each of a person's physical abilities is a specific tool in a toolbox. Although people with "disabilities" that impact seriously on daily living have fewer tools in their respective toolboxes, most people with "disabilities" still wish to live as full and as "normal" a lifestyle as their limitations allow. To do so, people with "disabilities" often adapt those tools that remain in their toolboxes to serve as many different purposes as possible, so that life can be as full as possible. They take the tools given to them and use those tools for far more than most others would.

Two simple examples may assist here. First, imagine that a person loses 10 percent vision in each eye. I suspect that many actuaries could calculate a standard damage award for such a loss. But should the answer be different depending on whether the 10 percent loss moves a person from 100 percent of "normal vision" to 90 percent, or from 10 percent of "normal vision" to total blindness? In my view, the latter is much more of a loss. Why? It is because the person with only 10 percent vision must have already adapted to the degree possible. In other words, the person with perfect vision who loses 10 percent of it can use corrective lenses or can move closer to objects to discover detail. In short, there are many ways in which a person can compensate for this 10 percent loss of vision.

However, a person with only 10 percent vision to begin with can adapt only in a limited number of ways to a total loss of vision. A number of cases have appreciated to some degree this greater impact on the plaintiff, and have attempted to compensate the plaintiff for it (see Kemp 1986, 11012-18, paras. 11-024 through 11-033; *Finbow* 1957). But, none of these cases goes so far as to say that the person has gone from having sight to having none and should be compensated on that basis. The 10 percent vision loss for this person means that there is none of that ability with which to adapt to the loss. Therefore, this loss may be just as great as that of a person who goes from 20/20 vision to total blindness. After all, the person has likely already used all the "tools" in their "toolbox" to adapt to the pre-existing condition. Someone with 10 percent vision typically makes more effective use of that 10 percent than someone with 20/20 vision would make of 10 percent of his or her vision. So, in that sense, each person has lost the same thing (all ability to see), whether he or she has a pre-existing condition. It is only because the law compares the actual plaintiff with some other "average" or "idealized" plaintiff that the pre-existing condition becomes relevant and the actual plaintiff's loss, irrelevant.

Now I turn to my second example. The way in which I perform my job as a law professor means that I need to be able to type my lectures and papers. My condition makes my right hand significantly more tense than average, and noticeably less dexterous than my left. However, I am still able to type. I use my left hand for more of the keyboard than would be standard for someone characterized as "able-bodied." Therefore, I have adapted to my physical limitations, and developed an effective system for typing.[1]

Why is this example relevant? Assume that a tort occurred that injured my right hand appreciably so that my system no longer worked, because my left hand could not cover the entire keyboard. In other words, before the tort, my adaptation to my situation allowed me to complete the tasks required in spite of my limitations. When compared with the "ideal" or "average" candidate for recompense, the tort system might contend, "Yes, you have lost this ability to type. But part of your loss is due to the pre-existing condition that afflicts you. Therefore, your damages should be less than the average person's, because the tort did not cause the initial loss of ability." In this example, under the "ideal candidate" approach, the person with a "disability" might not receive as much compensation as a person who is not so labelled.

When the same situation is viewed, not by comparing this plaintiff with the "ideal" or "average" plaintiff but, rather, from the perspective of the loss created for the particular plaintiff, the result could easily be different. Taken from the viewpoint of the "disabled" plaintiff, the loss is just as severe as for anyone else, because the system that the plaintiff established to compensate for physical limitations has been compromised by the subsequent tort. Therefore, the amount of damages, when viewed from this perspective, is the same regardless of whether the person seeking compensation is labelled as having a "disability" or not. This is really an explicitly "contextual" approach to damages in that one is focused not on comparing losses of the "average" (able-bodied) plaintiff against those of the actual ("disabled") plaintiff but on determining the abilities the plaintiff lost as a result of the tort, given the context in which the person operates.

A contextual approach to damages is not new. Some courts, while acknowledging the comparative analysis, have argued that the value ascribed to the plaintiff's "loss" depends on the number and quality of abilities that remain intact thereafter. In one case, a woman with a pre-existing mental condition was hit by a truck. The defence argued that "as [the plaintiff's] activities were so limited before the accident, she has been deprived of less than the 'ordinary' plaintiff as a result of her injuries and that the award should be lower than the norm to reflect that" (*Moody* 1992, 92). The judge appears to reject a comparative approach in the following terms:

My function is to not to make invidious comparisons between this plaintiff and, say, a "healthy, vigorous young woman who before her injury engaged in high-impact aerobics, tennis and other sports, as well as jogging and general outdoor activities." Rather, the task is to measure what this plaintiff has lost in terms of her own pre-accident capabilities.

A normal plaintiff who had suffered the injuries Nancy Moody had might have had other abilities and capacities to fall back upon. Nancy did not. Her injuries took away virtually all of her amenities for a year after the accident and to a reduced degree until the present and into the future. (*Moody* 1992, 94)

The court increased the quantum of damages by $10,000 to compensate for the plaintiff's loss.[2]

Therefore, as suggested by *Moody,* the law should move away from comparing one plaintiff against some "average" or idealized plaintiff. Instead, the law must give full value to the life that the plaintiff was able to lead before the tort. This requires a change of perspective and an appreciation of context. Simply stated, we must appreciate not only the existence of a "disability," but also how the person deals with the pre-existing condition in ways that ensure a fulfilling life. Losses should be judged by viewing the plaintiff as 100 percent of themselves, rather than some lower percentage of a notional plaintiff.

Focus on Inability
The law views a tort plaintiff with a pre-existing condition as two things: (1) a victim, and (2) someone who is less able than others. Let us examine each of these in turn.

The tort system views all successful plaintiffs as "victims." In one sense, the more "victimized" or injured the plaintiff is, the greater the damages. Space does not allow me to challenge this aspect of tort law here. Instead, I will focus on the law's characterization of the tort plaintiff as a "victim" of the pre-existing condition. The law treats the pre-existing condition as a victimizing event prior to the tort. Look at how we consider causation issues with respect to pre-existing conditions. One of the leading Canadian authors on personal injury awards deals with pre-existing conditions under the title of "Culpable and Non-Culpable Sufficient Causes" (Cooper-Stephenson 1996, 802-6). "Cause" is defined in part as "a person, thing, fact, or condition that brings about an effect or that produces or calls forth a resultant action or state."[3] The use of the word "cause" is, by its very nature, an assignment of responsibility. By making the pre-existing condition a "cause," the tort system essentially says: "It is the condition that is responsible for part of the loss. Therefore, you were victimized *prior to the tort* by the condition." In other words, the tort system views a person with a pre-existing condition as being a victim *before* dealing with the matter at hand (the tort). Essentially, a person with a pre-existing condition is considered to be a "victim" twice. First, the law says a person is victimized by the "disability." Second, the plaintiff is the victim of the tort. In fact, the following quotation from a unanimous decision of the Supreme Court of Canada demonstrates that the court thinks of a person with a pre-existing condition as "damaged": "The defendant is liable for the injuries caused, even if they are extreme, but need not compensate the plaintiff for any debilitating effects of the pre-existing condition which the plaintiff would have experienced anyway. The defendant is liable for the additional *damage* but not the pre-existing *damage"* (*Athey* 1996, 473, para. 35 [citations omitted; emphasis added]). The problem with this is obvious. It is true that the concept of "damage" is integral to tort law, and if a plaintiff comes to court having suffered no loss as a result of the tort, this person should receive little or no compensation. I do not wish to challenge the term "damage" at this level. But when the law assumes that a person is "damaged" prior to the tort – in this case, the plaintiff who comes to court with a pre-existing condition – the law is making an assertion about that person's value. When the law makes this assertion for no other reason than that the plaintiff is different from what is "normal," this is the essence of discrimination (*Andrews v. Law Society of British Columbia* 1989, 174-75). As discussed above, jurisprudence under the Charter indicates that if the common law is discriminatory, it should be adjusted to reflect Charter values, including the non-discrimination equality guarantee of section 15 of the Charter. Therefore, the ideas of "victimization" and perceiving an individual as "damaged," which are inherent in the concept of "pre-existing condition," need to be challenged.

I turn now to the issue of "ability." That the law views a person with a pre-existing condition as less "able" than others seems to me, in one sense, somewhat self-evident. After all, if the law started from the position that a person with a "disability" was not less able than others, why would we reduce damages as a result of the "disability"? Put less rhetorically, we reduce damages when the "loss" suffered by a plaintiff is not proven. One reason for saying the loss of the plaintiff is not compensable by the tort system is that the plaintiff was unable to do the particular activity prior to the tort and, therefore, causation is not established. Inherently, this focuses the issue of a pre-existing condition on what the "disability" takes away from a person.

But, many "disabled" people do not view themselves as less able than others. For example, as a law professor, I often have to settle down the occupants of a classroom before I begin a lecture. On one such occasion, I said something to the effect of, "Ladies and gentlemen, *when I walk into the room,* we need to start. There is a lot to be covered today." When I approached this project, one of my research assistants said that he was struck by the language I used to call the class to attention. He thought it unusual that I referred to myself as "walking" anywhere. After all, I am aware that I do not "walk." Technically, I "wheel" or "roll" to locations at any distance. However, by experience, I have learned to focus on my capacities (rather than on what I *cannot* do). That way, I tend to accomplish more. For me, the way I "walk" is different from that of most people. But, for me, *this is walking*. The difference lies in the mode of accomplishment, not the substance of what is accomplished.

In other words, for people who are defined as "able-bodied," the areas where I lack ability are my most evident characteristics. I am not attempting to cast aspersions on people who are "able-bodied." Many see past my limitations and deal with me on an equal plane. Nonetheless, the point remains that it is a very *different* experience for an "able-bodied" person to deal with a person with such obvious limitations. This is unusual and, in many ways, unexpected for the "able-bodied" person. For me, on the other hand, dealing with my limitations is a daily occurrence. If I were to view my limitations as my defining characteristic, I would probably stop trying to achieve my goals, because on that basis, I could never keep up. Put another way, focusing on the negative (my *dis*ability) distracts from progress on other, more positive, areas of my life. My self-image is not wrapped up in what I can*not* do. Rather, I choose to focus on my capacities, on what I *can* do. I know my limitations, but, left to my own devices, I choose to focus on the avenues available to me.

The empirical evidence appears to support such an idea of positive self-image. A study from 1998 suggests that children with either a learning or physical "disability" suffer no impact on their overall self-concept when compared with their peers without "disabilities" (Bohr 1998, 48). If one focused on the negatives in life, self-concept surely would be bound to diminish; if one were to focus on how much one is *un*able to accomplish, life would be very bleak, and one's opinion of oneself would be lowered. Indeed, "negative self-perceptions" and "negative worldview" have been used as two indicators of negative self-concept (Mrug and Wallender 2002, 276). Since the empirical evidence suggests that people with "disabilities" do not see themselves as less valuable than anyone else, it follows that people with "disabilities" see themselves as being no less able to accomplish things than is the "able-bodied" population.

Yet, the tort system is focused on what a "disability" takes away from the plaintiff. The fact of "disability" is used to provide a backdrop against which the tort system operates. The tort system takes an "able-bodied" perspective of those it labels as "disabled." The tort system looks first to the area where a "disability" has a negative impact on the plaintiff. The cases to which I have referred provide examples of this. Tort law focuses on the fact that a "disability" can sometimes remove a person from high-paying jobs (*Finbow* 1957, 504-5). It also assumes that, when there is a pre-existing condition, the loss of "amenities" does not have as great an effect as it otherwise would (*Haggar* 1972; Kemp 1986, 11001, para. 11-002). I suggest that the law should instead focus on the idea that people can adapt to their circumstances and are able to accomplish a great deal in spite of activity limitations. Once you place the "disability" in the context of the ability to adapt to limitations, then the amount that the "disability" takes away from a person is much less relevant to the discussion.

If Not This, Then What?

Where do we go from here? How do we adjust the tort system to better reflect the reality of people with "disabilities?" Below, I wrestle with these difficult questions, though some of the issues involved defy easy solutions.

A change in legal thinking can assist in the larger process of necessary societal change. Both the required societal shift, and the way in which law can be a positive force to further that end, merit attention.

Fundamentally, equality is about recognition and participation. Each of these elements must be sought to generate true equality. Recognition involves the idea that the term "different" need not necessarily require a comparative judgment of "better" or "worse." As the Supreme Court of Canada put it, "This historical disadvantage has to a great extent been shaped and perpetuated by the notion that disability is an abnormality or flaw ... ["Disabled" persons] have been subjected to paternalistic attitudes of pity and charity, and their entrance into the social mainstream has been conditional upon their emulation of able-bodied norms" (*Eldridge* 1997, 668, para. 56 [citations omitted]). As a society, we tend to categorize differences as being better or worse than the norm. Therein lies the required societal shift referred to above. This labelling tendency is a major contributing factor to the current assumptions of the tort system. Judges need to understand that there is no ideal candidate for recompense under the tort system. The tort system must become more sensitive to the way people with "disabilities" operate in their daily lives. If the presumption is that everyone is to be fully recognized as capable of accomplishment, the most important battle has already been won. In other words, although changes to legal thinking are still needed, the most important change one can bring about is attitudinal. Once society recognizes a person's limitations without needing to view the "disabled" person as being defined and, to a certain extent, subordinated by those differences, it will have made one of the necessary steps toward genuine equality.

The first way in which the law can assist in this change is to make explicit the idea that a disability is *not* about an "abnormality or flaw." In *Eldridge* (1997, 668, para. 56), for instance, the societal attitudes to "disabilities" were described as "unfortunate"; the case does not specifically say that this is "unacceptable." "Disability" is a *difference,* and should be recognized as such. People with activity limitations need to approach their lives differently than do those without such obvious limitations. To take another personal example, as I approached my university years, it became clear that I would choose a profession of some sort. Many employment choices were simply not feasible because of activity limitations and, even among the professional ranks, certain career choices were unrealistic. My lack of hand-eye coordination and dexterity meant that if I became a surgeon, I would likely kill more people than I saved. Therefore, I adjusted my expectations to make a more appropriate career choice ... a lawyer.

I recognize that my "disability" closes certain avenues to me, but I do not see it as being a flaw. This is the hand I was dealt. Consider the young person who dreams of being a professional athlete or musician but lacks the necessary talent. No matter how much that person practises, lack of talent prevents him or her from achieving the dream. Society, however, does not consider that person to be "flawed." The law is prepared to assume that the person can be successful in other ways. Why should the same not be said about people with "disabilities?" Ultimately, if the law starts from the perspective that "disability" is not a flaw, it can move away from many of the comparative, value-laden judgments that are currently so important to its decision-making process.

It is fine to say that the tort system we currently have is inadequate. But how does society begin the process of change? One way might be to change the language we use to describe the people who are the subject of this chapter. Readers will notice that every time I use the words "disabled" and "disability" in this chapter, I have enclosed them in quotation marks. Before this project, I was never concerned with labels. But I realized that the description I choose defines the subject matter. If a group defines itself (or allows itself to be defined) as less able than others (as being "*disabled*"), why should it be such a surprise that social institutions such as the law adopt a similar approach? A person with a "disability" is not flawed and does not have an abnormality. It is important to view him or her as a "person needing to adapt to activity limitations."

This may seem like semantics in the extreme. But, in my view, such a change would represent a shift in thinking. It places the emphasis not on what cannot be accomplished but, rather, on what allows accomplishment, that is, adaptation to new circumstances. It does not hide that there is a difference between this particular plaintiff and other possible plaintiffs. On the contrary, it recognizes the difference. But it places that difference in a particular context, alongside an acknowledgment that, through the necessary adaptations, a person with limitations can accomplish a great deal in spite of those limitations, rather than being *dis*abled from doing things. Once society as a whole recognizes this, it should facilitate the necessary adaptations to allow for accomplishment.

I also emphasize the term "participation." The tort system attaches monetary value to certain activities. The loss of the ability to perform those activities is a "loss" for which the tort system will provide compensation. In my view, the law must learn to place value on another key concept, that of independence. A person's independence allows him or her to choose how to participate in society.

Independence is important for at least two reasons. First, it is consistent with equality values. As I mentioned earlier, equality is about human dignity. Human dignity is about recognizing autonomy (Mill 1975, 53-69). The loss of independence should be compensable because autonomy of the individual should be recognized as a valuable commodity by the law. Put another way, if the law believes that autonomy is a value to be fostered, the loss of autonomy (the loss of independence) should be a compensable loss.

It is true that many of the decisions made by the Canadian courts say that they consider the loss of the plaintiff's independence suffered as a result of the tort. For example, in one case, it was found that after a catastrophic accident, the plaintiff would be unable to function independently. The judge held that there should therefore be no contingency to reduce damages for cost of future care (*Tucker v. Asleson* 1991, 68). In other words, independence is *indirectly* relevant to the calculation of losses. Because a plaintiff can no longer live an independent life, he or she will require more care than if able to live independently.

Nothing is wrong with this reasoning. What I am suggesting here is different, however. The loss of independence is a value beyond its pecuniary element, beyond its replacement cost. Again, an example might assist here. When I was injured by the collapse of the van lift, I lost the ability to ride horses and my all-terrain vehicle (my equivalent of a bicycle). There was no replacement cost for these losses; I simply spend more time in my wheelchair. Some may argue that this is the loss of a hobby and is thus a nonpecuniary loss for me in the same way as for anyone else. This argument, in my view, misses the point. For me, these two activities provided time in which I was not bound by my pre-existing condition. Few of the limitations that bound me in other arenas seemed to restrict me in these two activities. Thus, those two activities took on added value for me because of their ability to give me a sense of independence unrelated to my limitations. In other words, what is the loss of a "hobby" for one reasonable person may be a much more substantial loss for another reasonable person, depending on the circumstances, especially where independence is at issue. Therefore, independence should be compensable in and of itself.

Second, the concept of independence is not comparative. For one person to be independent does not require comparison with any "average" or "idealized" person. Judging the loss of independence involves multiple factors. In contrast, the current defendant-centred reasonable person standard, by its very nature, is focused on the particular act said to be negligent (Osborne 2000, 26). However, the idea of independence needs to be broader. In fact, it seems to me that the only way to judge the loss of independence is through examining the plaintiff's life in context. To return to my example, if one were to examine only the act said to be negligent (the faulty manufacture of the lift) and its effect on my physical well-being, the riding of horses would seem relatively inconsequential. But when viewed from the perspective of the loss of my independence, these elements take on a significance more indicative of the true "loss" suffered as a result of the tort. The broader the perspective, the less likely the court is to make the assumptions that contribute to the disadvantage under which tort law places those needing to adapt to limitations. Once limitations are placed in this context, it becomes much more difficult to argue that there should be any reduction in damages simply because the plaintiff has a pre-existing condition. That is, the recognition of the ability to adapt to limitation means that the idea of focusing on inability, and assessing the worth of the victim, are not as relevant. This change in perspective would ultimately have the effect of equalizing damages awards for people adapting to activity limitations with those for people without activity limitations.

Conclusion

The way the tort system views and compensates people adapting to activity limitations is important to me, both as a person with first-hand experience with the system and as a legal academic. My experiences opened my eyes to fundamental questions of how the law allows its doctrinal foundations to generate results similar to those that I experienced. My purpose here has been twofold. First, I wished to demonstrate that tort law can have certain unanticipated results, especially when dealing with those manufacturing products designed to assist with activity limitations. Second, I suggested that there are other ways that tort law fails to appreciate the reality of those adapting to activity limitations.

Unfortunately, there are no quick fixes to these issues. While some of my ideas for a solution are presented here, this is hardly the end of the story. After all, I suspect that some ideas put forward here are somewhat controversial, particularly given that my own experiences inform much of the analysis. Challenges to my assertions will inevitably be made. The fun will come in meeting them.

Acknowledgments
A draft of this chapter was presented at the conference of the Canadian Association of Law Teachers on 1 June 2003 in Halifax. Generous financial support for this project was received from the Legal Research Institute of the University of Manitoba. Trevor Anderson, Maryel Andison, Richard Devlin, Philip Osborne, Debra Parkes, Dianne Pothier, Lorna Turnbull, and Linda Vincent all reviewed earlier drafts of this chapter and provided valuable feedback. The brainstorming sessions with the participants in the Critical Disability

Theory subconference were also instrumental in developing my ideas. The research assistance of Matthew Burgoyne, Doug Schweitzer, and J. Graeme Young is also gratefully acknowledged.

Notes

1 Here, the word "limitations" is not used in the medical or functional sense rejected earlier. Instead, it is used in a more generic sense. I must acknowledge that I cannot do everything in the way that other people would ordinarily do things. In referring to "limitations," I simply wish to acknowledge the need to make adaptations in order to accomplish things. This fits with the idea of recognizing difference, which I refer to later in the chapter.

2 In other contexts, the courts have begun to recognize the difference of people adapting to activity limitations from others *without* allowing that difference to impact the substantive legal rights. On 2 May 2005, the Ontario Court of Appeal issued its judgment in *Ontario Nurses Assn. v. Mount Sinai Hospital*, [2005] O.J. 1739. In this case, a nurse was denied what would otherwise have been a statutory right to severance pay, based on the fact that the activity limitation that prevented her from working "frustrated" her employment contract. A challenge was brought to the constitutionality of the relevant section of *Employment Standards Act* (Ontario), R.S.O. 1990, c. E.14, para. 58(5)(c). The court held that the denial of severance pay violated s-s. 15(1) of the Charter and was thus unconstitutional. In certain ways, this situation is very different from my concerns here. First, this is a constitutional case considering the differential impact of a statutory provision. This chapter is concerned with the common law of torts. There was nothing in the judgment to indicate that the applicant in that case had a pre-existing condition prior to her accident. It was due to her accident that she was unable to work for an extended period. Despite these differences, however, the courts are becoming more sensitive to context. My contention here is that this sensitivity must also be applied in the law of tort.

3 As defined in *Webster's Third New International Dictionary of the English Language Unabridged* (Springfield, MA: Merriam-Webster, 1993).

References

Anderson, D.M., ed. 2002. *Mosby's medical, nursing, and allied health dictionary: 6th ed.* St. Louis: Mosby.
Andrews v. Law Society of British Columbia, [1989] 1 S.C.R. 143.
Athey v. Leonati, [1996] 3 S.C.R. 458 [*Athey*].
Bohr, Y. 1998. *Children with physical disabilities: Friendship, self-concept and the role of social attributions.* Toronto: University of Toronto Libraries.
Canada. Statistics Canada, Housing, Family and Social Statistics Division. 2002. *A profile of disability in Canada, 2001.* Ottawa: Minister of Industry.
Canadian Charter of Rights and Freedoms, Part I of the *Constitution Act, 1982,* being Schedule B to the *Canada Act 1982* (U.K.), 1982, c. 11 [Charter].
Cooper-Stephenson, K. 1996. *Personal injury damages in Canada.* 2nd ed. Scarborough, ON: Carswell.
Eldridge v. British Columbia (Attorney-General), [1997] 3 S.C.R. 624 [*Eldridge*].
Finbow et al. v. Domino et al. (1957), 11 D.L.R. (2d) 493 (Man. Q.B.) [*Finbow*].
Gateson v. Kiln Park Estates Ltd. (1980). Unreported decision of the English High Court, 25 February 1980 (Griffiths J.).
Haggar v. De Placido, [1972] 1 W.L.R. 716 [*Haggar*].
Hill v. Church of Scientology of Toronto, [1995] 2 S.C.R. 1130 [*Hill*].
Kemp, D.A. 1986. *Kemp & Kemp: The quantum of damages in personal injury and fatal accident claims – Special edition.* Vol. 1. London, England: Sweet and Maxwell.
Law v. Canada (Minister of Employment and Immigration), [1999] 1 S.C.R. 497 [*Law v. Canada*].
Mill, J.S. 1975. Of individuality, as one of the elements of well-being. In *John Stuart Mill on liberty: Annotated text, sources and background, criticism,* ed. D. Spitz, chap. 3. New York: W.W. Norton.
Moody (Guardian ad litem of) v. Windsor (1992), 64 B.C.L.R. (2d) 83 (B.C.S.C.) [*Moody*].

Mrug, S., and J.L. Wallender. 2002. Self-concept of young people with physical disabilities: Does integration play a role? *International Journal of Disability, Development and Education* 49: 267-80.

Osborne, P.H. 2000. *Essentials of Canadian law: The law of torts.* Toronto: Irwin Law.

[*Pepsi*]. *Retail, Wholesale and Department Store Union, Local 558 v. Pepsi-Cola Canada Beverages (West) Ltd.,* [2002] 1 S.C.R. 156. [*Pepsi*]

Simester, A.P. 2000. Can negligence be culpable? In *Oxford essays in jurisprudence,* fourth series, ed. J. Horder, 85-106. Oxford: Oxford University Press.

Tucker v. Asleson (1991). Unreported decision of the British Columbia Supreme Court, B.C.S.C. Order No. 091/122/025, Vancouver Registry B871616, 25 April 1991), (Finch J).

12
Beyond Compassion and Sympathy to Respect and Equality: Gendered Disability and Equality Rights Law
Fiona Sampson

The experience of gendered disability discrimination, within both equality rights theory and practice, is not well understood. As a result, the rights of women with disabilities are inadequately protected or advanced by the equality guarantees that are supposed to benefit them. In order to make equality rights law work for women with disabilities, analyses of gendered disability discrimination need to be developed that will expose the distinctive nature of the experience and will work to identify, address, and remedy the source of the disadvantage. My goal in this chapter is to improve the understanding of gendered disability discrimination so that equality rights law can be used more effectively to advance the rights of women with disabilities. I have not developed a definitive theory of gendered disability and the law. Because the experience of disability for women is so diverse, the development of a grand, unifying meta-theory of gendered disability should probably be avoided to prevent practices of universalism and essentialism. I have instead identified a framework for a gendered disability analysis, and then applied the analysis to the Supreme Court of Canada's decision in *R. v. Parrott* (2001). The *Parrott* case study is used as a prism through which to examine the theoretical rationale justifying the need for a gendered disability analysis. The application of a gendered disability analysis to *Parrott* exposes the importance of examining the distinctive experiences of gendered disability discrimination so as to maximize the value of equality rights law for women with disabilities.

The Framework for a Gendered Disability Equality Rights Analysis
Neither disability theory nor feminist legal theory provide an adequate framework for a gendered disability equality rights analysis. The primary concern with disability theory as it relates to the experience of gendered disability is its gender-neutral focus. Disability theorists have been virtually silent about the experience of gendered disability. This gap in disability theory may be a result of the fact that, internationally, the disability movement has tended

to be dominated by men (Sheldon 1999, 653), and that analyses of gendered disability have remained undeveloped as a result. The understanding of disability as a social and relational construction does represent a useful conceptual framework for consideration in the application of a gendered disability analysis (Bickenbach 1993; Pothier 1992). However, disability theory, as it has been developed to date, is not sufficiently complex to address the experience of gendered disability. Feminist theory offers a more developed understanding of the experience of subordination than does disability theory, as it has grown into a vast field of study that offers a wide breadth of knowledge relating to difference and inequality.

There are a number of different schools of feminist legal theory (see Comack 1999). Radical feminist legal theory is of particular significance to women with disabilities interested in the practice of equality rights law. Radical feminists are credited with successfully advancing a substantive analysis of women's equality rights. The primary goal of a substantive equality analysis is the achievement of an equality of results. Formal equality, under which women are treated the same as men, is rejected under a substantive equality analysis in favour of differential treatment intended to challenge the sources of women's oppression. Based on a substantive equality analysis, political – and legal – transformation, including major structural change, is the preferred means by which to achieve equality for women. A necessary component of a substantive equality analysis is the inclusion of a contextualized approach to equality questions. The contextualized approach to equality rights law requires the judiciary to consider the socio-historic roots of the inequality at issue in a given case (Fudge 1987, 497).

The primary problem with feminist legal theory, including radical legal feminism, is the feminist practice of essentialism. A significant body of critical race literature defines essentialism and addresses the need to recognize the diversity of women's backgrounds and experiences (Crenshaw 1991; Fuss 1989; Harris 1990; hooks 1982; Iyer 1993-94; Lorde 1984; Weedon 1999). Essentialism has been identified by Susan Williams as a modern manifestation of exclusion, somewhat more subtle if no less effective than explicit exclusion. Williams (1993) identifies social constructionism as an important antidote to the insidiously exclusionary implications of essentialism. Critical race theorists such as Williams have used the analytical tool of constructionism to advance understandings of racism as relational rather than inherent. In a critical race analysis, race is understood to exist as a relational category, not as a purely descriptive or inherent category. The question usually posed in exploring the construction of racial categories of difference is, who benefits from racism? (Comack 1999, 57; see also Minow 1990, 174 and 390). How difference is recognized and valued is another central concern of feminist critical race theorists (Comack 1999, 60). Feminist critical race theorists identify the general need to think about and explain the inability of different theories and practices to incorporate the diversity of women's experiences in their encounters with law and in society generally. These are important ideas to explore in relation to the experience of gendered disability discrimination (Razack 1994, 903 and 921).

Claims of gendered disability discrimination need to be informed by an analysis that addresses the distinctive experiences of gendered disability so that the rights of women with disabilities are recognized and protected. Gendered disability needs to be understood as a relational experience that is constructed to the disadvantage of women with disabilities. The contextualization of gendered disability equality claims is key to the exposure of power imbalances that are central to this experience. To contextualize an equality claim, it is necessary to describe and analyze the historical and contemporary socio-political experience of the specific claimant group, for example, women with disabilities, and to link that experience to the legal issues under examination in the claim. If equality is understood as the right of historically disadvantaged groups to have subordinating barriers removed, it makes sense that the historical disadvantage experienced by the group and its connection to the barrier being challenged must be clearly articulated as part of the claim. The historical disadvantage may vary depending on the facts of the case. However, the contextualization of gendered disability equality claims is likely to include a consideration of gender disability based poverty, extreme vulnerability to sexual violence, invisibility within public life, and a minimization of the value of the lives of women with disabilities.

Part of the attraction of the contextualized approach to equality for women with disabilities is that it diminishes the focus on the sameness/difference dichotomy (Jhappan 1998, 72-74). The goal of a contexualized equality rights analysis is to identify the source of the claimant's subordination in order to eradicate it. While the idea of subordination involves a comparative concept, the contextualized approach provides for some liberation from the more traditional equality rights analysis that is usually grounded in a rigid comparative analysis of two categories of experience. Using a contextualized approach to equality, women with disabilities need not necessarily argue that they are really the same as either non-disabled women or disabled men and so deserve the same treatment, nor that they are different from non-disabled women or disabled men so that they deserve different treatment. Through a contextualized analysis, women with disabilities can argue that their subordination has been socially constructed and legally enforced. The focus is thereby switched from the individual to systemic discrimination, allowing for a more comprehensive understanding of the experience of subordination for women with disabilities.

In dealing with a claim of discrimination against women with disabilities, the claim must articulate the relevance of the experience of gendered disability and the effect of the distinction at issue on the claimant. An analysis of the context of gendered disability needs to inform the analysis of the legal issues under review. The specificity of the discrimination analysis to gendered disability, rather than just an additive analysis of gender and disability, is imperative so that the relevant context is clearly and fully developed. In the application of a contextual analysis of gendered disability to the equality claims of women with disabilities, who may of course have other identity features relevant to a discrimination complaint, the goal should be to expose how the dominant norm maintains power relations that disadvantage women with disabilities. The application of contextualized equality rights analyses specific to the experiences of gendered disability does not guarantee the success of the claim, even assuming the analysis is a good one, as there is no guarantee that the judiciary will appreciate the significance of the experiential reality of the claimants' lives.[1] Dianne Pothier has concluded that "the ultimate question [about judicial assessments of human dignity] is whether the court 'gets' the context of the claimant in order to be able to make a sensible judgment about human dignity" (Pothier 2006, 5). However, without the advancement of contextualized gendered disability analyses, it is likely that the distinctive experiences of women with disabilities will be ignored, and that their entitlement to equal treatment will not be recognized, as was the case in *R. v. Parrott*.

Gendered Disability and the Missed Opportunity of *R. v. Parrott*

Factual Background and Judicial History

The facts in *R. v. Parrott* are relatively straightforward. The accused was charged with the kidnapping and sexual assault of a thirty-eight-year-old woman with Down's syndrome from the hospital in St. John's, Newfoundland, where she was a resident patient. The complainant's mental development was equivalent to that of a typical four-year-old. The complainant was forced by the accused into his car; this was witnessed by a hospital employee, who reported it to the police. The police found the woman seven hours later in a remote coastal area, in the passenger seat of the accused's car. The accused was immediately arrested and handcuffed. The woman's shorts were on backwards, her underwear was hanging out over the top of her shorts, she had bruises on her left cheek and left hand, she had scratches on her arms and legs, and her clothes were soiled and wet. The accused, Walter Parrott, was tried on a charge of kidnapping, under section 279(1) of the *Criminal Code,* and a charge of sexual assault causing bodily harm, under section 272(1)(c).

At issue in *Parrott* was the admissibility of the complainant's out-of-court statements for the truth of their contents. In her out-of-court statements made soon after the events, the complainant, when asked what happened to her, stated that "the man in handcuffs did it," and when asked what the man looked like, she said, "Man with black hat ... glasses ... police took him away." When she was asked who hurt her face, the complainant said, "Scratched me" and when she was asked who scratched her, she said, "The man." When asked where, she said, "In the car," and when asked what he did, she said, "Smacked me" (*Parrott* 2001, para. 12). The central issue on appeal was whether the Crown was obliged to call the complainant as a witness at the voir dire[2] held to determine the admissibility of the complainant's out-of-court statements that the Crown sought to rely on as hearsay evidence. The court's analysis focused primarily on the necessity and reliability of the hearsay evidence. That the complainant was a woman with a serious mental disability should have been central to the analysis of this case. However, the issue of gendered disability was not raised by any of the members of the judiciary who heard the case, including those of the Supreme Court of Canada.

At trial, the Crown took the position that the complainant was unable to communicate, and Crown counsel did not intend to call her as a witness. The Crown counsel submitted that she would seek to have the complainant's out-of-court statements admitted as evidence under an exception to the hearsay rule. The trial judge held the voir dire, at which the Crown introduced evidence to establish the required necessity for, and reliability of, the out-of-court statements made by the complainant to third parties, including her health-care practitioners and police officers. The complainant was not called as a witness on the voir dire – the very issue of the voir dire being her lack of competency to testify and the resulting necessity for the admission of the out-of-court hearsay statements. The trial judge relied on the evidence of several expert witnesses in making his decision on whether the complainant's out-of-court statements, including the complainant's video-taped interview with a police officer, should be admitted into evidence. The accused argued at trial that the evidence called at the voir dire established that the complainant was sufficiently competent to testify, and that the complainant should testify, as she would exonerate the accused on cross-examination (*Parrott* 1999, paras. 146-47). The Crown argued at trial that the evidence established that the complainant could not testify "in the traditional manner" (para. 149), and that it was appropriate to offer her evidence via hearsay in accordance with the practice established in earlier Supreme Court of Canada cases.[3] At the conclusion of the voir dire, the trial judge found that it was unnecessary to have the complainant herself called as a witness, and he admitted her out-of-court statements. The accused was convicted of kidnapping but acquitted of sexual assault, though convicted of the lesser and included offence of assault causing bodily harm.

The accused appealed the trial court's decision to the Newfoundland Court of Appeal, which found in his favour. The majority of the Court of Appeal found that the trial judge inappropriately relied on the observations and opinions of others in reaching his conclusion that the hearsay evidence met the required tests of necessity and reliability. The majority found that the trial judge erred in failing to make his own analysis of the narrative capacities of the complainant (*Parrott* 1999, 91-121; 2001, paras. 46-48). Chief Justice Wells dissented and accepted the trial judge's conclusion that, based on the evidence of the expert witnesses and the videotaped interview, the complainant did not understand the nature of the oath or affirmation and was unable to communicate in any coherent or understandable manner. Wells concluded that the complainant's out-of-court statements, made shortly after she was found by the police, exhibited sufficient circumstantial guarantee of trustworthiness to make them reliable for purposes of admissibility under the established exceptions to the hearsay rule. He rejected the accused's argument that the complainant was competent to testify, and he would have dismissed the appeal by the accused (*Parrott* 1999, 121-46; 2001, para. 49). The Court of Appeal dismissed the appeal of the kidnapping charge and ordered a new trial for the assault charge. The Crown appealed the setting aside of the assault verdict.

The Supreme Court of Canada's Decision
The Supreme Court of Canada's decision in *Parrott* provides a classic example of the judiciary's failure to understand the experience of gendered disability and, as a result, its failure to protect the equality rights of women with disabilities. The crimes at issue in *Parrott* – kidnapping, assault causing bodily harm, and sexual assault – were in these particular circumstances all crimes of gendered disability. The accused clearly targeted the complainant specifically because she was a woman with a mental disability, and the experience of gendered disability was therefore central to the case. However, the court did not appreciate the relevance of the multiple axes of identity that defined the complainant in *Parrott,* and entitled her to equality rights guarantees under section 15(1) of the Charter. The court in *Parrott* segregated the complainant's personal characteristics into independent, freestanding categories that did not represent the reality of her experience. The court neutralized the complainant's gender and dealt only with the issue of disability in a limited and somewhat patronizing fashion. The court's division of the complainant's identity into categories that did not accurately reflect the reality of her experience confirms the theory that judicial decision makers are ill-equipped to recognize the equality rights of those more than once removed from the dominant norm, such as women with disabili-

ties. The court's decision in *Parrott* didn't get the gendered disability equality rights analysis wrong; it didn't get it at all.

The majority of the Supreme Court found in favour of the accused in *Parrott*. The court held that the complainant's hearsay evidence was inadmissible and that she should have been made to testify at the voir dire to determine whether she was capable of testifying at the trial. The court did not appreciate the equality rights issues implicated by forcing the complainant to testify, exposing her to further disadvantage associated with her gendered disability status. Writing for a four-person majority of the court, Justice Binnie concluded that the expert evidence was improperly admitted at the voir dire. He found that the expert evidence was unnecessary, as the trial judge could have made the determination without the assistance of expert evidence (*Parrott* 2001, para. 52(1)). Justice Binnie concluded that the complainant's out-of-court statements were inadmissible because the trial judge had no admissible evidence on which to exercise a discretion to admit the statements and their admission was unnecessary (para. 52(2)). Justice Binnie's consideration of these issues appears to have been influenced by problematic misconceptions of disability and an unawareness of the relevance of gendered disability discrimination to the case at hand. Justice LeBel, writing for a three-person minority, concluded that the admission of the complainant's out-of-court statements was necessary, based on a flexible and principled interpretation of the rules governing hearsay evidence. LeBel seemed to maintain an awareness of the complainant's status as a person with a mental disability throughout his analysis; however, the complainant remained gender neutral in his analysis. Justice LeBel reached the right conclusion in this case, though his decision would have been more meaningful and robust if he had applied an equality rights analysis to the issue of gendered disability discrimination.

Both Justices Binnie and LeBel failed to analyze the *Parrott* case in the context of gendered disability discrimination. However, their decisions are more dissimilar than alike. The decision written by Justice Binnie constitutes the more problematic of the two, and it is the farthest removed from a gendered disability equality rights analysis. In dealing with the issue of the admissibility of the expert evidence at the voir dire, Justice Binnie concluded that the expert evidence on the voir dire was improperly admitted because it was unnecessary, as "trial judges are eminently qualified to assess the testimonial competence of a witness" (*Parrott* 2001, para. 52(1)). Unfortunately, Justice Binnie is wrong in his assumption that trial judges are qualified to assess the testimonial competency of a witness with a mental disability.[4] Trial judges, like the majority of the population, are generally unfamiliar with the wide range of mental disabilities experienced by people in Canada. Trial judges are not experts in mental disability, a condition that is often difficult to assess. The nature and degree of a mental disability represents exactly the kind of information that lies beyond the knowledge and experience of the average trier of fact. The stigma and stereotypes attached to the experience of mental disability mean that the experience is often misunderstood. Given that the general population, including judges, is ill informed about different conditions of mental disability, the trial judge's decision to rely on the evidence of expert witnesses to assist him in understanding the complainant's mental capacity seems entirely appropriate.

Justice LeBel, writing for the minority, reached a different conclusion from Justice Binnie on the issue of the admissibility of the evidence and whether it was necessary to introduce the hearsay statements. Justice LeBel concluded that the Court of Appeal should not have intervened in the trial judge's finding that the admission of a videotaped interview was rendered necessary by the evidence and facts of the case. However, Justice LeBel did not disagree with Justice Binnie on the issue of whether triers of fact are aware of issues of mental disability, and whether they need the assistance of expert evidence. Justice LeBel also missed the relevance of the disability analysis to the issue of experts. Instead, he grounded his analysis in an adherence to a flexible approach to the admissibility of hearsay evidence, as directed by the court in its earlier decisions relating to this issue.[5]

Justice LeBel concluded that the evidence justified the admission of the videotaped interview as necessary, since: "'evidence of the same value' would most likely not be obtained by *viva voce* testimony of the complainant. It was apparent that attempting to make the complainant testify would not only fail to generate any new evidence, but also that it would be demeaning and potentially traumatic to her" (*Parrott* 2001, para. 8). In the same vein, Justice LeBel stated later in his decision that "to require the Crown to call the complainant before the court in these circumstances, only to confirm her limited ability to convey evidence, would have been demeaning and traumatic to her" (para. 17).

Justice LeBel's reasoning did demonstrate a recognition of the complainant's status as a person with a disability.[6] However, his presumption about trauma is problematic. An image of persons with disabilities as pitiful inferiors may be generated by presumptions that they are vulnerable and presumed susceptible to trauma. This impression represents a construction of disability that disadvantages persons with disabilities. Justice Binnie raised legitimate concerns with the issue of potential trauma, and whether it constitutes a justification for the necessity of the admission of hearsay evidence in the context of this case. Justice Binnie cautioned that "the Court should not be quick to leap to the assumption that a person with mental disabilities is not competent to give useful testimony. Trauma should not be presumed, not only because such a presumption would deprive the accused of the ability to observe and cross-examine the witness, but also because stereotypical assumptions about persons with disabilities should be avoided" (*Parrott* 2001, para. 80). Justice Binnie was right that it is necessary to avoid stereotypical thinking about persons with mental disabilities (which is not to say that all persons should be subjected to traumatic cross-examinations on an equal basis). It is also important to avoid experts usurping the voices of witnesses with disabilities, and thereby silencing persons with disabilities. The court did demonstrate some awareness of the complainant's disability in its brief discussion of the issue of trauma. However, the consideration of the trauma issue in the context of a hearsay application provided insufficient opportunity to explore the complexity of the complainant's difference as a woman with a disability. The court addressed the issue of disability only superficially and in a gender-neutral way in its trauma discussion, without providing any meaningful insight into, or understanding of, the reality of the complainant's experience.

It is also important to note that both Justices LeBel and Binnie failed to address the difference between trauma and the humiliation the complainant might experience as a witness. Justice Binnie repeatedly noted there was no evidence to establish that the complainant would suffer trauma if she testified, but he did not address the issue of humiliation. The difference between trauma and humiliation is subtle yet significant. A cross-examination that humiliates a witness with a mental disability likely involves the exploitation of her mental incapacity by confusing her in order to make her appear less credible. By confusing and humiliating the complainant, she is made to appear as though she is mistaken about the facts and is unbelievable. In contrast, cross-examination that traumatizes a complainant of a gendered disability crime involves upsetting the complainant so that she suffers pain and distress. By traumatizing the complainant, she may be demeaned, and her attractiveness as a sympathetic, "good" victim may be diminished. She may also be compelled to abandon her complaint if the trauma of testifying creates an experience of revictimization that is too extreme to bear (Schmitz 1988; Blanchfield 1996). While experiences of both trauma and humiliation resulting from discriminatory cross-examinations are the kind of experiences that equality guarantees are expected to protect against, the significance of the humiliation experience needs to be understood as distinct from the experience of trauma. As an experience likely to be associated with the cross-examination of women with mental disabilities, humiliation should be addressed as an independent discriminatory practice. The failure to address the reality of potential humiliation in *Parrott* further demonstrates the way in which the full experience of gendered disability discrimination is overlooked by the court in its decision making.

The decision reached by Justice LeBel, that the complainant's hearsay evidence was admissible, was the right conclusion in this case. However, the value of Justice LeBel's decision is limited (aside from its status as a minority opinion), as it was not informed by an analysis of the discrimination associated with the case. It is important to note that Justice LeBel did comment in an aside that "the infringement of the witness's right to the preservation of her dignity and integrity may be inferred from the circumstances of the case" (*Parrott* 2001, para. 22). He concluded that to make the complainant testify would have "deprived her of that degree of respect that every disabled person is entitled to" (para. 17). However, he did not develop an equality rights analysis to support the appropriateness of the admission of the hearsay evidence and the complainant's right not to testify. The fact that *Parrott* was decided in the post-*Law* era makes the failure to link the relevant dignity and equality issues all the more contentious.[7] Justice LeBel's reasoning of the trauma issue raises concerns that his dignity analysis might be informed by problematic assumptions about disability. The absence of an equality rights analysis and the lack of acknowledgment of the significance of the dignity interests at issue in the case leaves Justice LeBel's decision open to misinterpretation and potential misapplication.

Justice Binnie did not include any reference to, or analysis of, equality or dignity concerns in his reasoning. But he did find that stereotypical assumptions about trauma and disability should be avoided. However, his judicial treatment of the complainant reinforced several other stereotypes about disability. His treatment of the complainant was characterized, in its best representation, as pity for an inferior person, rather than as respect for a person with constitutionally guaranteed equality rights. Justice Binnie stated that "compassion for the complainant must be balanced against fairness to the respondent" (*Parrott* 2001, para. 73), and that "it was kinder to the complainant to excuse her from appearing at the trial" (para. 73). The complainant does not need the court's compassion or kindness. The complainant needs the court to recognize and enforce her right to equal treatment before and under the law. Justice Binnie's reference to the complainant as someone deserving of compassion and kindness implies that the complainant is a weak and pitiful person. This representation provides a convenient cover for what's really happening between the court and the complainant as a woman with a disability. The court may appear to be acting out of a benevolent sense of paternalism when it calls for compassion for the complainant. However, it is in essence maintaining a significant power imbalance through the construction of the complainant as a pitiful and inferior person.

Cast in a philanthropic light, the paternalistic treatment of a woman with a disability may be considered virtuous and proper. The inappropriateness of this treatment becomes apparent once the relationship is exposed as one of domination rather than altruism. The characterization of women with disabilities as weak and pitiful, in need of compassion and kindness, is precisely the kind of negative social perception of disability that has historically determined the inferior value placed on the lives of persons with disabilities. The perception and characterization of disability as a negative attribute that warrants sympathy does not advance the equal treatment of persons with disabilities – it results only in their isolation from mainstream society. The characterization of disability as a negative attribute by a majority of the Supreme Court, and the majority's neutralizing the complainant's gender, results in the subordination of the complainant as a woman with a disability in the law – a result that works to reinforce the subordination experienced by women with disabilities in society at large. As the final decision maker on equality rights policy and practice, the court influences public opinion by its decisions; thus, the way in which the court treats gendered disability discrimination has an impact on the public's perception and valuation of the experience of gendered disability. The court's findings in *Parrott* act to legitimize the negative construction of gendered disability within the larger societal context. The court's fortification of the negative social construction of gendered disability works to entrench the power disadvantage experienced by women with disabilities, as the acceptability of their inferior status is reaffirmed. It contributes to the devaluation of women with disabilities, as their right to equal treatment is denied, and it contributes to the perception that women with disabilities aren't worthy members of society.

The court found that the complainant's out-of-court statements did not qualify for the application of an "exceptional procedure" regarding the admissibility of hearsay evidence. The justification for the application of an "exceptional procedure" was not recognized because the case was analyzed from a gender-neutral perspective and was informed by problematic constructions of disability. Had the court applied a contextualized equality rights analysis of the gendered disability discrimination at issue in the case, it might have come to a different conclusion. In consideration of all the circumstances, most notably the complainant's status as a woman with a mental disability, the decision that she should have testified on the voir dire represents a violation of her right to the equal protection and benefit of the law. If the court had considered the relevance of gendered disability discrimination to the issues under appeal in this case, perhaps the weaknesses in its own reasoning (both the majority's and the minority's reasoning) would have been apparent, and thus could have been avoided. The significance of the complainant's status as a woman with a mental disability is apparent if the case is examined in the context of an equality rights analysis, from a gendered disability perspective, as developed below.

The Application of a Gendered Disability Equality Rights Analysis

The equality rights issue in *Parrott* is the complainant's entitlement to the equal benefit and protection of the provisions of the *Criminal Code*, in this case, sections 279(1) and 272(1)(c) prohibiting kidnapping and sexual assault causing bodily harm. To ensure the complainant's equal benefit and protection of these laws, the evidentiary rulings made must respect the equality rights guarantees found in section 15(1) of the Charter. The complainant has the right to be protected from an application of evidence rules that advance discriminatory thinking about women with mental disabilities, or that unfairly disadvantage her because she is a woman with a mental disability. In *Parrott,* the accused clearly targeted the complainant, a woman with a mental disability, as evidenced by his premeditated abduction of the complainant from the psychiatric hospital where she lived (*Parrott* 2001, para. 31), making this a crime of gendered disability. An analysis of the complainant's right to substantive equality in the treatment of her evidence must be examined through an equality rights lens of gendered disability. The following analysis will apply this lens to the experience of sexual assault to demonstrate how and why a contextualized analysis is essential for the advancement of the equality rights claims of women with disabilities.

The context of gendered disability and sexual assault needs to be fully understood in order to make the required equality rights analysis work. Sexual assault has been repeatedly recognized by the court as a gendered crime (*R. v. Seaboyer* 1991, 648-49; *R. v. Osolin* 1993, 669). It should, therefore, not be a huge intellectual leap to recognize the kidnapping and assault of a woman with a disability as a crime of gendered disability. While sexual assault is, by definition, a gendered crime, other crimes can, in particular circumstances, be gendered crimes or gendered disability crimes. The basic socio-political attributes of sexual assault are generally well accepted today. Sexual assault as a form of violence against women is commonly understood to be a product of patriarchy, the system of male control over women. The act of rape is not an end in itself, but a means of enforcing prescribed gender roles in society and maintaining the social hierarchy in which men retain control. However, sexual assault is not experienced in a uniform and universal fashion. Racialized women have clearly articulated the differences associated with their experience of sexual violence as an exercise of power and control rooted in racism and sexism, the effects of which cannot be separated (Harris 1990; Crenshaw 1991; Monture-Angus 1999). The analyses of feminist critical race theorists represent useful models for exposing the problems with essentialized analyses of sexual assault that ignore the issue of disability. I will examine the relevancy for women with disabilities of feminist critical race theories relating to the experience of sexual assault, and the dominant conceptualization of sexual assault as the source of the problematic good/bad victim dichotomy. This examination of the socio-political context of the gendered disability experience at issue is the kind of analysis that needs to inform gendered disability equality rights challenges. It works to ensure that the complexity of their experience is understood, and that the source of their disadvantage is exposed.

The sexual assault of women with disabilities must be understood in terms of the experience of gendered disability, just as violence against women of colour demands an analysis that transcends the limitations of analyses devoid of a race perspective. The sexual assault of a woman with a disability is not the result of a disabled woman's "additive" status as a woman and as a person with a disability. These characteristics are indivisible and come together in a way that creates a distinctive life experience – one that puts women with disabilities at an increased risk of experiencing sexual assault and of being denied the full and equal benefit and protection of the criminal law. The complexities at issue in an analysis of sexual assault and gendered disability are different from the complexities at issue in an analysis of sexual assault involving women of colour. However, the need to recognize and explore the nature of these distinctive experiences is the same – the need to ensure that those who fall within the distinctive category are not erased from the analysis and that reform strategies are relevant and beneficial to those outside the dominant norm.

Some women with disabilities are exceptionally vulnerable to being the target of a sexual assault (Sobsey and Doe 1991, 248-49; Meekosha 1998, 178; Morris 2002).[8] There are several reasons for the increased vulnerability of some women with disabilities to sexual assault. Violence against women is an extreme application of social control. The commission of violence against women with disabilities represents an acute manifestation of the exercise of male power and, therefore, may be particularly attractive to some men. Some women with disabilities may be particularly vulnerable to sexual assault because they are so different from the norm that their status as Other, and their relative disempowerment, are especially amplified. Women with disabilities that are very different from the norm, such as women with a severe mental disability, may be viewed as so abnormal that they are not considered credible as a primary witness in a sexual assault trial. Their relative value as human beings may be so diminished, and their status as Other so heightened, that a sexual predator will consider them an especially easy target. Some women with disabilities may also be more physically susceptible to an attack if, for example, they are in an institution or have mobility impairments. While crimes of sexual violence against non-disabled women carry some social stigma, this stigma may not attach as much to crimes against women with disabilities because of their status as Other. A sexual predator may assume that women with disabilities can be attacked without consequence, as there is an ethos in our society that women with disabilities are not equally valued, so that they just don't count. These social realities make the experience of sexual assault for women with disabilities distinct from the sexual assault of non-disabled women, and make many women with disabilities especially vulnerable to sexual assault.

The dominant conceptualization of sexual assault, and the perception of the good/bad victim dichotomy, also operates to distinguish the experience of sexual assault for women with disabilities. Early analyses of rape law, argues Kimberle Crenshaw (1991, 1266), emphasized the "property-like aspect of women's chastity." This conceptualization of rape did not only result "in less solicitude for rape victims whose chastity had in some way been devalued," such as women of colour. It also legitimized a "good woman/ bad woman dichotomy" in the analysis of rape law (Crenshaw 1991, 1266). Women with disabilities have also experienced disadvantage as a result of the legitimization of the good/bad victim dichotomy in sexual assault law. The good/bad victim dichotomy works against women with disabilities in the context of sexual assault law in different ways. Throughout history, society has viewed mentally disabled women as hypersexual and more sexually promiscuous than other women (Tweddle, Robb, and Yereniuk 1993, 30-31). Because of this kind of stereotyping, women with mental disabilities are often viewed as oversexed "bad" victims of sexual assault, desperate for sex, and deserving of any abuse they may experience. They are unlikely, as a result, to experience equality of treatment in the criminal justice system. Alternatively, a woman with mental or physical disabilities may be viewed as a childlike asexual being who does not merit the full benefit and protection of the law usually reserved for the "good" or "normal" victim, because she may have "unwittingly" invited the assault. Women with disabilities who are perceived as asexual and childlike may attract the sympathy of the judiciary, but not necessarily the protection of the judicial system. As apparently happened in *Parrott,* a woman with a disability who alleges sexual assault may be considered asexual and basically gender neutral, so that the issue of her equality rights as a woman with a disability is ignored. A woman with a disability may also be denied the full benefit and protection of the law because she is so physically or mentally dissimilar to the norm that it is difficult for judicial decision makers to appreciate her sexual attraction (sexual assault in this instance being misinterpreted as an act of sex, rather than an act of power).

Crimes in which women with disabilities are targeted because of their vulnerability are crimes of gendered disability. The sexual assault of women with disabilities is one example of such a crime; however, it is not the only example. The kidnapping and physical assault of a woman with a mental disability, as was experienced by the complainant in *Parrott,* constitutes an exercise of gendered power over a woman with a disability. These crimes have specific origins and power differentials that distinguish them from other crimes in which gendered disability is not a factor. Crimes in which women with disabilities are targeted because of their specific identity constitute discrimination because of gendered disability, and should be legally recognized as crimes of gendered disability. Such recognition is important because it means that the section 15 equality rights of women with disabilities can be mobilized. Crimes of gendered disability should not be neutralized in their judicial treatment but should be recognized as crimes in which gendered disability matters so that the defining inequities can be addressed.

In the context of the *Parrott* case, if the issues had been considered with reference to the complainant's equality rights, the court's analysis would have been quite different. The complainant, as a woman with a mental disability, is a member of a recognized group protected against discrimination under section 15 of the Charter. Section 15 entitles the complainant to the equal benefit and protection of the *Criminal Code*. The complainant's right to the fair administration of justice in the context of sexual assault trials is now well established (*R. v. Mills* 1999, 668). It is also well established that the right of the accused to make full answer and defence does not include the right to information that would only distort the truth-seeking goal of the trial process. The Supreme Court of Canada stated in *R. v. Osolin* (1993, 669-70): "The provisions of ss. 15 and 28 of the *Charter* guaranteeing equality to men and women, although not determinative should be taken into account in determining the reasonable limitations that should be placed upon the cross-examination of a complainant ... A complainant should not be unduly harassed and pilloried to the extent of becoming a victim of an insensitive judicial system." Elsewhere the court held that "the accused is not permitted to 'whack the complainant' through the use of stereotypes regarding victims of sexual assault" (*R. v. Mills* 1999, 668, para. 90). In the prosecution of an assault of a woman with a mental disability, the accused should not be permitted to "whack the complainant" through a cross-examination, the sole purpose of which is to harass and demean the complainant. Nor should the accused be allowed to distort the truth-seeking process of the trial by conducting a cross-examination directed only at exposing the complainant's status as Other, thereby introducing prejudicial ideas about disability, such as the idea that inability to communicate effectively means that a woman's evidence is unreliable. If the court in *Parrott* had analyzed the Crown's application to enter the hearsay evidence in the context of gendered disability discrimination, such an analysis would have exposed the disadvantage experienced by the complainant as a woman with a mental disability, and would have justified the decision not to require the complainant's oral testimony. Evidence rules need to be responsive to the equality interests of complainants. Women with disabilities should not be forced to testify when the primary purpose of that testimony would be to exploit their disadvantage under the pressure of cross-examination and to introduce discriminatory beliefs about gendered disability. The application of evidence rules that disadvantage complainants who are the alleged victims of gendered disability crimes must be avoided – this can be achieved through the application of contextualized equality rights analyses that work to protect the equality rights otherwise guaranteed to these women.

Conclusion

Without a contextualized analysis of gendered disability discrimination, the inequality experienced by women with disabilities becomes invisible in the law. The *Parrott* case provides a good example of the consequences associated with a failure to consider the experience of gendered disability – the perpetuation of the invisibility and inequality of women with disabilities. As demonstrated by the court's one-dimensional perception of the complainant in *Parrott,* the challenge of perceiving a multi-faceted identity was beyond its ability. That the complainant was so different from the dominant norm of both the non-disabled judiciary and the "good" rape victim meant that the challenge of making the legal system work for her was particularly difficult. In *Parrott,* the social construct of a woman with a mental disability as a childlike being, deserving, perhaps, of kindness and compassion, essentially asexual in nature, operated to neutralize the complainant's gender. This construct allowed the court to focus exclusively on the complainant's mental disability or to ignore her personal characteristics altogether. While it is impossible to explain exactly why the court reached its different decisions, it is clear that the concept of gendered disability remained unexplored in *Parrott.* The court constructed a gender-neutral complainant whose identity was carved up, so that her disability eclipsed the other elements of her identity.

The development of gendered disability analyses is necessary so that women with disabilities are not subsumed within established legal discourses, and so that legal method can be transformed to allow women with disabilities to achieve the maximum value of equality rights law. The application of a contextualized gendered disability analysis, incorporating elements of disability and feminist legal theory, can be of assistance. By exploring the nature and extent of the subordination of women with disabilities within both society and the law, and by exploring how these different sites of subordination work to reinforce each other, it is possible to identify the law's shortcomings relating to gendered disability. The application of a gendered disability analysis to the equality claims of women with disabilities assists with unthinking the discriminatory reasoning that so often informs both society's treatment of women with disabilities and judicial decision making about women with disabilities. In the absence of the application of gendered disability analyses, there is a tendency simply to adopt the dominant legal paradigm. There are serious consequences attached to this kind of default analysis. It makes invisible the distinctive experience that is overlooked, leaving the needs of the group unidentified and unprotected. The default analysis represents a missed opportunity to expand the understanding of unexplored complexities. It means that the opportunity to develop analyses and legal arguments that would maximize the law's potential for women with disabilities is foregone, and that the security and equality interests of women with disabilities remain in legal jeopardy.

Notes

1 For a discussion of how contextualization can be done well or badly, see Dianne Pothier and Richard Devlin, "Redressing the Imbalances: Rethinking the Judicial Role After *R. v. R.D.S.*," *Ottawa Law Review* 31, 1 (1999-2000): 16-25.

2 A voir dire is an examination, separate from the main trial, conducted by the judge in the absence of the jury to determine the admissibility of evidence or the competency of a witness. Evidence called at the voir dire cannot be used in the trial itself, unless admitted again at trial.

3 See *R. v. Khan*, [1990] 2 S.C.R. 531; and *R. v. Smith*, [1992] S.C.R. 915. Under the *Khan/Smith* exception to the hearsay rule, the Crown is required to establish first that the admission of the complainant's out-of-court statements is necessary, and second, that the statements themselves are reliable.

4 The issue of gender does not directly factor into the debate on the capability of judges to assess mental disability and testimonial competence.

5 See *R. v. Khan*, [1990] 2 S.C.R. 531; *R. v. Smith*, [1992] 2 S.C.R. 915; *R. v. U. (F.J.)*, [1995] 3 S.C.R. 764; and *R. v. Rockey*, [1996] 3 S.C.R. 829.

6 While Justice LeBel does reference the potential trauma that might have been experienced by "her," the complainant, the use of the feminine pronoun does not, in my opinion, represent an awareness of the gendered disability nature of the crime or that the potential trauma was specific to that context. Justice LeBel's finding that "it was apparent that attempting to make the complainant testify would be demeaning and potentially traumatic for her" was grounded in his assessment of her status as a person with a disability based on the gender neutral evidence provided by the expert witnesses. There is nothing to indicate that Justice LeBel was alert to the fact that the context of the case was relevant to this assessment. It seems likely that Justice LeBel would have reached the same conclusion if the complainant were the primary witness in a break-and-enter trial instead of a sexual assault trial.

7 The *Law* decision (*Law v. Canada (Minister of Employment and Immigration)*, [1999] 1 S.C.R. 497) dealt with a challenge to the constitutionality of age restrictions for eligibility for survivor benefits under the *Canada Pension Plan Act* on the basis of age discrimination in violation of section 15(1) of the Charter. The framework for an equality rights analysis was redefined in *Law* to include an assessment of injury to dignity as a threshold requirement to a successful section 15(1) challenge.

8 The use of vulnerability as a concept carries some risk, as it may be understood to place the focus on the victim of the sexual assault, instead of on the perpetrator. It risks making the analysis about the individual, rather than about socio-political conditions and power imbalances that create an experience of vulnerability. I use the concept of vulnerability to refer to the socially diminished credibility, autonomy and devalued personhood of women with disabilities that can render them easy prey to perpetrators of sexual assault (see Martin 1994, 547; Razack 1994, 902).

References

Bickenbach, Jerome E. 1993. *Physical disability and social policy*. Toronto: University of Toronto Press.

Blanchfield, M. 1996. Courtroom warrior goes to battle for accused. *Lawyers Weekly* 15, 35 (26 January): 1.

Comack, Elizabeth. 1999. Theoretical excursions. In *Locating law: Race/class/gender connections*, ed. Elizabeth Comack, 19-68. Halifax: Fernwood Publishing.

Crenshaw, Kimberle. 1991. Mapping the margins: Intersectionality, identity politics, and violence against women of color. *Stanford Law Review* 43: 1241-99.

Fudge, Judy. 1987. The public/private distinction: The possibilities of and the limits to the use of Charter litigation to further feminist struggles. *Osgoode Hall Law Journal* 25, 3: 485-554.

Fuss, Diana. 1989. *Essentially speaking: Feminism, nature and difference.* New York: Routledge.

Harris, Angela P. 1990. Race and essentialism in feminist legal theory. *Stanford Law Review* 42: 581-616.

hooks, bell. 1982. *Ain't I a woman: Black women and feminism.* London: Pluto Press.

Iyer, Nitya. 1993-94. Categorical denials: Equality rights and the shaping of social identity. *Queen's Law Journal* 19: 179-207.

Jhappan, Radha. 1998. The equality pit or the rehabilitation of justice. *Canadian Journal of Women and the Law* 10: 60-107.

Lorde, Audre. 1984. *Sister outsider: Essays and speeches.* Trumansburg, NY: Crossing Press.

Martin, S. 1994. Some constitutional considerations on sexual violence against women. *Alberta Law Review* 32, 3: 535-56.

Meekosha, Helen. 1998. Body battles: Bodies, gender and disability. In *The disability reader: Social science perspectives,* ed. Tom Shakespeare, 163-80. New York: Cassell.

Minow, Martha. 1990. *Making all the difference: Inclusion, exclusion, and American law.* Ithaca, NY: Cornell University Press.

Monture-Angus, Patricia. 1999. Standing against Canadian law: Naming omissions of race, culture, and gender. In *Locating law: Race/class/gender connections,* ed. Elizabeth Comack, 76-97. Halifax: Fernwood Publishing.

Morris, Marika. 2002. Violence against women and girls – A fact sheet. Ottawa: Canadian Research Institute for the Advancement of Women. http://www.criaw-icref.ca/indexFrame-e.htm.

Pothier, Dianne. 1992. Miles to go: Some personal reflections on the social construction of disability. *Dalhousie Law Journal* 14: 526-43.

–. 2006 (forthcoming). But it's for your own good. In *Poverty: Rights, social citizenship and governance,* ed. Margot Young, Gwen Brodsky, Shelagh Day, and Susan Boyd. Vancouver: UBC Press.

R. v. Mills, [1999] 3 S.C.R. 668.

R. v. Osolin, [1993] 4 S.C.R. 595.

R. v. Parrott (1999), 175 Nfld. & P.E.I.R. 89 [*Parrott*].

R. v. Parrott, [2001] 1 S.C.R. 178 [*Parrott*].

R. v. Seaboyer, [1991] 2 S.C.R. 577.

Razack, Sherene. 1994. From consent to responsibility, from pity to respect: Subtexts in cases of sexual violence involving girls and women with developmental disabilities. *Law and Social Inquiry* 19, 4 (Fall): 891-923.

Schmitz, Cristin. 1988. "Whack" the sex assault complainant at preliminary inquiry. *Lawyers Weekly* 8, 5 (May 27): 22.

Sheldon, Alison. 1999. Personal and perplexing: Feminist disability politics evaluated. *Disability and Society* 14, 5: 643-57.

Sobsey, Dick, and Tannis Doe. 1991. Patterns of sexual abuse and assault. *Sexuality and Disability* 9: 243-59.

Tweddle, Margaret, Jim Robb, and Orest Yereniuk. 1993. Mental disability and the criminal justice system. *Health Law Review* 2: 28-34.

Weedon, Chris. 1999. *Feminism, theory and the politics of difference.* Malden, MA: Blackwell Publishers.

Williams, Susan. 1993. Feminist legal epistemologies. *Berkeley Women's Law Journal* 8: 63-105.

13

Infertility and the Parameters of Discrimination Discourse

Daphne Gilbert and Diana Majury

As indicated, we hope, by the appearance of a book such as this, disability theory is gaining new prominence in Canadian society. As is typical, law lags behind society in responding to trends in discrimination analysis. This is particularly true in the disability context. Canadian courts have considered very few disability cases under the *Canadian Charter of Rights and Freedoms,* and have offered unsatisfactory judgments in many of those. A 1999 decision by the Nova Scotia Court of Appeal in *Cameron v. Nova Scotia (Attorney General)* (1999) is an example. In *Cameron,* the court concluded that the medical condition of infertility is a disability for the purposes of analysis under section 15 of the Charter (which includes disability as one of its enumerated grounds).[1] We take issue with many of the assumptions that underlie the *Cameron* decision and with its approach to section 15 in the disability context.[2]

The claim in *Cameron* was brought by a heterosexual couple, Dr. Smith and Mr. Cameron, who underwent fertility treatments for Mr. Cameron's infertility that were not covered by the provincial health-care plan. They challenged the exclusion from the Medical Services Insurance plan as a violation of their section 15 rights under the Charter on the basis of disability discrimination.[3] The claimants were unsuccessful at both trial and on appeal, and leave to appeal to the Supreme Court of Canada was denied.[4] The majority decision by Justice Chipman of the Court of Appeal concluded that infertility is a disability, and that the funding disparity is discriminatory. He concluded, however, that the breach of equality rights was justifiable under section 1 of the Charter, which allows reasonable limitations on Charter rights.[5] The concurring opinion of Justice Bateman concluded that infertility is not a disability but offers virtually no analysis or explanation of why this is so.[6] Justice Bateman would also have found any discrimination to be justifiable.

The majority's reasoning in *Cameron* is problematic on many levels. In particular, it is illustrative of the weaknesses in the current approach for finding violations of the constitutional right to equality in section 15 of the Charter. The current test for violations of section 15 is derived from the Supreme Court of Canada's decision in *Law v. Canada (Minister of Employment and Immigration)* (1999). In *Law,* Justice Iacobucci emphasized that the equality guarantee deserves a purposive and contextual approach to its interpretation, involving three broad inquiries: (1) does the impugned law draw a formal distinction between the claimant and others on the basis of one or more personal characteristics?; (2) is the claimant subject to differential treatment based on one or more enumerated and analogous grounds?; and (3) does the differential treatment discriminate by imposing a burden upon, or withholding a benefit from, the claimant in a manner which has the effect of promoting the view that the individual is less capable or worthy of recognition or value as a human being, or as a member of Canadian society (*Law*, para. 88(3))? This last question has evolved into the human dignity test, requiring claimants to establish that the impugned law violates or demeans their dignity, or otherwise marginalizes them in Canadian society. As part of the human dignity determination, the court assesses whether the claimant's group carries a stigma that is exacerbated by the impugned law. As we will discuss, in the disability context the stigma analysis also arises in the second *Law* question in defining whether a claimant's condition is a disability. In our view, the *Law* test is ill-suited to a meaningful disability discrimination analysis.

In the next section, we consider an initial problem with the *Cameron* decision, namely, its conflation of the two claimants as an infertile unit. The majority judgment treats Dr. Smith as infertile, even though she has no diagnosed medical condition. The court fails to reason through the gendered history and medical treatment of female infertility, but applies it wholesale to male infertility as if the two situations are identical (indeed, as if infertility is a coupled problem). We then turn to section 15 of the Charter and address the problematic use of comparator groups in this case, and in equality analysis more generally, before exploring the under-theorized and underdeveloped enumerated ground of disability in section 15 and, especially, the inaccurate ascription of this ground to infertility in *Cameron*. We conclude by considering whether section 15 could be re-envisioned to better reflect developing disability rights advocacy. In the legal context, the medical model of assessing disability has prevailed, with only minor inroads by the social model. In disability literature and advocacy, the social model dominates, but has been critiqued and revised by postmodernism.[7] The effect of these models on the future jurisprudential treatment of disability is key to transforming law's response to disability discrimination and to improving section 15's assessment of the meaning of an equality right.

The Nature of the Claim

In our view, both Court of Appeal judgments run into immediate trouble by failing to fully examine the particular circumstances of the claimants. Before even deciding whether they fit into a ground, it is important to consider the nature of the discrimination claim. While the decision does not specify whether Mr. Cameron underwent any medical treatment associated with the funding claim before the court, it is certain that Dr. Smith received treatment.[8] The judgment indicates, however, that it is Mr. Cameron who received the medical determination as "infertile." He was diagnosed as having "severe male factor infertility," which led to the need for a specialized form of in vitro fertilization, ICSI, considered the treatment of choice for male factor infertility.[9] Before the treatment for which funding was claimed, each of the claimants had undergone surgery and participated in three cycles of intrauterine insemination. The next phase, ICSI, was not offered in Nova Scotia at the time, and so the couple travelled to Calgary and Toronto for the treatment. Dr. Smith went through four cycles of ICSI with no success. The claim before the court related to these out-of-province treatments.

Justice Chipman referred to the claimants as an "infertile couple," and as having "the condition of childlessness" and belonging to the group "the infertile," thus treating them as a unit. One cannot help but hear echoes of the old legal rule that when a man and woman marry, they become one, and that one is the husband.[10] Justice Bateman largely avoids this problem by referring mostly to the male appellant's infertility, though sometimes to just the appellant's infertility. She seems more attuned to the issue, though there is no mention or discussion of it in her reasons.

The judgment proceeds on the basis that, as a couple, they are infertile. While no further analysis is offered, this line of reasoning implicitly follows what Marjorie Shultz refers to as social infertility – individuals who are biologically able to conceive a child but lack or do not want a fertile partner.[11] The implication is that Dr. Smith is "socially infertile" in that she is married to a man who is unable to conceive a child. We reject the argument that a woman who lacks a fertile partner can be deemed infertile, either socially or otherwise. It is, however, perhaps a useful way of referring to Dr. Smith's situation in the context of this claim, given that she actually underwent fertility treatments. The category "social infertility" captures her claim, and explains why she is a part of the medical procedure. We think it important, however, especially in the context of a disability discrimination claim, to at least be aware of the exact nature of the claim. The problem with imprecision at this initial stage is that both judgments completely ignore the gendered history, context, and present reality of infertility and related treatments. This context has been the subject of much feminist critique of the gendered blame and medical treatment of the woman who is infertile, or whose male partner is infertile. Feminists have also raised questions as to the treatment's invasiveness and risk to the woman (Corea 1985; Dworkin 1983; Basen, Eichler, and Lippman 1993; Lacey 1998-99).[12] Understanding social conceptions of female infertility is crucial to any discussion on discriminatory infertility practices. It is relevant to any consideration of whether an infertile woman can claim a disability (and especially relevant to discussions on the stigma associated with the condition, as we outline below). This context must certainly be addressed when a man is infertile, and is even more pressing in the *Cameron* context, where Dr. Smith is "socially infertile."

Our view is that this decision perpetuates a problematic gender slippage and compounds the problems of slotting infertility into a disability category, as discussed below. The decision perpetuates the notion of women as natural reproducers, for the emphasis is on "fixing" Dr. Smith's failure to conceive a biological child. The court in *Cameron* treats male and female infertility as the same, both medically and historically. The judgment proceeds on this assumption without any evidence or argument to sustain it. While this is disheartening in itself, it is all the more so in light of the Supreme Court of Canada's recent section 15 decision in *Trociuk v. British Columbia (Attorney General)* (2003), which follows the same unfortunate line of reasoning.

At issue in *Trociuk* were provincial statutory provisions on birth registrations allowing a birth mother to declare her child's father as "unacknowledged," or "unacknowledged for valid reasons," or simply as "incapable or unknown" (*Trociuk* 2003, 11). Fathers were given no recourse in the decision to register or not register their names, and unnamed fathers could not participate in deciding the child's surname. Mr. Trociuk successfully challenged the provision as a violation of his equality rights. Justice Deschamps, writing for the court, held that the provision discriminated by treating fathers differently from mothers, in a manner that degraded or demeaned fathers on the enumerated ground of sex. She held that birth registration and the naming of children are significant interests, and that the arbitrary exclusion of the father from this process demeans his dignity (*Trociuk* 2003, 10-12). In so concluding, Justice Deschamps ignored two lengthy judgments from the British Columbia Court of Appeal that detailed the legislative and social history attached to the naming of children, discussions that emphasized the very different interests at stake between single mothers and fathers.[13] She paid no heed to arguments that single mothers are a particularly vulnerable group, and that there might be legitimate reasons to support a mother's decision to exclude the father from the birth registration process, especially in cases of sexual or physical assault, incest, or abuse.

Trociuk and *Cameron* are examples of formal equality at work: men and women should be treated the same, and necessarily have the same interests at stake – especially concerning reproduction and children. The resurgence of a formal equality model flies in the face of the court's insistence that section 15 is a purposive provision designed to further substantive equality ideals. Indeed, Justice Iacobucci emphasized this in *Law* (para. 38).

Comparator Groups

The initial failure to examine the circumstances of the claimants feeds into several of the problems in the Court of Appeal's section 15 reasoning. The court seems to accept many of the claimants' arguments without significant analysis, and its reasoning reads as premised on assumptions. This is clearly illustrated in the first step of the equality analysis: setting up the relevant comparison to determine whether the impugned regulation is discriminatory. Section 15 has been interpreted by the courts to require a comparison between the person who claims unfair treatment and another group posited as receiving better or more appropriate treatment, in order to assess the alleged differential treatment. Identifying the appropriate comparator can be problematic, yet it is an extremely significant part of an equality analysis.[14]

In the first post-*Law* Supreme Court decision on disability, *Granovsky v. Canada (Minister of Employment and Immigration)* (2000, para. 45), the court acknowledged that the identification of a comparator group is crucial. In *Granovsky,* the claimant suffered from a temporary disability that prevented him from working and contributing to the Canada Pension Plan. When his disability became permanent, he was excluded from disability benefits because of his lack of contributions. In his claim, he argued that he ought to be compared with an able-bodied member of the workforce during the contribution period. In his view, both able-bodied and temporarily disabled workers were expected to make the same level of contributions to the plan, which discriminated against those who are disabled and thereby unable to make CPP contributions (para. 46). Persons with a severe or permanent disability could take advantage of dropout provisions in the legislation, whereby periods of disability are not counted in the contribution calculation.

Justice Binnie, writing for the court, acknowledged that a claimant is given considerable scope to identify the appropriate comparator group, but emphasized it is ultimately the court's determination. In Binnie's view, the relevant comparator group in this case consists of those contributors who "suffered from severe and permanent disabilities," and who, therefore, benefited from relaxed rules to which the claimant wanted access (para. 52). He reasoned that the claimant was endeavouring to share the dropout benefit enjoyed by those with a severe or permanent disability and, therefore, should be compared with that group. Despite the claimant's insistence that he did not want to be compared with the permanently disabled, Binnie concluded: "If, as I believe, he has picked the wrong comparator group, the rest of his analysis collapses under the weight of an erroneous premise" (para. 64).[15] The dropout provision assists those with a history of permanent disability and is not targeted at those allegedly more fortunate (like the claimant). Binnie held that in subsidizing a particular group, Parliament does not demean the dignity of those who are not permanently disabled (paras. 61-70).

Granovsky illustrates a fundamental problem with comparator groups, one that is particularly evident in disability cases. Justice Binnie uses a formal equality model that would compare the claimant to the group whose benefits he wishes to share. If Mr. Granovsky wants the benefits accorded to those who are permanently disabled, he must fit into that category. The claimant's argument is more sophisticated and considers the actual impact of his condition. If his temporary disability has the same effect on his employability as a permanent disability, why should he not share the benefit of relaxed contribution conditions? Justice Binnie made an assumption that persons with temporary disabilities are better off financially than persons with permanent disabilities, an assumption that seemed to be at odds with the circumstances of the very case before the court.

The jurisprudential requirement that equality is a comparative concept also reinforces the medical model of disability, a model which, as we will discuss, disability rights advocates reject. The comparison between disabilities, or between the disabled and the abled, is not only an impossible task but one that perpetuates dominant notions of normalcy. In *Granovsky*, Justice Binnie relies on medical labels, rather than considering the actual impact of Mr. Granovsky's disability. This flies in the face of a substantive or purposive equality analysis. The claimant's chosen comparator group was based on his assessment of the reality of his situation. While it is still an awkward comparison, at least it captures the context of his claim. Justice Binnie's choice was based on medical assessments of the prospect of recovery (whether a disability is permanent or temporary). Such a comparison of impairments is antithetical to a meaningful equality analysis.

In *Cameron*, Justice Chipman identified the comparator groups as the infertile and the fertile. He found that a distinction was made on the basis that every aspect of having a child is covered by the provincial insurance plan, with infertile individuals or couples (Justice Chipman is unclear as to which) getting less than full coverage because they were unable to have a child. Justice Chipman argued that the claimants, who are disabled by their inability to procreate, are denied key treatments of choice (*Cameron* 1999, 651). This is a distinction based on their personal characteristic of infertility. The court compares the claimants – the "infertile couple" – to women who are pregnant or bearing children, for whom all treatments are insured.

This follows the medical model of assessing disability by comparing the disabled and the non-disabled on the basis of what Marcia Rioux and Fraser Valentine call "comparative incapacity" (see Chapter 2). Justice Chipman is essentially comparing a couple he considers disabled (infertile) with those who are not disabled (the fertile – those who have achieved the state of pregnancy) to decide what kind of treatment the disabled couple should be entitled to. In our view, this is extremely problematic in its strict comparison of disability and ability.

Even if we accepted a medical model, Justice Chipman's comparator choice seems unworkable. Are pregnancy and childbirth comparable with infertility treatments? In our view, the two conditions are dissimilar enough to make comparison meaningless. Once a woman decides to carry out a pregnancy, the well-being of a child is involved, and this adds a different element to the provision of medical services. Pregnancy is an ongoing condition that impacts dramatically on a woman's psychological and physical health. Once a woman conceives, treating a pregnancy (whether medically or through midwifery) is vital to her health and safety.

Justice Chipman's comparator choice is rooted in a formal equality argument that likes should be treated alike, and that in this case, the likes relate to reproduction. All reproductive issues cannot and should not be placed under the same umbrella, and certainly not in the context of an analysis around disability. The comparison is also of concern from a feminist point of view in our understanding of reproduction and reproductive services.[16] It is certainly not intuitive why Justice Chipman chooses that comparator, for there is no explanation why he made that choice.

If one has to retain the need for a comparator, a more logical one might be to other persons or couples who are infertile. Some fertility treatments were covered by the plan, others were not. It would remain an open question whether the legislative distinction was made on a discriminatory basis. Claimants could challenge the process of administrative decision making (as the claimants did in this case), which allows the government to respond with evidence on resource allocation, cost, success rates, and availability of treatment. Or, claimants could argue from a Charter perspective that the legislation improperly codified degrees of disability and imposed an artificial line for benefits. On the facts of this case, one is led to ask whether infertility is in fact a disability at all.

Is Infertility a Disability?

To us, the question of whether infertility can or should be considered a disability is key to the analysis. The difficult aspect of the question lies not so much in the answer reached, but in determining how to go about making the assessment. It is in this process that assumptions, expectations, and understandings about disability can be exposed. In pursuing this question, we first look at infertility as portrayed in the *Cameron* decision and the medical model of disability that it uncritically adopts. We then explore contemporary attempts to re-envision disability by looking at how other approaches – the social model and a postmodern approach – might help us think about infertility in relation to disability, and ultimately, critically reflect on disability as a legal category.

At the outset, we wish to note that a conclusion that infertility is not a disability would not necessarily foreclose the claim being put forward in the *Cameron* case. We do not explore the issue of alternative claims in the context of this chapter, but it is possible that some analogous ground or group characterization, other than disability, could carry the discrimination claim. Alternatively, there may be other administrative law or statutory interpretation grounds on which a challenge to the allocation of health resources in this type of situation could be successfully made.

Infertility in the *Cameron* Decision

Justice Chipman, on behalf of the majority, states emphatically and assuredly: "I do not think it can be seriously disputed that a person unable to have a child has a physical disability ... The perpetuation of the human race has, in almost all cultures and at all times, been assigned a very high value. One's inability to participate in this great plan must, for one willing to do so, be a major and deep felt disappointment" (*Cameron* 1999, 648). There are a number of readily apparent, major problems with this assertion. First, it *can* be seriously disputed that infertility is a disability. This is a complex question that requires serious investigation, not one that can be dismissed as intuitively obvious. In fact, a disability is intuitively obvious only to the extent that disablism has constructed it as such. Justice Chipman's ill-considered assertion allows him to avoid having to do any of the hard work or analysis of why infertility is a disability, and what it means to describe infertility as a disability.

Justice Chipman unreflectively adopts the medical model of disability whereby a serious physical impairment is, by definition, a disability. As a medical problem, infertility is a physiological condition that renders one unable to produce children. Infertility can be treated and perhaps[17] overcome by a variety of methods, depending on the cause and source of the impairment.[18] Stripped of social and historical context, infertility is completely contained within and by its medical diagnosis and prognosis.

As a corollary to his invocation of the medical model, Justice Chipman equates disability with "a major and deep felt disappointment." Infertility is no doubt a painful and difficult revelation for a couple that wants to bear a child, but personal disappointment does not transform a condition into a disability. Nonetheless, when the disability claim is related to treatment, the impairment is invariably depicted in tragic terms. This problem is writ large in Justice Chipman's judgment, which is full of the language of the tragedy of infertility. He describes infertility as "leaving its victims scarred and vulnerable," as "a very burdensome affliction," and as having "a serious impact on the mental and social well-being of couples that may result in detrimental social consequences such as divorce or ostracism" (*Cameron* 1999, 658). He refers to "overcoming the affliction of childlessness" (*Cameron* 1999, 661). This is quintessentially the medical model, presenting the condition as a devastating impairment, with medicine as the heroic rescuer valiantly attempting to right the wrong.[19] As descriptions of infertility, these types of statements are extremely troubling. As descriptions of disability, they are damaging and discriminatory in and of themselves.

According to the social model of disability, stigma would be a defining feature of disability. One of the ironies of the *Cameron* decision is that it – the decision itself – effectively constitutes evidence that infertility is a disability. The decision is loaded with statements about the stigma of infertility that serve to reinforce rather than challenge the stigma. Thus, if stigma is the key to the determination of an impairment as a disability, the *Cameron* decision is a significant piece in the construction of infertility as a disability. We are not sure that there is a stigma attached to infertility, at least, if infertility is stigmatized in 2003; nonetheless, this is a highly stigmatizing decision. This raises the troubling question of whether the language of this decision is sufficient answer to the question of stigma. To put a postmodern spin on it – law has spoken, medicine has spoken; the ruling disciplines have disciplined – infertility is a disability. We are not willing to concede the point to Justice Chipman and the medical model, nor are we willing to concede to the regulatory authority of the dominating disciplines.

We need to look further at the application of the social model of disability and the question of stigma and infertility. Justice Chipman engages with the question of the stigma attached to infertility as part of the third step in the section 15 assessment, that is, the determination of whether the differential treatment of not funding ICSI constituted discrimination. Having found differential treatment based on the ground of disability, the court, in this third part of the section 15 analysis, explicitly focuses on stereotypes, historical disadvantage, and stigma, under the rubric of promoting human dignity. But according to the social model of disability, these questions are part of the assessment of whether a condition is a disability, that is, the determination of the ground, which is the second step in the section 15 process. This is not merely a technical point or simply a matter of the order in which the determination is made. Under section 15 equality jurisprudence, issues of stigma and context go to the determination of discrimination based on the ground, not to the determination of the ground itself. This is the process Justice Chipman follows in *Cameron*, and which, as we argue above, is inappropriate because it assumes the ground as static, as without serious dispute, and thereby, forecloses an actual assessment of the ground. An assertion of the ground of disability is an assertion of stigma, stereotype, and disadvantage that needs to be decided in order for the matter to proceed as a disability claim.

To follow our logic and transfer the stigma assessment to the second step in the section 15 analysis would render disability a unique ground with its own section 15 process.[20] Perhaps, instead, this analysis should lead us to question the definitions of other grounds in a similar way. The law tends to see and treat these grounds/categories as fixed and immutable (or as close to immutable as possible), but they are only so to the extent that they have been essentialized and contained, that is, only to the extent that we have attached set meaning and consequences to them as categories. The categories are themselves stereotypes. The rigidity and inflexibility of these categories has been a source of much criticism in the human rights, as well as the Charter, context. According to Carolyn Tyjewksi, in Chapter 5, "the courts presum[e] the visibility and discreteness of these categories ... even when faced with evidence that these categories [are] not insular or necessarily visible." In questioning the fixed nature and the biological basis of the disability category and shifting the critical analysis to the ground itself, critical disability theory may, by implication and in its application, be destabilizing the grounds approach not just for disability but for all the grounds.[21]

But for now, the grounds remain stable and largely indisputable. Thus, in the *Cameron* case, the analysis that we are suggesting should have been brought to bear on the issue whether infertility as a disability was dealt with, following the section 15 three-step process, under the question whether there was discrimination. On this point, the claimants introduced historical evidence of stigma attaching to infertility: "The appellants refer to literature which shows that the commitment to parenthood in western civilization reflects a Judeo-Christian tradition which views children as blessings from heaven and barrenness as a curse or punishment. Like leprosy and epilepsy, they say, infertility bears an ancient social stigma. They say that the material shows the bigotry, ignorance and medieval thinking that they say have typified views of infertility and opposition to treatment of the infertile" (*Cameron* 1999, 656-57 [references omitted]). While "neither claimant" was able to testify to "any disadvantage suffered by them as infertile persons," the judge held that "the material [showed] that in various cultures and at various times, infertility – particularly in the female – has been regarded as a disadvantage – an unworthy state, the object of derision, banishment and disgrace" (657). According to Justice Chipman, "notwithstanding improved attitudes, [this] historical disadvantage cannot be denied" (657), and he found that a lesser but ongoing stigma did attach to infertile couples. Historical disadvantage is a critical component of inequality but, given the fluidity and indeterminacy of the categories and of the stigma that attaches to them, are past disadvantage and archaic stigma sufficient to ground a section 15 challenge in the absence of current evidence of stigma? In the contemporary context, Justice Chipman has perhaps confounded personal disappointment with social stigma.

In our opinion, the key is the historically gendered nature of the stigma that Justice Chipman refers to, but only in passing. A man's infertility does not share the pejorative historic context outlined by the claimants. It could be argued that, historically, a failure to reproduce resulted in less status for a man, and certainly complicated issues of lineage and inheritance for wealthy men. However, husbands were not traditionally blamed for their wives' failure to conceive; it was not men about whom "infertility has been equated to frigidity" (*Cameron* 1999, 658). It was infertile women who were accused of frigidity; women who failed to produce children were the ones to be labelled barren, to be stigmatized and devalued, and who were blamed for the loss of status and the curtailment of lineage. Justice Chipman's decision conflates male infertility with infertility generally, yet there are distinct considerations at play that deserve attention. A more subtle analysis would uncover the gendered assumptions we make about procreation and genealogy. The historical disadvantage and stigma attach to women and relate to their stereotyped role as reproducers, raising the question whether this case should have or could have been brought as a sex inequality claim.[22] Questions about how the claim is or should be framed bring us back full circle to our initial concerns about the characterization of the complainants as an infertile unit and the ascription of infertility to a woman on the basis of the infertility of her male partner. Does the stigma (or disappointment) alleged by the claimants derive from their combined inability to reproduce, or from their status as childless in a society that values descent and lineage? We do not know what other options may have been available, including, for example, donor insemination. Certainly they are not incapable of forming a family, either as a couple with extended family, or with adopted or foster children.[23]

In the absence of stigma about infertility, we are left solely with the medical model, which posits an impairment that needs fixing. Judith Mosoff distinguishes between women with disabilities and those who claim a reproductive disability.[24] This leads her to argue that those who claim a reproductive disability are not disabled, a conclusion to which we are similarly drawn. In part, this argument is based on what Mosoff describes as the different life experiences and different perspectives of each group on medicine and technology. Disability is a major factor in the life experiences of women with disabilities, affecting education, employment opportunities, living arrangements, and social relations, such that it is virtually inevitable that "women with disabilities experience the world in a fundamentally different fashion than women with fertility problems" (Mosoff 1993, 107). Women with disabilities have tended to adopt a well-founded distrust of medicine and science, and to reject the medical model of disability. On the other hand, women who claim a reproductive disability likely do so in the context of their active pursuit of medical solutions, having fully embraced the medical model. To the extent that they adopt a disability label, it is usually in order to gain access to medical technology; the identification of infertility as a disability is in response to the availability of the treatment, not vice versa. In this, Mosoff argues that "individuals with fertility problems have appropriated a disability rights discourse [in order] to gain access to resources and services forged by earlier efforts at advocating very different disability issues" (112). In doing so, they have substantially transformed the discourse they borrowed, especially as it relates to choice and medicalization.

Although there is very little in the way of explicit reference to choice in *Cameron,* a liberal individualist notion of choice underlies the decision in a way that transforms choice into entitlement. The individual choice to produce a child becomes a right to have the child you want in the way you want, a right, as argued in this case, that should be supported and funded by the state. The class, race, gender, and disability implications of choice as right remain unexamined, even unacknowledged.[25] This decontextualized understanding of choice runs counter to a contextualized, group-based understanding of equality.

Mosoff's analysis also raises a concern that relates to the data presented in other contributions in this book (for example, Chapter 1 and Chapter 6). In none of the surveys or data collections discussed would infertility be captured as a disability; none of the definitions used in these surveys would apply to infertility.[26] We expect that the only context in which an infertile individual or couple might self-identify as disabled is as a way to frame their claim for funding related to infertility. While we recognize that self-identification, as well as categorization by others, has limitations, it does seem contradictory to talk about the social construction of a disability that almost nobody, including those who have it, considers a disability.

Re-Envisioning Disability

We have rejected the medical model relied on by the majority in *Cameron* to ground the finding that infertility is a disability. We turn now to other approaches to disability to assist us in further exploring this question of infertility as a disability.

The social model of disability would focus on the social response to infertility and lead to the possible argument that, while infertility may constitute an impairment, in the absence of stigma, barriers, negative social response, or a history of disadvantage, it would not be considered a disability. The focus of the inquiry into whether infertility is a disability would be on social attitudes to infertility and the limitations placed by society on those who are infertile, rather than on individual limitations, feelings, or hardships related to the condition. Thus, Mr. Cameron may be considered to have an impairment, but that impairment, distressing as it might be, would not be characterized as a disability. Accepting the focus of the social model as appropriate, and given our skepticism that any of these negative factors currently apply to infertility, we argue that infertility is not a disability.

The social model raises interesting questions beyond the initial classification of a condition as a disability. The medical and social models have quite different implications for remedy. Even if infertility was understood as a disability, this does not mean that the appropriate solution would be the one sought by Mr. Cameron and Dr. Smith, that is, to fix the impairment. The social model might instead lead us to thinking about "fixing" the social attitudes that construct infertility as a disability. According to the social model, the problem is not the impairment itself, but the social response to it, which means that the appropriate solution would be challenging and shifting that social response. To respond to discriminatory social attitudes by trying to eliminate the disability is to revert to a medical model and, in so doing, to accede to the discrimination.

While this analysis may be helpful in understanding where the problem of disability lies, it may give rise to some practical problems in the context of a case in which those who have the impairment are not interested in changing social attitudes but simply want the impairment fixed. If an impairment-based claim is characterized purely in terms of a medical problem to be solved by medical means, then according to the social model of disability, it lacks essential features of a disability relating to negative social response, and remains simply a medical problem, the solution to which would lie other than in concepts of equality and discrimination. In these circumstances, the definition of disability may well take on the role of gatekeeper, potentially excluding claims that are exclusively treatment focused.[27] We do not, however, necessarily see this as a troubling role for the definition of disability because it would act as gatekeeper only for claims to services based on the section 15 ground of disability; the gate would remain open for claim to services on any other basis. In other words, while we recognize that almost any medical treatment can be associated with a single biological impairment or grouping of impairments such that denial of treatment for that impairment *could* be characterized as drawing a distinction on the basis of that particular disability, we reject the medical model conflation of disability into impairment on which such a characterization would be based.

Alternatively, if, rather than abandoning the infertile body to medicine, we instead explore a postmodern approach and the implications of Shelley Tremain's (2002, 42) point that the distinction between impairment and disability is a false one, such that "impairment has been disability all along," then we may be led down quite a different analytic path, one that would have us examining connections between the impaired/disabled, sexed/gendered body. The postmodern critique of the social model is the strict divide it imposes between impairment and disability. The social model accepts impairment as natural, as an actual condition onto which the social attitudes of disablism are ascribed. Impairment is accepted; disablism is critiqued.

We see the application of a limited version of the social model and the problems to which it can give rise in the decision in *Granovsky*. Justice Binnie draws a strict delineation between impairment and social response – "a proper [disability] analysis necessitates unbundling the impairment from the reaction of society *to* the impairment, and a recognition that much discrimination is socially constructed" (*Granovsky*, para. 30). While the recognition that the problem lies in the social responses and not in the condition or person is extremely important, it is undermined by an analysis that fails to recognize not only the interconnection and interdependence of these categories but even the existence of these categories. This version of the social model remains mired in the medical model, with the underlying implication that the impairment comes first, and "is then processed through a social lens ... [such that] the social bias is masked by categorization and language that purports to separate 'objective' from 'social' phenomena" (Mosoff 1993, 101). Thus, in *Granovsky*, the decision rests on a distinction between temporary disability and permanent disability, as if these labels have some objective meaning beyond their line drawing/benefit eligibility determining function.

Postmodernism rejects the impairment/disability distinction and its underlying objective-social framework, in much the same way that feminist theorists have collapsed the sex/gender distinction, arguing that there is no independent meaning to biological sex predating beyond that which gender has ascribed to it, that is, sex and gender are one and the same (MacKinnon 1989; Butler 1993; Franke 1995). The sex/gender divide helped us to see past the naturalized biological fact of sex to the socially imposed meanings of sex (gender), so that we can now see our way back to sex as gender, that is, to recognize that the fact of sex is a construct of gender. The recognition of disability as a social construct is playing the same role in facilitating the recognition of impairment, not as fact, but as a disablist construct. The social model of disability, however, is still firmly rooted in the impairment/disability distinction. Despite its powerful critique of the medical model, the social model's refusal to engage with impairment risks relegating impairment and the impaired body to the medical domain. A postmodern approach would reclaim impairment only to question its existence, in conjunction with questioning the existence of disability, arguing that both exist and sustain each other as regulatory practices.

While we are drawn to the insights of this postmodern approach, we are not clear how they translate in a legal context.[28] Law is all about defining, categorizing, line drawing, and remedies, about naming the problem and fixing it. This is why the medical model of disability aligns so smoothly with the law. The abstractness and instability of postmodernism are an anathema to law. Carol Smart (1994, 26) has noted that "in the legal forum," a postmodern analysis "would almost certainly be treated as incomprehensible ... The field of law therefore poses substantial problems for a feminist intervention which is influenced by structuralist thinking on matters of sex, gender and sexuality." Similarly, matters of impairment, disability, and the body, as well as the other section 15 grounds, will be difficult to dismantle under law when they are categories reified by law. Given the real life consequences that flow from these categories, it may be dangerous to try to dismantle them without first eradicating the subordination and discrimination attached to them. The categories provide a basis for naming and challenging the discrimination without which one might be left with the illusion of equality, with discrimination and subordination being seen as indiscriminate and ungrounded. Arguably, it is buying into disablism and reinforcing the construct even to frame a claim as disability (Tremain 2002, 44), but we are not ready to abandon the potential of law as a means to providing some immediate remedy and as a forum for debating new ideas. And we do not want to ignore the significant impact of impairment on the lives of people with disabilities. The challenge is to figure out how to incorporate the insights of postmodernism without totally vacating the disability category and its lived consequences.

Conclusion

We each read the *Cameron* decision in the context of other work we were doing on section 15, and both of us were uncomfortable with the equality analysis and the disability analysis (or absence thereof) in the case. We were intrigued that the notion that seemed intuitively obvious to Justice Chipman – that infertility is a disability – seemed to us, also intuitively, seriously amiss. Moreover, we were concerned by his, as well as by our own, willingness to defer to what seemed right and natural, and by our difficulty in articulating the reasons for our response. This case gave rise to many hours of discussion between us about infertility and reproduction, about disability and disablism, about our own attitudes and assumptions, about equality theory, and about section 15.

We wavered but ultimately did not shift from our original reaction that infertility is not a disability. We were assisted greatly by contemporary disability theory and the different approaches to conceptualizing disability, as well as by the critiques of the different approaches. What is clear to us is that if equality law is to move beyond the medical model of disability, then, at the very least, the section 15 test set out in *Law* needs to be reconfigured. If stigma is a defining feature of whether a condition is a disability, then a finding that the claimant has been treated negatively or disadvantageously, and that such treatment was related to her or his disability, would be sufficient to find a section 15 Charter breach. Any negative distinction based on disability would exacerbate the stigma and demean the individual's, as well as the group's, dignity. Much of the third step in the *Law* test would thus be unnecessary. But there are many more problems with the *Law* test. As *Cameron* illustrates, the comparator group requirement leads to arbitrary and inappropriate comparisons, which might in turn be related to the limited understanding of the grounds of discrimination. Slotting oneself into one of the proscribed grounds, or an analogous ground, unduly restricts the evidence and the analysis, such that in a case like *Cameron,* the gender and class dimensions of the issues are completely ignored. Disability theory is making major inroads into these problems and has the potential to dramatically improve the law's understanding of, and response to, claims brought by people with disabilities. The analysis and application of substantive equality would be significantly furthered by the integration of critical disability theory.

Notes

1   Section 15 states: (1) "Every individual is equal before and under the law and has the right to the equal protection and equal benefit of the law without discrimination and, in particular, without discrimination based on race, national or ethnic origin, colour, religion, sex, age or mental or physical disability.

    (2) Subsection (1) does not preclude any law, program or activity that has as its object the amelioration of conditions of disadvantaged individuals or groups including those that are disadvantaged because of race, national or ethnic origin, colour, religion, sex, age or mental or physical disability." See Part I of the *Constitution Act, 1982,* being Schedule B to the *Canada Act 1982* (U.K.), 1982, c. 11 [Charter].

2   Our critique of the decision in *Cameron* is less about the actual decision reached on the section 15 claim and more about the lack of analysis and engagement with the question of whether infertility is a disability and, implicitly, with the question of what is disability. We offer our perspective on these questions, but the issue of infertility is difficult and sensitive, and so we offer our views somewhat tentatively and cautiously in the hope of furthering discussion rather than answering questions.

3   The couple also claimed that the trial judge erred in not finding in vitro fertilization and intra cytoplasmic sperm injection (ICSI) to be insured services paid or reimbursed under the policy established by the *Health Services and Insurance Act* and the corresponding *Regulations.* The court held that under the act, there is no general right to receive insured hospital services outside the province, but such services will be paid if the treatment was medically necessary. The province argued that the treatments in question were not insured medical services in the province because they were not considered medically necessary or required, in that, having regard to costs, the limited success rate, and the risks, they did not

rank sufficiently highly to warrant payment for them from public funds. The court held it is not its function to determine which treatments are medically necessary or required.

This case also involves class and economic status issues relating to access to services that raise the spectre of slippage from a public health-care system to a private system whereby health services are available only to those who can afford them. We do not discuss these important issues in this chapter, as we see them as relating primarily to the discussion of medically necessary services dealt with in the other part of this claim. We do, however, think that there is a Charter dimension to that claim that was apparently not raised in this case.

4 See [1999] S.C.C.A. No. 531.

5 Section 1 of the Charter states: "The *Canadian Charter of Rights and Freedoms* guarantees the rights and freedoms set out in it subject only to such reasonable limits prescribed by law as can be demonstrably justified in a free and democratic society." After concluding that the denial of funding violated the claimants' equality right, the court found the government's actions justifiable under section 1, concluding that the violation of the claimants' right was rationally connected to the aim and policy of the legislation, and that it impaired the claimants' rights minimally because it denied only two procedures to the infertile, while leaving others available. In addition, there was proportionality between the effect of the exclusion of the procedures and the objective of the exclusion.

6 After quoting from *Eldridge v. British Columbia (Attorney General)* (1997) on the historic disadvantages endured by people with disabilities, Justice Bateman concluded: "The appellant Cameron suffers from male factor infertility with markedly reduced prospects of conceiving a child. In some contexts this dysfunction would be viewed as a 'disability.' In my view, however, it does not fall within the meaning of 'disability' for which protection is afforded by section 15(1). I am not satisfied, on the evidence, that the appellants (or their like group), by reason of infertility, are excluded from mainstream society" (*Cameron* 1999, 676). Justice Bateman's reasons are quite brief on this point and rely mainly on quoted passages from Supreme Court decisions. Since she does not engage in the kind of analysis we wish to advance on whether infertility is a disability, we will not focus on her decision.

7 We are not canvassing the models of disability analysis in this chapter, as they are surveyed in a comprehensive fashion elsewhere in this book. See for example, Rioux and Valentine, Chapter 2, "Does Theory Matter? Exploring the Nexus Between Disability, Human Rights, and Public Policy."

8 From a medical point of view, "infertility is the inability of a couple to achieve a pregnancy after repeated intercourse without contraception for 1 year" (Mark H. Beers and Robert Berkow, eds., "Infertility," in *The Merck manual of diagnosis and therapy*, 17th ed. Rahway, NJ: Merck, Sharp and Dohne Research Laboratories, 1999, chap. 245, sec. 18 (http://www.merck.com/pubs/mmanual/section18/chapter245/245a.htm.) We have heard anecdotal stories that women in their thirties might now be considered at risk for infertility after only six months of unprotected intercourse without conception, and allowed to undergo preliminary infertility treatment.

9 ICSI involves injecting a single sperm into an egg, which is then situated in a woman's fallopian tube or uterus. The sperm is collected either by masturbation or via a testicular biopsy, which involves a small incision if the male has a problem with blockages or sperm development. It is recommended that men who have little or no sperm in their semen undergo karyotyping also. Women must undergo daily hormone injections and monitoring to foster multiple egg production. Women must be frequently monitored by a doctor, and injections can be painful (see http://my.webmd.com/content/healthwise/198/63471).

10 Such a conflation certainly sets off feminist alarm bells.

11 In "Reproductive Technology and Intent-Based Parenthood: An Opportunity for Gender Neutrality," *Wisconsin Law Review* 297, 2 (1990): 297-398, Marjorie Shultz details how technology has allowed "individuals to choose procreative roles independent of ... their sexual or interpersonal intimacy" (297), arguing that "single persons of either gender could procreate without compromising their single status. Individuals in homosexual relationships, just as individuals in committed heterosexual relationships where one partner cannot or

chooses not to reproduce, could decide to procreate, without either betraying or abandoning the partner" (315).

12 For a feminist critique of these authors and an argument in favour of viewing infertility as a disability, see Linda Lacey, "O Wind Remind Him That I Have No Child: Infertility and Feminist Jurisprudence," *Michigan Journal of Gender and Law* 5 (1998-99): 163-203.

13 In *Trociuk v. British Columbia (Attorney General)* (2001), 200 D.L.R. (4th) 685 (B.C.C.A.), Justice Southin of the Court of Appeal engaged in an extensive review of the common law and legislative history of birth registrations in British Columbia (paras. 30-64). In her opinion, when taken in that historical context, the impugned modern provision reflects the legislature's purpose "of remedying whatever lingering stigma attached to being a child born out of wedlock" flowing from the differential rights accorded married and unmarried fathers (para. 68). To achieve this purpose, the legislature chose to deprive fathers of children born in wedlock of the right to be acknowledged and registered as such. She thus concluded that Mr. Trociuk was in no worse position than any other father (married or single) (para. 69). Southin's section 15 analysis is brief, for she argued it is difficult to fit Mr. Trociuk's claim into a Charter argument (para. 78). She concluded that a judicial revision of the statute to provide a right of inclusion for fathers in birth registrations would go well beyond any of the authorities on section 15, and constitute a serious diminution of the rights of single mothers, approaching discrimination (para. 84). Justice Newbury conceded that there is no doubt the impugned provision draws a formal distinction between mothers and fathers (para. 176), but she argued that requiring the mother to acknowledge the father against her wishes is "a serious incursion into the interests of the mother, who may have good reason for refusing to acknowledge (and disclose in a public document) the identity of the father" (para. 177). While acknowledging that the naming of children holds considerable significance for many members of Canadian society, Justice Newbury concluded that the differential treatment does not treat Mr. Trociuk as "less worthy of recognition or value. Rather, "if anyone has been historically regarded as 'less worthy,' it is single mothers, who until recently were treated as 'fallen women,' and their children who were stigmatized as illegitimate or worse ... The terminology employed by the court in *Law* is simply not apt to describe fathers in Mr. Trociuk's situation" (para. 179).

14 This is an area that has been academically under-theorized. While we cannot delve into it in depth in the context of this chapter, the issue of comparator groups merits further analysis.

15 Justice Binnie quotes from the claimant's factum, wherein Granovsky argued: "The appellant Granovsky wishes to make it clear that his submission is that he is relying on a comparison between temporary disabled persons and able-bodied persons. The fact that some adjustment has been made for 'permanently disabled' persons is not the gravamen of Mr. Granovsky's complaint" (*Granovsky* 2000, para. 64).

16 Justice Chipman describes the claimants' argument as follows: "The fertile woman who becomes pregnant gets full services for her pregnancy and childbirth. Every aspect of having children is covered by Medicare. She can even elect an abortion, an insured service. Sterilization is also an insured service. The infertile get less." He concludes: "In my opinion, the appellants belong to the group which may be classed as the infertile who need, but do not get, the full array of services for reproduction. The comparative group is the fertile who need, and do get, the full array of services for reproduction" (*Cameron* 1999, 651). This analysis is extremely problematic in its grouping of infertility treatments with pregnancy, abortion, and sterilization, suggesting that all reproductive issues involve the same interests and implicate the same governmental response.

17 This is a large "perhaps" and a source of major concern about the medicalization of infertility. Many of the treatments with very low "success" rates are highly invasive, potentially risky, replete with so-called side effects, and extremely costly.

18 Ironically, the medical model of infertility includes a diagnosis of infertility for unknown causes – that is, there is no discernible physiological impairment. Undaunted, doctors continue to treat even this form of infertility. This practice highlights the critiques of the medicalized approach to disability, which transforms impairment into a physiological problem to be treated.

19 This language of the tragedy of infertility is even more disturbing in light of the court's conclusion that the section 15 breach of not funding ICSI is justified under section 1 of the Charter. After finding that the "the impact of the denial of these procedures to the infertile perpetuates the view that they are less worthy of recognition or value. It touches their essential dignity and self-worth" (*Cameron* 1999, 660), the ruling that the denial is justified is painfully disrespectful and further damaging. This points to one of the many problems with the *Law* focus on dignity – once a court has held that the breach undermines a claimant's fundamental human dignity, how can that court, in good conscience, hold that the breach is justified? Moreover, the *Cameron* court, in its section 1 analysis of the question whether the violation of the section 15 right is minimal, asserts that the claimants are left with "not only the full panoply of medical services available to all, but a number of specific procedures available for their condition" (668). This is cruel in light of the court's earlier determination that ICSI was the only procedure that held out any "real hope of [Cameron and Smith] having a child" (661).

20 Disability has always been seen as unique among the list of prohibited grounds, in that it is the only ground that is described in terms that limit those who can bring a claim to members of the subordinated group. The other grounds, such as race and sex, are described in neutral terms, such that the members of the dominant group, as well as of the subordinated group, can and have brought discrimination claims. Importing notions of stigma and disadvantage into the definition of these other grounds would provide a way to offset the neutrality that currently characterizes the meaning of the ground itself.

21 Transgender advocates have been destabilizing the category of sex, but often in ways that reinforce rather than challenge gender constructs. In the current context, the most effective way to address transgender issues may be to introduce a new ground of gender identity. However, it may be more radical to explicitly destabilize or disrupt the grounds than to keep adding to the list. Such disruption might also resolve the group/grounds debate that, to a large extent, stems from the rigidity of the categories. And destabilized grounds might go a long way toward addressing some of the problems posed by intersecting grounds. To be clear, we are talking about destabilizing grounds, not eliminating them. While not innate, these categories are definitely real, with significant consequences.

22 This question was raised in the discussion following our presentation. While intriguing, such a claim would be complex and would risk further entrenching notions of women as the ones responsible for reproduction.

23 This is not to say that these alternative ways to create a family are unproblematic. They too involve difficult and complicated choices. As was pointed out by one of the participants at our session, adoption and fostering are themselves onerous, expensive, and invasive processes, with a number of hurdles that prove insurmountable for some people. Some people resort to in vitro fertilization because other options are foreclosed.

24 We quote from this work with the author's permission.

25 This failure to acknowledge the class, race, and disability implications of choice has been recognized by feminist reproductive rights advocates in the adoption of freedom of choice as a slogan for the abortion rights movement. For example, the simplistic focus on choice ignored the coerced abortions undergone by many poor, disabled, and/or racialized women, and made it difficult to raise concerns about prenatal testing and sex selection abortions.

26 For example, the surveys reviewed by McColl and colleagues in Chapter 1 focus on limitations in the kind and amount of activity because of a physical or mental condition, and on impairments related to mobility, agility, pain, cognition, and learning.

27 The potential for the definition of disability to play a gatekeeper role in this context was brought to our attention by Peter Carver in his paper "Disability and the Right to Medical Treatment," presented at a CALT panel on 31 May 2003 as part of the Critical Disability Theory: Legal and Policy Issues sessions at the 2003 Congress of the Humanities and Social Sciences in Halifax.

28 This dilemma was reflected in reverse in the discussions that arose in the critical disability theory workshop, where the questions raised by lawyers relating to the difficulties in applying these concepts in a legal context were dismissed as failures to understand the theory.

References

Basen, Gwynne, Margrit Eichler, and Abby Lippman, eds. 1993. *Misconceptions: The social construction of choice and the new reproductive and genetic technologies*. Hull: Voyageur.

Butler, Judith. 1993. *Bodies that matter: On the discursive limits of "sex."* London: Routledge.

Cameron v. Nova Scotia (Attorney General) (1999), 177 D.L.R. (4th) 611 (N.S.C.A.).

Canadian Charter of Rights and Freedoms, Part I of the *Constitution Act, 1982*, being Schedule B to the *Canada Act 1982* (U.K.) 1982, c. 11 [Charter].

Corea, Gena. 1985. *The mother machine: Reproductive technology from artificial insemination to artificial wombs*. New York: Harper and Row.

Dworkin, Andrea. 1983. *Right-wing women*. New York: Perigee Books.

Eldridge v. British Columbia (Attorney General), [1997] 3 S.C.R. 624.

Franke, Katherine. 1995. The central mistake of sex discrimination law: The disaggregation of sex from gender. *University of Pennsylvania Law Review* 144: 1-99.

Granovsky v. Canada (Minister of Employment and Immigration), [2000] 1 S.C.R. 703 [*Granovsky*].

Law v. Canada (Minister of Employment and Immigration), [1999] 1 S.C.R. 497 [*Law*].

MacKinnon, Catharine. 1989. *Toward a feminist theory of the state*. Cambridge, MA: Harvard University Press.

Mosoff, Judith. 1993. Reproductive technology and disability: Searching for the "rights" and wrongs in explanation. *Dalhousie Law Journal* 16: 98-124.

Smart, Carol. 1994. Law feminism and sexuality: From essence to ethics? *Canadian Journal of Law and Society* 9: 15-38.

Tremain, Shelley. 2002. On the subject of impairment. In *Disability/postmodernity: Embodying disability theory*, ed. Marian Corker and Tom Shakespeare, 32-47. London: Continuum.

Trociuk v. British Columbia (Attorney General) (2003), 226 D.L.R. (4th) 1 (S.C.C.).

Appendix
Legal Developments in the Supreme
Court of Canada Regarding Disability
Dianne Pothier

In the last two decades, the Supreme Court of Canada has considered disability issues on numerous occasions. Most of its discussion has been in the context either of human rights legislation or the *Canadian Charter of Rights and Freedoms*, 1982. The two streams have developed in tandem, with human rights legislation interpretation informing Charter interpretation, and vice versa (e.g., *Andrews* 1989; *BCGSEU* 1999). An important distinction between the two, however, is that while human rights legislation prescribes the conduct of both state and private actors, the Charter directly reaches only state actors (including legislatures adopting human rights legislation).

Section 15 of the Charter, the equality rights provision, came into force on 17 April 1985, three years after the rest of the Charter.[1] The delayed coming into force of section 15, including its express inclusion of physical and mental disability as enumerated grounds of prohibited discrimination, represented an admission that much needed to be done in order to achieve legal equality. For example, before 17 April 1985, a tribunal acting under the *Canadian Human Rights Act* could only make recommendations and not orders regarding a substantiated complaint involving mental disability, and its authority to make orders regarding physical disability was strictly limited (s. 65.1, added by S.C. 1980-81-82-83, c. 143, s. 25).

The social context underlying Charter and human rights legislation protection regarding disability was described by the Supreme Court of Canada in *Eldridge v. British Columbia (Attorney General)*:

It is an unfortunate truth that the history of disabled persons in Canada is largely one of exclusion and marginalization. Persons with disabilities have too often been excluded from the labour force, denied access to opportunities for social interaction and advancement, subjected to invidious stereotyping and relegated to institutions; ... This historical disadvantage has to a great extent been shaped and perpetuated by the notion that disability is an abnormality or flaw. As a result, disabled persons have not generally been afforded the "equal concern, respect and consideration" that section 15(1) of the *Charter* demands. Instead, they have been subjected to paternalistic attitudes of pity and charity, and their entrance into the social mainstream has been conditional upon their emulation of able-bodied norms; ... One consequence of these attitudes is the persistent social and economic disadvantage faced by the disabled. Statistics indicate that persons with disabilities, in comparison to non-disabled persons, have less education, are more likely to be outside the labour force, face much higher unemployment rates, and are concentrated at the lower end of the pay scale when employed. (*Eldridge* 1997, para. 56 [references omitted])

In *R. v. Swain* (1991), the Supreme Court of Canada commented on the social context of mental disability in particular:

The mentally ill have historically been the subjects of abuse, neglect and discrimination in our society. The stigma of mental illness can be very damaging. The intervener, C.D.R.C. [Canadian Disability Rights Council], describes the historical treatment of the mentally ill as follows:

For centuries, persons with a mental disability have been systematically isolated, segregated from the mainstream of society, devalued, ridiculed, and excluded from participation in ordinary social and political processes.

The above description is, in my view, unfortunately accurate and appears to stem from an irrational fear of the mentally ill in our society. (*R. v. Swain* 1991, 973-74, para. 39)

These statements from the Supreme Court of Canada signify important advances for persons with disabilities; they suggest that pity and charity are an inappropriate response to disability discrimination and they point the way toward a substantive understanding of equality for persons with disabilities. However, a careful analysis of the cases discussed below suggests that some of these advances may be more rhetorical than material, and that the story of disability in the Supreme Court of Canada is more complex than a one-way street of progress. Consequently, in this brief appendix, rather than providing a chronological account of the court's encounters with disability, I will identify six axes of analysis that demonstrate that the jurisprudence on disability signifies oscillations between understanding and ignorance, progress and retrenchment, hope and disappointment.

Challenging a Legacy of Marginalization
The Charter era has also been accompanied by non-Charter recognition of the rights of the disabled outside human rights legislation. *E. (Mrs.) v. Eve*

(*Eve* 1986) involved an application by the mother of a twenty-four-year-old "mentally retarded" woman to authorize non-therapeutic sterilization of her daughter. The daughter's lack of communication skills meant that it was not possible to ascertain her wishes. The Supreme Court ruled that there was no statutory basis to authorize the mother's request, so that the case turned on the court's exercise of its *parens patriae* jurisdiction, jurisdiction to protect children and mentally incompetent adults. Without specific reliance on Charter arguments, the Supreme Court ruled that sterilization should "never be authorized for non-therapeutic purposes under the parens patriae jurisdiction" (*Eve* 1986, 431, para. 86). In reaching this conclusion, the court expressly distanced itself from the openly eugenics-based history of compulsory sterilization:

> There are other reasons for approaching an application for sterilization of a mentally incompetent person with the utmost caution. To begin with, the decision involves values in an area where our social history clouds our vision and encourages many to perceive the mentally handicapped as somewhat less than human. This attitude has been aided and abetted by now discredited eugenic theories whose influence was felt in this country as well as the United States. Two provinces, Alberta and British Columbia, once had statutes providing for the sterilization of mental defectives; *The Sexual Sterilization Act*, R.S.A. 1970, c. 341, repealed by S.A. 1972, c. 87; *Sexual Sterilization Act*, R.S.B.C. 1960, c. 353, s. 5(1), repealed by S.B.C. 1973, c. 79. (*Eve* 1986, 427-28, para. 78)

The court emphasized that the *parens patriae* "discretion is to be exercised for the benefit of that [mentally incompetent] person, not for that of others" (427, para. 77), including a mother. In acknowledging that people have the right to choose whether to procreate or not, and whether to be sterilized or not, Justice La Forest, speaking for a unanimous court, called it a "fiction" to claim that any purported substituted decision making could represent the wishes of the mentally incompetent person (435, para. 95). Justice La Forest ultimately concluded that it was never safe for a court to assume that non-therapeutic sterilization was in the best interests of a mentally incompetent person (437, para. 99).

The Nature of Discrimination

Although not itself a disability case, *O'Malley v. Simpsons-Sears* (1985) marked an important development in the protection against disability discrimination under human rights legislation. Just as section 15 of the Charter was coming into effect, the Supreme Court of Canada, in the context of a religious discrimination case under Ontario human rights legislation, recognized that both direct and adverse effects discrimination are covered by the statute. Direct discrimination involves a rule or policy that makes a distinction on its face explicitly invoking the prohibited ground of discrimination. In contrast, adverse effects discrimination involves a rule or policy that is, on its face, neutral with respect to a prohibited ground of discrimination, but which nonetheless produces discriminatory consequences. In *O'Malley,* a rule requiring work on Saturdays at a retail store had a discriminatory effect on an adherent of the Seventh Day Adventist faith, for whom work on the Sabbath was contrary to her religious beliefs. In human rights legislation, the inclusion of adverse effects discrimination with respect to disability is crucial, since it is rare for a rule or policy to expressly exclude the disabled. Usually, barriers are created by the failure to respond to the different needs and circumstances of the disabled, for example, inaccessible premises or documents.

In *Eldridge* (1997, paras. 60-65), the Supreme Court of Canada reaffirmed that adverse effects discrimination is covered under section 15 of the Charter as well, specifically emphasizing the significance of countering adverse effects discrimination in order to protect the equality rights of the disabled.

Although *O'Malley* was important in the advancement of protection of the disabled from discrimination, there were also inherent limitations in the *O'Malley* analytical framework. The coverage of adverse effects discrimination under human rights legislation, as recognized in *O'Malley,* was accompanied by the requirement that employers or service providers render accommodation up to the point of undue hardship in order to avoid a finding of unlawful discrimination. In the Supreme Court's initial approach, accommodation was understood as involving the creation of exceptions to rules, rather than questioning the general rules themselves, as was dictated in direct discrimination cases. As a response to disability, accommodation by means of exceptions fosters tinkering, not fundamental transformation of an environment designed for the non-disabled.

The *O'Malley* approach was reconsidered in the *Meiorin* case (*BCGSEU* 1999), a sex discrimination case. In *Meiorin* the Supreme Court of Canada abandoned its bifurcated approach to direct versus adverse effects discrimination and adopted a unified approach to both types of discrimination. Under the unified approach, questioning of general rules is mandated for both direct and adverse effects discrimination. This creates at least the potential to challenge non-disabled norms in fundamental ways.

The *Meiorin* unified approach was applied in a disability context in *Grismer* (1999). *Grismer* involved the denial of a driver's licence without individualized testing to a person with homonymous hemianopia (HH), a condition causing loss of peripheral vision. Grismer was denied a driver's licence on the basis that his field of vision was less than 120 degrees. Persons with HH with less than 120 degrees of vision were automatically denied a licence in British Columbia, whereas those with less than 120 degrees of vision because of other causes might be able to obtain a driver's licence. The Supreme Court of Canada found a breach of British Columbia human rights legislation.

The *Grismer* case does not stand for the proposition that people have a right to drive irrespective of their ability to see. The result of the case was not that Grismer would necessarily have been entitled to a driver's licence had he lived long enough to personally benefit from the Supreme Court of Canada's decision.[2] The discrimination found was in the process of determining whether Grismer was entitled to a driver's licence. The finding was that Grismer had been denied a driver's licence on the basis of a rule found to be arbitrary. What was required instead was a more nuanced assessment that took into account the specifics of Grismer's particular circumstances; a proper assessment could still have resulted in a conclusion that he could not drive with reasonable safety.

Grismer recognizes the diverse nature of disability, mandating attention to difference, and proscribing arbitrary rules based on stereotypical assumptions about disability: "All too often, persons with disabilities are assumed to be unable to accomplish certain tasks based on the experience of able-bodied individuals. The thrust of human rights legislation is to eliminate such assumptions and break down the barriers that stand in the way of equality for all" (*Grismer* 1999, para. 26). The diverse nature of disability has also been emphasized in Charter cases, including *Eaton* and *Martin*, as will be discussed below.

The Meaning of Disability

Mercier (2000) involved Quebec human rights legislation in the employment context. The issue raised in three separate cases was whether it is necessary to manifest "functional limitations" for a person to have a "handicap." The municipal employers claimed that it is, entitling an employer, with impunity, to fire or refuse to hire someone with a (potential) disability even if he or she was not currently manifesting symptoms. The Supreme Court of Canada recognized the perverse implications of such an argument. This argument would allow employers who anticipated a future disability to escape the need to justify why someone could not perform a job. The court disallowed such a pre-emptive strike by concluding that there can be a handicap even in the absence of functional limitations. This conclusion was linked to perceptions of disability. Perception of disability can itself create barriers of the type that human rights legislation is designed to remove. Thus, a purposive interpretation makes it necessary to adopt a broad notion of handicap and disability in human rights legislation.

Models of Disability

In *Eldridge* (1997) and *Granovsky* (2000), both claims under section 15 of the

Charter, the Supreme Court recognized the distinction between a medical model of disability and a social model of disability:

> The *Charter* is not a magic wand that can eliminate physical or mental impairments, nor is it expected to create the illusion of doing so. Nor can it alleviate or eliminate the functional limitations truly created by the impairment. What section 15 of the *Charter* can do, and it is a role of immense importance, is address the way in which the state responds to people with disabilities. Section 15(1) ensures that governments may not, intentionally or through a failure of appropriate accommodation, stigmatize the underlying physical or mental impairment, or attribute functional limitations to the individual that the underlying physical or mental impairment does not entail, or fail to recognize the added burdens which persons with disabilities may encounter in achieving self-fulfilment in a world relentlessly oriented to the able-bodied.
>
> It is therefore useful to keep distinct the component of disability that may be said to be located in an individual, namely the aspects of physical or mental impairment, and functional limitation, and on the other hand the other component, namely, the socially constructed handicap that is not located in the individual at all but in the society in which the individual is obliged to go about his or her everyday tasks ...
>
> The primary focus is on the inappropriate legislative or administrative response (or lack thereof) of the state. Section 15(1) is ultimately concerned with human rights and discriminatory treatment, not with biomedical conditions. (*Granovsky* 2000, paras. 33, 34, 39)

In *Eldridge,* the Supreme Court of Canada rejected the analysis of the majority of the British Columbia Court of Appeal, which had held there was no Charter breach because the state has not caused the deafness of the claimants. The Supreme Court held that the medical cause of deafness was irrelevant to a claim that the delivery of health-care services needed to be accessible to the deaf. A breach of section 15 of the Charter was found in the failure of the province to fund sign language interpretation for visits to doctors and hospitals. To expect the deaf to pay for sign language interpretation would amount to the state's imposing a social burden on deaf patients inconsistent with the required non-discriminatory delivery of a service. This amounted to the adoption, for legal purposes, of a social model of disability.

Later, however, in *Auton* (2004), the social model of disability was not apparent in the court's analysis. The case involved claims by parents of autistic children for funding of a particular treatment, Lovaas, a form of Applied Behavior Analysis. The claim itself was framed in terms of a medical model, in support of a therapy designed to train children out of autistic behaviours. Moreover, the trial did not provide an opportunity to assess Lovaas for its compliance with equality principles, despite substantial critiques from the autistic community. There was no autistic voice in the case until the Supreme Court hearing, where Michelle Dawson, an autistic person, was granted intervenor status. While not endorsing the British Columbia government's inaction, Michelle Dawson strenuously opposed Lovaas treatment as antithetical to the humanity of autistic children. Another intervenor first appearing at the Supreme Court of Canada, a joint intervention by the Women's Legal Education and Action Fund (LEAF) and the DisAbled Women's Network (DAWN Canada), for whom the author was counsel, made a point of not endorsing Lovaas. LEAF and DAWN argued instead that the section 15 breach arose from the failure to respond to the needs of autistic children.

The Supreme Court's finding of no section 15 breach in *Auton* did mean that there was no uncritical endorsement of Lovaas specifically, or ABA generally. Yet, the more fundamental reason for the court's rejection of a section 15 breach in *Auton* has a more profound significance, which undermines the earlier incorporation into legal analysis of a social model of disability.

Chief Justice McLachlin, speaking for a unanimous court in *Auton* (2004, para. 31), began her analysis by rejecting the proposition that the health-care scheme provides anyone with coverage for all medically necessary treatment, a proposition no one argued before the court. What was argued instead was that the health-care system disproportionately meets the needs of some, the non-disabled, thereby under-including the disabled. The court avoided this argument. The court found that *Auton* involved no "benefit of the law" within the meaning of section 15, because the statute did not cover what was claimed: "In summary, the legislative scheme does not promise that any Canadian will receive funding for all medically required treatment. All that is conferred is core funding for services provided by medical practitioners, with funding for non-core services left to the Province's discretion. Thus, the benefit here claimed – funding for all medically required services – was not provided for by the law. More specifically, the law did not provide funding for ABA/IBI therapy for autistic children" (paras. 35-36). This analysis is circular. A challenge to under-inclusiveness is met with the answer that what is claimed is not included. The court leaves no room for argument that what is not included produces discriminatory effects. The court did not even acknowledge the argument, made by LEAF and DAWN as intervenors, that a health system privileging services provided by doctors and hospitals is geared to the typical needs of the non-disabled population.

Auton can be distinguished from *Eldridge* on the basis that *Eldridge* involved the general means of accessing health services, not accessing particular health services. Nonetheless, the ultimate basis for rejecting the section 15 claim in *Auton* was a rejection of the *Eldridge* notion, critical to a social model of disability, of the requirement that the state respond to the different needs of the disabled.

Equality as a Comparative Concept

The Supreme Court of Canada has emphasized that equality is a comparative concept (*Andrews* 1989). That still leaves for determination who is to be compared with whom, and the nature of the comparison.

In a human rights act context in *Gibbs* (1996) and in a Charter context in *Martin* (2003), the Supreme Court accepted that inequality could be established using within-disability comparisons. *Gibbs* found a contravention of human rights legislation where an employer's disability insurance policy provided greater coverage for physical disability than for mental disability. *Martin* involved a challenge to the almost complete exclusion of coverage of chronic pain under Nova Scotia workers' compensation legislation, compared with comprehensive coverage of other disabilities. The Supreme Court commented in *Martin:*

> Due sensitivity to these differences [among disabilities] is the key to achieving substantive equality for persons with disabilities. In many cases, drawing a single line between disabled persons and others is all but meaningless, as no single accommodation or adaptation can serve the needs of all ... The equal participation of persons with disabilities will require changing these situations in many different ways, depending on the abilities of the person. The question, in each case, will not be whether the state has excluded all disabled persons or failed to respond to their needs in some general sense, but rather whether it has been sufficiently responsive to the needs and circumstances of each person with a disability. If a government building is not accessible to persons using wheelchairs, it will be no answer to a claim of discrimination to point out a TTY (teletypewriter) telephone for the hearing impaired has been installed in the lobby. (*Martin* 2003, para. 81)

A within-disability comparison, however, can sometimes be fatal to a claim of discrimination. *Granovsky* involved a section 15 Charter challenge to the dropout provisions of the Canada Pension Plan that relax the requirements for length of recent contribution for those with severe and prolonged disabilities. Granovsky sought to challenge his inability to access these provisions as someone who had had a temporary disability. He sought to make the comparison between those with temporary disabilities and those without disabilities. However, the Supreme Court of Canada found that the proper comparison was between those with temporary disabilities and those with permanent disabilities. That comparison revealed no discrimination because the statutory regime was responding to the different and greater needs of those with permanent disabilities. Ultimately, Granovsky was not sufficiently disabled to take advantage of a statutory regime targeted to disability.

In *Eaton* (1997) it was accepted that the proper comparison was between the disabled and the non-disabled, but the underlying issue was the perspective from which to make that comparison. *Eaton* involved a claim by parents of Emily Eaton, a twelve-year-old girl with cerebral palsy. The parents wanted Emily to be integrated into a mainstream age-appropriate class, with supports for her special needs, but the educational authorities thought Emily should receive segregated education for disabled students. The Eatons lost their case when the Supreme Court of Canada rejected a presumption of integrated education:

> Segregation can be both protective of equality and violative of equality depending upon the person and the state of disability. In some cases, special education is a necessary adaptation of the mainstream world which enables some disabled pupils access to the learning environment they need in order to have an equal opportunity in education. While integration should be recognized as the norm of general application because of the benefits it generally provides, a presumption in favour of integrated schooling would work to the disadvantage of pupils who require special education in order to achieve equality. Schools focussed on the needs of the blind or deaf and special education for students with learning disabilities indicate the positive aspects of segregated education placement. Integration can be either a benefit or a burden depending on whether the individual can profit from the advantages that integration provides. (*Eaton* 1997, para. 69)

Underlying this analysis is an assumption of the limited capacity of an integrated educational setting to meet diverse needs, including the needs of disabled students. The comparison between the disabled and non-disabled is made from an able-bodied frame of reference:

> The principal object of certain of the prohibited grounds is the elimination of discrimination by the attribution of untrue characteristics based on stereotypical attitudes relating to immutable conditions such as race or sex. In the case of disability, this is one of the objectives. The other equally important objective seeks to take into account the true characteristics of this group which act as headwinds to the enjoyment of society's benefits and to accommodate them. Exclusion from the mainstream of society results from the construction of a society based solely on "mainstream" attributes to which disabled persons will never be able to gain access. Whether it is the impossibility of success at a written test for a blind person, or the need for ramp access to a library, the discrimination does not lie in the attribution of

untrue characteristics to the disabled individual. The blind person cannot see and the person in a wheelchair needs a ramp. Rather, it is the failure to make reasonable accommodation, to fine-tune society so that its structures and assumptions do not result in the relegation and banishment of disabled persons from participation, which results in discrimination against them. (*Eaton* 1997, para. 67)

I previously commented:

Examining Justice Sopinka's examples illustrates the difficulty with the analysis. Justice Sopinka identified the characteristic of blindness as the source of the inability of a blind person to succeed in a written test rather than identifying the problem as the inaccessible format of the test. The significance of that point is illustrated by an alternate scenario – most sighted persons would be incapable of success in a test in Braille. Thus the real barrier in Justice Sopinka's example is not blindness but the design of the test according to able-bodied norms. Similarly the need for a ramp to enable a wheelchair user to enter a library arises only if the initial design did not incorporate level access. (Pothier 1998, 271-72)

Where comparison is made from an able-bodied reference point, inequality for the disabled is likely to go unrecognized.

Auton presents further difficulties in establishing discrimination because of the approach to choosing comparators. Although the Supreme Court did not need to address this issue, having found there was no benefit of the law at issue, Chief Justice McLachlin did go on to offer another reason for there being no section 15 breach: "I conclude that the appropriate comparator for the petitioners is a non-disabled person or a person suffering a disability other than a mental disability (here autism) seeking or receiving funding for a non-core therapy important for his or her present and future health, which is emergent and only recently becoming recognized as medically required" (*Auton* 2004, para. 55). Framing the comparator in such terms inevitably produced the conclusion that there was no such comparator who was provided with health services. Such detailing in the description of comparators will frequently make discrimination on the basis of disability impossible to establish. The needs related to a particular disability will often be unique, so no one else will be receiving anything like the benefit claimed. Such detailing in the description of comparators fosters recognition of only formal equality – treating likes alike. Substantive equality – that is, responding to different needs – cannot be accomplished where the comparison is so detailed as to preclude the identification of a relevant comparator. The diversity of disability highlighted in previous cases becomes a basis in *Auton* for avoiding a finding of discrimination. For equality law to respond to the different needs of persons with disabilities, a higher level of abstraction is required to show comparative disadvantage. *Auton* presents major challenges to the advancement of disability rights in Canada.

Disability Issues in Criminal Law

Disability issues in criminal law include questions arising from an accused having a disability, a victim of crime having a disability, and crimes with indirect implications for persons with disabilities.

R. v. Swain (1991) held that it was unconstitutional, by virtue of section 7 of the Charter, to allow the Crown to raise an insanity defence at any stage of a criminal trial.[3] It is up to the accused to decide whether to raise the defence of insanity during the trial. The Crown is entitled to lead evidence about the accused's sanity only in two circumstances: if the accused raises the issue during the trial, or at the end of the trial if it has been concluded that the accused would otherwise be guilty. Moreover, a further breach of sections 7 and 9 of the Charter was found in *R. v. Swain* in the provisions providing for automatic detention under a Lieutenant-Governor's warrant for anyone found not guilty by reason of insanity.[4] The Charter breach was attributed to the failure to ensure that the detention under a Lieutenant-Governor's warrant was limited to the minimum time needed to determine whether the person is dangerous. While those found not guilty by reason of insanity might be dangerous, it could not be assumed that this is inevitably so.

An overbroad response to the possibility of a danger to the public was also the basis of the finding of a Charter breach in *R. v. DeMers* (2004), in which the accused was found to be unfit to stand trial. His mental disability was such that it was assumed he would never be fit to stand trial. Persons permanently unfit to stand trial were subject to indefinite appearances before a review board. It was held that this is unconstitutional under section 7 of the Charter for the failure to restrict these provisions to accused persons who are dangerous. Those who are permanently unfit to stand trial but who are not dangerous are constitutionally entitled to an absolute discharge that ends their subjugation to the criminal process.

R. v. Latimer (2001) involved a father convicted of second degree murder of his severely disabled twelve-year-old daughter, Tracy. Robert Latimer claimed that his killing of Tracy was an act of compassion and therefore not a crime. The Supreme Court of Canada did not, as invited by several intervenors, use this case as an opportunity to discuss section 15 rights of disabled victims of crime. Nevertheless, the court unequivocally rejected Robert Latimer's attempt to invoke a defence of necessity. Furthermore, the Supreme Court rejected Robert Latimer's claim that the mandatory minimum sentence (life imprisonment, with no eligibility for parole for ten years) is cruel and unusual punishment under section 12 of the Charter.[5] The court did, however, express sympathy for Robert Latimer, while indicating that any account of the circumstances of his case was a matter for the Cabinet, exercising the Royal Prerogative of Mercy.

R. v. Parrott (2001) is another case involving a disabled victim of crime. This case, concerning charges of kidnapping and sexual assault of a woman with a mental disability, dealt with the question of whether the woman was required to testify in the voir dire about her competence to testify at trial. The gendered disability issues in this case are the subject of Chapter 12.

Rodriguez (1993) involved a constitutional challenge to the crime of assisted suicide. Sue Rodriguez claimed a constitutional right, under either section 7 or section 15 of the Charter, to assistance in committing suicide. Because of amyotrophic lateral sclerosis (ALS), Rodriguez anticipated becoming physically unable to commit suicide at a time when she would choose to end her own life. She argued that decriminalizing assisted suicide was necessary to uphold a right to die with dignity. By a five-four split, the Supreme Court of Canada rejected Rodriguez's claim. The majority of the court concluded that the recognition of a constitutional right to assisted suicide was unwarranted because it would be too easily open to abuse. The majority was not convinced that there could be adequate safeguards to prevent a slippery slope; that is, they feared that decriminalizing assisted suicide would lead to the killing of vulnerable people who had not genuinely decided to commit suicide.

Conclusion

Although decisions of the Supreme Court of Canada in the last two decades have involved significant advances for persons with disabilities, there is much to be done to achieve substantive equality. As Devlin and Pothier argue in the Introduction to this book, persons with disabilities in Canada experience a regime of dis-citizenship. While the Supreme Court has, on occasion, demonstrated an awareness of the nature of the problem and sometimes articulated inspiring exhortations, it has remained remedially timid, refusing to fully come to terms with the egalitarian needs of many persons with disabilities.

Acknowledgments
I would like to thank Richard Devlin for his encouragements and helpful comments.

Notes
1 Section 15 of the Charter reads:

> (1) Every individual is equal before and under the law and has the right to the equal protection and equal benefit of the law without discrimination and, in particular, without discrimination based on race, national or ethnic origin, colour, religion, sex, age or mental or physical disability.
> (2) Subsection (1) does not preclude any law, program or activity that has as its object the amelioration of conditions of disadvantaged individuals or groups

including those that are disadvantaged because of race, national or ethnic origin, colour, religion, sex, age or mental or physical disability.

2 Terry Grismer died shortly after the Member Designate of the British Columbia Council of Human Rights ruled in his favour. Given the significance of the case, the Superintendent of Motor Vehicles sought judicial review, and Grismer's estate was granted standing throughout all the court proceedings.

3 Section 7 of the Charter reads:

Everyone has the right to life, liberty and security of the person and the right not to be deprived thereof except in accordance with the principles of fundamental justice.

4 Section 9 of the Charter reads:

Everyone has the right not to be arbitrarily detained or imprisoned.

5 Section 12 of the Charter reads:

Everyone has the right not to be subjected to any cruel and unusual treatment or punishment.

References

[*Andrews*]. *Law Society of British Columbia et al. v. Andrews et al.*, [1989] 1 S.C.R. 143 [*Andrews*].

Auton v. British Columbia (Attorney General), [2004] 3 S.C.R. 657 [*Auton*].

[*BCGSEU*]. *British Columbia (Public Service Employee Relations Commission) v. BCGSEU*, [1999] 3 S.C.R. 3 *(Re Meiorin)* [*BCGSEU*].

Canadian Charter of Rights and Freedoms, Part I of the *Constitution Act, 1982*, being Schedule B to the *Canada Act 1982* (U.K.) 1982, c. 11 [Charter].

Canadian Human Rights Act, s. 65.1, added by S.C. 1980-81-82-83, c. 143, s. 25.

E. (Mrs.) v. Eve, [1986] 2 S.C.R. 388 [*Eve*].

Eaton v. Brant County Board of Education, [1997] 1 S.C.R. 241 [*Eaton*].

Eldridge v. British Columbia (Attorney General), [1997] 3 S.C.R. 624 [*Eldridge*].

[*Gibbs*]. *Battlefords and District Co-operative Ltd. v. Gibbs*, [1996] 3 S.C.R. 566 [*Gibbs*].

Granovsky v. Canada (Minister of Employment and Immigration), [2000] 1 S.C.R. 703 [*Granovsky*].

[*Grismer*]. *British Columbia (Superintendent of Motor Vehicles) v. British Columbia (Council of Human Rights)*, [1999] 3 S.C.R. 868 *(Re Grismer Estate)* [*Grismer*].

[*Martin*]. *Nova Scotia (Workers' Compensation Board) v. Martin; Nova Scotia (Workers' Compensation Board) v. Laseur*, [2003] 2 S.C.R. 504 [*Martin*].

[*Mercier*]. *Quebec (Commission des droits de la personne et des droits de la jeunesse) v. Montréal (City) (Re Mercier)*, [2000] 1 S.C.R. 665 [*Mercier*].

O'Malley v. Simpsons-Sears, [1985] 2 S.C.R. 536.

Pothier, D. 1998. *Eldridge v. British Columbia (Attorney General)*: How the deaf were heard in the Supreme Court of Canada. *National Journal of Constitutional Law* 9: 263-76.

R. v. DeMers, [2004] 2 S.C.R. 489.

R. v. Latimer, [2001] 1 S.C.R. 3.

R. v. Parrott, [2001] 1 S.C.R. 178.

R. v. Swain, [1991] 1 S.C.R. 933.

Rodriguez v. British Columbia (Attorney General), [1993] 3 S.C.R. 519 [*Rodriguez*].

Contributors

Dana Lee Baker is an Assistant Professor at the Harry S. Truman School of Public Affairs at Washington State University. Dr. Baker did her PhD work at the University of Texas at Austin and does research primarily in the area of children's disability policy.

William Boyce is Director of Queen's Social Program Evaluation Group. Dr. Boyce's research focus is on youth health risk behaviours, land mine survivor programs, and community health education in developing countries.

Richard Devlin is Professor of Law, Dalhousie University. He is editor of *Canadian Perspectives on Legal Theory* and has published more than forty articles in various Canadian, American, and British journals.

Catherine Frazee is Co-Director of the Institute for Disability Studies Research and Education at Ryerson University. A long-time disability activist, she served as Chief Commissioner of the Ontario Human Rights Commission from 1989 to 1992.

Daphne Gilbert (LLB, Manitoba; LLM, Yale) is an Assistant Professor at the University of Ottawa, where she teaches primarily constitutional law and comparative constitutional law. Her main research interests are equality rights and freedom of expression. Daphne clerked for Chief Justice Antonio Lamer at the Supreme Court of Canada.

Joan Gilmour, LLB, JSD, is Associate Professor at Osgoode Hall Law School, York University, and a member of the bars of Ontario and British Columbia. She teaches and writes on health law and disability and the law, and is Director of Osgoode Hall's masters program in health law.

Teri Hibbs (LLB, Queen's) is a graduate student in Dispute Resolution at the University of Victoria. She is a trained mediator and facilitator, and has been a long-time disability and anti-poverty activist. Her primary interests include advocating for changes to policy and practice to promote the full inclusion and participation of disabled people in all aspects of community life.

Alison James has been a Research Associate in the Centre for Health Services and Policy Research at Queen's University in Kingston, Ontario. She has extensive experience with large national datasets on health and disability issues.

Jon Johnson completed his BA and MA in socio-cultural anthropology at the University of Western Ontario. He is currently working toward a PhD in the Communication and Culture program at York University. He is interested in the intersections between social justice, health policy, and health communication.

Kari Krogh is a Canadian Institutes of Health Research Senior Research Fellow and Assistant Professor at the School of Disability Studies, Ryerson University and a temporary advisor to the World Health Organization. The Royal Society of Canada's Alice Wilson award recipient, she investigates disability and health policy.

Theresa Man Ling Lee is an Associate Professor in the Department of Political Science at the University of Guelph. Lee is a political theorist who has published in postmodernism, feminism, human rights, multiculturalism, and modern Chinese political thought. Her current project is a study of cultural crisis and political identity.

Mary Ann McColl is Associate Director for Research at the Queen's Centre for Health Services and Policy Research, and a Professor in the departments of Community Health and Epidemiology, and Rehabilitation Therapy at Queen's University in Kingston, Ontario.

Darcy L. MacPherson (LLB, Dalhousie; LLM, Cantab.) is an Assistant Professor, Faculty of Law, University of Manitoba, and a member of the Ontario bar. He has taught courses in administrative law, commercial law, contracts, constitutional law, and corporations. His current research interests include the law of directors' duties, corporate criminal responsibility, the law of sentencing, and issues for people adapting to activity limitations. He is a member of the Board of Directors of the Canadian Centre on Disability Studies.

Diana Majury is a white, non-disabled, lesbian feminist. She teaches in the Law Department at Carleton University in Ottawa. Her research and activism are primarily in the areas of human rights and Charter equality.

Ravi A. Malhotra is an SJD candidate at the University of Toronto Faculty of Law and, as of 2006, will be an Assistant Professor at the Faculty of Law, University of Ottawa. He completed his LLM at Harvard Law School. His areas of interest include globalization, labour law, and critical legal studies. His work has appeared in the *Harvard International Law Journal, New Politics,* and *Canadian Dimension.*

Roxanne Mykitiuk is an Associate Professor at Osgoode Hall Law School. She is the author or coauthor of a number of articles and book chapters investigating various legal and social implications of new reproductive technologies and the new genetics and the legal construction and regulation of embodiment.

Dianne Pothier is a Professor at Dalhousie Law School, having joined the faculty in 1986. She has taught, written, and been involved in litigation on equality and disability issues.

Marcia Rioux holds a PhD in Jurisprudence and Social Policy. She is Chair of the School of Health Policy and Management and Director of the graduate program MA (Critical Disability Studies) at York University. Her research includes disability, human rights, universal education, globalization and welfare, literacy, and social justice issues.

Fiona Sampson (BAH, Queen's; MA, Trent; LLB, Queen's; PhD, Osgoode Hall) is Director of Litigation at the Women's Legal Education and Action Fund (LEAF). Fiona's practice and research interests relate primarily to women's equality rights and gendered disability discrimination.

Sam Shortt is Director of the Centre for Health Services and Policy Research at Queen's University. He is the author of numerous books and papers on medicine, history, and health policy.

Carolyn Tyjewski's work has appeared in various academic journals, including *Politics and Culture* and *Disability Studies Quarterly*. She is known for her work pertaining to civil rights law, identity politics, and identification/misidentification of disabled, gendered, raced, sexed, and sexualized subjects. Carolyn is also a creative non-fiction writer. She is pursuing her PhD in cultural studies at the University of California, Davis.

Fraser Valentine is trained as a political scientist. His primary academic interests lie in examining the relationships among people with disabilities, disability rights organizing, and the state. He is an instructor at the School of Disability Studies, Ryerson University, and a senior policy analyst in the Strategic Policy Branch at Social Development Canada.

Robert D. Wilton is an Associate Professor in the School of Geography and Geology at McMaster University. His research is focused on the social geographies of disability and mental health, with particular interest in access to paid employment.

Index

Cameron, Alexander. *See Cameron v. Nova Scotia (Attorney General)*
Cameron, Colin, 180
Cameron v. Nova Scotia (Attorney General), 285-300, 300n3, 300n5
Canada Health Act (2003), 153
Canada Health and Social Transfers, 153-54
Canada Pension Plan (CPP), 67n1, 140, 283n7, 289, 312-13
Canadian Charter of Rights and Freedoms: autism, 192n1; common law, 234, 249, 259; denial of severance pay, 265n2; equality rights, 11, 13, 63, 72, 121-22, 281, 300n1, 301n5; fertility treatment coverage discrimination, 293-95; formal citizenship rights, 197-98; history and wording of, 1, 305, 316n1, 317n3, 317n4, 317n5; home support policy, 154, 174n5; HSAG views on, 174n5; human dignity, 249; multiculturalism, 87-88; and persons with disabilities, 48-49, 60, 103n3, 285; potential for dismantling, 108, 121; right to privacy, 234; university accommodation policies, 208-9, 216n1. *See also* court cases; human rights legislation
Canadian Council on Social Development, 28
Canadian Election Survey (CES, 1997), 25, 29-32
Canadian Human Rights Commission, 72, 103n15
Canadian Medical Association, 159
Canadian National Institute for the Blind (CNIB), 145
Carl, Lisa, 124n17
Carver, Peter, 303n27
caste system, 119
categories: disability, 4-5; essentialism, 294, 299; legal, 121; patronizing nature of, 272; rigidity of, 303n21. *See also* identity categories
Central Alberta Dairy Pool v. Alberta (Human Rights Commission) (1990), 103n16
cerebral palsy, 124n17, 313
charitable privilege, 56-57, 61, 63, 65, 66
charity, as response to disability, 11, 166, 174n6, 192, 306
Charter of the City of Cincinnati, 109
charter schools, 190
Chatterji, S., 28
child care, 55
children with disabilities: access to education, 65, 72; accommodation, 184;

civil rights, 184-85; institutional living, 64; learning disabilities, 260; murder of, 11. *See also* autism
Chinese Canadian National Council, 100
Chipman, David R. (Justice), 285, 287, 290-95, 300, 302n16
choice, notion of, 296, 303n25
chronic illness, 226
chronic pain, 72, 209, 312
Cincinnati, Ohio, 108-9, 115-17
citizenship: citizen rights, 151, 168; citizenship/dis-citizenship, 17-18, 55, 316; concept of, 1-2, 54-56, 66; and disability, 17-18, 56-58, 61; full citizenship, 48, 121-22, 129, 153, 160-61, 163; and human rights, 62, 64; *In Unison* agreement, 64, 68n17; inclusion/exclusion, 55; judicial decisions, 61; Kymlicka on, 55; support systems, 55, 167-70, 172, 173; US definition of, 107-8
civil disability, 56-57, 62, 66
civil rights: and ADA, 120; based on physical traits, 119-20; bisexuals/homosexuals, 109, 123n11; of children, 184; civil rights-based disability policy (US), 186-87; developmentally disabled (US), 186; hybrids, 106-23; invisible "other," 106-23; social disability model, 78. *See also* human rights
Civil Rights Act (US), 107
clerical occupations, 135(t), 136
clinical encounter, 223-45; as dehumanizing experience, 237; dialogue, 231-32; gaze, 231; judgment, 232, 236, 240; objectification of body, 234-37; Ontario focus groups, 228-32; personal narratives, 228-30, 234-35; social assistance assessment reliance on, 237-44; treatment of health information, 224-25, 229, 232-44, 245n5; women with disabilities, 233-37
Coalition of Provincial Organizations of the Handicapped, 103n3
cognitive/learning disability, 33(t), 135(t), 136(t), 137
Colker, Ruth, 111, 116, 119, 123n5
common law, 234, 249, 259
community participation, 154, 160-61, 168, 171, 262-63
community-based services (US), 183
comparative concept of equality, 255-58, 289-91, 300, 302n15, 312-15
compensation levels, 250-57, 259, 261, 262
computer technology, 6, 13
Connecticut, autism waiver, 191

damages, compensation levels, 250-54,
260-61, 264
Dart, Justin, Jr., 124n17
Davis, John M., 228
Davis, Leonard, 112
Dawson, Michelle, 311
Day, Shelagh, 95-96
D'Cunha, Colin, 100
deaf/deafness: access to health care, 13,
62-63, 68n16, 310; as cultural minority,
92-95, 100-2; disability survey results,
33(t); hearing aids, 205, 217n9; personal
narrative, 201-2
degenerative conditions, 226
DeMers, R. v. (Supreme Court of Canada,
2004), 315
democracy, 77, 82
demographics: ADA population figures
(US), 118; age groups, 35, 36(f), 38;
autism, 4; Canadian disabled population, 1, 32-49, 132, 237, 248-49, 254;
disability surveys, 25-26, 29-35, 134-36,
148n1, 170-72; education, 37(t), 38;
gender comparisons, 35(t); health and
disability, 33-35; income, 37(t); Ontario
focus groups, 228-30; precarious work,
132, 134-38; socio-economic characteristics, 35, 37-38; unemployment rate for
persons with disabilities (US), 120-21
depression, 242
Deschamps, Marie (Justice), 288
developmental disabilities, 64, 178, 186-87,
191-92
Dewsbury, G., 27
diabetes, 124n16, 144
dialogue, clinical encounter, 231-32,
235-36, 240
difference: hierarchies of, 10-11, 12;
inevitability of, 20
Difference Principle, 70, 75, 79, 81, 84-85
disability: as cultural group, 91, 99-100,
101; definitions, 4, 27-28, 103n2, 183,
240; demographic characteristics, 1,
31(t), 32-49, 132, 237, 248-49, 254;
disability/impairment dichotomy, 226;
diverse nature of, 47, 242, 308-9;
evolution of, 26-28; fraudulent claims,
209, 211; functional analysis, 251-53;
inclusion/exclusion dichotomies, 14-15;
individual pathology of, 49(f), 50-51, 54,
56, 57(f); judicial/legal developments,
61-63, 261-64, 305-16; medicalization
of, 40, 164-65, 203, 208, 210-11, 251-52;
notion of prevention, 10-12, 52;
oppressive nature, 79-80, 172, 225, 244;
re-envisioning, 178, 296-99; social and

scientific formulations, 39-40, 49(f),
50-53; socio-economic characteristics,
26, 35-38; value of embodied experience, 174n7, 223, 227-28; visibility/
invisibility, 15-16, 99, 124n16. *See also*
infertility; stereotypes; stigmatization
disability discrimination: court cases, 306,
307-8; disability-based, 14, 57-58, 113,
209, 303n20; in employment, 71-74, 98,
103n15, 109; human rights commissions,
85; infertility, 287-88, 296-99; legislation,
133; nature of, 307-8; prohibition of, 72;
summary of legal developments, 307-8;
women, 270. *See also* discrimination
disability models. *See* medical-based
model of disability; social construct
model of disability
disability policy: civil rights-based (US),
186-87; debt containment, 158; disabled
descriptor as federal policy, 3; evidence
base for, 25-43; human rights policy
(US), 186-87; multiple jurisdictions, 48,
181; participation in making, 152, 154-
56, 173n1; power relations, 203-5. *See
also* accommodation/accommodation
policy; autism; home support policy
and services
disability rights movement: and citizenship, 55-56; as group rights, 88, 91;
integration as goal, 90-91, 93, 95, 101-2;
international agreements, 58-60; male-
dominated, 267-68; Ontario disability
programs, 53; policy formation, 180-81;
political action, 60-66, 72, 82; reclama-
tion of term "disability," 4; recognition
of, 56-58, 60-66; social construct model
of disability, 72, 77, 225
disability studies programs, 89-90, 103n8
Disability Studies Quarterly (2002), 88-89
disability surveys, 25-43; design, 28-29,
31(f), 32(f); evaluating, 25-28; methodology, 28-32; purpose, 30(f); results/data
analysis, 32-43
DisAbled Women's Network (DAWN)
Canada, 165, 311
discrimination: conduct-based, 123; court
cases, 85, 103n15; justifications for, 179;
legal definition (US), 115; nature of,
307-8; pre-existing conditions, 259;
prevention of, 186; religious, 96; social
bias, 298-99; and visibility, 116; workplace, 71-74. *See also* disability discrimination; gendered disability; stereotypes;
stigmatization
distributive justice theory (Rawls), 74-85,
104n17

doctors. *See* medical profession
domestic service, 142-44
Down's syndrome, 236, 270
driver's licence, 308-9
Dyck, Isabel, 210
Dyment, R. v. (Supreme Court of Canada,
   1988), 234

E. *(Mrs.) v. Eve* (Supreme Court of Canada,
   1986), 61, 306-7
early diagnosis, autism, 183-84, 190
earned income allowance, 148
Eaton, Emily, 62, 68n15, 313
Eaton v. Brant County Board of Education
   (Supreme Court of Canada, 1997), 14,
   62-63, 68n15, 313-14
economic capital, 157, 159, 160
economic model of disability, 39-42
education system: access, 65, 72, 195,
   197-99; Braille instruction, 65-66; and
   Canadian Charter of Rights and Freedoms,
   195-97; citizenship rights, 55; civil
   disability, 62; cost-cutting measures, 65,
   197-98, 217n10; court challenges to, 14;
   functional model, 62; inclusive programs,
   65-66, 68n15; integrated education/
   mainstreaming, 14, 62, 65, 313-14;
   levels of education, 71-72; right to (US),
   186; students with disabilities, 195-215.
   See also post-secondary education
egalitarianism/egalitarian values, 9, 54, 94
Eldridge v. British Columbia (Attorney General)
   (1997), 62-63, 102, 216n1, 249, 301n6,
   305-6, 308, 309-12
embodied experience, 174n7, 223, 227-28
emotional impairment, 33(t)
employment: Aboriginals, 71, 79; barriers
   to, 71-72, 129-30; changing nature of,
   130-33; classification schemes, 64; court
   cases, 307-8; criteria for, 13, 114-15;
   employment law, 83-85; full citizenship,
   129; hiring quotas, 80; labour force
   participation, 71-72, 84, 129-48, 132-33,
   148, 170; low-wage jobs, 146; occupation
   types, 134-36, 146; patterns of, 133-34,
   135(t), 136, 137; salaries/hours, 136,
   137(t), 146; unemployment rates (US),
   120-21; unions/union shops, 73, 133,
   139-40, 148; work speed-up orders, 143.
   See also precarious work; short-term
   contract/temporary work
employment agencies, 141
Employment Equity Act (1986; 1996), 60
empowerment. *See* empowerment, *under*
   power relations
England, 61

the Enlightenment, 89
entitlements: charitable privilege, 65-66;
   as civil right (US), 187; or "discretionary
   benefits," 48; evaluation for, 237-44;
   humanitarian relief, 65; Medicaid (US),
   190; neo-liberalism, 64; recognition of,
   63; theoretical constructs, 54-58, 57(f), 65
environmental model, 49(f), 52, 57(f)
Equal Rights Not Special Rights, 109
equality: access to post-secondary
   education, 197-99; achievement of, 66;
   barriers to, 122; as comparative concept,
   255-58, 289-91, 300, 302n15, 312-15;
   and disability, 11-12, 56-58, 66, 268-70,
   286; equal rights law, 267-83; equal
   treatment standard, 54; formal equality,
   289, 290, 291; idea of, 3-4, 10, 53-54,
   57(f), 67n12, 122, 249, 261; *In Unison*
   agreement, 64, 68n17; justice as fairness
   theory (Rawls), 74-77; medical-based
   model of disability, 300; and women,
   267-70
Equality Foundation of Greater Cincinnati,
   Inc. v. City of Cincinnati (1995), 107-9,
   115-17, 121
equality rights analysis, 267-70, 277-82
equity: approaches to, 197-99; concept of,
   213; negotiating for, 211-15. *See also*
   accommodation/accommodation policy
essentialism: autism, 177, 190; exclusionary practices, 14-15, 56; in feminist
   theory, 268; and identity, 20n1; legal
   grounds/categories, 294, 299; race, 268;
   sexual assault analysis, 278; social
   construct model of disability, 14-15,
   226; Tremain on, 6-7
eugenics, 307
evaluation process. *See* assessments for
   disability determination
evidence, rules of, 281
evidence-based advocacy, 42-43
exclusion: based on individual pathology,
   56; engendering of, 12; essentialism and,
   56; inclusion/exclusion, 55, 62; practices
   of, 7-8, 14, 15-16, 56, 177, 202

family: alternate structures, 303n23;
   autism support services, 187-89; privacy
   issues, 238; therapy participation,
   184-85
Federal Supplemental Security Income
   (SSI) (US), 191
Federalist Papers (US), 182
feminism/feminist theory, 9, 83, 89,
   267-69, 282, 298-99
fibromyalgia, 209

Finkelstein, V., 132
firefighters, 73
First Nations, 64, 67n10. *See also*
  Aboriginals
food and beverage service occupations,
  135(t)
Foucault, Michel, 152, 159-61, 164, 165,
  196, 201-3
France, quotas for workers with disabilities,
  80
French, Sally, 226
functional limitations. *See* handicaps;
  impairments
functional model of disability, 49(f), 57(f),
  62
funding constraints. *See* cost-cutting
  measures

Garland-Thompson, Rosemarie, 227-28
Gateson v. Kiln Park Estates Ltd. (1980)
  (UK), 255
gays and lesbians, 67n10, 92, 100, 109,
  115-17, 123n11
"gaze": administrative, 160-61, 166;
  Foucault's theory of, 152; medical, 160,
  161, 163-65, 231, 240
gender: assumptions about, 232; and
  disability, 14; equality, 10, 267-83; gender
  comparisons, 35(t); gender/sex distinction, 10, 298; occupation patterns, 134,
  135(t), 136; and power differential,
  236-37; reproduction as gender neutral,
  301n11; salary patterns, 146. *See also*
  sex/sexual orientation
gendered disability, 267-83; contextual
  analysis, 282; and disability theory, 268;
  discrimination, 273, 280-82; equal rights
  law, 267-83; infertility, 286-89, 294-95;
  negative constructions of, 11, 277; as
  relational experience, 269; sexual assault
  as crime of, 279-82
General Social Survey (GSS, 1994), 25-26,
  29-35, 170-72
genetics, 5
Georgia, Olmstead planning committee,
  187
Germany, quotas for workers with
  disabilities, 80
Giant Steps program (Quebec), 185
Gibbs case (Supreme Court of Canada,
  1996), 312
Gill, Carol, 234
glasses, 205
Glenn, Evelyn Nakano, 107
Gordon, Avery, 106, 111, 122
Gough, Dwayne, 170

government of Canada: *Canada Health Act*
  (2003), 153; Canada Health and Social
  Transfers (1994), 153-54, 237; Canada
  Pension Plan (CPP), 67n1, 140, 283n7,
  289, 312-13; *Canadian Employment Equity
  Act* (1986; 1996), 60; Health Canada,
  182; Human Resources Department,
  139; *Human Rights Act* (1977), 60, 72,
  305; *In Unison* agreement, 64, 68n17;
  legislative framework for human rights,
  60-61, 72-73, 98, 214; Ministry of
  Health, 159; *Multiculturalism Act* (1988),
  92. *See also Canadian Charter of Rights
  and Freedoms*; Supreme Court of Canada
Granovsky v. Canada (Attorney General)
  (2000), 13, 20n4, 289-90, 298, 302n13,
  302n15, 309-10, 312-13
Grismer, Terry, 317n2
Grismer case (Supreme Court of Canada,
  1999), 308-9
Guelph, University of, 87

Habermas, Jürgen, 82
habitus, 157-58, 165, 166, 169
Haggar v. De Placido (1972) (UK), 255
Hamilton, Ontario, 130, 133-38
Hammar, T., 2
handicaps, 20n3, 90, 97, 192, 309
Haraway, Donna, 226
Harlan, John Marshall (Justice, US), 106,
  117
Health and Activity Limitation Survey
  (HALS, 1991), 25, 29-34, 148n1
Health Canada, 182
health-care system: access to, 13-14, 40-41,
  62-63, 68n16, 310-11; confidentiality of
  information, 224-25, 229, 232-44, 245n5;
  cost-cutting measures, 153-54; and
  disability, 27, 33-35, 159, 164, 231-32,
  241-44; medicalization of disability,
  40, 164-65, 203, 208, 210-11, 251-52;
  occupations, 135(t); ongoing surveillance, 164-66, 174n12, 207, 215, 238;
  personal narratives, 241-42; public/
  private programs, 158, 300n3; self-
  reported conditions, 34(f), 238-39. *See
  also* clinical encounter
Health Services and Insurance Act, 300n3
hearing aids, 205, 217n9
hearsay evidence, 271, 273-76, 281-82,
  283n3
hegemony, Gramsci's notion of, 158
Helms, Jesse (US Senator), 118-19
Hendriks, A., 132
Hill v. Church of Scientology of Toronto
  (1995), 249

Nagel, Thomas, 81
National Population Health Survey
(NPHS, 1998-99), 29-34
neo-liberalism: citizenship rights, 151;
and disability, 51, 61, 63-65, 121-22;
economic efficiency, 172; entitlements,
64; home support policy revisions, 153;
human rights, 66; individualism, 107-8;
role of private sector, 158; welfare state,
64. *See also* liberalism
Neuhauser, D., 28
neurodiversity, 179
neurological experiments, 235-36
Newfoundland Court of Appeal, 272
Newfoundland and Labrador, 181, 185, 188
non-standard work, 130-32
normalcy, presumptions of, 15-16, 203,
290; disability as abnormality, 261-62;
need to conform to, 204-5, 206, 236,
238; "normal" lifestyles, 255-58. *See also*
ableism/ableist attitudes
Norman, Wayne, 55
North Carolina, 190
Nova Scotia, 312; Court of Appeal, 285-300
Nozick, Robert, 70
nursing homes, employment, 144-46

occupations: gender divisions, 134, 135(t),
136; salaries/hours, 136, 137(t), 146;
types, 134-36, 146. *See also* employment;
precarious work
O'Connor, Sandra Day (Justice; US), 118,
120
Oklahoma, Olmstead Strategic Planning
Committee, 187
Oliver, Michael, 225, 228
Olmstead v. L.C. (US Supreme Court,
1999), 186-87, 192n2
O'Malley v. Simpsons-Sears (1985), 307-8
ombudsman, 213
ongoing surveillance, 164-66, 174n12,
207, 215, 238
Ontario: accommodation guidelines, 98,
103n15; Autism Society, 184; Court of
Appeals, 62, 265n2; disability rights
movement, 53; Disability Support
Program (ODSP), 230, 238-44; disabled
women's focus groups, 228-32; Family
and Children Services, 188; Human
Rights Commission, 72, 103n15, 184;
human rights legislation, 307-8; income
support programs, 238-44; labour force
studies, 130, 133-38; Ontario Works,
239; *Policy and Guidelines on Disability
and the Duty to Accommodate*, 98, 103n15;
SARS outbreak, 100

Ontario Direct Funding Program (ODFP),
53
Ontario Disability Support Program Act
(ODSPA), 239-40
Ontario Human Rights Code, 88
Ontario Nurses Assn. v. Mount Sinai Hospital
(2005), 265n2
oppression, disability as, 79-80, 172, 225,
244
Osolin, R. v. (1993), 281
the Other, 279, 281
out-of-court statements, 271-77

pain, 33(t), 72, 209, 312
paraplegia, 170
Parrott, R. v. (1999; 2001), 11, 14, 270-82,
316
Parrott, Walter, 270
"partial," as visual impairment label, 112
Participation and Activity Limitation
Survey (PALS, 2001), 25, 29-34, 148n1
part-time work, 130-33, 140
passing as, 15-16. *See also* accommodation/
accommodation policy
paternalism: charitable privilege, 13, 57,
234, 261, 276; medical-based model of
disability, 64; patriarchy system, 278;
and US policy, 183, 190
Paterson, Kevin, 204
pathology, formulations of disability, 49(f),
50-53, 57(f), 62
person-first language, 3-4
personal assistance. *See* home support
policy and services
personal care, 33(t)
personal health information. *See* confidentiality of information, *under* health-
care system
personhood, 3-4
persons with disabilities: adaptations to
live full life, 169, 255-58, 260-62, 264,
265n1, 265n2; body as text, 227-28;
cultural capital, 172, 174n8; as cultural
minority, 88-95, 100-2; demographics,
1, 237; descriptor as federal policy, 3;
devaluing expertise of, 161-62; economic
status, 71-72, 146; employment patterns,
129-48, 170; media depictions of, 82;
negative connotations, 4, 55, 80, 163,
166, 170, 172, 178, 276-77, 306; objectification of body, 234-38; passive role,
167; as plaintiffs, 251-61, 270-77;
precarious work histories, 138-46; self-
image, 259-60; as special interest group,
198; UN initiatives on behalf of, 59(f),
60; unemployment rate (US), 120-21

Sandison v. Michigan High School Athletic Association (US, 1995), 123n12
SARS outbreak, 100
Saskatchewan, autism handbook, 181
Scales-Trent, Judy, 111
Scott, David, 104n22
seasonal work, 137, 141
self-employment, 131, 142
self-identifying as disabled: disadvantages, 207; medical-based model reliance on, 208, 215; requests for accommodation, 197, 203, 205-8; self-reported health conditions, 34(f), 238-39
self-identity: and assistive technologies, 169; Rawls on self-respect, 76, 94, 104n17; self-image, 16, 236, 259-60
self-reliance, 65
sensory disability, 135(t), 136(t), 137
separate but equal concept, 113, 120
service sector employment, 131-33, 146
Seventh Day Adventists, 308
severance pay, 265n2
sex/sexual orientation: bipolarity approach, 117, 119; bisexuals, 109, 115-17, 123n11; categories of, 110, 117, 124n15, 303n21; civil rights, 109, 123n11; cultural identity, 92-93; as gender construct, 298; homosexuals, 92, 109, 116, 123n11; "intersexed," 124n13; same-sex marriage, 10-11; sex/gender distinction, 10, 298; sexism, 112, 278; sexuality as human right, 88-89, 103n6, 115-17, 123n10; transgender, 124n14, 303n21. *See also* gender
sexual assault: as gendered crime, 270, 278-82, 283n8; *Parrott* case, 11, 14, 270-82, 316
Shakespeare, T., 132, 226
Shapiro, Joseph P., 118
Shapiro, Lawrence, 88-89
sheltered workshops, 64
shopping, 33(t)
short-term contract/temporary work: employer accountability, 142; lack of benefits, 140; multiple work tasks, 141; prevalence of, 130-33, 137, 147; workplace accommodation, 141. *See also* precarious work
Shultz, Marjorie, 287, 301n11
sign-language/sign-language interpreters, 13, 68n16, 92-93, 102, 217n9, 310
Singer, Judy, 178
Sixth Circuit Court of Appeals (US), 109, 116-18, 123n12
slavery, 3
Smart, Carol, 299

Smith, Cheryl. *See Cameron v. Nova Scotia (Attorney General)*
social assistance programs: assessments, 237-44; cost-cutting measures, 238; earned income allowance, 148; limitations in, 129
social capital, 156-57, 159
social construct model of disability: British, 78; Brown on, 91; civil rights paradigm (US), 78; context of impairments, 119, 165, 179, 204, 226, 243-44, 298; cultural minority, 98; in disability theory, 6-7, 13-16, 27, 39(f), 85; essentialism, 14-15, 226, 268; gendered disability, 277; home support policy, 152; infertility, 286, 293-94, 296-99; mental illness, 282; race as, 123n5; and self-identification, 296; social barriers, 84, 163, 225-28, 240, 244-45; societal culture, 101, 162-63; summary of legal developments, 309-12; workplace barriers, 70-72
social contract: autism, 183, 192; Rawls on, 11, 74-83; rights-based policy, 179, 192
social pathology: and equality concept, 57(f); formulations of, 49(f); responsibility of disability, 50-53
social safety net, 180, 183, 190
Social Security Disability Insurance program (US), 241
societal responses to disability, 4-8, 11-12, 170, 172
socio-political model, 39(f), 90, 102, 204
Somerville, Siobhan, 122
Sopinka, John (Justice), 314
Southin, Mary (Justice), 302n13
special education, 65, 68n15, 186, 313
speech impairment, 33(t), 87, 97-100
speed-up orders, 143, 145, 147
sports disabled lists, 4
Statistics Canada, 25, 29-32, 148n1, 248-49
steel industry, 133
stereotypes: and human dignity, 293-94; infertility, 294-95, 303n19; labour force, 98, 141; patients or paupers, 178; perceptions of disability, 207, 309; perpetuation of, 107, 110, 118, 121-22, 197, 261-64, 273-77; prejudicial ideas of disability, 281; of women with disabilities, 229-30, 244, 280. *See also* stigmatization
sterilization, 61, 306-7
Stevens, John Paul (Justice; US), 114-15, 119
stigma analysis, 286

Randy K. Lippert, *Sanctuary, Sovereignty, Sacrifice: Canadian Sanctuary Incidents, Power, and Law* (2005)

James B. Kelly, *Governing with the Charter: Legislative and Judicial Activism and Framers' Intent* (2005)

Dianne Pothier and Richard Devlin (eds.), *Critical Disability Theory: Essays in Philosophy, Politics, Policy, and Law* (2005)

Susan G. Drummond, *Mapping Marriage Law in Spanish Gitano Communities* (2005)

Louis A. Knafla and Jonathan Swainger (eds.), *Laws and Societies in the Canadian Prairie West, 1670-1940* (2005)

Ikechi Mgbeoji, *Global Biopiracy: Patents, Plants, and Indigenous Knowledge* (2005)

Florian Sauvageau, David Schneiderman, and David Taras, with Ruth Klinkhammer and Pierre Trudel, *The Last Word: Media Coverage of the Supreme Court of Canada* (2005)

Gerald Kernerman, *Multicultural Nationalism: Civilizing Difference, Constituting Community* (2005)

Pamela A. Jordan, *Defending Rights in Russia: Lawyers, the State, and Legal Reform in the Post-Soviet Era* (2005)

Anna Pratt, *Securing Borders: Detention and Deportation in Canada* (2005)

Kirsten Johnson Kramar, *Unwilling Mothers, Unwanted Babies: Infanticide in Canada* (2005)

W.A. Bogart, *Good Government? Good Citizens? Courts, Politics, and Markets in a Changing Canada* (2005)

Catherine Dauvergne, *Humanitarianism, Identity, and Nation: Migration Laws in Canada and Australia* (2005)

Michael Lee Ross, *First Nations Sacred Sites in Canada's Courts* (2005)

Andrew Woolford, *Between Justice and Certainty: Treaty Making in British Columbia* (2005)

John McLaren, Andrew Buck, and Nancy Wright (eds.), *Despotic Dominion: Property Rights in British Settler Societies* (2004)

Georges Campeau, *From UI to EI: Waging War on the Welfare State* (2004)

Alvin J. Esau, *The Courts and the Colonies: The Litigation of Hutterite Church Disputes* (2004)

Christopher N. Kendall, *Gay Male Pornography: An Issue of Sex Discrimination* (2004)

Roy B. Flemming, *Tournament of Appeals: Granting Judicial Review in Canada* (2004)

Constance Backhouse and Nancy L. Backhouse, *The Heiress vs the Establishment: Mrs. Campbell's Campaign for Legal Justice* (2004)

Christopher P. Manfredi, *Feminist Activism in the Supreme Court: Legal Mobilization and the Women's Legal Education and Action Fund* (2004)

Annalise Acorn, *Compulsory Compassion: A Critique of Restorative Justice* (2004)

Jonathan Swainger and Constance Backhouse (eds.), *People and Place: Historical Influences on Legal Culture* (2003)

Jim Phillips and Rosemary Gartner, *Murdering Holiness: The Trials of Franz Creffield and George Mitchell* (2003)

David R. Boyd, *Unnatural Law: Rethinking Canadian Environmental Law and Policy* (2003)

Ikechi Mgbeoji, *Collective Insecurity: The Liberian Crisis, Unilateralism, and Global Order* (2003)

Rebecca Johnson, *Taxing Choices: The Intersection of Class, Gender, Parenthood, and the Law* (2002)

John McLaren, Robert Menzies, and Dorothy E. Chunn (eds.), *Regulating Lives: Historical Essays on the State, Society, the Individual, and the Law* (2002)

Joan Brockman, *Gender in the Legal Profession: Fitting or Breaking the Mould* (2001)